Communications
in Computer and Information Science   177

Reggie Kwan   Carmel McNaught
Philip Tsang   Fu Lee Wang
Kam Cheong Li (Eds.)

Enhancing Learning Through Technology

Education Unplugged: Mobile Technologies and Web 2.0

International Conference, ICT 2011
Hong Kong, China, July 11-13, 2011
Proceedings

 Springer

Volume Editors

Reggie Kwan
Caritas Institute of Higher Education, Hong Kong SAR, China
E-mail: rkwan@cihe.edu.hk

Carmel McNaught
The Chinese University of Hong Kong, Hong Kong SAR, China
E-mail: carmel.mcnaught@cuhk.edu.hk

Philip Tsang
Hong Kong Web Symposium Consortium, Hong Kong SAR, China
E-mail: ptsang@cihe.edu.hk

Fu Lee Wang
Caritas Bianchi College of Careers, Hong Kong SAR, China
E-mail: pwang@cihe.edu.hk

Kam Cheong Li
Open University of Hong Kong, Hong Kong SAR, China
E-mail: kcli@ouhk.edu.hk

ISSN 1865-0929   e-ISSN 1865-0937
ISBN 978-3-642-22382-2   e-ISBN 978-3-642-22383-9
DOI 10.1007/978-3-642-22383-9
Springer Heidelberg Dordrecht London New York

Library of Congress Control Number: 2011931464

CR Subject Classification (1998): H.5, H.4, H.3, I.2, C.2, D.2, K.6.5

Typesetting: Camera-ready by author, data conversion by Scientific Publishing Services, Chennai, India

Printed on acid-free paper

Springer is part of Springer Science+Business Media (www.springer.com)

Preface

Welcome to the proceedings of ICT 2011.

The conference was the sixth event in the ICT conference series and was combined with the 15th Web Symposium. Many exciting things have happened in the past two years and now we are able to share our reactions to them. The conference in Singapore last year was a blast. Colleagues at the SIM U did a great job and participants stayed until the closing keynote session. Following that success we extended the past practice of the two-day and two-and-a-half-day conferences into this year's three-day event. Of course this meant a reduction in shopping time, so please forgive us for that.

The conference theme was "Education Unplugged: Mobile Technologies and Web 2.0." Indeed, learning with the help of technologies is ubiquitous and learners are now, not only able to be active but also deeply immersed in their own learning. We were delighted to see the ICT Conference continue to offer practitioners, developers and researchers the opportunity to share teaching and learning experiences and facilitate exploration of the ways these technologies can be used to support and enhance lifelong learning.

The papers in this volume explore the new and emerging practices required or enabled by Web 2.0 through mobile technologies. The 30 papers document e-learning projects from many parts of the world. On behalf of the editors we would like to thanks all the authors for their conscientious and scholarly efforts. Much credit should also be dedicated to the Programme Committee and those tireless reviewers who provided the green light for inclusion. Last but not least, we would like to express our gratitude to all the organizations that support our effort to ensure the continuous success of this conference. We acknowledge (in alphabetical order):

* Apple Asia Ltd.
* Computer World HK
* Croucher Foundation
* Education Bureau, Hong Kong SAR
* eHealth Consortium Ltd.
* Fuji Xero
* Hong Kong Information and Technology Federation
* Hong Kong Institute of Engineers
* Hong Kong Police Information Society
* Hong Kong Society of Medical Information Ltd.

* Hong Kong Tourism Board
* International World Wide Web Conference Committee, IW3C2
* Internet Special Project Group, Australia
* Internet Society
* Institute of Electrical and Electronics Engineers
* Pearson Education Asia Ltd.

July 2011

R. Kwan
C. McNaught
P. Tsang
F.L. Wang
K.C. Li

Organization

Organizing Committee

Chair

Reggie Kwan — Caritas Institute of Higher Education, Hong Kong, SAR China

Co-chairs

Sr. Margaret Wong — St. Paul's Convent School, Hong Kong, SAR China

K.S. Yuen — The Open University of Hong Kong, SAR China

Members

F.T. Chan — HKU School of Professional and Continuing Education, Hong Kong, SAR China

Li Chen — Beijing Normal University, China

K.S. Cheung — The Open University of Hong Kong, SAR China

Paul Corrigan — City University of Hong Kong, SAR China

Ken Eustace — Internet Special Project Group Australia

Nigel Evans — Li & Fung Ltd., Hong Kong, SAR China

Bob Fox — The University of Hong Kong, SAR China

Qin Gao — Tsinghua University, China

Stefan Hammond — Computer World Hong Kong, SAR China

Michael Jacobson — University of Sydney, Australia

Kai S. Koong — University of Texas, USA

Andrew Lai — St. Paul's Convent School, Hong Kong, SAR China

Jeanne Lam — HKU School of Professional and Continuing Education, Hong Kong, SAR China

K.C. Li — The Open University of Hong Kong, SAR China

Sharen Liu — SIM University, Singapore

Titus Lo — Centre for Advanced and Professional Studies, Hong Kong, SAR China

Carmel McNaught — The Chinese University of Hong Kong, SAR China

David Murphy — Monash University, Australia

Kongkiti Phusavat — Kasetsart University, Thailand

Marianna Sigala — University of the Aegean, Greece

Teddy So — Caritas Bianchi College of Careers, Hong Kong, SAR China

S.H. Tong	Hong Kong Baptist University, SAR China
John Traxler	University of Wolverhampton, UK
David Triggs	Greensward College, UK
Eva Tsang	The Open University of Hong Kong, SAR China
Philip Tsang	The Hong Kong Web Symposium Consortium, SAR China
Sandy Tse	Caritas Institute of Higher Education, Hong Kong, SAR China
Susan Verberne	Radboud University Nijmegen, The Netherlands
Philips Wang	Association for Computing Machinery (HK Chapter), SAR China

Programme Committee

Programme Co-chairs

Philip Tsang	Caritas Community and Higher Education Service, Hong Kong, SAR China
Bebo White	Stanford University, USA
Philips Wang	Association for Computing Machinery (HK Chapter), SAR China

Members

F.T. Chan	HKU School of Professional and Continuing Education, Hong Kong, SAR China
Li Chen	Beijing Normal University, China
Simon Cheung	The Open University of Hong Kong, SAR China
Paul Corrigan	City University of Hong Kong, SAR China
Peter Duffy	Hong Kong Polytechnic University, SAR China
Ken Eustace	Internet Special Project Group Australia
Geoff Fellows	Charles Sturt University, Australia
Bob Fox	The University of Hong Kong, SAR China
Mary Ho	Caritas Institute of Higher Education, Hong Kong, SAR China
Helena Hong Gao	Nanyang Technological University, Singapore
Kai S. Koong	University of Texas, USA
Jeanne Lam	HKU School of Professional and Continuing Education, Hong Kong, SAR China
Peter Lam	Beijing Normal University, China
Kat Leung	Caritas Institute of Higher Education, Hong Kong, SAR China
K.C. Li	The Open University of Hong Kong, SAR China

Organizers

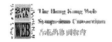

The Hong Kong Web Symposium Consortium

The Open University of Hong Kong

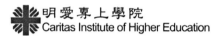

Caritas Institute of Higher Education

Caritas Bianchi College of Careers

St. Paul's Convent School

School of Professional and Continuing Education, The University of Hong Kong

Sponsors

The Education Bureau, HKSAR

Meetings & Exhibitions Hong Kong

ComputerWorld Hong Kong

Table of Contents

Technological Practice and Change in Education 1
   Robert Fox

Encouraging Student Learning through Online E-Portfolio
Development 8
   Tan Eik Chor Christopher

First Steps towards an Integrated Personal Learning Environment at
the University Level 22
   Martin Ebner, Sandra Schön, Behnam Taraghi,
   Hendrik Drachsler, and Philip Tsang

Integrating Scholarly Articles within E-Learning Courses 37
   Bee Bee Chua and Danilo Valeros Bernardo II

Web 2.0 Divide among Naughty Insiders, Worried Outsiders, and
Invisible Monitors: A Case Study 51
   Mingmei Yu, Allan H.K. Yuen, Jae Park, Hoi Ching Lam,
   Kai Kwong Lau, and Wilfred Lau

The Organization of Mobile Learning in Higher Education of
Kazakhstan 63
   Daniyar Sapargaliyev

Learning of Algorithms on Mobile Devices through Bluetooth, SMS
Technology.. 71
   Ricardo José dos Sanos Barcelos and
   Liane Matgarida Rochembach Tarouco

An Innovative Application for Learning to Write Chinese Characters
on Smartphones 85
   Vincent Tam and Chao Huang

GoPutonghua: An Online Learning Platform for Self-learners to Learn
Putonghua 96
   Vanessa Sin-Chun Ng, Andrew Kwok-Fai Lui, and Fu-Hong Wong

Construction and Evaluation of a Blended Learning Platform for
Higher Education 109
   Lisa Beutelspacher and Wolfgang G. Stock

Development of Engineers' Social Competences in the Settings of Web
2.0 Platform.. 123
   Malinka Ivanova

Students' Self-reported Assessment of E-Dictionaries 138
    Yoko Hirata and Yoshihiro Hirata

Leveraging Low-Cost Mobile Technologies in Bangladesh: A Case
Study of Innovative Practices for Teacher Professional Development
and Communicative English Language Teaching 152
    Christopher S. Walsh, Prithvi Shrestha, and Claire Hedges

Addressing Some Quality and Effectiveness Issues in E-Learning 167
    Kin Chew Lim

Peer Assessment Using Wiki to Enhance Their Mastery of the Chinese
Language 177
    Carole Chen, Kat Leung, and Gordon Maxwell

E-Learning Design for Chinese Classifiers: Reclassification of Nouns for
a Novel Approach 186
    Helena Hong Gao

Using a Conversational Framework in Mobile Game Based Learning –
Assessment and Evaluation 200
    Faranak Fotouhi-Ghazvini, Rae Earnshaw, David Robison,
    Ali Moeini, and Peter Excell

Knowledge, Skills, Competencies: A Model for Mathematics
E-Learning 214
    Giovannina Albano

Building an Effective Online Learning Community: An Ethnographic
Study 226
    Ken Eustace

Constructing of ePortfolios with Mobile Phones and Web 2.0 243
    Selena Chan

University Students' Informal Learning Practices Using Facebook:
Help or Hindrance? 254
    Rebecca Vivian

Piloting Lecture Capture: An Experience Sharing from a Hong Kong
University 268
    Keng T. Tan, Eva Wong, and Theresa Kwong

Generation of Hypertext for Web-Based Learning Based on
Wikification 280
    Andrew Kwok-Fai Lui, Vanessa Sin-Chun Ng, Eddy K.M. Tsang, and
    Alex C.H. Ho

The Impact of E-Learning in University Education: An Empirical
Analysis in a Classroom Teaching Context 291
  José Albors-Garrigos, María-del-Val Segarra-Oña, and
  José Carlos Ramos-Carrasco

The Enhancement of Students' Interests and Efficiency in Elementary
Japanese Learning as a Second Language through Online Games with
Special Reference to their Learning Styles 305
  Ng Kwan Keung Steven, Chow Kin Man Charles, and
  Chu Wai Kee David

Using Web 2.0 Technologies in K-12 School Settings: Evidence-Based
Practice? 319
  Khe Foon Hew and Wing Sum Cheung

Going Beyond Face-to-Face Classrooms: Examining Student Motivation
to Participate in Online Discussions through a Self-Determination
Theory Perspective 329
  Wee Sing Jeffrey Sim, Wing Sum Cheung, and Khe Foon Hew

Uncoupling Mobility and Learning: When One Does Not Guarantee
the Other 342
  Shelley Kinash, Jeffrey Brand, Trishita Mathew, and Ron Kordyban

e-Assessment System as a Positive Tool in the Mastery of
Putonghua 351
  Kitty Siu, Y.T. Woo, Kat Leung, Kenneth Wong,
  Reggie Kwan, and Philip Tsang

Reconciling "human touch" with "high tech"? 366
  Madeleine Tsoi, Reggie Kwan, Kat Leung, and Sandy Tse

Author Index 375

Technological Practice and Change in Education

Robert Fox

Centre for Information Technology in Education
The University of Hong Kong

Abstract. Today more than at any other time, the potential for technology to act as a major catalyst for educational change in what we do and how we do it has never been more apparent. This chapter explores one case within an institution in Hong Kong that rose to the challenge of doing things differently and providing students and teaching staff with new ways of working, taking into account new technological practices and changing educational needs.

1 Introduction

We live in exciting times with many opportunities and challenges for reform and advancement in education. Today more than at any other time, the potential for technology to provide a major catalyst for change in what we do and how we do it in education has never been more apparent. Few students today come to university without ownership of powerful mobile technologies, whether these are laptops, tablets or hand-held devices such as smart phones. All these devices have enormous computing capabilities and offer access to thousands, of often free, applications, readily downloadable over the Internet. Many students regularly and frequently access their networks, including but not limited to, Facebook or iTunes, YouTube, Skype, Blog, Twitter, many times each day.

Universities have observed this trend towards mobility and personal learning environments (PLEs) is made possible by the easy access to multiple software applications and have begun to recognize the potential to link into, and communicate with, students through these new applications. For example, universities such as Stanford have for several years run extended induction programs, sample lectures, special interest groups, course materials and assignments and many more activities via Facebook (http://www.facebook.com/stanford). These are open, not only to their own students, but to potential and future students and interested people across the world.

Increasingly, universities have installed free wifi access in their: classrooms, lecture theatres, libraries, on-campus cafes and corridors, to complement free wifi access or relatively cheap 3G access off-campus. This trend is no more apparent than in universities in Asia, notably in Korea, Japan, and Hong Kong. The rhetoric that stated we are at the crest of a technological wave that could soon transform our higher education environments is true today.

In Hong Kong, this potential for change is especially apparent. We are just one year away from a major once-in-a-lifetime reform of our education curriculum at both

R. Kwan et al. (Eds.): ICT 2011, CCIS 177, pp. 1–7, 2011.

school and university levels. Our students will complete their school education one year younger and commence their university education one year earlier. The standard university programs will change from a predominantly three year to a four year degree. All undergraduate programs will provide outcomes-based courses where students will be required to show evidence of their capabilities benchmarked against a clear set of learning outcome statements. At the same time, the numbers of students in the major universities is expected to increase in 2012 by one-third, requiring universities to create many new physical learning spaces to accommodate this extended influx. At my university, this increase in numbers is expected to be around 3,500 students. Universities are asking what new kinds of teaching and learning places are needed? Do we need to duplicate existing classrooms, computing laboratories and lecture theatres, designed prior to the introduction of PLEs and ubiquitous mobile devices or should we re-think our physical environmental needs, taking into account changing student study habits, changing curriculum requirements and emerging technological and pedagogical practices.

This chapter is based on an ICT 2011 conference presentation that explores one case within an institution in Hong Kong that rose to the challenge of doing things differently and providing students and teaching staff with new ways of working, taking into account new technological practices and changing educational needs.

2   Trends and the Impact of Changing Technological Practices in Education

Since the early 2000s, the annual Horizons Report has identified emerging technologies and their likely impact on teaching and learning in education. The report this year (Johnson, Smith, Willis, Levine, & Haywood, 2011) continues this trend, highlighting the increasing importance of the following over the next few years: (learning) resources and easy access to multiple applications that lend themselves to education; an increasing expectation and ability for students to learn when and where they need, often through access to mobile devices; a continuing growth in importance of new collaborative ways of working, leading to emphasize on the need for higher education to re-think the ways we do things and the need for creating more opportunities to facilitate and stimulate meaningful learning tasks that engage students in collaborative projects; and a shift towards using cloud-based computing and decentralized information technology services. All of this emerging as we all move more towards taking advantage of powerful, ubiquitous and cheaper (and increasingly mobile) digital technologies and their applications. Along with these trends are many challenges, not least those related to helping teachers and their students understand and use technology to support student learning. Researchers and practitioners such as Koehler, Mishra and Henriksen (2011) through their applied work with the technological pedagogical content knowledge framework (TPCK www.tpck.org/) are helping us to understand the complexities of this challenge. Their framework identifies four additional types of teacher knowledge (technological knowledge (TK), technological-content knowledge (TCK), technological-pedagogical knowledge (TPK) and technological-pedagogical-content knowledge (TPCK) that are required by teachers to successfully integrate digital technology use in their teaching

These come on top of (pedagogical knowledge (PK), content knowledge (CK) and pedagogical-content knowledge (PCK)) proposed by Shulman (1986).

Increasingly, new technologies are changing our everyday practices. For example, where the printed word was once king, the new digital multi-media of text, audio, image, animation and video is taking over. No longer do we first 'read' the news in printed news*papers*. Now we watch Internet TV, access online news sites such as TIME.com or Newsy.com or WikiLeaks. We subscribe to news related groups via our preferred social network using our mobile devices, as we go about our everyday work and play. A recent example is the way the news first broke concerning the death of Bin Laden via Twitter (Harlow, 2011). These ongoing changes in our everyday practices need to be used to our advantage in leveraging changes in today's educational practices.

As earlier mentioned, the major opportunity we have in Hong Kong for effecting change in what we do is provided by the new 3+3+4 curriculum, which constitutes six years of secondary school followed by four years at university (Tang, 2010). Each of the main universities in Hong Kong is planning their own unique ways of adapting to the extra year of study, the outcomes-based curriculum and the criterion referenced grading system accompanying this move. What is important is that this is the major watershed event for Hong Kong education as well as a 'unique opportunity for universities to move from a specialized focus to a more holistic student-oriented approach to undergraduate education.' (University Design Consortium, Arizona State University, n.d.).

> The increased duration of undergraduate degrees is posing opportunities and challenges for Hong Kong institutions. The additional undergraduate year will provide the possibility to offer students a more flexible learning experience, giving them time and space to build a broader knowledge base and to develop a more solid foundation for their holistic development. It is hoped that this will help nurture capable people to drive the development of a knowledge-based economy and to meet society's rapidly changing needs. (University of Aberdeen, Curriculum Reform Initiative, n.d.).

Despite the focus for undergraduate education, the philosophy of curriculum change and restructuring is also being encouraged in taught post-graduate programs and courses.

3 Changing Educational Practices through Technology: A Case Study

The new outcomes-based curriculum requires the development of clear principle learning outcomes (PLOs) statements, identifying what our students should be able to do to successfully complete the degree they have taken. These degree PLOs must be broken down into Learning Outcomes (LOs) for every course, identifying how each course contributes to the program PLOs. The courses that make up a program or degree then require activity and assignment tasks for students to complete which will go towards evidencing student capabilities defined in the PLO/LOs. An example, described in a course is outlined below in Figure 1.

Module Learning Outcomes (LO)

LO No.	LO Statement	Related PLO*	Related Assessment Task(s)
1	Identify challenges in implementing change in organizations	1, 2	1
2	Evaluate and apply models of change to a learning organization	5	1, 2
3	Develop strategies to support sustainable change in a learning organisation	1, 3, 5	2

*List of Program Learning Outcomes (PLO) and links to the University's Educational Aims is available in course student guides: MITE: http://mite.cite.hku.hk/course/view.php?id=10&topic=5 and MLIM: http://mlim.cite.hku.hk/course/view.php?id=5&topic=5

Fig. 1. Course or module learning outcomes and links to program outcomes

Each topic in the course is related to a face-to-face or an online session with clearly identified content and student activities to be covered. Students normally initiate work on the activities in class then complete the work out-of-class through their ePortfolios which may be in the form of a blog or a proprietary system such as Mahara. At regular intervals individual students and groups present their work to the class, either online or in the face-to-face class, evidencing their work within the online environment. The ePortfolios are linked to the course learner management system, illustrated in Figure 2.

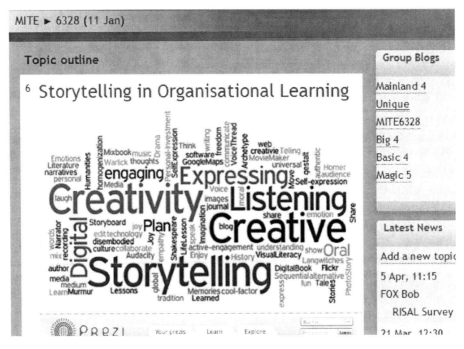

Fig. 2. Group ePortfolios linked to the course Learner Management System

The assignment tasks, both individual and group-based are explained in the course outline and discussed in class with samples of marked student work with grades provided online to enable students to understand better what is expected in terms of their potential grades. In the first class, the assessment marking framework is outlined, enabling students to understand what levels of work will constitute different grades. The framework used is based on the 'Structure of Observed Learning Outcomes' or SOLO (Biggs & Chan, 2007). In addition, each student task and assignment is accompanied with a list of key considerations taken into account in marking the work. The structure of the course and the continuous activities students are expected to complete during the semester, evidenced online as video, audio, image, photo, animation and text offer a way of working not possible before the use of new digital technologies.

4 Physical Collaborative Environment

The previous section focused on the eLearning environment in this case study. The physical environment used afforded collaborative work within a technologically advanced learning room. The layout of this innovative room is provided in Figure 3 and is supportive of the learner needs and learning theories (Oblinger, 2006) within the course.

The room is designed to support the seating of students in groups around separate tables positioned around the room. These tables are well equipped with technology

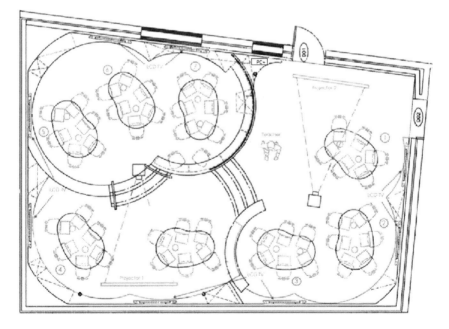

Fig. 3. Layout of the collaborative classroom

and the room has excellent wifi, allowing students who use their own mobile devices (mostly tablets, iPads and laptops) to connect to their PLEs, ePortfolios and the various eLearning sites. The grouping of seats in this room do not highlights a single focal point. The room provides multiple focal points, enabling students sitting in groups to remain seated and yet able to present their work to the entire class by remotely linking their table digital devices to display their work on all eight 42 inch LCD screens and the two projectors around the room, as needed. The lighting in the room is adjustable and remotely controlled, enabling teachers and students to change the lighting used for different types of activities creating different moods. There are potentially two teacher stations in the room. The teachers can either select one of eight tables or position their remotely controlled devices on a ledge at the side of the room. In classes given in this case study, the teacher preferred not to take over one of the eight tables. This enabled the teacher complete freedom to roam and when teacher-led periods of the class were required, the teachers were able to stand in the middle of the room. This may cause unease for the teachers as they face just half the class at any one time. Yet at the same time, it puts pressure on a teacher to keep the teacher-centred components of the class to a minimum and instead to stimulate student group work. Yes, the design of this special classroom could be improved, but it does afford a new way of working and interacting in class, privileging collaborative group work and student-centred activities.

5 Conclusion

The opportunities we have in Hong Kong to make major changes in education have never been greater than they are now. The technology at our disposal is ubiquitous and becoming cheaper and easier to use. Students are buying ever faster and smarter mobile technologies that complement potential changes to the curriculum and to our changing needs in society and education. Our institutions are re-thinking the use of physical spaces. Teachers and their students have already begun to show a lead in taking up new approaches to their academic work.

This paper has introduced one case study that highlights some of the changes possible, though there are many new opportunities, thanks to the ever increasing technology innovations and applications being created daily. This paper has explored some changing practices using new technologies to drive the changes and has outlined changing needs for university physical and virtual learning spaces and the resultant designs to maximize opportunities for student learning.

References

1. Biggs, J.B., Tang, C.: Teaching for Quality Learning at University. Open University Press/McGraw-Hill Education (2007)
2. Harlow, S.: Twitter First to Break News of Bin Laden's Death.Knight Center, Journalism in the Americas Blog, The University of Texas, Austin (2011),
   http://knightcenter.utexas.edu/blog/
   twitter-first-break-news-bin-ladens-death
3. Johnson, L., Smith, R., Willis, H., Levine, A., Haywood, K.: The 2011 Horizon Report. The New Media Consortium (2011),
   http://www.nmc.org/pdf/2011-Horizon-Report.pdf

4. Mishra, P., Koehler, M.J., Henriksen, D.: The Seven Trans-disciplinary Habits of Mind: Extending the TPACK Framework towards 21st Century Learning. Educational Technology 11(2), 22–28 (2011)
5. Oblinger, D.: Space as a Change Agent. In: Oblinger, D. (ed.) Learning Spaces. Educause (2006), http://net.educause.edu.ir/library/pdf/pub7102.pdf
6. Shulman, L.: Those who Understand: Knowledge Growth in Teaching. Educational Researcher 15(2), 4–14 (1986)
7. Tang, H.H.: Higher Education Governance and Academic Entrepreneurialism in East Asia: The Two Episodes of Hong Kong and Macau. Research Studies in Education 8, 106–124 (2010)
8. University Design Consortium, Arizona State University(nd.): Hong Kong Undergraduate Education Reform Under "3+3+4". Hong Kong Council for Accreditation of Academic and Vocational Qualifications, China, http://universitydesign.asu.edu/db/hong-kong-undergraduate-education-reform-under-201c3-3-4201d
9. University of Aberdeen, Curriculum Reform Initiative (nd): Briefing on Curriculum Reform in Hong Kong, http://www.abdn.ac.uk/cref/uploads/files/hong_kong_briefing.doc

Encouraging Student Learning through Online E-Portfolio Development

Tan Eik Chor Christopher

School of Digital Media and Infocomm Technology
Singapore Polytechnic
tanec@sp.edu.sg

Abstract. This paper introduces some ideas on how various interactive Web 2.0 tools can be used by students to build their e-portfolios. The importance of creating portfolios, in particular, e-portfolios is emphasized throughout this paper. Examples are drawn from actual assignments that were set for students during the past semester from the Web Publishing module. The advantages and disadvantages students publishing their works online are also highlighted.

Keywords: Portfolio, Digital Portfolio, E-portfolio, Web 2.0, Web Publishing.

1 Introduction

In this paper, I shall be highlighting efforts done in the Web Publishing module that I was the module coordinator of in the previous semester and present ideas on how various Web 2.0 tools can be used effectively by students to create or supplement their e-portfolios.

I will start with the definition of a portfolio, following by an elaboration on its importance. Next, I will discuss about the advantages and disadvantages of publishing an online portfolio.

I will then proceed to describe the efforts made in using various Web 2.0 tools in the teaching of the Web Publishing module. Lastly, I will highlight some relevant websites that I have created as part of my own portfolio.

2 Definition of a Portfolio

According to Campbell (2010), "*a portfolio is an organized, goal-driven documentation of your professional growth and competence.*" Campbell further defines a **working portfolio** as "*unabridged versions of the documents you have carefully selected to portray your professional growth*" and a **presentation portfolio** as a portfolio that is "*compiled for the expressed purpose of giving others an effective and easy-to-read portrait of your professional competence*".

This is perhaps comparable to a curator of a museum who might have thousands of exhibits in the storeroom (working portfolio) but carefully selects a subset of these exhibits for public display (presentation portfolio).

R. Kwan et al. (Eds.): ICT 2011, CCIS 177, pp. 8–21, 2011.
© Springer-Verlag Berlin Heidelberg 2011

An e-portfolio or electronic portfolio, according to Campbell serves to same purpose as a portfolio, *"but artifacts are created and presented using electronic technologies and they appear in a variety of media formats: audio, video, digital photographs, graphics and text"*. Furthermore, *"links are created to show the relationship between the artifacts and standards"*.

According to Campbell, artifacts are *"tangible evidence of knowledge that is gained, skills that are mastered, values that are clarified, or dispositions and attitudes that are characteristic of you. Artifacts cannot conclusively prove the attainment of knowledge, skills, or dispositions, but they **provide indicators of achieved competence**."*

3 Importance of a Portfolio

Having a credible presentation portfolio is extremely important for students in the digital media field. An excellent presentation portfolio will give students an edge when applying for higher education or jobs in the digital media industry. The tools and technology of the digital media industry are constantly changing. However, having a credible portfolio remains a constant requirement.

A professional presentation portfolio is much more impressive than academic grades on a transcript or a diploma or degree certificate. It conveys to the potential employer that the student has the necessary skills and talents to get the job done. Thus, having a good portfolio increases the students' chances of employment.

Fig. 1. An example of a student portfolio

Many universities today require students to submit a portfolio of their work for evaluation before accepting them into university courses. This is especially true for digital media degree programmes. A good portfolio is essential for clinching a place in higher education.

By creating a portfolio, the student naturally applies his or her knowledge and skills to create a tangible product. The portfolio allows the student to showcase his talents, strengths and accomplishments. It facilitates self development and independent learning as well. Figure 1 shows an example of a student portfolio.

With portfolio creation being so important for students studying in the field of digital media, many modules in the Diploma of Digital Media are strongly focused on portfolio creation, particularly e-portfolios.

4 Advantages and Disadvantages of Getting Students to Publish Their Digital Work Online

Clazie (2010) highlights the benefits of having a digital portfolio as follows: *"..anyone can access your work at any time, making it highly portable. A quick email from one reviewer to another is all it takes to spread word of your capabilities, creativity, and contact information. Other advantages include the ability to change details and content rapidly and easily without having to redistribute any physical material. You also gain the ability to link to relevant information, websites, live projects, and collaborators online."*

The following are some more advantages of getting students to publish their digital portfolio work online:

- It encourages students to reflect on their work – Before publishing work online for other to see, students are more likely to review and reflect on the quality of their work.
- It encourages greater work ownership – By publishing their work online, students take greater ownership of their work. They are made responsible for maintaining their own online portfolios.
- It builds confidence – Once students achieve some success at publishing their work online, they gain confidence and will be more willing to continue the process of updating and refining their online portfolios.
- Students gain skills at using Web 2.0 tools – New online Web 2.0 tools available seem to be ever increasing and evolving. Ultimately, it does not matter which tools students choose to use. What is important is that students develop the ability to learn how to use the tool properly and effectively.

Some of the disadvantages of using an online environment are as follows:

- Students publish low or negative value posts – There is a tendency for students to publish items of trivial value online. This is made worse when students publish derogatory remarks or statements about their lecturers, peers or the institution that they are studying in. Lecturers need to constantly look out for such occurrences and to correct students appropriately.
- Mainly used for socializing – A myriad of social networking sites exist such as Facebook. As its name implies, such sites are used for online socializing. These sites are useful for building social networks and for finding people of similar interests. As for building a credible online e-portfolio, students may be better off with a website or a blog as these allow for better control of the content published online.

- Addiction – There is an ever present danger of students getting addicted to the Internet, wasting many precious hours online.

It is not possible for lecturers to have total control over students' online activity. However, I believe that lecturers can make a difference and help students make positive choices when it comes to the usage of the Internet.

One way is to encourage students to create their own online e-portfolios. By getting students to create useful digital content which can be published online, students have a clear positive goal to focus on, rather than wasting time online.

5   Portfolio Creation in Web Publishing Module

Over the past semester, I have had the privilege and opportunity to be the module coordinator of the Web Publishing module (ST7106/ST3106). In this module, students are taught the technical skills of using HTML (Hypertext Markup Language) and CSS (Cascading Style Sheets) in order to create web pages.

Learning to code in HTML and CSS can be a potentially boring and tedious task. Therefore, in order to make the module more interesting and relevant, the assignments set were made **portfolio-centric**. In other words, students do not make learning HTML and CSS code an end in itself but use their skills to create web pages about themselves, in effect creating a basic online e-portfolio.

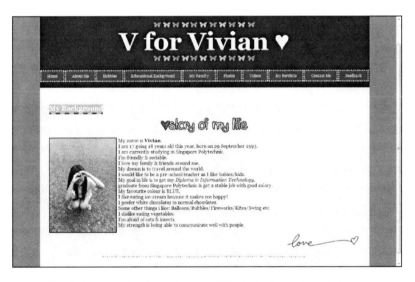

Fig. 2. An example of a student portfolio in the form of a website

In the first assignment, students were given the task of creating a single "About Me" page using HTML and CSS. In the second assignment, they were tasked to expand this single web page into a complete website. Finally, in the third assignment, they were asked to write a report about their website and to present survey results of their own website. They were also expected to publish their websites online.

Most students took to this approach well. They found the assignments to be relevant and interesting and enjoyed creating their e-portfolios in the form of a website. Figure 2 shows an example of an e-portfolio in the form of a website.

6 Student Feedback

Some qualitative feedback which I have obtained from students are as follows:

"I have completed my website and it is uploaded on the web. Looking back at what I did, I felt a great sense of achievement. I want to thank my teacher Mr. Tan for teaching and helping me out to make such a great website. It may not be a great deal to other but it is to me. I enjoyed the assignment and wish to do it again."

(Teo Jia Hao)

"The MY WORK gallery is my favorite part of this website! Because I can show the work pieces that I have done in school to my fellow friends and viewers online. I think my users are very satisfied with my website as shown in their feedback."

(Wong Kok Fai)

"For this assignment, the main problem that I faced was the lack of information. What I was achieving to do was to make a website to keep all my works, so that I can show to others. It was something like my portfolio. Being only year one, I didn't have enough notable works to show. Also, I didn't want to make the website seem like a blog, with too much personal information."

(Joan Tan)

Students taking the Web Publishing module were only first year students and only had limited portfolio work to display on their web pages. Nevertheless, they still managed to successfully complete their assignments. Some students were initially uncomfortable about publishing their work online but with some encouragement they all managed to do so.

7 Online Photo Galleries

Solis (2011) says that *"one of the most understated categories of social networks is also one of the most established. Online photo sharing encourages views and interaction around images, transforming pictures into social objects."* Also, *"some of the more successful companies are already sharing art and customer-focused, exclusive content in communities such as Flikr and Facebook Photos."*

There are many free online photo galleries that students can use to publish their work on.

These include:

- Flickr (http://www.flickr.com)
- Google Picasa Web Albums (http://picasaweb.google.com)

- Photobucket (http://www.photobucket.com)
- Facebook Photo Galleries

These services allow users to upload their digital photos online and arrange them into virtual albums. These virtual albums can then be shared with anyone using the Internet in the form of online slideshows.

For example, one of my students created an online slideshow on Flickr which can be found at http://www.flickr.com/photos/tuesdaymrngs/sets/72157625770654013/show/. She embedded her slideshow into her website as shown in Figure 3 below.

Fig. 3. An online slideshow embedded in a webpage

Many modules being taught in the Diploma in Digital Media involve the creation of digital design and artwork. If these digital creations were simply stored on the student's computer, they would not be seen by many people other than the student's lecturer who would mark the student's work. In contrast, if their digital artwork were published on the Internet on an online photo gallery, they could be seen and admired by a much wider audience.

Some time ago, one particular student decided to upload some of his portfolio work on *Flickr*. A manager from an IT company browsed some of the work that he uploaded and liked his work. Eventually, this led to the student getting employed by the company for freelance work.

In addition to digital artwork, some students also uploaded photographs of a field trip which was taken in Vietnam in 2010. Shown in Figure 4 is an example of a **Picasa Web Album**.

Thus, online photo galleries are an excellent web 2.0 tool for showcasing a students' digital artwork and photography skills. Lecturers should strongly encourage their students to upload their digital creations or photographs online. Of course, care has to be taken not to infringe any copyright.

Fig. 4. Photographs of Vietnam trip uploaded online to Picasa web album

8   Dropbox

Dropbox (http://www.dropbox.com) is a very useful Web 2.0 tool that can be used to create an e-portfolio almost instantly. It is basically on online storage website which gives users 2GB of online storage. Once the Dropbox utility has been downloaded and installed, users need only drag and drop folders on their computers to their specified Dropbox folders into order to have them uploaded and synced online.

Users also have the ability to make a folder Public or share folders with other. Making a folder Public allows users to quickly publish their work online. Virtually any sort of file can be uploaded and made public. The screenshot below in Figure 5 shows an example of a Public folder.

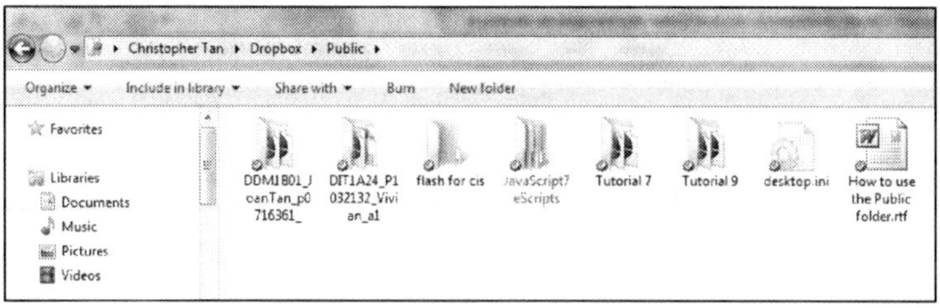

Fig. 5. Dropbox Public folder

Last semester, for the Web Publishing module, students were asked to upload their assignments online using Dropbox. Marks were awarded if the students managed to successfully complete this task. The task involved uploading HTML and CSS files along with image files. Most students managed to successfully upload their web publishing assignments online. By submitting a link to the starting HTML file, the entire website could be viewed online using a web browser.

An example of a hyperlink to the public Dropbox folder is http://dl.dropbox.com/u/ 19783443/DDM1B01_JoanTan_p0716361_/index.html. The screenshot is shown in Figure 6.

Fig. 6. Online website hosted using Dropbox

9   Google Forms

An excellent way of gathering feedback on the web is by using Google forms. This Web 2.0 tool is available free of charge when one signs up for a Google account. This tool can be accessed via Google Documents (http://docs.google.com).

In the third assignment of the Web Publishing module, students were asked to create a web survey form in order to gather feedback from their fellow classmates about their website. I encouraged students to use this Web 2.0 tool in order to gather feedback. If fact, many students had not used Google forms before and were pleasantly surprised at how easy and convenient it was to create a form and gather feedback on the Internet.

After publishing a form online, students were able to ask their classmates for feedback on their own websites. The results of the survey are conveniently captured in a spreadsheet format. A screenshot of a sample survey form is shown in Figure 7.

Hi, I'm doing a usability survey for my website. Please help me by filling in the questions in this form. Thanks!

* Required

Name *

Email

Contact Number

Gender

○ Male

○ Female

Please rate each question accordingly. *

	1. Strongly Disagree	2. Disagree	3. Neutral	4. Agree	5. Strongly Agree
My website is easy to navigate.	○	○	○	○	○
My website has an attractive theme.	○	○	○	○	○
The content of my website is meaningful and interesting.	○	○	○	○	○

Fig. 7. An online Google form

Gathering feedback from others is important as it allows students to better gauge their own work and to make improvements where necessary. It also encourages students to improve their standards of work as they know that their work will be seen and evaluated by their peers.

10   Video Sharing Websites

Video sharing websites also allow students to showcase their talents in the area of video editing. In the Diploma in Digital Media, first year students take a module entitled Video and Audio Fundamentals. I was pleasantly surprised when some students embedded the assignment done in the Video and Audio Fundamentals within the Web Publishing assignment as part of their portfolio. (see Figure 8)

It is a fairly easy task to create an account and upload videos to these video sharing website. Using the Embed or Share functions, students can share their video creations anywhere on the web.

The challenge then is for lecturer to properly guide students to publish worthwhile and substantial content on these video sharing sites which add to the quality of the students' portfolios.

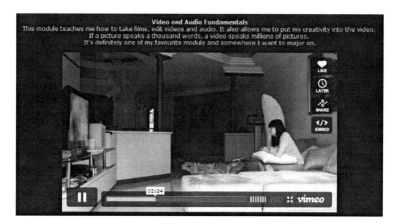

Fig. 8. VIMEO video sharing website

The School of Digital Media and Infocomm Technology, Singapore Polytechnic also currently maintains a YouTube channel (http://www.youtube.com/dmitvideo) to publish video works done by students.

11 Blogs

Blogs offer a convenient way of publishing portfolio work online. One can sign up for a blog in a matter of minutes and begin publishing on the Internet almost instantly.

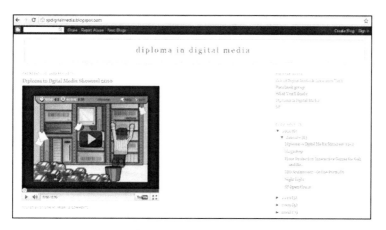

Fig. 9. The Diploma in Digital Media blog

The Diploma in Digital Media maintains a blog (http://spdigitalmedia.blogspot.com), see Figure 9, which contains many embedded YouTube videos of student work. Every semester, students taking the Final Year Project are asked to submit a video trailer promoting their project. The videos are then uploaded to YouTube and displayed on the blog.

This blog provides a convenient way for the public to view the portfolio works of the Diploma and Digital Media students. It also serves as a free online marketing tool.

12   Student Blogs and Websites

The School of Digital Media and Infocomm Technology, Singapore Polytechnic has an annual Graduation Show event where students display their work for the public to view. Every year, a Graduation Show website (http://www.render.sg) is updated, where a mini portfolio of each student is shown. For example, the screenshot in Figure 10 shows an example of a student from the Diploma in Digital Media together with a link to her website.

Fig. 10. A student profile from the GradShow 2011 website – http://www.render.sg

Some Diploma in Digital Media students maintain their own blogs and websites and use these resources to publish their portfolio work online. Some examples are as follows:

- Maizurah Kasim (http://maisnapshots.tumblr.com/)
- Neo Xian Zhen (http://zxoen.carbonmade.com/)
- Ong Ching Wen (http://minsooyi.deviantart.com/)
- Ong Li Teng (http://kazerain.deviantart.com/)
- Delconi Quek (http://delconi.daportfolio.com/)
- Randy Ng (http://www.youtube.com/watch?v=08pBjrx5qvg)
- Siti Mariam (http://sitimariambab.tumblr.com/)
- Siti Suhaila (http://suhailaaris.tumblr.com/)
- Su Xiang Ting (http://www.linkedin.com/pub/xiangting-su/2a/923/635)
- Tan Li Ping (http://smallbottled.tumblr.com/)
- Teo Sheng Yang (http://www.silverbtf.com/)
- Tong Shi Hui (http://www.tongtongchiang.com/)

The links to the various websites and blogs are all public links which contain more e-portfolio works which the student wishes to display.

13 My Own Portfolio

Besides encouraging students to create their portfolios, it is also important for lecturers to continually build their own portfolios. This allows the lecturer to "practise what he preaches" and "walk the talk". It is also helpful to share these project works with students as it helps them see the relevance and usefulness of the knowledge and skills that they are acquiring in their modules.

Personally, I have used my web publishing skills to create a few website for Singapore Polytechnic which are highlighted as follows.

14 SIWF Website

The following screenshot in Figure 11 shows the website for the Singapore International Water Festival (SIWF) (http://www.siwf.sg).

Fig. 11. Singapore International Water Festival (SIWF) website

It was constructed using HTML and CSS and incorporates some of the Web 2.0 tools which are mentioned in this paper:

- Online photo galleries
- Embedded YouTube video
- Links to online registration forms

In addition a Facebook page was created at http://www.facebook.com/ SingaporeInternationalWaterFestival.

This website is used to demonstrate to students the practical applications of HTML and CSS code when teaching the Web Publishing module. The Facebook page is used to demonstrate how Social Media tools can be used to promote an event.

15   DesignWorks Website

The following screenshot in Figure 12 shows the DesignWorks website (http://www.designworkssingapore.com).

Fig. 12. DesignWorks Singapore website

I was privileged to be given the opportunity to help set up this website. This involved some of the following skills:

- HTML and CSS
- Registering the domain name
- Acquiring the web hosting service
- Translating a given Photoshop template into webpages.

This website can also be used to demonstrate relevant web publishing skills that are taught in the web publishing module.

16   Conclusion

Getting students to build their own portfolios is an important educational goal, especially for students in the School of Digital Media and Infocomm Technology. Furthermore, portfolios are much more conveniently accessed if they were digital and online. It is my hope that this paper has helped to increase the awareness of this goal.

The same idea of portfolio building can be applied to almost any subject or module being taught at Singapore Polytechnic or at any tertiary institution. A myriad of Web 2.0 tools also exists. These tools enable students to publish their portfolio works online. Many of these tools do not require much technical knowledge to use. Students need only create an account to begin publishing content online.

Lecturers should actively encourage students to publish the portfolio works online. One of the most effective ways of doing this is to lead by example and to maintain a professional personal online portfolio.

References

1. Campbell, D.: How to develop a professional portfolio. Pearson, New Jersey (2010)
2. Clazie, I.: Creating your digital design portfolio. RotoVision, UK (2010)
3. Solis, B.: Engage! The complete guide for brands and businesses to build, cultivate and measure success in the new web. John Wiley & Sons Inc., New Jersey (2011)

First Steps towards an Integrated Personal Learning Environment at the University Level

Martin Ebner[1], Sandra Schön[2], Behnam Taraghi[1], Hendrik Drachsler[3], and Philip Tsang[4]

[1] Graz University of Technology, Computing and Information Services,
Division of Social Learning, Graz, Austria
{martin.ebner@tugraz.at,b.taraghi@tugraz.at}@tugraz.at
[2] Salzburg Research, Information Society Research, Salzburg, Austria
sandra.schaffert@salzburgresearch.at
[3] Open University of the Netherlands,
Center for Learning Science and Technology (CELSTEC), Heerlen, The Netherlands
mhendrik.drachsler@ou.nl
[4] Caritas Institute of Higher Education, Office of the President, HKSAR, China
ptsang@cihe.edu.hk

Abstract. Personalization is seen as the key approach to handle the plethora of information in today's knowledge-based society. It is expected that personalized teaching and learning will efficiently address learner needs. The education of the future will change as a result of the influence of Web 2.0 content typified by a steadily increasing supply of data. This means that the students of tomorrow will regularly have to deal with sharing and merging content from different sources. Therefore, mashup technology will become a very important lens by which to focus on individual learning needs and enable personalized access to particular information. The following paper describes the challenges of Personal Learning Environments at higher education institutions. In the first section, the concept of Personal Learning Environments is presented, while the second section discusses the new challenges that arise for learning with the help of Personal Learning Environments. The third section describes the technical background of Personal Learning Environments and the widget standard in general. In section four, a first prototype of a personal learning environment will be presented, which is integrated into the learning culture at the Technical University of Graz. A detailed description of the available widgets for the prototype, along with a first expert evaluation, is provided. Finally, the conclusion of the article consolidates the main points of the paper and present plans for future research together with the prospective developments.

Keywords: adult learning; architectures for educational technology systems; distributed learning environments.

1 Introduction

Since Tim O'Reilly (O'Reilly, 2006) referred to the booming possibilities of interaction and communication within the Internet as 'Web 2.0', a new era of the

R. Kwan et al. (Eds.): ICT 2011, CCIS 177, pp. 22–36, 2011.
© Springer-Verlag Berlin Heidelberg 2011

World Wide Web began. Interaction among people, as well as content-sharing, has increased dramatically. Sharing and collaborating by way of social software has become a common activity. By the same token, communication and debate through social networks is nowadays almost as normal as e-mail. It is a fact that our social life and our working environment, along with our learning and teaching behavior, are increasingly influenced by Web 2.0 technologies, due largely to its ubiquitous availability and pervasive use (Holzinger et al., 2006; Klamma et al., 2007). Downes labeled the use of Web 2.0 technologies for teaching and learning purposes as E-learning 2.0 (Downes, 2005). Numerous research papers have established several different possibilities of didactical settings for this new approach (Ebner, 2007). Apart from web-based software – wikis (Augar et al., 2004), weblogs (Farmer & Bartlett-Bragg, 2005), or podcasts (Towned, 2005) – the integration of Web 2.0 elements into current learning and teaching scenarios generates a vast potential for creating new learning environments. Nowadays, not only social software like Facebook (social networking) or Twitter (micro-blogging) is important for learning (Ebner & Maurer, 2008), but also platforms for sharing different kinds of media, like YouTube (video), Slideshare, Scribd (presentations and documents) or Del.icio.us (bookmarks) make up for an integral part of the innovative teaching methods that strengthen informal learning processes (Mason & Rennie, 2007).

Considering the enormous number of rapidly growing applications intended for the purposes mentioned above. Efficient management of these tools can become extremely challenging. Therefore, it is understandable that teachers and learners may be overwhelmed by the extensive possibilities that Web 2.0 tools offer. Surprisingly enough, various studies on Web 2.0 technologies have shown that first-year university students are largely unaware of the existence of numerous Web 2.0 tools (Nagler & Ebner, 2009).

Personal Learning Environments (PLEs), also referred to as mashups, can be of great assistance in managing multiple tools, along with handling information and the cognitive overload that comes with it (Kulathuramaiyer & Maurer, 2007). "The possibility to connect different resources in one environment should help to maintain the overview of all activities. Mashups merge content, services and applications from multiple websites in an integrated, coherent way" (Tuchinda et al., 2008). Therefore, PLEs offer a new form of personalized learning (Wild, Mödritscher & Sigurdason, 2008).

This paper describes the challenges that Personal Learning Environments present for higher education institutions. In section two, new challenges for learning and the information overflow will be discussed, whereas section three will describe the technical background of Personal Learning Environments and the widget standard in general. In section four, a first prototype of a personal learning environment for higher education systems will be presented, which has been integrated into the learning culture at the Technical University of Graz. This section will also give a detailed description of the available widgets for the prototype and provide a first expert evaluation. Finally, the conclusion of the article will consolidate the main points of the paper and present the plans for future research, including prospective developments.

2   The Development and Concept of 'Personal Learning Environments'

The challenge and possibility to connect and mash-up different web-based applications was the cradle for developing a new concept in the field of technology-enhanced learning. In this way, the idea of a 'Personal Learning Environment', in short PLE, was born (Olivier & Liber, 2001). Existing technological concepts of learning and teaching by using the Web, like the Learning Management System (LMS), have mainly been developed to support formal teaching needs, such as student management and course organization. In contrast, the PLE concept focuses on the individual learner and his/her personal learning interests. This means that within a PLE, learners arrange and use web-based (learning) content and web-based (learning) tools to support their personal knowledge management and learning.

Olivier and Liber (2001) were among the first scholars to examine the idea of a personal learning environment. A few years later, Wilson (2005) sketched an image of a future 'virtual learning environment, where he integrated external services and enhanced them through applications. By 2006, PLEs had gained in popularity. This fact was proven by the results of an analysis of the search term 'personal learning environment', carried out by Google Insights (Google Insights, 2009) and was supported in several publications. (Attwell 2007; Liber & Johnson, 2008).

To sum up, the current definitions of PLEs are defined as learning applications that enable learners to integrate and organize dispersed online information, resources and contacts, and furthermore allow for content and other elements developed in a PLE to be applied in other online environments (Schaffert & Kalz 2009).

PLEs are not the first attempt to personalize learning content; on the contrary, there is a long tradition of Instructional Design and Adaptive Learning. Instructional Design follows the idea of fostering the learning outcome on the basis of bite-sized, sequenced instruction bits. Particularly in the field of artificial intelligence, the possibility of an automatic 'personalization' of the content is considered as an automatic adaptation of the learning content by a system, pre-defined by an expert model. For several reasons, the aforementioned ideas seem to have become outdated or not further applicable (Schaffert et al., 2008): "(i) learning is mainly dynamic, permanently under development and only shallowly categorized; (ii) referring to current learning theories, the learners are to be seen as active, self-organized creators of their learning environment, and (iii) social involvement and interaction is crucial for learning." Additional arguments for applying new forms of personalized learning focus on new ideas of learning (Wild, Mödritscher & Sigurdason, 2008, p. 2): "learning to learn is more important than (re-)constructing field-specific knowledge, therefore the establishment of a (networked) learning environment can already be seen as a learning outcome. From a pragmatic point of view, a system that was built on emergence should be more powerful than 'programming' by rules."

New possibilities, perspectives, insights and challenges, have catapulted interest in the PLE concept. But while it seems to be an interesting but not a very well developed or elaborated concept it seems that there is limited practical implementation as an innovative approach within technology-enhanced learning and especially within the field of higher education.

2.1 How the PLE Concept Challenges Higher Education

First of all, PLE is a technological concept because it describes the functionalities that a system should have to actively support personalized learning on the Web. It challenges the educational organization of traditional LMSs and the formal learning style.

Teachers and educational institutions are interested in supporting and fostering learning processes and activities of their learners. It can be observed that the selection of suitable tools has a pronounced impact on the students if the institutions offer them engagement in virtual learning phases.   Nevertheless, this decision may inhibit learning and teaching processes, for example as a result of the limited possibilities of interaction among the students or a lack of opportunities for learners to create their own content.

Terry Anderson (2006) identified the disadvantages and advantages of PLEs over LMSs. He gave six advantages in comparison with LMSs, namely: identity (learners have various identities outside the formal school environment), ease of use (customization by the users themselves), control and responsibility of ownership (content belongs to the user), copyright and reuse (the owner and not the institution has to make these decisions), social presence (support of communication and 'online culture') and capacity of speed and innovation (new applications evolve rapidly and new features invade the PLE conglomerate in the learning setting).

The following table provides an overview of seven crucial aspects of the shift from the LMS to a PLE that are identified as important changes and challenges (Schaffert & Hilzensauer, 2008).

Schaffert & Hilzensauer (2008) observe that the shift from a LMS to a PLE challenges several norms: The role of learner has to shift from consumer to 'prosumer', which means that self- organization is possible and necessary; learner need certain competencies to organize their learning, to search, find and use appropriate sources; and also, knowledge of personal data is required. What is more, a shift in educational and learning culture is not only a precondition but also a consequence of actively supporting and implementing PLEs.

According to what has been established so far, currently there no real shift from LMS to PLE is taking place. Instead, it is more likely that the concept of PLE will gradually gain ground. In the sphere of higher education transformation is difficult, because managerial requirements will be higher in formally organized learning environments than in higher education. Nevertheless, available on the Web of a plethora of tools and content will encourage educational institutions to support the concept of PLEs.

2.2 Challenges of PLEs for Learners

A common problem for mashups and PLEs is the amount of data gathered within a short time span. Depending on the type of widget that is integrated into a PLE and the number of people adding content to the widget, an enormous amount of information can be collected, which may have an overwhelming effect on the user. This particularly applies to a widget acting as a window for online communities that frequently contribute content to the widget. Particularly text-based widgets that are based on blog posts, social bookmarks or micro-blogging statements, are frequently

Table 1. An overview of seven crucial aspects of the shift from a LMS to a PLE (Schaffert & Hilzensauer, 2008)

		LMS	PLE	challenges & shifts
1	Role of learner	learner as consumer of predefined learning materials, which depend on the 'creativity' of the teacher	active, self-directed, creator of content	shift from consumer to 'prosumer' self-organization is possible AND necessary
2	Personalization	... is an arrangement of learning assignments and materials according to a (proposed or predefined) learner model, based on an underlying expert system	... means to get information about learning opportunities and content from community members and learning services corresponding to learner interests (via tags/RSS)	competence for the usage of several tools and self-organization are necessary
3	Content	developed by domain experts, special authors, tutors and/or teachers	the infinite 'bazaar' of learning content on the Web, exploring learning opportunities and services	competences necessary to search, find and use appropriate sources (e.g. Weblogs)
4	Social involvement	limited use of group work, focus on the closed learner group (e.g. in the LMS), collaboration and exchange not in the centre	community and social involvement (even in multiple communities) is the key for the learning process and the recommendations for learning opportunities	community and collaboration as central learning opportunities
5	Ownership	content is generally owned by the educational institutions or the students; for technological reasons, this ownership cannot always be claimed	content is organized in multiple, web-based tools, ownership is held by the learners themselves and/or (commercial) service providers	knowledge of personal data is needed
6	Educational & organizational culture	imitation of classroom learning course-orientated, teacher-orientated features	self-organized learner in the centre	change of learning culture and perspective – move towards self organization and self determination
7	Technological aspects	classic learning content needs interoperability between LMS and data repositories	Social software tools and aggregation of multiple sources	required interoperability between LMS and social software

updated. Therefore, a significant time has to be invested to follow them. Yet not every learner or student can afford to invest the required amount of time on a daily basis; that is why a pre-selection of information might be an efficient solution to direct learners to find the required information more quickly. In the long run, the overwhelming effect also applies to media-driven widgets (videos, pictures, presentations) that address public web-services such as YouTube, flickr and Slideshare. Moreover, the size of the community is a critical factor for the overwhelming effect. On the one hand, if the community is small, the learners are not able to gain a broad enough overview of the information needed. On the other hand, when the community is too large, the learners are not able to cope with the amount of information since it is updated too frequently. In the latter case, the learners need to structure and filter the information flow, otherwise it becomes difficult to gain an overview of the available content and identify the most suitable items for certain tasks (Hummel et al., 2007).

The recommender system technology, known from e-commerce systems, could aid learners to establish their priorities and filter through the information overflow. The main purpose of e-commerce recommender systems is to pre-select information that users might be interested in, in order to offer suitable products that fit their personal taste. The most prominent example is the Amazon.com recommender (Linden, Smith, & York, 2003), which suggests related products based on the product search history of a user. Drachsler et al. 2009 applied the recommender system approach from e-commerce and implemented it in a mashup PLE for non-formal learning to suggest most suitable Web 2.0 items to learners. In the so-called ReMashed system[1] , a recommender system was integrated, which suggests the most suitable content, showing up in various Web 2.0 services within a PLE to a learner by using his/her tags and ratings (Drachsler et al. 2010).

3   Technological Background of the PLE

The goal of a PLE cannot be reduced to a platform for accumulating distributed learning applications used at university or on the Internet. One of the goals is certainly that the students are able to adapt the learning environment to their preferences, so that they can make their own decisions on which applications they want to use and integrate into their environment. By the same token, each application or service that is integrated into a PLE should be flexibly configurable to meet the individual needs of the student. From the technical point of view, a PLE is a client-side environment (Rich Internet Application) that comprises a mashup of different small independent web applications and services selected by the user. These distributed applications are configurable and can communicate with other web applications within the PLE environment. What is more, Hoyer (Hoyer, 2008) noted some existing mashup tools with different emphases, such as Yahoo Pipes and Microsoft Popfly. Aumueller and Thor (Aumueller & Thor, 2008) describe three main components of a mashup application: data extraction, data flow and presentation. They categorize mashup tools according to one or several of these components.

---

[1] http://remashed.ou.nl (last visited 10.03.2011).

At the Technical University of Graz a PLE is being developed that is based on a mashup of widgets according to W3C widget specifications. To end-user mashups, it can be classified as described in Gamble and Gamble (Gamble & Gamble, 2008). Applying widgets in a PLE can have several advantages. Widgets represent independent web applications and hence they can be implemented independently from a PLE. The W3C widget specifications, which are explained briefly in the next section, introduce a unique standard for widgets. If this standard is applied, it could result in many open source widgets that can be employed across PLEs and other learning systems, supporting the W3C widget specifications. Another issue is the distributed knowledge transfer from different servers, along with diffusion. Remote servers provide widgets with the corresponding services through their API (Application Programming Interface). Widgets cannot send 'cross-site' requests to remote servers because of browser security restrictions. Yet, there are some techniques that enable bypass of these restrictions, such as JSONP[2] or HTTP Access Controls[3]. In our case, a proxy script is used on the PLE server to enable cross-site communication between widgets and remote services.

In the following section, widgets in general as well as the widget specifications of World Wide Web consortium (W3C) are described.

3.1 Widgets

Widgets are small embedded front end applications that can be included in any (X)HTML page. They include the client-side programming logic and the presentation layer. They can be developed in any common client-side language, such as (X)HTML + JavaScript, and Java-applets. The server-side logic of the applications is no longer responsible for the presentation layer. Its only task is to provide the clients (widgets) with the data and resources they need for using an API in a Service Oriented Architecture (SOA). Widgets are very often used on personalized web sites or personal desktops where users are supported to aggregate and create their own configuration of widgets. iGoogle[4], Netvibes[5], Protopage[6] and Pageflakes[7] are some examples of such personalized desktops. The most famous projects that provide developers with tools to develop widgets are the Konfabulator from yahoo widgets, Dashboard from apple project, Desktop widgets from Opera, and Google gadgets.

3.2 The W3C Widget Family of Specifications

Different types of widgets require different widget engines. Widgets of one widget engine, like iGoogle cannot be applied in others, like Netvibes. The W3C widget family of specifications contains a series of specifications to gain a standard for

---

[2] http://en.wikipedia.org/wiki/JSON#JSONP (last visited: 10.03.2011).
[3] http://www.w3.org/TR/cors/ (last visited: 10.03.2011).
[4] http://www.google.com/ig (last visited: 10.03.2011).
[5] http://www.netvibes.com/ (last visited: 10.03.2011).
[6] http://www.protopage.com/ (last visited: 10.03.2011).
[7] http://www.pageflakes.com/ (last visited 10.03.2011).

widgets and remove the lack of interoperability among widget engines. 'Widget Packaging and Configuration'[8] 'The Widget Interface'[9] and 'Widgets 1.0: Digital Signatures'[10] are three W3C candidate recommendations that are described here briefly for the sake of completeness:

- 'Widget Packaging and Configuration' needs the zip packaging format to include all the widget files, folders and the XML configuration file, along with some mandatory and non-mandatory elements. It also specifies the behavior and means of error handling for widget user agents.
- 'The Widget Interface' defines a set of APIs and events and deals with the functionality within the widget scope. It defines the corresponding methods to access meta-data that are declared in the widget configuration file and methods to receive events related to changes in the state of the widget.
- 'Widgets 1.0: Digital Signatures' deals with the digital signing of widgets. It defines a profile of XML signature syntax and processing specification to allow a widget to be digitally signed by widget authors or distributors.

4 Proof of Concept - A PLE for Higher-Education Institutions

At the TU Graz we implemented a first prototype of PLE that offers centralized access to various University services, like administration systems, LMS or blogospheres in one overview. The users can personalize the PLE to their individual information and learning needs. In addition, public services of the Internet are also offered in the PLE. For each of these services, a widget has been developed that can be integrated into the PLE. Fig. 1 shows a conceptual view of the PLE of the TU Graz that integrates University portals and other Internet services.

The widget engine used in the TU Graz PLE is an extension of the widget engine that was first implemented within the scope of the IST Palette project[11] for the Palette web portal. The widget configuration file, which is specified in W3C Widget Packaging and Configuration, has been extended to add some default user preference values in order to facilitate widget customization. What is more, the W3C Widget Interface has been extended to enable widget intercommunication within the PLE environment. Communication can run in the background automatically or can be directed manually by the user, for instance as a drag and drop event for data flow between two widgets. The TU Graz PLE represents a web portal that students can fully adjust to their personal needs by adding and removing widgets as well as modifying widget preferences. The PLE widget engine distinguishes between local widgets, which are installed on the PLE server, and remote widgets, which can be installed on any remote server. By using this extension, widgets do not need to be installed on the PLE server.

---

[8] http://www.w3.org/TR/widgets/ (last visited: 10.03.2011).
[9] http://www.w3.org/TR/widgets-apis/ (last visited: 10.03.2011).
[10] http://www.w3.org/TR/widgets-digsig/ (last visited: 10.03.2011).
[11] http://palette.ercim.org/ (last visited: 10.03.2011).

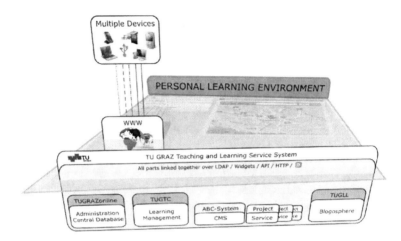

Fig. 1. PLE concept: aggregation of different services from distributed university portals and other applications on the Internet

The following sections examine the structure of the user interface and demonstrate some widget prototypes that have already been implemented in the TU Graz PLE.

4.1. User Interface (UI)

The PLE Graphical User Interface (GUI) is a combination of a traditional UI with a sidebar element and banner for orientation and navigation. In addition, it offers a widget-based UI with the so-called 'widget zones', which require an adjustment by the user (Fig. 2).

Widgets are categorized according to pre-defined topics. Each widget topic (category) has its own widget zone. The sidebar elements contain the main widget topics and help the user to switch between widget zones. The topics are easily extendable if the number of widgets is increasing. Furthermore, the sidebar also updates the user on the status of the widgets by means of color and numerical indicators. The sidebar can be switched off in favor of the unfamiliar widget-based UI and replaced by another navigation element, which resembles the Mac Dock menu on the bottom part of widget zones. The widget topics include different areas related to formal and informal learning: 'Communication Center' for emails, chats and news groups; 'TeachCenter' for all services related to the TU Graz LMS system, such as course materials, podcasts etc.; 'LearnLand' for services related to the TU Graz blogosphere system social bookmarking, file sharing, etc.; and 'Help and Support' for the help desk as well as FAQ. Widget zones contain widgets and are structured in columns. The user can switch between widget zones, add (open), close, customize, position and arrange the widgets in different columns according to her/his personal learning preferences. Moreover, the user is able to create a mashup of the most frequently used interesting widgets from different widget zones in a special interface called 'Personal Desktop'. The personal desktop is always available to the user and can be activated at any time. When the user activates the personal desktop it overlays

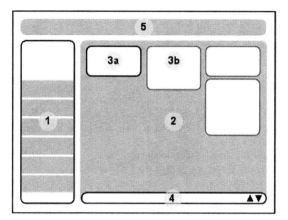

Fig. 2. PLE User Interface. 1) Sidebar elements contain widget topics; 2) Widget zone contains the widgets that belong to a widget topic; 3a and 3b) Widgets within the corresponding widget zone; 4) Hidden 'Personal Desktop' containing a mashup of widgets from different widget zones selected by the user. 5) Banner displays information in context of the active widget zone from the network.

the whole screen from the bottom of the page upwards (Fig. 2 part 4). Users can add or remove widgets from all widget zones to a personal desktop and arrange them in columns according to personal needs. On the top of the page there is a graphic element called 'banner' (Fig. 2 part 5), which contributes to brand a site and help the user to locate contents and orientate himself. But its main purpose is to display information from the network in a user-profile-sensitive way. It also keeps track of the currently active widget zone. The widgets consist of a front side and a rear side, where the rear side contains the widget preferences that can be modified by the user.

4.2 Widget Prototypes

Some first widget prototypes have been developed by computer science Master students according to their interests. The widgets vary from different distributed applications of the Internet to various services within the University to enhance formal learning and foster informal learning scenarios.

Some university widgets

- The "blog" widget allows users to read weblog postings from the blogosphere of the university (Fig. 3). Users can customize the widget to their favorite blogs, a specific blog community, or to all items from the blogosphere.
- LMS widget (Learning Management Widget), for instance, presents a view on the existing LMS system of the TU Graz (Fig. 4). The widget presents a list of courses a student has access to. Selecting a course displays the e-learning materials related to that course. In addition, some supplementary widgets, such as a timetables and a location widget, can be auto-synchronized in the background to provide the user with information regarding the place and the time schedule of

the course. An alert widget informs the student as soon as a course is cancelled or new notifications are coming in.

- LO widgets (Learning Object Widgets) linked to several courses are suitable to be used in the PLE. As an example, a widget was developed for the course *Design and Analysis of Algorithms* that demonstrates different algorithms (Fig. 5). The "Truth table" widget is used for Informatics students in first semester to try out and learn logical mathematical operations. There are some more LO widgets currently under development, such as a 2D and 3D function plotter for mathematic courses.

Some useful widgets from the Internet

- The Twitter widget enables users to follows twitter streams. The users can customize the widget to be able to follow the tweets of every other user. What is more, a tag-based search module in the public stream of twitter is provided.
- The "RSS Feed Reader" widget allows users to aggregate and follow published Internet content through RSS feeds in the PLE.
- "Google Maps", "Google Calendar" and "YouTube" widgets represent the corresponding services from Internet.
- "Translation" and "TODO" widgets are some other examples of running widgets.

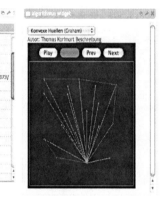

Fig. 3. Blog widget displaying blogs from the blogosphere system

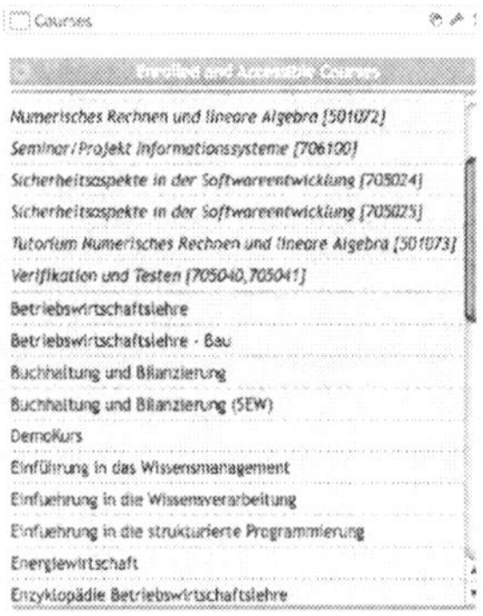

Fig. 4. LMS course widget displays the list of accessible or enrolled courses to a user

Fig. 5. LO widget displaying the functioning of the Graham Scan algorithm

5   Conclusions and Future Work

This paper described the challenges that the introduction of Personal Learning Environments pose for higher education institutes. In section two, new challenges for learning and the information overflow were discussed. In the following section, the technical background of Personal Learning Environments and the widget standard in general was presented. A proof of concept was presented in section four, namely a personal learning environment that has been integrated into the learning culture at the

Technical University of Graz. A detailed description of some of the available widgets for the prototype was also provided. In the final section that follows, we conclude with an outlook on future research and developments plans.

As already mentioned, a common problem for mashups and PLEs is the amount of data that is quickly gathered in a short time span. To overcome the overwhelming effect and help the users to structure and filter the information flow within the PLE, we plan to investigate four possibilities to apply the recommender system technology within the PLE of the Graz University of Technology.

1. A study path recommender system: The University of Stanford in the US developed a study path recommender system that suggests alternative courses to students to improve their study time. The CourseRank system (Bercovitz et al., 2009) is a free study planner that offers the students access to information about their courses, lectures and alternative choices. It supports the students in selecting the most suitable course by demonstrating the decision of the students on certain courses through the recommender system. CourseRank uses feedback information of the students (indirect ratings) about the courses offered and makes this accessible to all the students at the campus. In that way, CourseRank makes the tacit knowledge about courses only available by word-of-mouth, while the brief course descriptions are made explicit and widely available to all students. The students can anonymously rate courses they have taken, add comments and rate the accuracy of other comments. They receive personalized recommendations and are able to organize their courses in their study schedule. CourseRank extends the knowledge base of the students by identifying the most efficient and effective study path through a selection of courses at the university. The implemented recommender system technology sets CourseRank apart from traditional study planner tools. A similar approach could be considered for the TU Graz PLE. The recommender system could also be designed as a widget and integrated into the PLE.

2. A widget recommender system: Nowadays, an increasing number of recommender systems are no longer designed to recommend content or persons, but rather recommend certain web services, applications or widgets to individual users (Kokash, Birukou, & D'Andrea, 2007). Depending on the amount of widgets available for a university PLE, a recommender system for widgets should be a reasonable choice; especially in case the university follows an open policy that allows the students to integrate and develop their own widgets for the PLE. Such a widget recommender could be integrated into the dashboard interface of the PLE suggesting certain widgets to particular students. It could also recommend different sets of widgets to a student on the basis of study domain or course selection. For instance, a computer scientist student that has subscribed to a course in computer algorithms could take advantage of the algorithm visualization widget (Fig. 4a). Thus, with subscription to the course, the recommender will suggest this particular widget to the student. The recommender would be based on a top-down knowledge-driven recommender technology, as in e-commerce systems for complex products like insurances (Felfernig, 2005). But it can also be combined with bottom-up technology, like collaborative filtering, and allow the students to assess if a widget is valuable or not.

3. A peer student recommender system: Another scenario to apply a recommender system at university level is to increase the connections among the students on the campus. This could be done either for short problem-solving issues, as Van Rosmalen et al. (2007) demonstrated with a 'question-answering' tool that recommends the user a list of other students to be considered to solve a certain question. But that could also be applied to complex problems or themes to which the students are committed. Similar to the CourseRank system, knowledge about specialist areas according to distinct topics can be made explicit and returned to the students. That way, special interest groups throughout different semester levels could be created and bring together students who are interested in the same topics. The system could recommend peer learners to meet and prospective candidates to create learning groups or communities of practice. Nevertheless, this approach requires student agreement to allow other students to contact them over their e-mail or phone number. Shared interests of students could be established by comparing their tag cloud, search terms and documents used in the past.

4. A hybrid recommender system: Finally, there is a real possibility to create a hybrid recommender widget that combines aspects of other scenarios in one recommender widget. Such a hybrid approach could be sensitive to various activities within the PLE. It could for instance be sensitive to search terms entered in the search widget of the PLE environment. Or it could request a combination of information related to the search term and present them in one overview. Apart from that, it could also request a definition for the search term from the Web (Wikipedia), recommend documents (from the Web or the university repository), and suggest peer students for learning groups.

In addition to the recommender research perspectives, we will extend the PLE to mobile clients. From the technical point of view, the PLE and the widgets are implemented on the basis of MVC design architecture (Model View Controller). This pattern makes it possible to extend the whole logic, user interface or client-side data layer without interfering with other modules. One of our next steps will be to extend the view modules so that the PLE and the widgets can also be applied in mobile clients.

- What is more, the extension of the model modules to local storage or database storage that are specified in HTML 5 makes it possible to build offline widgets. Following these extensions, the PLE can be used offline and in mobile clients.
- The overwhelming flood of information and distributed services on the WWW and within universities, means there is a need to provide PLEs for higher education. Combining mashups with appropriate recommender systems would support students in finding the required services easily and filter the flow of information in the PLE efficiently.

References

Anderson, T.: PLEs versus LMS: Are PLEs ready for Prime time? In: Virtual Canuck – Teaching and Learning in a Net-Centric World (2006), http://terrya.edublogs.org/2006/01/09/ples-versus-lms-are-ples-ready-for-prime-time/

Attwell, G.: The Personal Learning Environments – the future of eLearning? E-Learning Papers 1, 2 (2007)

Augar, N., Raitman, R., Zhou, W.: Teaching and learning online with wikis. In: Atkinson, R., McBeath, C., Jonas-Dwyer, D., Phillips, R. (eds.) Beyond the comfort zone: In: Proceedings of the 21st ASCILITE Conference, Perth, Australia, December 5-8, pp. 95–104 (2004)

Aumueller, D., Thor, A.: Mashup-Werkzeuge zur Ad-hoc-Datenintegration im Web. Datenbank-Spektrum 8, 26 (2008)

Bercovitz, B., Kaliszan, F., Koutrika, G., Liou, H., Mohammadi Zadeh, Z., Garcia-Molina, H.: CourseRank: a social system for course planning. In: Binning, C., Dageville, B. (eds.) Proceedings of the 35th SIGMOD International Conference on Management of Data, SIGMOD 2009, Providence, Rhode Island, USA, June 29-July 02, pp. 1107–1110. ACM, New York (2009)

Drachsler, H.: Adaptation in Informal Learning Environments. In: Presentation at IATEL Conference, June 19-20. TU Darmstadt, Darmstadt (2009)

Drachsler, H., Pecceu, D., Arts, T., Hutten, E., Rutledge, L., Van Rosmalen, P.: ReMashed - An Usability Study of a Recommender System for Mashups for Learning. International Journal on Emerging Technologies in Learning, iJET (2010)

Downes, S.: E-learning 2.0. ACM e-Learn Magazine 10 (2005)

Ebner, M.: E-Learning 2.0 = e-Learning 1.0 + Web 2.0? In: Second International Conference on Availabilty, Reliability and Security, ARES 2007, pp. 1235–1239. IEEE, Los Alamitos (2007)

Ebner, M., Maurer, H.: Can Microblogs and Weblogs change traditional scientific writing? In: Proceedings of E-Learn 2008, Las Vegas, pp. 768–776 (2008)

Farmer, J., Bartlett-Bragg, A.: Blogs @ anywhere: High fidelity online communication. In: Proceeding of ASCILITE 2005: Balance, Fidelity, Mobility: Maintaining the Momentum?, pp. 197–203 (2005)

Felfernig, A.: Koba4MS: Selling complex products and services using knowledge-based recommender technologies. In: Seventh IEEE International Conference on E-Commerce Technology (CEC 2005), München, Germany, pp. 92–100 (2005)

Gamble, M.T., Gamble, R.F.: Monoliths to Mashups: Increasing Opportunistic Assets. IEEE Software 25(6), 71–79 (2008)

Google Insights: Search term 'personal learning environment' (2009-07-20)

Holzinger, A., Nischelwitzer, A.K., Kickmeier-Rust, M.D.: Pervasive E-Education supports Life Long Learning: Some Examples of X-Media Learning Objects (2006), http://www.wccee2006.org/papers/445.pdf

Hoyer, V.: Ad-hoc-Software aus der Fachabteilung, Report. Enterprise Mashups iX(10), 98 (2008)

Hummel, H.G., Van den Berg, B., Berlanga, A.J., Drachsler, H., Janssen, J., Nadolski, R.J., et al.: Combining Social- and Information-based Approaches for Personalised Recommendation on Sequencing Learning Activities. International Journal of Learning Technology 3(2), 152–168 (2007)

Klamma, R., Chatti, M.A., Duval, E., Hummel, H., Hvannberg, E.T., Kravcik, M., Law, E., Naeve, A., Scott, P.: Social software for life-long learning. Educational Technology & Society 10(3), 72–83 (2007)

Kokash, N., Birukou, A., D'Andrea, V.: Web service discovery based on past user experience. In: Abramowicz, W. (ed.) BIS 2007. LNCS, vol. 4439, pp. 95–107. Springer, Heidelberg (2007)

Kulathuramaiyer, N., Maurer, H.: Current Developments of MashUps in Shaping Web Applications. In: ED-Media 2007, Vancouver, pp. 1172–1177 (2007)

Liber, O., Johnson, M.: Special Issue on Personal Learning Environments. Interactive Learning Environments 16, 1 (2008)

Mason, R., Rennie, F.: Using Web 2.0 for learning in the community. Internet and Higher Education 10, 196–203 (2007)

Nagler, W., Ebner, M.: Is Your University Ready For the Ne(x)t-Generation? In: Proceedings of 21st ED-Media Conference, pp. 4344–4351 (2009)

O'Reilly, T.: Web 2.0: Stuck on a name or hooked on value? Dr. Dobbs Journal 31(7), 10 (2006)

Olivier, B., Liber, O.: Lifelong learning: The need for portable Personal Learning Environments and supporting interoperability standards (2001), http://wiki.cetis.ac.uk/uploads/6/67/Olivierandliber2001.doc

Schaffert, S., Kalz, M.: Persönliche Lernumgebungen: Grundlagen, Möglichkeiten und Herausforderungen eines neuen Konzepts. In: Wilbers, K., Hohenstein, A. (eds.) Handbuch E-Learning, pp. 1–24. Wolters Kluwer, Köln (2009)

Schaffert, S., Bürger, T., Hilzensauer, W., Schaffert, S.: Underlying Concepts and Theories of Learning with the Semantic Web. In: Kalz, M., Koper, R., Hornung-Prähauser, V., Luckmann, M. (eds.) TSSOL 2008, Technology Support for Self-Organized Learners, Proceedings, EduMedia Conference 2008, Salzburg, Austria, May 26, pp. 67–83 (2008)

Schaffert, S., Hilzensauer, W.: On the way towards Personal Learning Environments: Seven crucial aspects. In: elearning Papers, p. 9 (2008)

Towned, N.: Podcasting in Higher Education, Media Online focus 22, British Universities Film & Video Council (2005), http://www.bufvc.ac.uk/publications/mediaonlineissues/moF22_vf61.pdf

Tuchinda, R., Szekely, P., Knoblock, C.A.: Building Mashups by example. In: Proceedings of the 13th International Conference on Intelligent User Interfaces. ACM, Gran Canaria (2008)

Van Rosmalen, P., Brouns, F., Sloep, P., Kester, L., Berlanga, A., Bitter-Rijpkema, M.: Question answering through selecting and connecting peer-students. In: ePortfolio 2007 Conference (2007)

Wild, F., Mödritscher, F., Sigurdason, S.: Designing for Change: Mashup Personal Learning Environments. In: eLearning Papers, p. 9 (2008)

Wilson, S.: Future VLE – The Visual Version, http://zope.cetis.ac.uk/members/scott/blogview?entry=20050125170206

Integrating Scholarly Articles within E-Learning Courses

Bee Bee Chua and Danilo Valeros Bernardo II

Human Centred Technology Design
University of Technology, Sydney
1 Broadway P O Box 123
Australia NSW 2007
bbchua@it.uts.edu.au, bernardan@gmail.com

Abstract. E-learning systems support course-based learning. Inadequate course materials provided to learners can result in a decline in effective learning. The designed framework discussed in this paper illustrates that learning can be advanced and assist learners through a better method of learning. In turn, it helps learners build diversified skills including research, aptitude and analysis. This framework is based on the notion that an educational theory can foster a circle of educational knowledge building and sharing between educators and learners emphasizing a better understanding of scholarly articles. Three case studies have validated this framework and in each case study the result highlighted the fact that students' learning and motivation to learn was significantly increased.

Keywords: Scholarly articles, e-learning, learners.

1 Introduction

E-learning is gaining popularity faster in Western countries than in Eastern countries, according to a European survey report [1]. Large European organizations and universities have progressively prepared themselves for the implementation of e-learning in education and training, and investment in e-learning systems is substantial. Because of the competitive advantage to be gained by establishing an early foothold in the market, many e-learning suppliers and designers around the world are striving to produce good e-learning systems.

It has always been a challenge to design an e-learning system that can meet its goal of satisfying learners and educators. More than one researcher [2,3] has recommended using quality frameworks and/or criteria to develop effective e-learning systems. Levis' research [3] is a good example. He introduced criteria that would be appropriate for developing a good e-learning system and they include 1) good learning management software; 2) flexible and collaborative platforms; 3) interesting catalogue content; 4) a good customized learning programme; 5) an effective system integrator and consulting group; and 6) support from training companies which include technology in their blended offerings.

Although these categories are already familiar to academic educators, there is still a desire for an e-learning system that can provide good functionality and learning

R. Kwan et al. (Eds.): ICT 2011, CCIS 177, pp. 37–50, 2011.
© Springer-Verlag Berlin Heidelberg 2011

support to online learners. They sought ways to improve their teaching including course design methods and teaching strategies. Nonetheless none seems to add much value towards contributing to learners' motivation and their learning ability as they find the learning materials that are presented on e-learning systems are superficial learning and not deep learning which is of an intrinsic value considered to be more important for them.

The objective of this paper is to provide a constructive guided learning scholarly articles framework to support this goal. The focus of this paper places heavy emphasis on research, its integration and incorporation within learning activities, and on allowing learners to build their research, analytical and critical review skills. It is based on the concept of scholarly articles as the key subject context integrated within courses as part of a test assessment or a tutorial-based activity in an e-learning environment, as an alternative approach for maintaining educational sustainability. In turn, the aim of this framework is to help learners understand scholarly articles by encouraging them to discuss challenging issues online with other global learners and, through the appropriate use of a tool for collaboration, to generate inventive and innovative ideas.

In this paper, 'scholarly articles' will be frequently mentioned; however, the framework itself is the main topic of discussion. The structure of the paper is as follows: Sections 2 and 3 highlight issues of teaching and learning challenges faced by educators and learners. Section 4 outlines e-learning systems' characteristics and limitations. Our framework, SOAR (Scholarly Articles) is introduced in section 5. Section 6 describes framework validation and case studies are presented in section 7. The last section is an update of our future direction.

2   Challenges Faced by Educators

Educators believe that there are challenges to educating learners. Teaching materials, in particular, must be well-prepared so that learners can understand them. Because learners' learning objectives vary and not all educators design their courses to satisfy all learners, consequently, educators could have been exploring new teaching approaches to try to improve themselves. However, in some cases, the blame is not placed on educators' teaching approach. It could be either a problem of assessment or poor development of the course design. The consideration of materials to be added to e-learning systems involves time and thinking similar to developing a teaching strategy to help learners understand; hence it is equally difficult for educators. In this respect, educators fail to realize how to make learners think and analyze subject matter critically, and helping them identify learning can be more than just understanding concepts.

It is understandable that educators immersed in a learning culture based on traditional teaching methods may be strongly influenced to believe that the fundamental aim is for every student to learn concepts before they attempt to apply those concepts [4]. In reality, not all learners can solve problems even if they have a good knowledge of concepts. This is due to the lack of an integrated learning process that builds their cognitive learning more creatively through blending concept learning and problem solving.

To remain competitive at the cutting-edge of technology, the integration of a research component within any e-learning course should be strongly encouraged. Research drives innovation, and new technologies push improvements to our lives through newly created products, processes and services.

Importantly, in order to maintain a high quality of online teaching, learners must aim not only to learn past theories and their present applications, but should also focus on their own future works. In other words, learning is not simply an act, a process or an experience of gaining knowledge and skills; it should be a lifelong process of transforming information and experience into knowledge, skills, behaviour, and attitudes [5].

3 Challenges Faced by Learners

Two challenges are faced by learners when using e-learning systems: 1) uninteresting course materials fail to promote learners into deep learning and 2) learning approaches [6] are insufficient to increase knowledge that extends beyond theories and concepts.

4 Characteristics of E-learning Systems

Moodle [7] and Blackboard [8] are two popular Learning Management Systems (LMS) [9] that support SCORM specifications [10]. They have similar characteristics with respect to a set of homogenous settings. For example, the prerequisite for every system is a basic setting to allow educators to upload, download and perform course backup. A course announcements and calendar administration tool provides educators with the ability to manage users, roles, courses, instructions and facilities, and to generate reports.

Assessment features such as the grading of coursework, testing, and the ability to handle pre-/post-assessments and individual grades are provided. Unique features found in some e-learning systems include access tracking of learners; for example, how many articles have they posted/read; which pages have they accessed; how many tasks have been submitted? Other tracking facilities include showing how many learners have accessed a page, and when. The introduction of forums enables collaborative work and topic discussions, and good functional support is provided for learners' needs. No matter how easy and flexible e-learning functionalities are, however, they cannot promote deep learning.

Observing educators uploading online course materials shows that they routinely follow a structured and step by step approach. Their first task in uploading to any e-learning tool is usually to name a folder. All course materials are classified and categorized into topics and titles for learners to download and read. Next is the upload of test assessments in which learners take part.

Little research has found that course content alone is beneficial to learners in enabling them to excel, to become involved in critical reviews or develop the ability to think and devise new solutions. If educators choose the conventional method in Figure 1, which focuses on course-based materials, the learning curve for learners is likely to remain broad and fail to promote learning in depth.

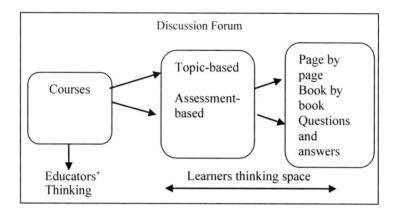

Fig. 1. Steps for uploading materials in e-learning

5 Framework

Scholars all over the world publish scientific articles, and getting a paper published is the first step toward achieving academic success. It is not a scholar's responsibility to find out what learners like to read and to write; similarly, it is unrealistic for every learner to expect to understand each scholar's work easily. This can be a controversial issue in understanding the fundamental concepts of learning. However, from a research perspective, it is not at all controversial for learners to acquire ideas from scholarly papers. The goal in this paper is to seek a way to enhance the learning process as effectively as possible, and to encourage students to learn widely and deeply beyond the concepts level.

Our framework allows learners a thinking space in which to develop creativity and apply it by enabling them to build their problem solving and research skills. This framework is designed based on Brown et al.'s [11] educational theory and framework (figure 2), which aims to foster a circle of educational knowledge building and sharing. It emphasizes three key terms: create, use and remix, each of which is explained as follows:

Create: is the support of the development of reusable and shareable learning content and scenarios

Use: is the encouragement of teachers and lecturers to discover, review, critique and build on others' work

Remix: is the enabling of teachers and lecturers to integrate others' work into their own teaching

Brown's framework provided an existing concept on which we could successfully base our framework [12] because it is aligned closely with our understanding of learning. The goal in developing this framework is to guide educators through the process of integrating a research component within their courses. It addresses the issue that quality online teaching should be well-supported by a good facilitation

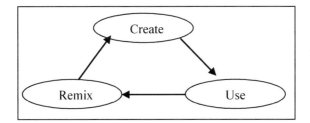

Fig. 2. Brown and Adler's [11] framework on the circle of educational knowledge building and sharing

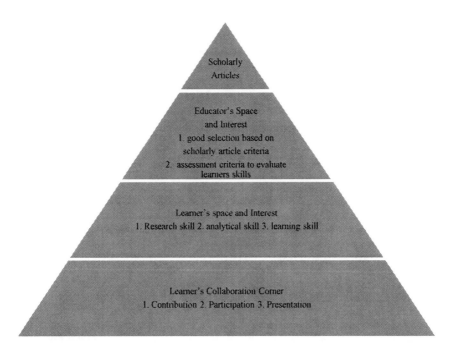

Fig. 3. SOAR Framework

process so that online learners can trust that the e-learning system is a good system through which they can excel at other social skills, including networking.

Our framework in Figure 3, the SOAR Framework requires a subject as an input. Scholarly articles are picked because past, present and future works in each field are clearly presented. This *creates* an educators' thinking space in which to decide whether to *use* scholarly articles [12] as a 1) class activity, 2) a test assessment or 3) whether to integrate it and *remix* it into a tutorial. The e-learning interface acts as a middle process or agent to facilitate open discussion via social networking and as a process to promote a learners' space which will encourage more collaboration, participation and presentation.

6 Framework Validation

Two post-graduate courses from different faculties have validated SOAR. Because these subjects have a large number of student enrolments the use of an online learning tool is highly demanded. Educators aim to help learners develop an interest in understanding their subjects and having research that is integrated within their courses. Certainly they support the idea of testing SOAR framework and evaluate that its value is of benefit to students in terms of critical review and improving their ability in thinking, writing and talking.

To validate this practice-based framework, two stakeholders are required, i.e. educators and learners, a subject input, scholarly articles and a tool to support learners' collaboration and participation. Without an appropriate e-learning system, managing scholarly articles for a large class size would be difficult, especially if critical discussions and online participation are required. It is essential to have a learning tool to test the framework.

The framework consists of the basic procedure and steps below which outlines that they are not difficult to follow: an educator **creates** his or her thinking space to decide where to **use** scholarly articles when using an e-learning system. He asks whether it is for a class activity, 2) a test assessment or 3) to integrate it and remix it into tutorials. With regard to two post-graduate courses, educators prefer to **remix** it into tutorials.

1. Educators create a subject folder for materials to be uploaded to an e-learning system.
2. Every topic is attached with a document, e.g. a scholarly article for learners to download and read and assessment criteria are attached for completing the task.
3. A group discussion board is created for learners to discuss weekly papers.
4. Learners are assigned to read weekly scholarly articles.
5. Learners upload their questions which relate to the industry context with reference to the paper.
6. Learners can upload their questions on a discussion board.
7. Learners invite other learners on the same course to provide their inputs and comments.
8. Educators use their skill and knowledge to review learners' research questions and other learners' comments as to whether they are valid or invalid. Educators can make comments to correct or clarify matters on the discussion board.
9. Learners are required to deliver a presentation online. In the presentation, learners must discuss the paper's topic and their questions relating to an industry case, and provide a summary or outline the statistics of other learners' comments on the questions asked on the discussion board.

- Steps 1, 2, 3 and 4 Educator's thinking space and interest (1. good selection based on scholarly article criteria, 2. assessment criteria to evaluate learners' skills)
- Steps 5 and 6 Learners space and interest (rresearch skill, analytical skill and thinking skill)
- Steps 7, 8 and 9 Learners' collaboration corner (1. contribution 2. participation and 3. presentation)

7   The First Case Study

One author of this paper is a subject coordinator who coordinates a post-graduate subject offered to information technology students. A past survey result showed high ratings for the teaching, but not for the subject. In order to validate our proposed framework, we selected a postgraduate subject with two classes, A and B, as the main focus of the case study and as part of the unit analysis. We carried out an experiment on 50 students from both classes in five weeks and, according to what was observed, data were analyzed from surveys and information that was posted by students on an online discussion board using an e-learning tool.

Past feedback from many students expressed concern about the difficulty in understanding scholarly articles. Many could not interpret what the authors discussed in the paper. As a result, students did not like the subject or the support materials handed out by the subject coordinator. Rather than re-design the whole subject, the coordinator analyzed all aspects of the learning factors that impacted on the students' learning, and reviewed all processes, including tools and techniques. The learning environment was the first area to be evaluated to discover whether there were any missing or inappropriate resource supports for the students.

The learning tool that was provided to the students provided good functionality and adequate features, according to our observation, and was therefore not believed to be the cause of the problem. As such, the tool was retained. Next, the coordinator reviewed ten different scholarly articles, carefully selected by us, to determine whether they were difficult for students. This review confirmed that there was no replacement of the existing articles, as that was not the primary teaching goal. The teaching goal was to encourage students to undertake deep learning, rather than surface learning and the objective was not, therefore, to change the ten papers being used. Instead, the coordinator revisited the presentation structure, as a result of which it was recognized that it was necessary to re-engineer the presentation process so that the subject matter would be explicitly clear to students, both informatively and intuitively. It was decided to outline any missing steps between the old and new presentation structures, in order to achieve improvement in the subject.

Our objective is to ensure that students are more engaged in their learning and hence we proposed the development of a collaborative interface between students at group and class levels for questions and discussions. This interface acted as a two-way communication process that made groups responsible for posting their designed questions and the class responsible for feedback on the designed questions.

Fifty students from two classes in one semester took part in the new process. Ten scholarly articles were chosen, on topics ranging from understanding Michael Porter's framework on the five forces to strategic information planning. Papers published by ACM, MISQ and IEEE were the focus. Students listened attentively to the settings for the paper discussion in the first lesson. Each group was made up of five students. Ten groups of five students per group were formed, and each group was given a different paper topic to read, analyze and discuss. Of the concerns raised, some students were confused about the actual process because it was the first time they had experienced such a framework. A minority of students felt insecure and lacking in confidence because detailed data had to be collected and interpreted in one of the steps, and they had no prior knowledge of research skills.

There were no negative responses from students about the learning process, but acceptance of change was not readily forthcoming when the new framework was introduced

7.1 Result from the First Case Study

The first week of presentations by the two classes went well. Students knew what to do for each paper. They had to: 1) identify a problem issue discussed in the paper (a process equivalent to requirements gathering [13]) 2) contribute their opinions or comments on the paper (a process equivalent to requirements elicitation [14]), 3) ask the class for feedback on questions they have asked (a process equivalent to requirements clarification [15]), 4) respond to comments from their classmates (a process equivalent to requirements review [16]), 5) know how to summarize their findings and propose a strategy (a process equivalent to that of requirements changes [17]), and 6) present their data or findings in a class presentation (a process equivalent to requirements traceability [18]).

The presentation structure, the learning tool and the interface for group discussion are the events on which we sought understanding. Students claimed that class A's papers were more difficult than class B's papers. The statistics report showed that class A received more responses than class B, even though the papers were difficult. We believe that class A students received a high response rate due to the fact that the topic interested them and thus they focused on that, rather than on the paper's difficulty. The same group of students had to analyze data (feedback) from the class and summarize their findings in one presentation slide. Two of the five questions had to involve a critical review of the research into technology and an analysis of the data collected from their classmates. They were also required to propose ideas for solutions to a particular problem based on their classmates' feedback.

In other words, they had to be able to think of a strategic approach and show why it was useful, thought provoking, innovative and interesting. Most importantly, they were asked to summarize findings from the five questions and to conduct an oral presentation to the class the following week in order to leverage knowledge and knowledge transfer of the topic, ideas and solutions for the class.

After week five, an anonymous survey was distributed to all students to evaluate their responses to the framework. Forty-one out of 50 students completed and returned the survey. Nine students did not complete it as they did not attend the class. The survey findings are shown in Table 1, Figures 4 and 5.

Difficult papers were rated with an asterisk, indicating that students had difficulty reading them and understanding the scope, and that they had to read them more than once. Before we reviewed the learning process, we were convinced by our students

Table 1. Classes A and B data with students' responses to the paper

	Class A (16/20)					Class B (25/30)				
Paper	1	2	3	4	5	1	2	3	4	5
Difficulty	*	*	-	-	*	-	-	*	*	*
PaperLength	8	15	6	5	24	13	7	8	6	11
Responses	8	3	2	2	1	4	3	9	4	5

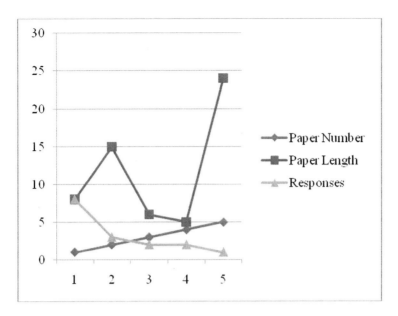

Fig. 4. Class A Data with students' responses to the paper

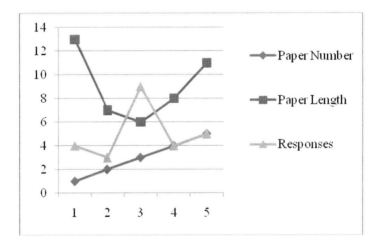

Fig. 5. Class B data with students' responses to the paper

that scholarly papers were too hard to read. We think that this is the same belief that drove a similar situation in software development, in which the team always found it difficult to understand some of the users' requirements because they were vague or incomplete. In fact, a well-developed process to help developers understand requirements simplifies the situation and makes users' requirements understandable. This learning framework underpins the process for assisting students to overcome the barrier of reading difficult papers. The aim is to make them realize that academic papers are not complicated or hard to understand. It is a guiding process on the 'how' and 'what' of reading scholarly articles.

We were also keen to know whether students liked the presentation structure. The process for the presentation was to have them read an article, post designed questions and then analyze data from the class feedback and comments from the subject coordinator for an oral presentation. In this question, we were able to gain many valuable insights from students' responses. Most of their comments are similar and we summarized them in relation to four aspects: 1) article topics, 2) paper discussion, 3) questions posted on the forum, and 4) their oral presentation. We were pleased to find that feedback from the students was positive. For the article topics, the words used repeatedly were:

'Topics are current significant, clear and interesting', 'good knowledge', 'It sharpened our thinking', 'Topics are thought-provoking', 'They give us business aspects of a technical field', 'They broadened our knowledge of IT strategies'. The comments on the paper discussion showed that students felt it was *'informative'*, and that *'team dynamics were unique'*. They agreed that the process involved two-way discussion and they *'enjoyed it'*. They also believed that such discussion helped them *'not only get to know each other better but also able to share their experience and knowledge within the group level and class level'*. On the questions posted on the forum, one student commented that *'questions are a good help to think critically and relate to the paper and real life experiences'*. As for the oral presentation, many students claimed that the purpose was to *'help understand the topic well'*, *'stimulate discussion in class and feedback from the subject coordinator'*. Students commented that *'there was a lot of information'* and *'argumentative and critical evaluation'*. They felt that they learned how to *'build oral communication skills, negotiation skills and analytical skills, as well'*.

As a supplementary question, we wanted to know whether students found the presentation structure helpful to their learning, for example, whether it led to better understanding of the scholarly articles. Ninety-eight percent of students agreed that the presentation structure did help them to understand the scholarly papers better. One student offered a comment that was not negative about the presentation structure, but rather concerned the length of the paper. He felt that some articles were slightly longer than others and thus took longer to read. Another student believed that some students' answers in the forum discussion showed a lack of clarity: either their answers were incomplete or the meaning was not clear and it would have been better if they had provided resource links to justify their findings clearly from journals or books.

7.2 Result from the Second Case Study

One semester later, the same technique was validated in the same subject. The total number of students enrolled was 50 and each group had ten students. They were given scholarly articles to read and told to use the framework in Figure 3 to assist their understanding. At the end of the teaching semester, students were asked to complete a survey designed by the subject coordinator. Students' responses in the result findings (see Table 2 and Figure 6) are similar to those of the first case study.

Table 2. Class C data with students' responses to the paper

Class C					
Paper	1	2	3	4	5
Difficulty	*	*	*	*	*
Paper Length	7	8	15	10	11
Responses	9	10	8	10	10

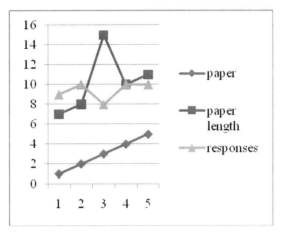

Fig. 6. Class C data with students' responses to the paper

Some constructive comments were made in this semester, particularly in relation to the questions posted on the forum, and their oral presentation. Two students commented that the questions posted on the forum by groups analyzed them *quantitatively*, which did not provide useful insights on the paper's topic. Ideally, it would be helpful for groups to provide in-depth answers.

7.3   Result from the Third Case Study

It is highly recommended that the framework should be cross validated in different subjects in order to evaluate its results. In another faculty, a research-based subject with heavy emphasis on scholarly articles did not receive a good subject rating; hence the subject coordinator wanted to seek subject improvement. He agreed to use the framework for a trial period during one semester to see whether this would help to improve his subject rating level. He was interested to discover whether the length of scholarly articles affected students' ability to read and understand.

In total, 20 students were enrolled in the subject (Class D). Although the enrolment was not large, the number of students seemed sufficient for us to analyze the results, as long as they were new students learning how to read and understand scholarly articles for the first time.

Fifteen students took part and completed surveys. The information in the returned surveys enabled us to explicitly investigate whether there was any validity threat to the technique. Not to our surprise, the students' feedback was similar to that of students in the first subject. The following Table 3 and Figure 7 illustrate the Class D data.

Table 3. Class D data with students' responses to the paper

	Class D (15/20)				
Paper	1	2	3	4	5
Difficulty	*	-	*	-	*
Paper Length	9	15	7	6	14
Responses	3	2	5	2	3

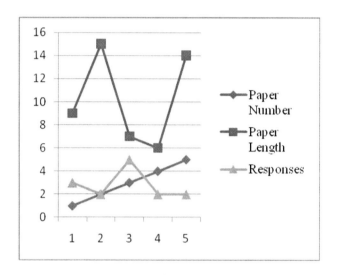

Fig. 7. Class D data with students' responses to the paper

The results shown in this table and diagram clearly identified to the subject coordinator that there is no significant evidence that students' difficulty in understanding scholarly articles is due to the length of the paper. Three students mention that papers 1, 3 and 5 were difficult despite their length and size. Paper 1 had 9 pages, paper 3 had 7 pages and paper 5 had 14 pages. The most highly rated by students was paper 3. Five students felt that it was difficult. In the survey, we asked students to comment on the usefulness of the presentation structure. Fifteen students agreed that the process of presentation really helped them to better learn the concepts and theories discussed in the papers. One student commented that the presentation can be time-consuming but is nevertheless thought-provoking.

In order to establish the framework reliability and effectiveness, it must be validated in more than one case study. The more case studies involved in the validation, the more accurate and reliable that the framework can be considered to be.

8 Conclusion and Future Works

In this paper, we introduced the feasibility of integrating scholarly articles into e-learning courses. We presented our framework drawn from the works of Brown [17]. The framework has been validated in a small learning environment of an e-learning system. Validation on a large-scale environment, particularly of students using e-learning systems for programming subjects, will be part of our future work in the next phase. Existing case studies reveal that the technique can be applied effectively in research-based and coursework-based subjects in which students might be experiencing difficulty in understanding scholarly articles. The framework appears to be convincing enough to be suitable for use in small classes.

Our future research study will seek to validate this framework in large classes and in programming subjects, to establish whether it is suitable for use in such contexts. Many concerns remain to be addressed: for example, is this technique able to support a large class of, say, 600 students? Is a learning tool a necessary aid for supporting resources and setting up a forum discussion? What are the limitations of this technique? These questions will roll into the next phase of our research investigation, which will be more in-depth and analytical.

References

1. Matusu, R., Vojtesek, J., Dulik, T.: Technology-Enhanced Learning Tools in European Higher Education. In: Proceedings of the 8th WSEAS International Conference on Multimedia Internet and Video Technologies (2008)
2. Chua, B.B., Dyson, L.E.: Applying the ISO 9126 model to the Evaluation of an e-Learning System. In: Proceedings of the 21st ASCILITE Conference, pp. 184–190 (2004)
3. Levis, K.: The Business of (e) Learning. A revolution in training and education markets. Published by Screen Digest (2002)
4. Galbraith, M.: Community-based organization and the delivery of lifelong learning opportunities. Paper Presented at the National Institute on Postsecondary Education, Libraries and Lifelong Learning, Office of Educational Research and Improvement, U.S. Department of Education (1995)
5. Marton, F., Dall' Alba, G., Beatty, E.: Conceptions of learning. International Journal of Educational Research 19(3), 277–300 (1993)
6. Saljo, R.: Learning in the learner's perspective-some common-sense conceptions. Reports from the Department of Education, University of Goteborg. No. 76 (1979)
7. Dougiamas, M., Taylor, P.C.: Moodle: Using Learning Communities to Create an Open Source Course Management System. In: Proceedings of World Conference on Educational Multimedia, Hypermedia and Telecommunications (2003)
8. Blackboard Inc. (2005), http://www.blackboard.com
9. IMS, Learning Design Specification, IMS Global Learning Consortium, Inc. (2003), http://www.imsglobal.org/learningdesign/index.html
10. ADL, SCORM, Advanced Distributed Learning (2004), http://www.adlnet.org
11. Edu-sharing.net. The association edu-sharing.net (2010), http://www.edu-sharing.net/mcportal/web/edu-sharing/technologien
12. Chua, B.B., Bernardo, D.V.: Introducing Scholarly Articles: A Way for Attaining Educational Sustainability. In: Proceedings of the Second International Conference on Mobile, Hybrid, and On-Line Learning (2010)

13. Ambler, S.W.: Agile Modelling: Extreme Practices for eXtreme Programming and the Unified Process. John Wiley and Sons, New York (2002)
14. Cockburn, A., Highsmith, J.: Agile software development: The people factor. IEEE Computer 34(11), 131–133 (2001)
15. Kotonya, G., Sommerville, I.: Requirements Engineering Processes and Techniques. John Wiley and Sons, New York (1998)
16. Kotonya, G., Sommerville, I.: Requirements engineering with viewpoints. Software Engineering 1(11), 5–18 (1996)
17. Vonk, R.: Prototyping: The Effective Use of CASE Technology. Prentice Hall, New York (1990)
18. Young, R.R.: Effective Requirements Practices. Addison Wesley, Boston (2001)

Web 2.0 Divide among Naughty Insiders, Worried Outsiders, and Invisible Monitors: A Case Study

Mingmei Yu, Allan H.K. Yuen, Jae Park, Hoi Ching Lam, Kai Kwong Lau, and Wilfred Lau

Faculty of Education, The University of Hong Kong
mmyu@hku.hk

Abstract. Through focus group interview, this paper carried out a case study in a secondary school in Hong Kong on the use of Web 2.0 technologies among students, parents, and teachers. Findings suggest that there was no divide in terms of access and usage but a divide of web 2.0 technologies use among them. In conclusion, our research team speculated the roles that all these stakeholders were playing and attempted to describe them as: naughty insiders, worried outsiders, and invisible monitors.

Keywords: digital divide, Web 2.0, technology integration.

1 Introduction

Web is playing an indispensible role in modern education as more and more schools are connected to the Internet [1]. Accompanied by the popularity of blogs, the Facebook, Wikis and other tools or social networks, a new era in the progress of the Web has arguably dawned—Web 2.0. Its sharing and participatory essence purportedly exerts ever increasing influence on teaching and learning, a claim that opened up debates over young people's engagement in these tools and websites under the educational context. It has also been argued that related studies are both imperative and meaningful because of the fact that young people are increasingly active Web 2.0 users, and their interactions through these technologies are altering their social identities, styles of learning, and exchanges with others around the world [2].

However, available researches seem to be soles than satisfying in two respects. Firstly, related debates tend to centre merely on what young people are doing with these technologies; where, how and for what purpose they are using them and how such activities might usefully be harnessed in formal educational settings [3]. Few studies attempted to scrutinize or decipher those findings in a wider scope where both teachers' and parents' engagement with these technologies should be taken into consideration as part of children's development environment. To understand the surroundings of students' participation with new technologies could probably provide us more possibilities of better utilizing them for the purpose of student development. In fact, adults' influence has always been a hot issue when explaining children's information and communication technology (ICT) use [4] [5] [6].

R. Kwan et al. (Eds.): ICT 2011, CCIS 177, pp. 51–62, 2011.

Secondly, researches on Web 2.0 applications in education appear to converge on higher education [7] [8] while secondary school education is seldom put into research agenda. Partly this phenomenon could be attributed to the fact that one of the big ideas behind Web 2.0 technologies is collaboration and open access to information resources, which may be more visible in senior grade students. Instead of such a simplified view, the ever increasing time devoted by secondary school students to being online deserves researchers' attention without easy labeling them as digital natives[9] and trying to figure out its connection to the process of education as a whole.

This study attempts to probe the link between secondary school students' Web 2.0 useand the possible influence from parents and teachers. The research not only concentrates on the self-reported information from students, teachers and parents but also tries to synthesize the findings from these three groups to get an overall and all-sided picture. Researches questions are: What Web 2.0 technologies do secondary school students, parents or teachers use? Is there any relationship between students' use of Web 2.0 and parents' or teachers' use of it?

1.1 Web 2.0 Applications in Education

As ICT develops, digital technology does not only mean computer or internet, especially, when the term of Web 2.0 is emerging to describe new read-write websites. "The term Web 2.0 is associated with web applications that facilitate participatory information sharing, interoperability, user-centreed design, and collaboration on the World Wide Web. A Web 2.0 site allows users to interact and collaborate with each other in a social media dialogue as creators (prosumers) of user-generated content in a virtual community, in contrast to websites where users (consumers) are limited to the passive viewing of content that was created for them. Examples of Web 2.0 include social networking sites, blogs, wikis, video sharing sites, hosted services, web applications, mashups and folksonomies" [10].

Although the first Web 2.0 tools did hit the market over a decade ago, e.g. blogging software in 1998, RSS feeds in 1999, and Wikipedia in 2001, the term Web 2.0 did not emerge until 2004 when it was coined by Dale Dougherty. However, "no matter how often educators run across the term (Web 2.0), many remain confused" [11]. Besides the popular binary of describing teachers as digital immigrants while students as digital natives takes into account only their distinct growing-up time without giving much importance to individual capabilities and distinctiveness. Individual teachers' knowledge and perceptions about and attitude towards Web 2.0 technologies' educational application might determine their intention to use them or not. Lovejoy [12] seems to describe a conflict between digital native students and Luddite teachers:

The digital divide between students and adults (including teachers and parents) continues to widen. Students are powering down to go to school and powering up after school to re-enter the digital world…Teachers are so busy with their daily drudgery of preparing their lessons, quizzes, tests and then marking them, that they have little time or initiative to become as tech-savvy as their students…Some teachers lack the confidence to learn from their most tech-savvy students. One such teacher was heard saying 'If I hear the word INTERNET one more time I am going to hit somebody' …Some senior teachers don't give a damn about ever using the internet and just want to continue in their old teaching mode.

However, the same account does not seem incompatible with many other senior teachers who could well be tech-savvies but opted out in terms of ICT use in classrooms. It invites us to rethink critically about our own assumptions and focus our attention on how Web 2.0 tools are affecting social relations and how these technology-mediated social relations (parents and teachers) exert influence on the education of their students: "With all of the attention paid to Web 2.0 tools these days, it is important to both explore their uses and evaluate their effectiveness in supporting student learning"[13]. Web1.0 websites' impact on students' achievement was found to be mostly in digital literacy with mixed results in academic achievements. Due to the characteristics of Web 2.0 tools that allow better interactions between students and teachers, it is worthwhile to discuss Web 2.0 technology and its impact on learning outcomes. Unfortunately, research on educational use of Web 2.0 technology is not too much in literature and the few focus on the benefits of a specific Web 2.0 technology and its impact on learning and teaching. However, the differences between those who are advantaged and disadvantaged in terms of Web 2.0 access were not clearly addressed.

Obviously, to benefit from Web 2.0, one needs to have the traditional digital divide bridged by getting computer equipment and internet access first. If basic inequalities could not be addressed, it is just unlikely that digital divide in Web 2.0 could be solved. From a unique and subtle perspective, [14] suggested that Web 2.0 technology including video conferencing through a virtual private network in three education systems in six remote western Australia schools, not only improved learning opportunities for students and administrative services for staff but it also alleviated the digital divide between rural, regional and remote schools.

Although it is true that the arrival of new technologies could create opportunities for learning, it is uncertain whether this would result in remission or deepening of early stages of digital divide. No simple explanation could provide with all-round answer to this question because distinct outcomes would turn up due to diverse patterns of working of the affecting factors. Rudd and Walker [15] found that Web 2.0 technologies were used extensively by some young people who feel confident and safe while some others did not use, raising the question of Web 2.0 divide among students. Their findings showed that much of the use of these tools takes place in informal or peer-supported context, that is, the development of digital skills takes place mostly outside schools. Clearly, there is a need to look into this far less known and reported home use of Web 2.0 tools.

1.2 Parents' and Teachers' Influence

In literature, students from lower social-economic status (SES) family are usually identified as disadvantaged in terms of computer skills and knowledge [16]. They have lower confidence in their digital skills and opportunities to develop digital competence [6] and smaller number of such students testifies positive effect of computer use in their learning outcomes [17]; even when they have had exposure to technology later [18].

All these studies seem to indicate that lower SES family with poorer access and social empowerment might have less chance to use ICT and get benefits at home.

Some other researchers do not agree with these findings. For instance, Zhao[19] revealed that teenager children of less educated parents are as either as likely as or even more likely than their counterparts with high education parents to seek online health information, which may indicate that these teens are seeking online health information on behalf of their less educated parents. Furthermore, students from lower socioeconomic and cultural background families benefited more from individual use of computers than their counterparts and this could imply that individual use of ICT could reduce, at least relatively, the academic achievement gap caused by social and education inequalities [20].

Although these findings are far from being even, they all raise the issue of family factors in the use of the Web 2.0. Indeed, while providing children with physical access to ICT only without attention to other socio-political aspects will not do as much to close the digital divide [18]. If we were to use an ecological discourse, the ICT adoption in education as a whole have to take the border social and cultural contexts into consideration, among which the family or home factor appear as even more apparent. Some other researchers call on all schools to consider the dynamic relationship between school and families when performing technology planning process because this relationship could increase the social capital and empowerment of citizens and families, which will affect the outcomes of the students in their schools [21]. Based on two years' data analysis, Zhong[22] found the role of home computer access as crucial. Its influence on enhancing adolescents' digital skills and self-efficacy does not change in different countries with either high or low ICT penetration rates. A possible reason for this may depend on the way how children use computer at home, including game playing, downloading, emailing and so on, that are more closely related to digital skills enhancement than school-based learning. Furthermore, schools ICT integration efforts were reminded the need to take into account student differences in prior experience and to be coordinated with students' home computer use [6].

Literature also discusses school teachers' influence on students' ICT use. Teachers' professional development has been firmly related with their ability to integrate technology into teaching and learning, with the ultimate goal of students' development [23]. Teachers' pedagogical decisions, including the adoption of ICT, depend on their assessment of the appropriateness for subject matter content and student characteristics [24]. Oliver [25] further suggested that different Web 2.0 tools could be leveraged to assist teaching and learning in respectively different subjects, for example, Gliffy, Flickr, Mind Meister, Prezi, Prezo and so on could be used for teaching 'Science 2.0' while Quizlet, Shelfari, Diigo, LetterPop and so on might be adopted for learning English. Johnson [11] wrote a book verifying and instructing that Web 2.0 tools could assist teaching with primary historical sources. It has also been proven that there is relationship between school SES level and the connection between school, community and family [21].

To sum up, existing researches suggest our present study that there could be a relationship between parental uses of ICT, be it at home or work, and their children's use of ICT. In the same vein, teachers' uses of ICT at school and in daily could have comparable impact on their students' use of ICT, especially in the use of Web 2.0 technologies.

2 Method

Case study is a research strategy which focuses on understanding the dynamics present within single settings. Case studies typically combine data collection methods such as archives, interviews, questionnaires, and observations and one of the aims is to provide description [26]. To understand the research issues better, it is necessary to describe the background of this study because it is conducted in the specific context of Hong Kong Education. According to a systematic report on Hong Kong education changes of ICT in education for the past one decade, The changing face of Education in Hong Kong [24], there have been great improvements in the accessibility to computers and the Internet for teaching and learning in schools worldwide between 1998 and 2006, Hong Kong inclusive. The mean student-computer ratio in Hong Kong decreased from 23:1 in 1998 to 6:1 in 2006, indicating a substantial improvement. And pedagogical support and technical support available for ICT-use in schools have also improved significantly in Hong Kong over the same period.

This study reports a part of a large five-section educational project supported by Hong Kong Education Bureau, which commenced in September 2010 and is supposed to end in September 2012. This project was designed to obtain people's attitudes, beliefs, values, behaviors towards ICT use under the context of education, aiming to address the issue of digital divide in education. Students, teachers and parents' access, use, attitude, and vision of ICT are to be analyzed. This project adopts a mixed methodology, including a range of quantitative and qualitative methods that have obtained ethical clearance from the university. This paper specifically reports the findings from the qualitative research sections, which contain desk-based literature study and focus group interviews section.

This case study was conducted in a middle school located in a suburban district of Hong Kong. It was selected as a convenient sample since one of our research team member works as an IT teacher in this school. This school was built in 1983 and was ranked as one of the band one middle school in Hong Kong. As far as ICT facilities are concerned, this school is digitally well equipped with 30 standard classroom with a full range of IT support, 2 multimedia learning centres, 4 laboratories, 6 special rooms, library resources centre, English learning centre, multimedia production centre, campus TV studio and so on.

The students participating in this study were in their second year in secondary school, all the parents were those with a child in their secondary year and all the teachers were teaching students at secondary level. For the interview section, five focus group interviews were organized with a total of 28 participants separated into the following groups: 2 students groups with 16 participants in all, 2 teachers groups with 7 teachers in all and 1 parent group with 5 parents attended

Two features of the focus group interview are: it could offer variety and versatility to both qualitative and quantitative research method and it could offer opportunities for direct contact with subjects [27]. This method was originally developed for use in marketing, later applied in the social sciences, and in recent years, it has been used to obtain information from consumers, caregivers and healthcare service providers [28]. Focus group interview is to carry out interviews with several participants to discuss some specific issues, usually 5 to 8 participants. The method provides researchers with the possibility of generating large amounts of narrative data from the participants' perspectives during a small amount of time [29]. From the desk-based literature review, our research team prepared a list questions for those three groups interviews and got consent letter signed by them before interviews.

3 Results

Since the focus of this study is on the home Web 2.0 technology access and use and its impact on children's academic achievement, the followings data analysis are going to present results by drawing the images of self-reported views from the participants: first, to look into students' access and use of computer at home; second, Web 2.0 technologies used by students at home and for what reason? Then we will find out how Web 2.0 technologies were used to assist learning and teaching at school and at home; finally, we will work out what are teachers and parents' perception and concerns on technologies.

The findings of this study is coherent with the hypothesis that the first and the second digital divide in education has been bridged, thus every student has access to computer and internet and they use them every day. But the third digital divide has not been resolved; parents, students and teachers do not seem to be not fully making use of the benefits of technologies to assist learning and teaching and did not achieved the quality of use. When it comes to the Web 2.0 technologies, all of them appeared to be out of their expected position, hence, we speculated over the roles that all of these stakeholders were playing and attempted to describe them metaphorically as: naughty insiders, worried outsiders, and invisible monitors.

3.1 The Naughty Insiders

Naughty insiders refer to the students who used Web 2.0 technologies almost every day but seldom for academic reasons. They were wild about new technologies and showed high passion to these Web 2.0 technologies. They are the group that supposed to be digital natives. However, their knowledge was so limited that they did know close to nothing about the possible gains in their studies if adopting technologies properly. They surely know the convenience or functions of these interactions brought by the Web 2.0 tools. However only few of them realize that blogs could be used to assist writing ability practice through which others' valuable comments could also be obtained—the very essence of instructiveness of the Web 2.0. Since many of the students spent most of their online time entertaining and playing at home, strategies could be thought of by identifying the underlying reasons and then designing effective changes based on the findings. When asked about their opinions about the causes that attracted students to play online games, one of the teachers mentioned the interest aroused by the games, and which indicated more space for our research on how to take complete advantages of the existing motivation of children to get online and chat on Facebook.

Rather clearly, the early digital divide of access could be regarded as bridged, at least when referring to the sample of our interview participants. Every student in our interviews has access to computer and internet at home and some even have more than one computer. Most of them could use computer freely except three students.

One of the students could not because the computer was put in the living room for public use. Another student owns an individual computer at home but her younger brother always plays online games so her parents switched off the electricity for all the computers, which indeed caused a lot of inconvenience and delay of her online assignments. For the other student who does not own a private computer is because his computer at home was always seized by others and would break down constantly. Meanwhile, others students expressed their preference for using computer at home than at school. Reasons were as following: using computer at home is more comfortable. And there are more software installed in home computer than that in school computers. Others complained that much software was blocked in school computer.

However, all the children admitted they used home computer for entertainment reasons other than for learning purpose. Several students even stated that they sometimes cheated their parents by saying that they need to use the computer to do assignment and actually these excuses were falsehoods. Although sometimes they use home computer to search for learning materials or do assignments, their attempts mainly focused on no-study intention. For example, most of them use internet for Facebook, MSN, online games, news, watching pop stars, and so on.

Because they spent much time for non-study purpose, no wonder all the student participants complained their use of technology at home is not enough because their parents imposed restrictions both on the time and content. According to parents' further acknowledgement, the commonly allowed frequency of their children being online at home is from one hour to three hours per day. When asked about their children's reaction to these regulations, one of the parents stated proudly: "It all depends on your (the kid's) self-control; you (the kid) are such a big boy now. Two and a half hours every day is just as it is said so just schedule it well. Do not try to talk to me (to get longer time). Sometimes several minutes or ten minutes more would be ok but it does not mean to let you be addicted (to internet). After all, my son could manage this."

Both the time and content of being online was restricted by parents. Apart from parents' daily education and warnings on the proper content that the kids should be limited to, all the parents reported their monitoring on their children's internet use in private and indeed their children have not noticed this. When we asked the parents whether they usually check the websites that their child browsed, they all answered with "Yes". However, it turned out that their children did not notice this or believe that "They may not to do that (check the websites) deliberately."

Questions related to which Web 2.0 technologies are used and the reasons for using them by students were answered by two focus groups of students with sixteen students in all. As stated before, home use of Web 2.0 technologies might be an unknown whereas important area to look into the real situation that technologies are influencing students' lives and why they choose to use them. According to the interviews, we found the most frequently referred Web 2.0 technologies used by students at home were: Facebook, Blog, You tube, Twitter, and Yahoo knowledge. They always use these technologies for social communication: chatting with familiar or unknown friends, expressing ideas about current events or news, joining discussion forum to find the newly hot affairs, and so on. Those kids all perceived the usefulness of these technologies for social communication but not for learning. One student even indicated there cheating on examination, sharing answers with others on Facebook. The children all considered the Web 2.0 websites to be "useful for communication" because they could "know more friends."

Although they also agreed that Web 2.0 tools could be beneficial for their study, the way they referred to it is quite surprising. When we asked "Do you think them (the Web 2.0 websites) are useful for your study?" One of the students replied "Yes (Pointing at another student)…sometimes, I ask him to tell us examination answers, he will put answers on Facebook". And the one who announce the exam answers did not mind to spread it to other because he insisted that "helping others does not matter." Students' communication online is also limited since their interaction scope were mainly between peers and seldom with family member or their teachers. Only few students confessed that they talked with other siblings in their family via Facebookwhile others did not because they were used to traditional ways of communication: e-mail or face-to-face talk. It must be true that both the students and the teachers admitted they added each other on Facebook, but the only function used by the teacher is to check students' opinions spread on internet in order to avoid negative comments on the school.

And among all these Web 2.0 technologies used by student at home, only the Yahoo knowledge, English Builder, and Blog were used for academic reasons. It must be so weird to use English Builder to assist learning at home that all of the students blasted into laughter when one of the students told the interviewer that he use internet for English Builder. While another boy declared that he usually used blog to write articles online and wait for other peers to give him advice. Yahoo knowledge was so popular that many students stated they used it for searching for materials but no contribution for it was found among these students.

3.2 The Worried Outsiders

The worried outsiders refer to parents from our interviews that knew little about Web 2.0 technologies but really care about their children's development. They seldom use Web 2.0 technology even though some of them added their sons of daughters' Facebook account. Some of them were houses wives and knew little knowledge or skills about digital technology. Others were working parents, who face computers in their working places and would never turn on the power button again when arriving at their home, let alone to teach their children to use computer for academic practice or digital skills. As we dig into the literature, we found the important impact of students' family members' use of computer on their use [6]. What they all emphasize is their worries about the negative impact or risks of being online. What is worse, they all seem to agree that the more their kids are exposed to internet, the less communication between them. It was apparent that parents were also lagging behind their children in term of ICT skills. A suggestion might be to invite parents to use Web 2.0 technologies with their children together, for examples, the first step could be talking with them on Facebook and then they could explore the possible academic benefits that these Web 2.0 technologies could offer.

In general, parents considered their IT skills as beginner level. Some of them knew and used the function of information searching on the internet; one parent mentioned that she only knew Google after her child told her about that. Other from information searching, most parents did not use Web 2.0 applications to interact with their children. When asking whether they use Face book to communicate with their children, they said they do not or seldom do so as they prefer face-to-face as the communication channel. It seems that parents are still at the Web 1.0 stage and not familiar with the Web 2.0 applications. When they had inquiries on using computer, they sought help from their children and they thought that their children are quite talent in IT aspect.

Every parent in our interviews acknowledged the conveniences, rich resource, and other benefits of technologies on their children's learning. At the same time, parents were also concerned: they were afraid of their children relying on online resources, which could go against their thinking ability development; they were also worried about the hidden health danger if their children spent a lot of time playing online games, which might cause lack of sleep and the abnormal shape of the growing bodies; they raised another question about the less and less communication between parents and children because these young kids felt annoyed and refused to talk to parents if interrupted by their parents when they were using computers; parents also cared a lot about the possible risks that their children might come across online, for example, knowing some bad persons; they also felt anxious about their children's future since they were so fond of computer entertainment, like games, movie star news. One of the parents complained: "I am so scared if he could not find a job when he grow up because he faces the computer screen all the time and do not study".

3.3 The Invisible Monitors

The invisible monitors were the teachers who used Web 2.0 technologies solely for monitoring their students and seldom interacted with them. They all found that the Web 2.0 was a very good channel to observe students because their students were passionate about them and would occasionally write and upload something about them. As a teacher, the role as a monitor never equals to facilitator and the later one is the role that could be needed to create a sound environment for students' learning. Integrating technologies into curriculum has always been the popular slogan floating in front of the building of modern teaching. We asserted that teachers in our interviews actually could not follow the pace of students in terms of Web 2.0 technologies use because they seldom used it for learning or teaching, even for social network.

For ICT in teaching, teachers did use some Web 2.0 applications to supplement face-to-face teaching, such as YouTube, wise news, question writer, Google earth. Yet, there was mainly input from teachers and not much interaction between teachers and students was involved. Some teachers have added students on Facebook, interestingly, their purpose was not for communication or academic use, but to supervise students' online behavior. One teacher stated that "it (Facebook) is a good channel for understanding our students more, not for communication...you can see what they write and comment, nowadays students are more willing to express on the internet than at school." Another teacher further extended that Facebook helped teachers to give guidance to students; she noted that "If I find a student post some negative comments, I will tell our school counselor and she will talk to the student". Teachers generally seldom use Web 2.0 applications for communication with students. Facebook is mainly used to supervise students and email is seldom used as well; their interaction is mainly face-to-face.

For teachers, they agreed that the upgraded technologies helped their teaching job a lot. But they cared about something else rather than the benefits of negative impact of technologies on their teaching or students' learning. They cared about students' misbehaviors or negative comments on their school. When referring to students' home access of computers, they reported: "As far as I know, I think nobody has no (computers at home)". Both parents and students themselves proved that students would use more than one hour a day at home. So the teachers added students' Facebook account but seldom talked to them because the only reason is that they want to monitor what the students were stating online and what wrong behaviors they were carrying out.

4   Discussion

Through focus group interviews, the findings of this study suggest there is a Web 2.0 divide among students, teachers, and parents who were also described as naughty insiders, worried outsiders, and invisible monitors. The findings from this study might be useful for other researchers, policy makers to know the real situation and to be addressed the needed improvement about quality of Web 2.0 technology use both at home and in school. All of the stakeholders should fasten their moving steps for the sake of student developments. Joint efforts must be made by school and home together to ensure the positive impact of Web 2.0 technologies on students.

Some suggestions emerged here for both parents and teachers. At home, children play the role as a 'teachers' in regard to IT skills. They transfer the IT knowledge learnt from school to their parents. As internet has become so common and children do often communicate with each other online, it would be useful for parents to know more about some Web 2.0 applications such as social networking sites and instant massagers. On the one hand, it gives another channel for parents to interact with and know more about their children. It equips parents with more advanced IT skills which could be useful in their daily life. Realizing that students talk and express more on the internet, teachers could make use of the online channel not only to understand them more or supervise them, but also can attempt to raise students' incentives in learning by initiating some online discussion. In this way, besides one-sided input from the teachers in the lesson, the online platform provides opportunities for students and teachers to share information and ideas. Student-student and student-teacher interactions are likely to increase. In addition, improving teachers' professional development of ICT integration into curriculum has been discussed for years as a long-run vehicle to benefit students' information literacy enhancement.

Although the hardware in our sample school is quite well equipped, the teachers showed little enthusiasm about adopting new technologies to assist their teaching. Our finding are coherent with Law and Chow's conclusion that despite the apparent increase in the presence of lifelong learning pedagogy in Hong Kong schools based on principals' reports, teachers' survey results indicate that Hong Kong teachers' general teaching practice were largely traditional [30]. Part of the reason might be the reality in Hong Kong that the teachers were not confident in pedagogical use of ICT because the number of professional development courses for training in the general use of ICT is much higher than the pedagogical use of ICT [24].

Finally, it is also very significant to report the limitation of this study. Due to limited sample participants and the weakness of the focus group interview research method itself, we could not suggest that these findings should reflect the whole scene because these were just a reflection of a case under a specific context. More empirical studies with a larger sample and both quantitative and qualitative research methods must be needed in the future to understand the problem well.

Acknowledgments

This research was supported by a competitive research grant awarded by CPU/RGC Public Research Funding Scheme (HKU7025-PPR-10).

References

1. Kuiper, E., Volman, M., Terwel, J.: The Web as an Information Resource in K–12 Education: Strategies for supporting Students in Searching and Processing Information. Review of Educational Research 75(3), 285–328 (2005)
2. Schuck, S., Aubusson, P., Kearney, M.: Web 2.0 in the Classroom? Dilemmas and Opportunities Inherent in Adolescent Web 2.0 Engagement. Contemporary Issues in Technology and Teacher Education 10(2), 234–246 (2010)
3. Luckin, R., Clark, W., Graber, R., Logan, K., Mee, A., Oliver, M.: Do Web 2.0 tools really open the door to learning? Practices, perceptions and profiles of 11-16 year-old students. Learning, Media and Technology 34(2), 87–104 (2009)
4. Giacquinta, J.B., Bauer, J.A., Levin, J.E.: Beyond technology's promise: examination of children's educational computing at home. Cambridge University Press, Cambridge (1993)
5. Livingstone, S., Bober, M.: UK Children online: final report of key project findings, http://eprints.lse.ac.uk/399/
6. Vekiri, I.: Socioeconomic differences in elementary students' ICT beliefs and out-of-school experiences. Computers & Education 54, 941–950 (2010)
7. Anderson, P.: What is Web 2.0? Ideas, technologies and implications for education. JISC Technology and Standards Watch, 1–64 (February 2007)
8. Thompson, J.: Is Education 1.0 Ready for Web 2.0 Students, http://www.innovateonline.info/ http://innovateonline.info/index.php?view=article&id=393
9. Prensky, M.: Digital Natives, Digital Immigrants Part 1. On the Horizon 9(5), 1–6 (2001)
10. Wikipedia.: Web 2.0, http://en.wikipedia.org/wiki/Web_2.0
11. Johnson, M.J.: Primary source teaching the Web 2.0 way K-12. Linworth Books, Columbus (2009)
12. Lovejoy, F.: Digital Divide between Students and Teachers, http://www.classroom20.com/forum/topics/digital-divide-between
13. Meyer, K.A.: A comparison of Web 2.0 tools in a doctoral course. Internet and Higher Education 13, 226–232 (2010)

14. Trinidad, S., Broadley, T.: Using Web 2.0 Applications to Close the Digital Divide in Western Australia. Education in Rural Australia 18(1), 3–11 (2008)
15. Rudd, P., Walker, M.: Children and young people's Views on Web 2.0 Technologies. NFER, Slough (2010)
16. Tien, F.F., Fu, T.-T.: The correlates of the digital divide and their impact on college student learning. Computers & Education 50(1), 421–436 (2008)
17. Attewell, P., Battle, J.: Home computers and school performance. The Information Society 15(1), 1–10 (1999)
18. Angus, L., Snyder, I., Sutherland-Smith, W.: ICT and Educational (Dis)Advantage: Families, Computers and Contemporary Social and Educational Inequalities. British Journal of Sociology of Education 25(1), 3–18 (2004)
19. Zhao, S.: Parental education and children's online health information seeking: Beyond the digital divide debate. Social Science & Medicine 69(10), 1501–1505 (2009)
20. Ferrer, F., Belvís, E., Pàmies, J.: Tablet PCs, academic results and educational inequalities. Computers & Education 56, 280–288 (2011)
21. Hohlfeld, T.N., Ritzhaupt, A.D., Barron, A.E.: Connecting schools, community, and family with ICT: Four-year trends related to school level and SES of public schools in Florida. Computers & Education 55(1), 391–405 (2010)
22. Zhong, Z.-J.: From access to usage: The divide of self-reported digital skills among adolescents. Computers & Education, 1–11 (2010)
23. Lawless, K.A., Pellegrino, J.W.: Professional Development in Integrating Technology Into Teaching and Learning: Knowns, Unknowns, and Ways to Pursue Better Questions and Answers. Review of Educational Research 77(4), 575–614 (2007)
24. Yuen, A., Law, N., Lee, M.W., Lee, Y.: The Changing Face of Education in Hong Kong: Transition into 21st Century. Hong Kong: Centre for Information Technology in Education, Faculty of Education, The University of Hong Kong (2010)
25. Oliver, K.: Integrating Web 2.0 Across the Curriculum. Techtrends 54(2), 50–61 (2010)
26. Eisenhardt, K.M.: Building Theories from Case Study Research. The Academy of Management Review 14(4), 532–550 (1989)
27. Vaughn, S., Schumm, J.S., Sinagub, J.: Focus Group Interviews in Education and Psychology. Sage Publications, Thousand Oaks (1996)
28. Owen, S.: The practical, methodological and ethical dilemmas of conducting focus groups with vulnerable clients. Journal of Advanced Nursing 36(5), 652–658 (2001)
29. Esposito, N.: From Meaning to Meaning: The Influence of Translation Techniques on Non-English Focus Group Research. Qualitative Health Research 11(4), 568–579 (2001)
30. Law, N., Chow, A.: Pedagogical Orientations in Mathematics and Science and the Use of ICT. In: Law, N., Pelgrum, W.J., Plomp, T. (eds.) Pedagogy and ICT Use in Schools Around the World, pp. 121–179 (2008)

The Organization of Mobile Learning
in Higher Education of Kazakhstan

Daniyar Sapargaliyev

Eurasian National University, Kazakhstan
dsapargalieff@gmail.com

Abstract. Mobile learning, through the use of wireless mobile technology lets learners and educators to access necessary information from anywhere and at anytime. Despite that the most researches of mobile learning are still in the beginning phase, the using of portable, wireless and handheld devices are gradually increasing in every sector of education. Mobile learning has growing evidence and significance in higher education. There is the big size of international dedicated conferences, seminars and workshops. Nowadays we can see the rising numbers of universities that use special mobile service systems, develop mobile version of own sites and create education applications for all type of mobile devices. Nevertheless this type of learning needs in special research for identification the pedagogical conditions of using M-learning in higher education. The leading idea of our research is the mobile learning in the modern university will improve the organization of education process through the detection necessary pedagogical conditions. The progressive popularity of mobile learning will give new quality for education process in higher schools.

Keywords: pedagogical conditions, pedagogical forms, organization of m-learning.

1 Introduction

The modern society, thanks to prompt development of mobile communication facilities has entered during a new mobile age. In this new time the great attention is given to process of an individualization of learning. Several years ago was appeared a new trend in pedagogical science - the mobile form of education.

The first scientific researches that started to discuss about problems of mobile learning appeared from the beginning of 2000. Mike Sharples's article "The Design of Personal Mobile Technologies for Lifelong Learning" (2000) [1] provides the potential of personal mobile technologies that could improve lifelong learning programs and continuing adult educational opportunities.

Today we can find so many definitions of mobile learning in different sources. Polsani (2003) described mobile learning as "a form of education whose site of production, circulation, and consumption is the network" [2]. Mike Sharples (2004) defined it as "learning away from one's normal learning environment, or learning involving the use of mobile devices" [3]. Geddes (2004) tried to define mobile

R. Kwan et al. (Eds.): ICT 2011, CCIS 177, pp. 63–70, 2011.

learning as "the acquisition of any knowledge and skill through using mobile technology, anywhere, anytime, that results in an alteration in behaviour" [4]. John Traxler (2005) considered it like "any educational provision where the sole or dominant technologies are handheld or palmtop devices" [5]. Keegan (2005) suggested that mobile learning by the size of the mobile device: "Mobile learning should be restricted to learning on devices which a lady can carry in her handbag or a gentleman can carry in his pocket" [6]. Mike Sharples (2007) describes mobile learning as "It's the learner that's mobile; learning is interwoven with everyday life. Mobile learning can both complement and conflict with formal education." Sharples also accentuates "the importance of context, constructed by learners through interaction" [7].

Some scientists have tried to classify types of mobile training. Frohberg (2006) [8] indicates classification in the context of learning, which describes as digital, formalized, free, physical, and social contexts. John Traxler, professor of mobile learning at University of Wolverhampton, expanded this classification (Traxler, 2009) [9]:

- Remote/rural/development mobile learning.
- Miniature but portable e-learning.
- Mobile training/performance support.
- Connected classroom learning.
- Informal, personalized, situated mobile learning.
- Technology-driven mobile learning.

More and more of scientists in the whole world starts to focus of their attention to pedagogical aspects of mobile learning. Many scientists in Kazakhstan are trying to find conditions and forms of electronic learning and distance education. It is obvious that process of implementation the mobile learning in Kazakhstan is only at beginning stage. This trend of learning demands many scientific explanations and special pedagogical investigations. We tried to find and analyzed in our article the main views of Kazakhstan pedagogical scientists, who interested in developing of information and communication technologies in education.

The scientists in Republic of Kazakhstan spend a wide range of individual and collective researches in this area. In research fields of Kazakhstan investigations special attention is given in formation of students' readiness to work with information technologies [10, 11]. There were described the problems in organization of various studies at computer science studying [12] and the method in organization self-study works of students [13].

Many research works devote to computerization of distance learning education [14-17]. In investigations of other Kazakhstan scientists are reflected on the didactic problems of learning process with using information technologies [18, 19]. For example, the dissertation thesis of A.K.Mynbayeva (2001) dedicated on studying of pedagogical regularities in educational process with using information technology. The researcher had presented the package of measures for humanization of information's process in higher education, there was showed the new definition - "information-didactic preparation". In research work of T.M.Saliy (2006) were presented the didactic conditions in using of multimedia technologies in education. The problems of widespread using in computer technologies for monitoring of students' grade results and creation of check quality system in education also ware reflected in scientific works of E.A.Bateshov [20] and K.L.Polupan [21].

We have analyzed the scientific and special literature and sources that cover the mobile learning questions and define our research problem as pedagogical conditions in organization of mobile learning in higher education. We are interesting in this theme because we found the basic contradiction - modern system of Kazakhstan higher education needs in the development mobile education environment. It is necessary reveal pedagogical conditions in organization of mobile learning. We will try to identify the methods and forms of M-learning.

2 Developing of Mobile Learning in Kazakhstan

The population of the Earth is approximately 6.5 billion people and the users of Internet are about 2 billion ones. At the same time in the USA and the other Western European countries is the glutted market in the telecommunication sphere. This means that the growth of Internet users in these countries has already stopped. The leaders of growth Internet audience are other world regions - Asia, Africa and the South America. In these regions the growth of Network connections has explosive character. Many people from developing countries access to Internet firstly by their mobile phones, not laptops or desktops. The main of all reasons is the prices of mobile phones that more cheaply and accessible than computers ones.

The Republic of Kazakhstan, according to the Kazakh State Agency of information, has 15.7 million users of mobile communication in 2009. Herewith general number of the population country is about 16 million persons. In the article "The Global Competitiveness Report 2009-2010" [22] Kazakhstan on an indicator "The quantity of mobile communication users" has risen on 20 points and occupies 59 place, among 133 countries.

Nevertheless the dynamic of development Internet and mobile communications are actively worked in all directions of information services in Kazakhstan. The number of mobile Internet users steadily grows. We can constant that in a modern Kazakhstan society the mobile technologies become the main source of information.

The Government of Kazakhstan declares about strategic directions in developing the modern information society. In December of 2010, there was presented the «Government program of development education since 2011 to 2020 years» [23]. The main objects of this program are the increase of competitiveness in education sphere and development of the human capital. The special attention in this program is given to active development of electronic learning. It will be done by supporting an equal access for all participants of educational process at anytime from any place. According to the Program- more than 90 % educational organizations will access to Global Network. As we see from the program text, in the next decade in Kazakhstan will be done big work in adoption of new education technology (as mobile learning) for all educational levels.

Last years the Ministry of Education and Science of Kazakhstan carried out the special conferences that focused on challenges and problems of distance education. This spring in Karaganda city was conducted by Ministry of Education the Second International Conference "Distance Technology in Education - 2011". There were presented many universities from Russia, Ukraine, Belarus, Kyrgyzstan, Tajikistan and more than 70 educational institutions Kazakhstan. On this conference the scientists from different countries discussed, for the first time, about the problems in implementation of mobile learning.

It should be noted, that any implementation activities of distance learning in Kazakhstan educational institutions should be regulated according to the State standard № 34.016-2004 named as «Hardware and software of distance learning. The general technical requirements of distance learning". And also should be approved by the Ministry of Education and Science that created the "Government rules of organization the distance forms of learning at educational institutions of the Republic of Kazakhstan".

There are some examples of the beginning the realization of new educational projects focused on mobile learning. In 2010, the Ministry of Education and Science together with the software company «Crystal Education» [24] have presented the new project «Mobile education». The project will be realized the decisions for mobile technologies in education. In Almaty city was presented educational project «SMS-Diary» in 14 schools. Every parent can receive short reports about study progress of schoolchild by using a mobile phone. Next years all schools in the country will be joining to this mobile technological service. Though the similar projects have realized in many countries, in Kazakhstan it is for the first time.

Some commercial services of mobile learning were introduced at the beginning of 2011. These services help Kazakhstan subscribers to teach foreign languages on their mobile phones. British Council and GSM Kazakhstan have presented the mobile service "Phrase of the day", with the use of which all subscribers will be able to learn English through SMS, using the materials of the British Council. By subscribing to the service, the users will receive each day within the entire week a new word in the English language, including its translation into Russian and Kazakh, and the phrase, based on which the use of a new word will be demonstrated. At the end of the week the users will receive the fault detection test in respect of usage of new words. Each subscriber will be able to select the appropriate level: elementary, intermediate or advanced [25].

It is necessary to notice that in higher education sphere of Kazakhstan the implementation of mobile learning is not so intensive. There are some attempts in introduction of separate mobile technologies elements in several universities, but it is not system conception. Some universities in Kazakhstan are beginning to create new structures for implementation and studying systems of mobile learning in higher education. For example, at Kokshetau State University was created the learning laboratory of innovations in education and management spheres. The main goal of this structure is the searching of new ways for effective functioning of educational process at the university. The main activities of this sector focus on innovative solutions for promotion of electronic and mobile learning. As example of successful work in this direction can be presented at Eurasian National University (ENU is main scientific and educational center of Kazakhstan).

In 2010 ENU and South Korean company AHA I & C have developed the conception of «ENU Smart School» - the digital platform that will allow to implementing E- and M-learning technologies at university. By this conception, all campuses and hostels are equipped by free access to wireless networking. Today the teachers and students are actively participants of university's local network not only using laptops but also connect to it by mobile and handheld devices. According to the project «Mobile University» that will start in 2011 there will be created mobile electronic catalogue of university's library. By this project, many books and audio- and video-lectures and other teacher content will be transform in digital formats (PDF, EPub, MPEG-4 and MP3). Nowadays the news and educational information about ENU translate on system of microblogs - Twitter and social network - Facebook. It was made for students that using these services on smartphones and other mobile devices.

Today is possible to notice that in the modern development of mobile technologies - mobile devices successfully provide interaction among all participants of learning process. It is necessary that Kazakhstan researchers start to focus their attention on the realization of new scientific projects in pedagogical and educational fields.

3 Pedagogical Conditions of Mobile Learning

Mobile technologies became an integral part of everyday lifestyle in our society; they offer new possibilities and attractive prospects which were absolutely inaccessible several years ago. Today the world becomes the witness of rapid growth in the field of mobile technologies. The pervasive information which surrounds us should serve improvement process of lifelong education. Nowadays person who studies at schools or universities has already got accustomed to be in access to global information area, this is new generation distinguishes from the last decades' one. In our opinion the growth of standard living for each person in the nearest future will depend directly on his knowledge, competence, and ability to react to instantly changing conditions. Probably mobile technologies that have unlimited possibilities on penetration and constancy access will help people to acquire all new knowledge at anytime in any places.

Certainly, the main tools of mobile learning are compact wireless devices, but usage such ones sometimes limited by their technical characteristics. Important condition of convenience in use mobile device is individual adaptation to the person. The success in studying educational material depends on intuitive measuring in usage without the previous experience in work with mobile technology. The learner in studying of teaching content and searching of knowledge should have constant access to educator.

During our research work we have identified the pedagogical conditions in organization of mobile learning:

1. It is availability in constant access to various educational resources (directories, catalogues, databases etc.);

2. It is constant dialogue among all participants of learning (the teacher-student, the teacher-teacher, the student-student) by digital form for exchanging information (a chat, a forum, a blog, a micro-blog, e-mail);

3. It is everyday updating of digital educational resources and creating content for mobile devices (applications, books, quizzes and tests);

4. It is possibility for both - educator and student to manage the individual schedule and learning trajectory.

Important condition of mobile learning is - interactivity that allows a student to make interaction as between an educator and teaching material, and also interactive actions of students among themselves. At the learning process in a mobile mode the knowledge should be got by initiative of a student. A students that use mobile technologies also must have the capable to operate of own development. When student use mobile technology of education, he can learn not only himself, but also other students. He becomes a significant participant of education process and a manager in knowledge receiving. It is important that the students understand the personally convenience in using of mobile learning. They clearly see the advantages and freely access to any information. All of these factors become powerful stimulus for self-education of each person.

The creation of mobile learning becomes evolution process of transformation electronic education system in the whole world. Obviously, that using mobile technologies in higher schools connects with finding an optimum combination of traditional and innovative forms in organization of learning process.

In our research work, we suppose that mobile learning has some pedagogical forms:

1. It is the dialogue form (chat, forum, e-mailing, web-conference, file exchanging);

2. It is the form of studying material (text document, audio-video lecture, presentation);

3. It is the form of control (testing system, chat poll, project report).

The process of mobile learning implementation in higher education is in stage of formation. The introduction of mobile technologies in learning process constantly changes. We should trace in time and sensitively react to all striking changes which occur in educational area. The primary aim of all participants of educational process - should be in accurately using abilities of new technologies in individual mobile learning with a glance of pedagogical conditions.

4 Conclusion

We are on the threshold of new decade of the twenty first century. For the last decade the distribution of information technologies has strongly changed our everyday life. We observed explosive development of mobile communication technologies, huge popularity of social networks and growing by huge rates worldwide society of Internet users. All of this has affected on possibilities in exchange, access and delivery of information.

The new generation that in different media sources named as – "digital natives" or "homo mobilis" is growing up. These people (from different age, social groups and countries) are united by one very important quality - they have unlimited access to any information. Probably, people from developing countries still feel restrictions in acquisition of digital content due to various reasons. But today we very often hear about the increasing distribution of mobile technologies in all corners of the planet.

Today our education period does not end with graduated from universities and with beginning of work activity. We compel to receive knowledge and new skills constantly and to raise our qualifications throughout all life. Modern persons in different occupations must have to permanent access to actual knowledge and receiving new information, otherwise they become noncompetitive in their professional spheres. So, it will automatically lead to decrease of income level, career growth and work productivity.

Since the earliest period of life, modern person receives the increasing volume of the information that grows in geometrical progression. The information constantly increases, expanding of penetration into all spheres of our life by distribution of information technologies. In our opinion, the development of information technologies is constant, it process really becomes an integral part of our society. The "digital revolution" has changed our relation to educational and learning process. We are witnesses of global changes - information sources such as television, newspapers, magazines and even radio, are still popular but in new "digital format". We can establish that transformation of information sources occurs in education sphere. Books, encyclopedias, dictionaries and other educational literature are there libraries in digital format. For the modern students these types of data are easier, faster for consumption and more clearly convenient for usage. There is global process of "digitalization" of different information's sources.

Today educational process in higher schools changes promptly and irreversible. More and more high schools introduce systems of mobile learning and expand use of mobile technologies in educational process. Process of transition to individual mode of study is provided with new mobile technologies. Mobile learning becomes the main education criterion of universities to deliver its knowledge. In the twenty first century there comes an age of penetration of education in all spheres of life. Learning passes through all our life. This process hardly ever to come to the end, but constant studying of mobile learning will give possibilities to realized effectively ways of lifelong education.

References

1. Sharples, M.: The Design of Personal Mobile Technologies for Lifelong Learning. Computers and Education 34, 177–193 (2000)
2. Polsani, P.: Network learning. In: Nyiri, K. (ed.) Mobile Learning Essays on Philosophy, Psychology and Education, pp. 139–150. Passagen Verlag, Vienna (2003)
3. Sharples, M. (2004), http://www.lsri.nottingham.ac.uk/msh/Papers
4. Geddes, S.J.: Mobile Learning in the 21st Century: Benefit for Learners. Knowledge Tree e-Journal 6 (2004)
5. Traxler, J.: Defining Mobile Learning. In: Proceedings IADIS International Conference Mobile Learning 2005, Malta, pp. 261–266 (2005)
6. Keegan, D.: Mobile Learning: The Next Generation of Learning. Report, Distance Education International (2005)
7. Sharples, M.: A Short History of Mobile Learning and Some Issues to Consider. Online presentation. mLearn, Doctoral Consortium (2007)
8. Frohberg, D.: Mobile Learning Is Coming of Age: What We Have and What We Still Miss. Paper Presented at DeLFI, Conference (2006)
9. Traxler, J.: The Evolution of Mobile Learning. In: Guy, R. (ed.) The Evolution of Mobile Teaching and Learning, pp. 1–14. Informing Science Press, Santa Rosa (2009)

10. Спирина, Е.А.: Формирование готовности студентов информационных специальностей к работе с сетевыми технологиями: Дис... к.п.н.: 13.00.08. - Караганда (2003),143 с
11. Антонова, Н.А.: Алгоритмическая подготовка студентов информационных специальностей к решению профессионально-ориентированных задач: Дис... к.п.н.: 13.00.08. - Караганда (2007), 175 с
12. Дузбаева, Р.М.: Дидактические основы формирования готовности студентов к интерактивному обучению (на примере изучения курса "Экономическая информатика"): Дис... к.п.н.: 13.00.01. -Алматы (2002), 161 с
13. Нурмуханбетова, Г.К: Совершенствование методики организации самостоятельных работ студентов при обучении предмету информатики: Дис... к.п.н.: 13.00.02. - Шымкент (2002), 137 с
14. Шипачев, С.А.: и др. Организация дистанционного обучения в Казахском национальном техническом университете им. К.И. Сатпаева: Отчет о НИР (заключит.) / Дистанц. ун-т (ДистанцУ); Руководитель С.А.Шипачев. - Алматы (2007), 32 с
15. Темирбеков, Н.М.: и др. Современные информационные технологии в университетском образовании: Отчет о НИР (промежут.) / Вост.-Каз. гос. ун-т им.С.Аманжолова (ВКГУ); Руководитель Темирбеков Н.М. - Усть-Каменогорск (2005), 77 с
16. Султанова, Б.К.: Активизация самостоятельной работы студентов дистанционного обучения на основе образовательного портала: Дис... к.п.н.: 13.00.08. - Караганда (2007), 134 с
17. Изтлеуова, Г.К.: Методические основы использования сетевых технологий в дистанционном обучении информатике: Дис... к.п.н.: 13.00.02. - Жанаозен (2003), 125 с
18. Мынбаева, А.К.: Дидактические основы информационных технологий обучения студентов: Дис..к.п.н.: 13.00.01.- Алматы (2001), 198 с
19. Салий, Т.М.: Дидактические условия использования в учебном процессе вуза мультимедийных технологий обучения: Дис... к.п.н.: 13.00.08. - Павлодар (2006), 129 с
20. Батешов, Е.А.: Педагогические основы компьютерного контрольно-обучающего тестирования качества знаний студентов на примере физики: Дис... к.п.н.: 13.00.08. - Кокшетау (2006), 149 с
21. Полупан, К.Л.: Управление качеством образования студентов на основе развивающей компьютерной диагностики: Дис... к.п.н.: 13.00.08. - Караганда (2006),136 с
22. http://www.weforum.org/reports/
23. http://www.edu.gov.kz/ru/proekty/gpro_na_2010_2020_gody/
24. http://www.cred.kz/
25. http://www.kcell.kz/en/?l=press&p=display&idx=325

Learning of Algorithms on Mobile Devices through Bluetooth, SMS Technology

Ricardo José dos Sanos Barcelos[1] and Liane Matgarida Rochembach Tarouco[2]

[1] IFF-Instituto Fedral Fluminense, RJ, Brasil
[2] UFRGS-Universidade Federal do Rio Grande do Sul, Porto Alegre, Brasil

Abstract. Teaching Institutions are up against challenges of an advanced technology of learning with the objective of improving the efficiency of the teaching-learning process. Joining the students' learning style to the technologies is important to improve the educational process. This work presents the advantages of using mobile devices, associated with the students' learning styles. The learning which is carried out with the use of mobile devices makes it possible for users to learn at anytime and anywhere.

Keywords: algorithms, mobile devices, mobile education.

1 Introduction

The use of ICTs in the teaching of algorithms was made possible through the supervision of the teaching-learning process of this subject at Instituto Federal Fluminense, in Campos dos Goytacazes, when it was able to verify the huge difficulty experienced by the students. The creation of environments which support this learning is of great interest, since the knowledge construction process necessary to the production of algorithms for programming constitutes an arduous task to the student, as [1] emphasizes.

There is consensus, among the teachers of the area, that it is not enough to present an algorithm in an explanatory way on the board in order to be able for the student to comprehend it completely, and to create similar or derived algorithms from that, neither to become capable of resolving problems with these instruments [2]. This work presents the use of mobile devices to the teaching-learning process of algorithms.

The use of mobile devices as an educational resource is not trivial because the features of the pieces of equipment differ substantially from the ones which are normally used at home and in labs at schools, chiefly by the size of the presentation area of the visual pieces of information. Another factor to consider is the process of transference of the educational content in a thriftier way, because the cost of access to the Internet, via cell phone network, is still very high in Brazil. In this work, it is related an experience in which it was explored another way to transfer learning material to students' mobile device, using the wireless technology called Bluetooth and SMS.

R. Kwan et al. (Eds.): ICT 2011, CCIS 177, pp. 71–84, 2011.
© Springer-Verlag Berlin Heidelberg 2011

[3] states that mlearning can be defined as learning through the use of devices and the wireless technology. According to [4], this learning through mobile devices (Mobile learning) is observed due to the fact it is without the permanent physical presence within the educational process.

To make explicit mobile learning is to define the use and possibilities about the way how the mobile technologies will be inserted into the educational process. [5] points to the potential that these technologies enable in terms of learning strategies such as constructivism, interaction, curiosity, complexity, collaboration, challenge.

In a learning context for mobile learning, even if the mobility is one of the pillars, various other factors must be considered like: i) learning along the time; ii) the informality and iii) the appropriation of knowledge by the student.

The use of mobile devices within the learning process has been performed as a support to the presential learning, though, the purpose of this work is to make observed the formal learning of the school environment, that is, the students have got the possibility to "download" the learning objects onto mobile devices for, from then on, these to be accessed for learning at the moment when the users consider it to be more appropriate.

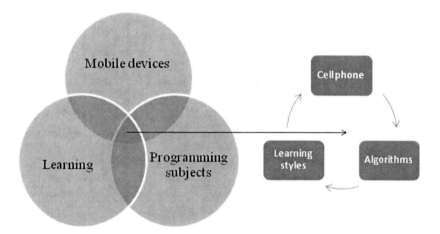

Fig. 1. The convergence Technology and Education, shows the investigations of this work, which embody the programming subjects, in particular in the learning of algorithm, the learning styles, in particular the students' ways of learning, as well as the mobile devices technology, besides the insertion of the mobile technologies for the learning refinement. The intersection of these areas is investigated in the teaching of algorithm and corresponds to the way how the students learn by using technologies.

This work investigated the use of the Bluetooth connection that is faster, of easy access for the student to share data among the various mobile devices, like: from cell phones to cell phones, laptop to PDAs, laptop to cell phones, laptop to smatphones. The SMS technology was also used, which is the transmission of text messages – maximum of 160 characters for the sending of solution of problems, incentive messages, notices of tasks already performed.

According to [6], the future educational applications and services will need resources to make it easier its use, like: to download materials in different types of format, text, voice and video, to "run" without the use of adaptations, as well as to make feasible the reduction of the cost of access to the Internet because the characteristics of the functionality of the devices differ from manufacturers.

The learning of algorithm has been presenting at IFF one of the largest indexes of failing. A survey carried out by the author, at IFF-Campos-RJ, in the technical course and higher education courses, points out the presented results in Graphic 1, encompassing the four late semesters between the first semester of 2008-1 and the second semester of 2009-2.

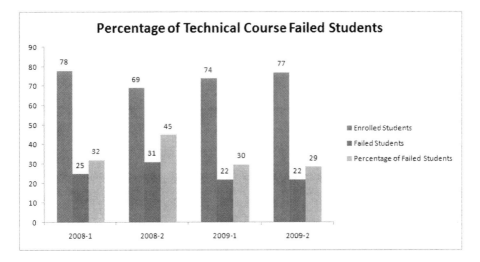

Graphic 1. Failed ones in Algorithms, shows in the semesters 2008-1 to 2009-2, the percentages of failing in the Computer Science Technical Course, from 2008-1 to 2009-2, the average of 34% of the failing of algorithm students. This has become a motivation for an investigation work aiming at the improvement in students' learning. This work investigated the use of new technologies in groups of this universe for the improvement of the teaching-learning process.

The reasons for this high level of lack of success are not specific ones of the area. In general, [5] and [7] observe that the students do not present self-assurance in the organization of reasoning, elaboration of strategies for solving problems, attention, concentration, stimulus to the process of mental calculation. Thereby, the skills involved in this process, such as trying, observing, conjecturing, deducing, and that constitute what we call logical reasoning, not being appropriately developed, they interfere in the learning of practically all cognitive areas, but, especially, they affect this area of knowledge.

On the other hand, the students show a unique self-assurance concerning the use of technological resources. To nullify this difficulty, taking advantage of the students' motivation and vocation for the use of technology, new strategies have been investigated regarding the use of computer science resources in education, in order to enhance skills which aim at the development of the reasoning, according to [8].

2 Objective

The objective of this work is to make it available, through the Bluetooth technology, the pedagogic materials of algorithms to the mobile devices. In parallel, the students are registered by their cell phone number so that they receive short texts and messages through the SMS. Texts are sent to absent students from presential classes, informing them about the topics taught in presential lesson and assignments to be developed. Also it was used the sending of educational objects by MMS.

The use of this learning way is considered, in this work, as being a support to the classroom lesson. According to [9], this resource is indicated to the improvement of learning in two moments essentially different: (1) right after the initial learning, when part of the forgetting of the content can occur, in order to consolidate the content learned in a more efficient way and, also, to originate the learning of gradations and subtle implications, not learned in the first presentation; (2) after a certain time, when a considerable forgetting can occur, making it possible for the student an opportunity to take advantage of (to avoid posterior presentations) his/her own awareness of negative factors (such as ambiguity or confusion with similar ideas) responsible for the possible forgetting.

Various peculiarities are important in the learning process of algorithms as it follows: i) coherence with the fundamental objectives of algorithms and that the teacher must build in the operationalization of this learning for the students: i.1) to express in an objective way the ideas, the concepts and the techniques to the students because if the teacher presents the algorithms in a confusing way (confusing ones) in the presential class or by using transparencies, the students do not understand the resolution of problems involving this learning and the expected results of the proposed algorithms are not clear in students' responses; i.2) to highlight the importance of the theoretical results and show formal rigor in the situations, even in the simpler ones; and i.3) to valorize the use of techniques in the resolution of problems; ii) to highlight the critical thinking, a care to be observed, because the students own little experience in the resolution of problems involving mathematics and tend to believe any demonstration. This kind of behavior must not be stimulated. It is essential that the students have critical thinking on any resolution of problems and are stimulated to obtain new solutions for the same problem. It will be from healthful doubts and of a new resolution and perception that the importance of the theoretical work will be presented. Still in that sense, a valuable resource is the set of exercises which make it possible for the students to identify argumentation failures, errors in algorithms or algorithms that would be made better; iii) the theory put into practice. The experience shows that the students, in general, do not feel themselves motivated as they consider the learning of algorithms to be extremely abstract, then, it is believed that it is important to use real examples as a didactic resource.

That group of factors is the one that makes it possible the improvement or the lack of success of the learning. First of all, it is essential to comprehend what an algorithm is. Its definition becomes, thus, important to have a perfect comprehension of these peculiarities, because the algorithm is a sequence of instructions in order, without ambiguities, presented in a logical way for the resolution of a determined task or problem. The algorithm is a mathematics formulation, a piece of code, and finds itself located between the input and output to transform the first into the second. It is the way for the solution of a problem and, in general, through these ways several solutions can be obtained.

3   Characterizing the Target Public

Initially, it was investigated the students' age of two Computer Science Technical Course class groups Level 1 – Morning and Level 2 – Afternoon at Instituto Federal Fluminense.

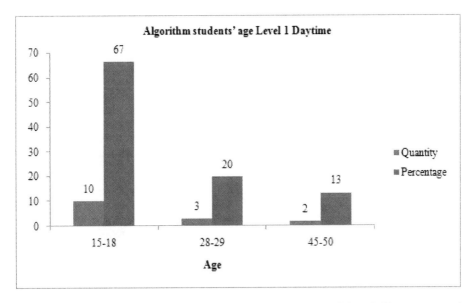

Graphic 2. Presents four eighteen-year-old students, six students of the 16-17 age group and three of the 28-29 age group. In this case, there is a heterogeneity with regard to the group of students, because whereas the 15-19 age group can be regarded as being digital natives, the 45-50 age group, according to [10], is characterized as digital immigrants

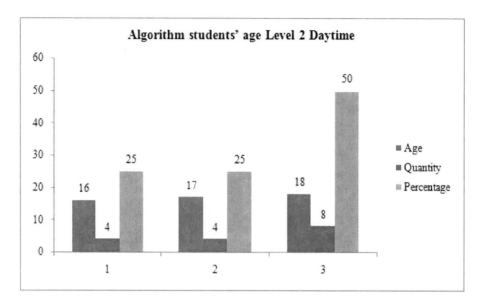

Graphic 3. Algorithm students' age Level 2 Daytime, with the Level 2 students, this discrepancy of age does not take place, because all students can be characterized as digital natives since the age is between sixteen and eighteen years old

4 Methodology

Using MLE, Bluetooth and SMS – In stage 1, the construction of a quiz (questions) about algorithms with images and sounds using the MLE (Mobile Learning Engine) was the solution presented in this work. This system is open source (code free font); free of charge and with capacity of personalization, and the access to MLE by cell phone is done through Bluetooth technology. The MLE is available in two languages, German and English and offers various tools, as it is shown by following the items: i) Didactic Material: It constitutes of a set of pages, ending with a question with answer alternatives. ii) Quiz: It is a multiple choice test, true or false, and questions of short answers. Each attempt is automatically checked and the teacher can choose by which way the interaction with the student will occur, i.e. the answers will be sent, or to present the right responses to the immediate student's correction.

Through the MLE, a special learning object is constructed called Mobile Learning Objects (MLOs) that can be stored into the cell phone and subsequently used, without any connection to the Internet. This way is considered as off-line. The learning through the MLOs implements all the MLE functionalities, including: interactivity among instantaneous questions with automatic correction, answer to quizzes, simple and multiple choice questionnaires.

Learning objects – shaped like videos – were sent and made available to the students with the following topics and time duration: i) introduction, time – a minute and six seconds; ii) types of data, time – two minutes and thirty-six seconds;

iii) sequence, time – two minutes and fifty seconds; iv) repetition, time – two minutes and sixteen seconds; v) decision or selection, time – three minutes and six seconds; vi) refinement, time – two minutes.

The use of SMS technology in this project was used in various categories. Three categories of themes to send SMS messages by cell phone were selected.

1. Administrative Messages: They are content messages specifically about the operational and administrative part of the course. For instance, messages informing the availability of the contents, activity hand-in deadline, and the contents taught at the presential lesson etc. Example of messages sent: i) Two days left to hand in the assignment about If...Then...Otherwise; ii) The content of the August 04th presential activity was the construction If...Then...Otherwise; iii) Today, August 11th, we are starting the If...Then...Otherwise.

2. Pedagogic Messages: Content messages related to the subject of the course. For example, tip about sites with related content, reading suggestions etc. Example of messages: i) Send a message to a classmate about which questions of the assignment you have already done; ii) Ask another classmate which questions of the assignment he/she has done; iii) Do you have any difficulty about the problems to be solved?

3. Motivational Messages: They are messages that enable the motivation for the learning and the resolution of proposed problems and the individual objectives: i) messages which rouse students' interest in the learning of algorithm. ii) messages that are usually out of the context of the course like, for instance, "have a good holiday" or "U had a good performance in the activities grade 8,5" iii) Are you going to solve problems this holiday?; iv) When you are to solve problem 5, try If...Then; i) Have a good weekend!; Enjoy the holiday!.

The work had as a return text messages sent by SMS, by phone-call or by e-mail. Example of messages of replies sent by students: i) Thanks for the Information; ii) Nice holiday! 4U2.

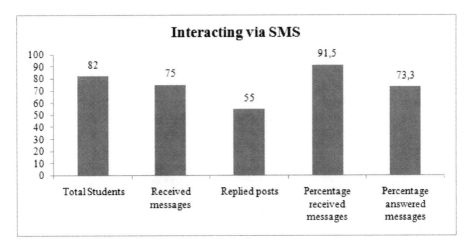

Fig. 2. Interacting via SMS

The **Figure 2,** It is observed that 91.5 received the messages, this percentage was not higher because the students have exchanged mobile phone number not provided or the number and 73.3% of the students interacted via SMS, that is, answered the messages requested other information and that these interactions occurred between teacher-student and student-student.

The learning object constructed to be used on mobile devices demanded a series of observations like: size of characters, colors, sounds, among others.

Figures 3,4,5,6 provides educational materials on various mobile devices.

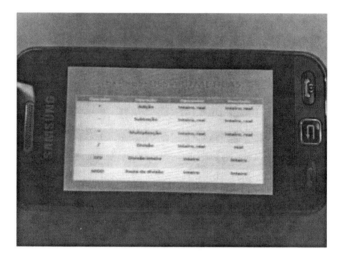

Fig. 3. Presents the contents on the mobile device, representation of data types

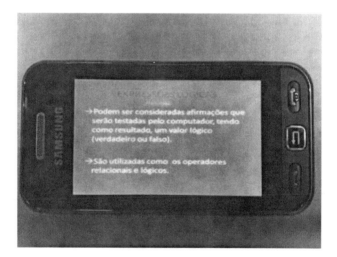

Fig. 4. Presents the contents on the mobile device, example of algorithm using logical expressions

Fig. 5. Presents the contents on the mobile device, example of sequencing algorithm

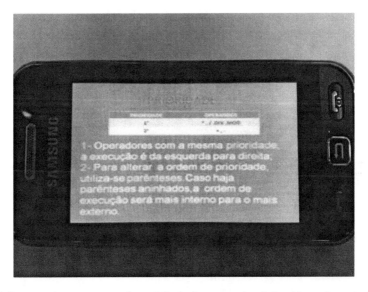

Fig. 6. Presents the contents on the mobile device, example of algorithm using priority

Besides this technique of videos with contents of algorithms, demonstrative videos of functioning were produced using one of the techniques called Table Test, presented by [11] and [12], that consists of following instructions of the algorithm in a sequential and accurate way, storing the possible values of the variables to verify the procedures used in the designing of the algorithm.

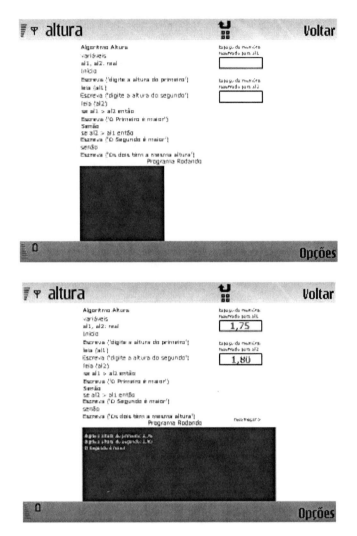

Fig. 7. and 8. Show the construction sequence of the table test. This test makes it possible to compare the results to the objective of the algorithm and the possible errors during the execution. The teachers also use them in learning environments through the *web*. It is a technique which prioritizes the visual perception.

5 Difficulties and Discussion

As soon as the students were informed about the cell phone use as an educational device, the reaction was very reticent because they do not "believe" and also do not understand how the cellular could be used in educational activities. In so far as they acquired knowledge about the methodology to be used, it was observed that the learning with the use of technological resources and the attitude changed.

The results appeared from individual interviews with the students, taking into consideration punctual questions like the use of the student's cell phone (access, didactic-pedagogical perspectives, interface, cooperation, synchronous and asynchronous tools, adequacy and usability. It was observed that only one of the students did not have a cell phone with the Bluetooth function. Initially, the students were apprehensive with regard to learning by using the mobile devices for the learning and also how the pieces of information about this content, that is, how to learn using these devices, not only with theory, but also to resolve problems. Miscellaneous students' accounts were important in this work: Student F1: "I did not have a hard time using my cellular, but how are we going to learn?". Student M1: "The activity was very interesting, because the classes are always the same". Student M2: "I was convicted of not having a flowchart of algorithm in the cell phone".

[13]The use of SMS for question/answer on learning has become an instrument that enabled the improvement in the learning process. The interaction using interactive SMS contributed to help students accomplish tasks or achieve a goal in their learning.

The results obtained showed that students own a developed technological view, and the relations of them with the videos were the best ones because they manifested the desire to access and watch the video related to the content to be taught in the presential lesson of the day.

We can state that the students identified themselves with the format of the objects, mainly when they had entire knowledge of their learning styles. Thus, they requested the materials that would better provide them with learning; however they also accessed other format of objects.

Under the aspect of the used technology, the students presented difficulty in the transmission of videos notebook/cell phone. In this methodology, they pointed out the delay to "download" the files into the devices. In the execution of the system, problems appeared due to the low memory of the cell phones regarding the size of the file to be sent.

Some of the difficulties in the construction of the educational objects are related as it follows: i) the diversity of cell phone models. In relation to the materials to be consulted by the students, there was the necessity of installing the software Java in two cell phones – program required for the mobile devices, as they did not contain the necessary "plugins" to run the materials, that is, the devices which do not 'run' files with .doc, .pdf. format. The solution found was to convert the files with .txt extension (in text format), though, in a short way, because in this format they do not contain the illustrations of the original material, serving just as fast consultation about the concepts over specific subject.

Another difficulty reported by students was the cost, in the case of the sending of SMS to other students and teachers, impairing the interactivity. Concerning the educational difficulties, the students "would like to have more consultation material during the learning out of the classroom", more didactic material, i.e. videos with other contents of algorithms.

In a general way, the students understood that the use of this technology for the learning was of great importance and they expect that its use converts itself into positive results in their performances in the learning. The fifteen students answered the questions on a Saturday and Sunday and on their way work/school and, mainly, when they did not have access to the computer.

6   Results

With regard to the male students' learning styles, only one with visual and kinesthetic learning style as well as male student with preference to the auditory learning style did not obtain approval. Concerning the female students' learning styles, only one with visual and kinesthetic learning style as well as male student with preference to the auditory learning style did not obtain any approval.

The failed students were interviewed and reported that the experience regarding the knowledge of their own learning styles was beneficial to the learning and attributed the weak performance to extra-class problems, because they missed the examination. Though, they even reported that would like to keep on in the process and be re-evaluated based on the support with educational objects.

Through accounts, the students attributed to the satisfactory performance in this subject several factors, as it follows: i) the use of mobile devices making it available the access to the course content, what enhances the motivation and learning opportunity, as the performance shows. Practically by just one click, contents are found which permits students to learn wherever they are, despite the limitations of the home responsibilities, work hours, trips etc. Besides, since the students achieved the success and progress through exercises, they state that they have being motivated to learn more by the use of pieces of technology; ii) Another factor was the strategy of learning of algorithms in an individual way made possible by the convergence of information and communication technology with the strategy used; iii) the learning of algorithms through the opportunity of interaction among the students. The availability of the learning objects must include the opportunity for the students to interact with other students and with the teacher in order to report the difficulties and the solutions found in the resolution of the proposed problems. The students understand that the mobile devices are becoming integral part of the teaching.

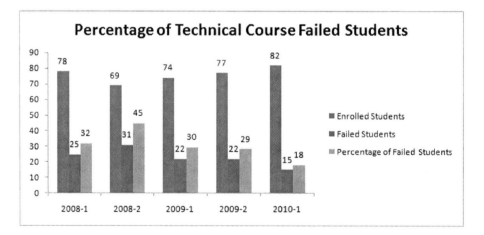

Graphic 4. Shows the result in the subject of Algorithms of the students of the Computer Science Course in the year 2010-1 that the performance was satisfactory, because in the year 2009-2 the index of failing was of (29%) and in the year 2010-1 this index was of 13%

7 Conclusion

The use of mobile learning in the teaching of algorithms led to a significant improvement on the students' performance, because it made possible the collaboration, giving a good opportunity for the support of multimedia such as videos, graphics. The learning through the mobile devices in consonance with the students' learning styles, as well as their motivation with the insertion of this technology made the teaching of algorithms more attractive and, consequently, made it possible to improve the learning. In this work we observed that with the introduction of SMS the learning process had positive results such as improved collaboration and cooperation between students and teachers.

Regarding the fifteen level 1 students, fourteen students participated actively of the assignments and thirteen obtained approval without need of a third exam to be retaken. It can be, therefore, stated that the experience contributed to the development of the logical thinking and made it easier the supervision of the academic trajectory. It was verified in these students the improvement of the abstraction, of the logical reasoning and of their learning performance, confirming a differential with regard to the ones who did not take part into the project, even though, evidently, other factors can also have interfered into the learning.

References

[1] Bercht, M., Ferreira, L.F.E., Silveira, S.R.: Aprendendo a construir algoritmos através da mediação digital. Cinted-UFRGS Novas Tecnologias na Educação 3(1) (Maio 2005)
[2] Barcelos, R.J.S., Tarouco, L.M.R.: O uso de mobile learning no ensino de algoritmos. CINTED-UFRGS NovasTecnologiasnaEducação 7(3) (Dezembro 2009)
[3] Caudill, J.: The Growth of M-learning and the Growth of Mobile Computing – Parallel Developments. International Review of Research in Open and Distance Learning (2007)
[4] Boyinbode, O.K., Akinyede, R.O.: MOBILE LEARNING: An Application Of Mobile And Wireless Technologies In Nigerian Learning System. International Journal of Computer Science and Network Security 8(11), 386–392 (2008)
[5] Valentim, H.: Para uma Compreensão do Mobile Learning. Reflexão sobre a utilidade das tecnologias móveis na aprendizagem informal e para a construção de ambientes pessoais de aprendizagem. Tese de mestrado em Gestão de Sistemas de e-Learning, Universidade Nova de Lisboa, Lisboa (2009)
[6] Sharples, M.: Big issues in mobile learnin, Report of a Workshop by the Kaleidoscope Network of Excellence. Mobile Learning Initiative, University of Nottingham (2007)
[7] Jenkins, T.: On the difficulty of learning to program. In: Annual LTSN-ICS Conference. Proceedings.., pp. 53–57. Loughborough University, Leeds (2002)
[8] Grabe, M.E., Kamhawi, R., Yegiyan, N.: Informing citizens: How people with different levels of education process television, newspapers, and web news. Journal of Broadcasting & Electronic Media 53(1), 90–111 (2009)
[9] Azubel, P.D.: Aquisição e retenção de conhecimentos: Uma perspectiva cognitiva, 1.a Edição pt-467-Janeiro de 2003 ISBN 972 - 707 - 364 – 6 tradução (2002)
[10] Prensky, M.: Digital Natives Digital Immigrants Marc Prensky Digital Natives, Digital Immigrants, Marc Prensky From On the Horizon (2001)

[11] Szwarcfiter, J., Markenson, L.: Estruturas de Dados e seus Algoritmos, LTC (1994)
[12] Medeiros, C.L., Dazzi, R.L.S.: Aprendendo algoritmos com auxilio da web. In: II
      Congresso Brasileiro de Computação – CBComp 2002 (2002)
[13] Yengin, I., Karahoca, A., Karahoca, D., Uzunboylu, H.: Is SMS still alive for education:
      Analysis of educational potentials of SMS technology? In: Procedia Computer Science.
      World Conference on Information Technology, pp. 1439–1445 (2011) ISSN=1877-0509,
      http://www.sciencedirect.com/science/article/
      B9865-527GFKD-4J/2/5c9358138bc902fdd991116bc8f12966,
      doi:10.1016/j.procs.2011.01.027

An Innovative Application for Learning to Write Chinese Characters on Smartphones

Vincent Tam and Chao Huang

Department of Electrical and Electronic Engineering, The University of Hong Kong,
Pokfulam Road, Hong Kong
vtam@eee.hku.hk

Abstract. With the fast economic development in China, learning Chinese becomes very popular and significant worldwide. To most foreigners and even local students, one of the major challenges in learning Chinese is to write Chinese characters in correct stroke sequences that are considered as crucial in the Chinese culture. However, due to the potentially complex structures of Chinese characters together with their stroke sequences, there were very few available character recognition techniques that can tackle this training task well in a flexible and efficient manner. In this paper, we propose an extendible and intelligent e-learning software based on learning objects to facilitate the learning of writing Chinese characters in correct stroke sequences. Furthermore, the basic features including the evolution and pronunciation of each Chinese character can be encapsulated as part of the learning object metadata to better students' understanding. To demonstrate the feasibility of our proposal, a prototype of our proposed e-learning software was built on smartphones such that students can learn anytime and anywhere. Our proposal represents the first attempt to reduce the complexity while increasing the extendibility of the e-learning software to learn Chinese through learning objects. More importantly, it opens up numerous opportunities for further investigations.

Keywords: Chinese characters, e-learning systems, innovative applications, learning object metadata, stroke sequences.

1 Introduction

The learning of Chinese has become very crucial for both Chinese and foreigners due to the amazingly fast economic development and increasing political influence of China in the past decade. Among the four basic skills including listening, reading, speaking and writing to master any language, learning to write Chinese characters with the correct stroke sequences is often the most challenging task for foreigners, or sometimes Chinese students themselves, taking into account of the complicated structures and diversity of Chinese characters with their unique stroke sequences. Even with the latest advance in the development of intelligent character recognition techniques [5], the complexity of structures of Chinese characters together with their stroke sequences impose a serious challenge to many sophisticated e-learning software [5, 6] developed for learning to write Chinese characters. As a result, there were very

R. Kwan et al. (Eds.): ICT 2011, CCIS 177, pp. 85–95, 2011.

few available e-learning systems [1, 2] integrated with intelligent character recognition techniques to effectively handle both complex structures and correct stroke sequences of Chinese characters in a timely manner. To reduce the complexity of the underlying knowledge domain in many practical e-learning systems, the IEEE Learning Object Metadata (LOM) standard [7] is frequently adopted to construct a systematic organization of learning objects for the specific knowledge domain. For the complex and diverse structures of Chinese characters, there are a fair number of such characters that can be decomposed into some basic constructs or sets of strokes containing specific semantic meanings, thus ideal for being represented as 'learning objects'. Accordingly, with the aid of learning object management subsystem, course or software developers can easily maintain and update the apparently complex structure of the underlying Chinese characters by breaking them down into basic sets of strokes specified as learning objects in our proposed e-learning system. Clearly, this will promote students' appreciation of the meaning of a specific Chinese character through the semantic meanings of the involved basic constructs represented as learning objects contained inside the character. Ultimately, the set of stored Chinese characters can be easily shareable with other learning content management system (LCMS) [3] that strictly follows the IEEE LOM standard. More importantly, this will help to reduce the computational complexity of the character recognition technique used in the e-learning system which can be more 'extendible' to define new Chinese characters in terms of basic sets of strokes represented as learning objects stored in its local repository.

Although the structural complexity of any Chinese character is reduced through the concept of learning objects, students may not have sufficient time to practice the writing of Chinese characters in correct stroke sequences during classes. Conventionally, web-based e-learning software [3, 5] has been developed for students to practise the writing of Chinese characters mainly on desktop computers with the Internet access. However, with the reducing prices and increasing processing speeds of mobile devices nowadays, smartphones [8] are very convenient e-learning platforms for students to practise the writing of Chinese characters at their own pace anytime and anywhere. Therefore in this project, we propose to develop an extendible and learning object based platform, namely the iWrite system, for foreigners or Chinese students to practise the writing of Chinese characters in correct stroke sequences on iPhones. Furthermore, the basic features including the evolution and pronunciation of each Chinese character can be encapsulated as part of the learning object metadata to better students' understanding.

To demonstrate the feasibility of our proposal, we implemented a prototype of the iWrite system as an extension from a previous work [10, 11] using the Objective C and the Xcode development tool for the iPod Touch™ device or iPhone. Our prototype of the iWrite system can systematically categorize all the stored Chinese characters in its database according to the predefined basic constructs as learning objects, and include Chinese characters of all the basic structures into each training exercise. In each step of the training exercise, a template of the selected Chinese character will be displayed for the students to write with their fingers in the correct stroke sequence on the touch screen. After the student finishes writing the concerned character, the iWrite system will use an efficient and heuristic-based method to check whether the stroke sequence of the inputted Chinese character is correct or not. In case the sequence of inputted strokes is incorrect, an error message will be displayed. At the end, the student will receive an evaluation report showing at which specific structure(s) of the Chinese characters that the concerned student is relatively weak. A preliminary evaluation was conducted with some encouraging feedbacks collected. A more careful evaluation was planned around the upcoming May in which the iWrite system would be available for foreign students for trials in some selected Chinese courses in the University of Hong Kong. All in all, there are many interesting directions for further investigation including the integration of relevant multimedia or pointers to online databases about a specific Chinese character into our system, and a thorough study of the pedagogical impacts brought by our integrated system for mobile learning.

This paper is organized as follows. Section 2 reviews the basic structures of Chinese characters, some existing e-learning systems for learning to write Chinese characters, and previous works about the use of learning objects in education. Section 3 details the system design of our proposed learning object based Chinese writing system, iWrite, on iPhones to enhance learners' experience on mobile devices for learning to write Chinese, especially for foreigners. We give an empirical evaluation of our proposal on various criteria in Section 4. Lastly, we summarize our work and shed lights on future directions in Section 5.

2 Preliminaries

In the following subsections, we will review preliminaries on the basic structures of Chinese characters. Then, conventional features of existing e-learning systems that may hinder the progress of learning to write Chinese will be considered. Lastly, previous works about the possible uses of learning objects in e-learning systems will be discussed.

2.1 The Basic Structures of Chinese Characters

Chinese characters are highly structural, as totally different from the alphabetical languages such as English and Greek used in other parts of the world. Nevertheless, each Chinese character is intrinsically made up of sets/types of basic strokes as its components. There are around 30 types of basic strokes for which the following table shows the 10 common types of basic strokes.

The above types of basic strokes as components of Chinese characters totally make sense semantically and phonetically. For instance, the Chinese character for river, lake, sea and ocean are 河，湖，海，洋 respectively. It can be easily observed that all these characters share the basic component of "three dots" which is the symbol of water on the left-hand-side. Therefore, through these basic components/structure, a learner can more easily identify how various Chinese characters are related to one another, and possibly guess the meanings of new characters. Besides, in most cases, the remaining parts such as "可" and "胡" in the above examples for river and lake will also give some hints about the pronunciations of the whole Chinese characters.

2.2 Existing E-Learning Systems for Learning to Write Chinese Characters

The existing e-learning systems [5, 6] for learning to write Chinese characters can be divided into two major categories. The first category is the view-only e-learning system in which students can only see how a Chinese character should be written yet no practice is provided. For instance, the famous eStroke [6] provides the online and offline viewing of the stroke sequences for Chinese characters. In addition to showing the stroke order of every Chinese Character, the eStroke system also translates phrases in a Chinese text passage into English or German as according to its predefined dictionary. This will greatly facilitate foreigners to understand the whole text instead of each individual character. Besides, eStroke can display the animation of the stroke sequences for both simplified and traditional variants of the same Chinese character. All in all, it can only provide guidance to students by showing how to write Chinese characters with correct stroke sequence **without any actual practice**.

Table 1. The 10 common Types of basic strokes

	Pronunciations in Pin-yin (Chinese meaning)	Types of Basic Strokes
1.	Heng (横)	
2.	Ti (提)	
3.	Shu (竖)	
4.	Shuzhe (竖折)	
5.	Shugou (竖钩)	
6.	Pie (撇)	
7.	Hengzhe (横折)	
8.	Henggou (横钩)	
9.	Dian (点)	
10.	Xiegou (斜钩)	

On the other hand, the second category allows the student to practise their writing and also gives some feedback to indicate if there are errors in the students' handwriting. However, there is no display or animation on how a Chinese character can be written with its correct stroke sequence for education purpose. An example is an automated Chinese handwriting error detection system [5] using the attributed relational graph matching. The system can be used to identify the stroke production errors, sequence errors and errors in spatial relationship between the strokes for a specific user's handwritten input. However, the system cannot provide useful statistics such as the average rate of errors after writing a number of Chinese characters, or a group of characters containing specific structures. Furthermore, the processing speed of the system can be slow when the characters are complicated with a lot of strokes. Therefore, in this project [10, 11, 12], we aim to design and build a more complete e-learning system with both facilities for viewing and practising the writing of Chinese characters with correct stroke sequences, and also giving reasonable performance for complex characters with a fairly large (> 13) number of strokes. Moreover, our ultimate e-learning system would provide more detailed and informative feedbacks including the aforementioned error statistic for each individual student to practise the Chinese characters with specific structures that (s)he is weak at.

2.3 Learning Objects for E-Learning Systems

A learning object is "a collection of content items, practice items, and assessment items that are combined based on a single learning objective" in an e-learning system. By following the IEEE-1484 LOM standard [7], the LOM management subsystem of the underlying e-learning system can facilitate the searching of learning objects using the standardized metadata format. Basically, LOM is used to capture explicit knowledge, context, perspectives, and opinions. Learning objects in the form of text, image or video can be imported and searched by keywords. Therefore, each user is free to access, discover and find information using the LOM. In this way, the process of learning and knowledge creation will be significantly enhanced and smoothed.

After a user uses any keyword(s) to query the LOM management system, the e-learning system can redistribute the specific query to all connected LOM repositories and then respond to the user by displaying the resulting LOM when the search is successful. For efficiency of the search, the implementation of LOM for our designated e-learning system in this work is simplified since the subjects are mainly restricted to Chinese characters and their structures. As most of the LOM search is in the form of keyword(s), the LOM management system will try to match any LOM with the provided keyword(s) at the title, description or keyword field. Accordingly, we only need to implement the corresponding search function on a relatively small subset of fields as defined in the original IEEE-1484 LOM schema, including the title, description, keyword and technical related fields.

3 Our Proposal

As considered in Section 2, most of the Chinese characters are constructed by basic structures or sets of ordered strokes that can actually be implemented as learning objects as according to the IEEE-1484 LOM schema [7]. In fact, all such basic structures/radicals have specific meanings that can be expressed as learning objects with related keywords and linked multimedia files for pronunciation and/or animation of relevant concepts in the local repository.

Our proposed e-learning system, based on smartphones for higher portability, has implemented the concepts of learning objects since the basic strokes of Chinese characters will be implemented as learning objects with animations to promote the students' appreciation of the specific semantic meanings of the concerned basic strokes. In addition, the basic features including the evolution from the pictogram to the traditional form and also the pronunciation of each Chinese character can be easily encapsulated as part of the learning object metadata to better students' understanding. The proposed system has three main components to serve for the functions of illustration, practice, and feedbacks as clearly shown in Figure 1.

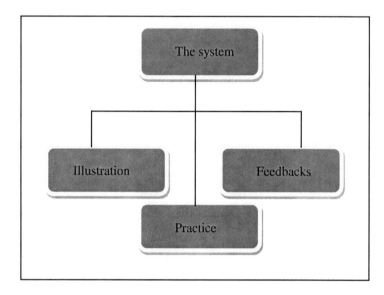

Fig. 1. The basic system architecture of our proposed e-learning system for smart-phones

For the illustration part, the e-learning system will provide motion pictures of writing Chinese characters with their correct stroke sequences. For the practice part, the system will provide Chinese character templates for students to follow in writing. The system will check the stroke sequences after (s)he finishes writing on the template. In the returned result, the system will give a detailed analysis of the student's performance including the average rate of errors over all the Chinese characters the student has practiced, and also providing suggestions via the feedbacks subsystem to each individual student on the specific structure(s) that (s)he may work hard to improve.

4   An Empirical Evaluation of Our Proposal

To demonstrate the feasibility of our proposal, we implemented a prototype of the smart e-learning platform [10, 11, 12] using the Objective-C programming language and the Xcode Integrated Development Environment (IDE) [9] tool for execution on iPhones for its high popularity and portability. The current prototype implementation consists of approximately 2,500+ lines of source codes with 30 templates of Chinese characters for practice. It took around 4 man-months for the design and implementation of our e-learning system.

For a better evaluation, the templates of Chinese characters were built into one of the four basic structures of the underlying Chinese characters. The four basic structures include single structure, up-down compound, left-right compound and bounded structure. Table 2 shows some of the examples for each of the four basic structures.

Table 2. Examples of 4 Basic Structures of Chinese Characters Used in Our iWrite System

Structure	Examples
Single Structure	天, 上, 下, 中, 大, 甘, 日, 早
Up-down Compound	美, 金, 合, 雷, 笑, 哭
Left-right Compound	地, 和, 換, 江, 河, 明, 清, 好
Bounded structure	圓, 周, 同, 國, 回, 風

Fig. 2. The User Interface of Our iWrite System for the Template of a Chinese Character (i.e. Moon) Displayed on the iPhone Simulator

The Microsoft™ Paint program is used to build the templates of Chinese characters for our extendible e-learning system. Fig. 2 shows the graphical user interface of our iWrite system with a selected template being displayed and ready for the user to

Fig. 3. The User Interface of Our iWrite System After a User Wrote the Chinese Character (i.e. Moon) with Incorrect Stroke Sequences on the iPhone Simulator

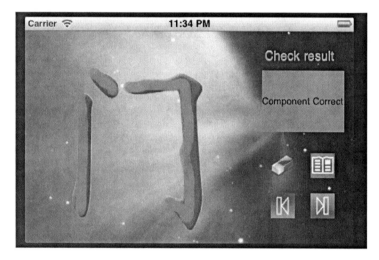

Fig. 4. The User Interface of Our iWrite System After a User Wrote the Chinese Character (i.e. Door) with Correct Stroke Sequences on the iPhone Simulator

practice on the iPhone simulator of the Xcode IDE tool. Basically, the interface of the system is divided into three parts. The left panel of the interface is the input area which will provide the template for a student to write on it. The right of the system will have two functions. The upper part is the control panel with the demonstration part being under it. On the other hand, Fig. 3 gives the user interface of our e-learning system run on the iPhone simulator of the Xcode IDE when invalid inputs for the stroke sequence are provided. Fig. 4 shows the user interface of our iWrite system when a Chinese character with the correct stroke sequences is written on the touch screen by following the displayed template. For each stroke of the displayed template, the user's input is regarded as correct if the starting and ending points, and also direction of the user's input are consistent with those defined in the concerned stroke of the template with at least 70% of its area overlapped with that of the template. For the whole inputted character to be recognized as "correct" by our prototype, each of the inputted strokes must be correctly written in the correct stroke sequence. Furthermore, Fig. 5 illustrates the evolution of a Chinese character (i.e. horse) to better the students' understanding of

Fig. 5. The User Interface of Our iWrite System to Show the Evolution of the Chinese Character (i.e. Horse) on the iPhone Simulator

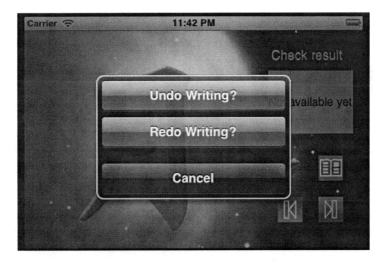

Fig. 6. The User Interface of Our iWrite System After a User Triggers the G-sensor on the iPhone Simulator to Undo/Redo the Writing of A Chinese Character

the specific meanings of basic constructs involved in this character while Fig. 6 demonstrates the unique of using the G-sensor (by shaking) on the iPhones (or smartphones) to redo or undo the writing of a Chinese character during the training process.

An evaluation plan was already formulated and would be conducted in a Chinese course offered to foreign students in the upcoming Fall Semester in the School of Chinese, the University of Hong Kong. A more detailed analysis will be performed with its result to be published by the end of that semester.

5 Concluding Remarks

In this paper, we propose to develop an adaptive and extendible e-learning platform based on the concept of learning objects for foreigners or Chinese students to practise the writing of Chinese characters in correct stroke sequences on smartphones [8]. To demonstrate the feasibility of our proposal, we implement a prototype of our e-learning system using the Objective-C and the Xcode IDE tool [9] for execution on iPhones/iPod touch. Our prototype of the targeted e-learing system can systematically categorize all the stored Chinese characters according to four basic structures, and also include Chinese characters of all the basic structures into each training session. In each step of the training session, a template of the selected Chinese character will be displayed for the students to input the correct stroke sequence using the touch-screen of iPhones. After the student finishes inputting the stroke sequences, our e-learning system will use an efficient and intelligent algorithm to check whether the stroke sequences of the inputted Chinese character are correct or not. In case the direction of any stroke or the sequence of strokes is incorrect, an error message will be displayed. At this instant, the student can click on the animation button to display the correct stroke sequence of writing the specific Chinese character through animated GIF files. At the end, the student will receive an evaluation report showing at which specific structure(s) of the Chinese characters that the concerned student is relatively weak. In this way, our e-learning system may adaptively provide more such structures for the concerned student to practise.

Basically, there were some initial and positive feedbacks about our work collected from different researchers in the Faculty of Education, and also the School of Chinese in our university or other institutions in Hong Kong. A thorough evaluation will be conducted in a Chinese course offered to foreign students in the upcoming Fall Semester in the University of Hong Kong for a careful analysis. All in all, our work is very promising, and shed sheds light on many interesting directions including the integration with existing online course materials for further investigation on both the pedagogic and technological impacts.ï

Acknowledgments. The authors are grateful to the generous supports from Department of Electrical and Electronic Engineering, the University of Hong Kong. Furthermore, the authors would like to express their gratitude to Dr. Daniel Churchill and Ms. Sue Meng for their fruitful discussions on e-learning systems for writing Chinese.

References

1. Forsberg, A., Bragdon, A., Joseph, J., LaViola Jr., J., Raghupathy, S., Zeleznik, R.: An Empirical Study in Pen-Centric User Interfaces: Diagramming. In: Proceedings of the Eurographics Workshop on Sketch-Based Interface and Modeling 2008, Annecy, France, pp. 135–142 (2008)
2. Li, C.J., Miller, T.S., Zeleznik, R.: AlgoSketch: Algorithm Sketching and Interactive Computation. In: Proceedings of the Eurographics Workshop on Sketch-Based Interface and Modeling 2008, Annecy, France, pp. 175–182 (2008)
3. Goh, T.T.: Kinshuk and Lin, Taiyu: Developing an adaptive mobile learning system. In: Lee, K.T., Mitchell, K. (eds.) Proc. of the International Conference on Computers in Education 2003, Hong Kong, December 2-5, pp. 1062–1065 (2003)
4. Foster, I., Kesselman, C., Nick, J., Tuecke, S.: The Physiology of the Grid: an Open Grid Services Architecture for Distributed Systems Integration. Technical report, Global Grid Forum (2002)
5. Hu, Z.-h., Xu, Y., Huang, L.-s., Leung, H.: A Chinese Handwriting Education System with Automatic Error Detection. Journal of Software, Special Issue on Advanced Distance Learning Technologies 4(2), 101–107 (2009)
6. The eStroke development team: The eStroke Animated Chinese Characters Site (2011), http://www.eon.com.hk/estroke/ (retrieved: March 10, 2011)
7. The Learning Object team: The Learning Object Site (2011), http://www.learnactivity.com/lo/index.htm (retrieved: March 11, 2011)
8. The Wikipedia development team: Smartphone – Wikipedia, the free encyclopedia (2011), http://en.wikipedia.org/wiki/Smartphone (retrieved: January 10, 2011)
9. The Xcode development team: the Xcode - Developer Tools Technology Overview website (2011), http://developer.apple.com/technologies/tools/xcode.html (retrieved: January 21, 2011)
10. Yeung, K.W.: Mobile Learning of Writing Chinese Characters on UMPCs. A Final-Year Project Report 2008-09, Department of E.E.E., The University of Hong Kong (2009) (revised: March 10, 2009)
11. Yeung, K.W., Tam, V.: An Adaptive Learning Platform to Practise the Writing of Chinese Characters on Ultra-Mobile PCs. In: Proceedings of the International Conference on ICT in Teaching and Learning (ICT 2009), Hong Kong, July 6-8 (2009)
12. Yeung, K.W., Tam, V.: Learning to Write Chinese Characters with Correct Stroke Sequences on Mobile Devices. In: Proceedings of the IEEE 2nd International Conference on Education Technology and Computer (ICETC 2010), Shanghai, China, June 22-24, vol. 4, pp. 395–399 (2010)

GoPutonghua: An Online Learning Platform for Self-learners to Learn Putonghua

Vanessa Sin-Chun Ng, Andrew Kwok-Fai Lui, and Fu-Hong Wong

School of Science and Technology
The Open University of Hong Kong
30 Good Shepherd Street, Homantin, Hong Kong
scng@ouhk.edu.hk

Abstract. Internet has become a part of our life. Online learning offers us convenience, flexibility and collaboration. In this paper, a new online learning platform – GoPutonghua is introduced for self-learners to learn Putonghua. The online platform includes components like learning materials, online exercises, online assessment, learning tools and communications tools. The platform allows learners to conduct online exercises that are related to the lecture contents in e-books and online lectures. An online assessment system is developed for learners to know their performance and seek for improvement. A character dictionary (zidian) and a phrase dictionary (cidian) are built to support mapping from Chinese characters to Pinyin. Learning tools like Pinyin converter and Text-to-Pinyin Speech have been developed to search for the Pinyin (with tone marks) of Chinese characters and produce the correct pronunciations in Putonghua. The two types of communication tools (asynchronous and synchronous) are also included in the platform. GoPutonghua is developed to provide more resources and services for self-learners to learn Putonghua in a hassle-free manner. This paper explains why there is a need of developing the new online platform. The components and the architecture of the platform will be introduced. The implementation details of some components will be discussed in this paper. Finally, an evaluation on the usefulness and the quality of the online platform will also be reported.

1 Introduction

Learning a new language is not an easy task. Learners should expose to the environment with a lot of exercises, practices and training. E-learning systems promote lifelong learning by enabling learners to learn anytime, anywhere and at the learners' pace [1, 2]. Online learning has no time zones, and location and distance are not an issue. Learners can use the Internet to access the learning materials through the online learning platform, and can communicate with the cyber teachers. Situated learning is facilitated, since learners can learn while they are working on the job or in any environment at their own pace.

J. Yong (2005) [3] defines four main functions for e-learning systems based on four participants – lecturers, learners, administrative personnel, and technical staff. In this case, the e-learning system is sub-classified as teaching workflow system,

R. Kwan et al. (Eds.): ICT 2011, CCIS 177, pp. 96–108, 2011.
© Springer-Verlag Berlin Heidelberg 2011

learning workflow system, administrative workflow system, and infrastructure workflow system. For example, in teaching workflow system, the teaching activities include assessment, materials preparation, student learning services and support, etc. In learning workflow system, the learning activities include assignment, discussion, evaluation, examination, etc.

Based on the principles of e-learning system, an online learning platform namely "GoPutonghua Online Self-Learning Platform" has been developed for self-learners to learn Putonghua. This online learning platform allows learners to conduct online exercises which are related to the lecture contents. An online assessment system is developed for learners to know their performance and seek for improvement. A character dictionary (zidian) and a phrase dictionary (cidian) are built to support mapping from Chinese characters (Hanzi) to Pinyin. Learning tools like Pinyin converter and Text-To-Pinyin Speech has been developed to search for the Pinyin (with tone marks) of Chinese characters and produce with the correct pronunciations in Putonghua. Online lectures and e-books are also included in the platform.

As for the online assessment system, it provides the learners with a reference on how they are acquiring their knowledge and skills, and the topics/areas where they need to seek clarification or invest more effort [4, 5]. Online assessment system has the advantages of instant feedback to students, greater flexibility with respect to location and timing, improved reliability, and enhanced question styles which incorporate interactivity and multimedia. According to R Trillo, et. al (2008) [6], an online assessment system should include the support of automatic corrections, different roles, different types of questions, random generation of tests and questions, etc. The online assessment system of "GoPutonghua Online Self-Learning Platform" allows teachers to set questions, and allows learners to view their results. It supports automatic marking and corrections of online tests.

There are two types of communication tools – asynchronous and synchronous. Synchronous tools allow collaboration and discussion among a group of people at the same time. Asynchronous tools allow communication and collaboration among people at different time. [7, 8] For the synchronous tool, the online platform uses Windows Live Messenger to allow learners to have instant messaging with cyber teachers. For the asynchronous tool, a forum is used for asking and answering questions, and to initiate discussions on topics related to Putonghua. It foments interactivity among learners and opportunities for learners to lead discussions.

2   Existing Online Putonghua Platforms

Two existing Putonghua online learning platforms are available in the market. They are "PLW" CUHK Online Putonghua Platform [9] and TEENS platform [10]. The following table shows a comparison of the two existing platforms and the new one - "GoPutonghua Online Self-Learning Platform". It can be seen that the TEENS platform has learning tools such as Text-To-Pinyin Speech and Pinyin dictionary that "PLW" platform does not have. It is also observed that both of the two existing platforms do not provide communication tools like instant messaging and discussion forum. However, they are important learning tools as learners may encounter problems while learning. The provision of communication tools can facilitate the

Table 1. Comparison of "GoPutonghua Online Self-Learning Platform" with existing platforms

Functions / Features		"PLW" CUHK Online Putonghua Platform	TEENS Platform	GoPutonghua Online Self-Learning Platform
Learning materials		✔	✔	✔
Lab sessions / exercises		✔	✔	✔
Online assessment		✔	✔	✔
Learning tools	TTS	✗	✔	✔
	Pinyin dictionary	✗	✔	✔
Communication Tools	Instant messaging	✗	✗	✔
	Discussion forum	✗		✔

interaction between teachers and learners. In short, the new online learning platform includes the learning materials, lab exercises, online assessment, learning tools and communication tools so as to provide more resources and services for self-learners to learn Putonghua in an easy and convenient way.

3 System Architecture

The architecture of this online learning platform can be visualized by Figure 1.

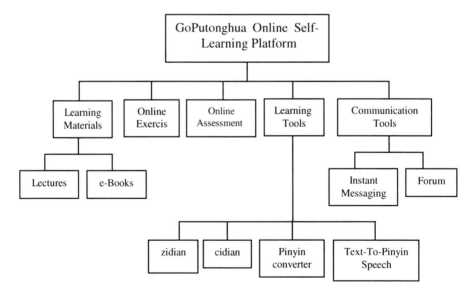

Fig. 1. The platform architecture

4 Methodology

The techniques used in the platform include HTML, CSS, PHP, MySQL. HTML is used to create web pages. CSS is used to define layout of HTML documents. PHP is used to create dynamic web pages and support database. MySQL is used to build a database system used on the platform.

The online platform involves online assessment system, learning tools, learning materials and communications tools.

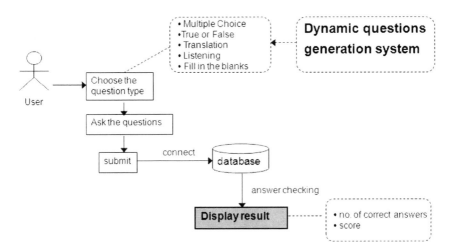

Fig. 2. The implementation of Online Assessment System

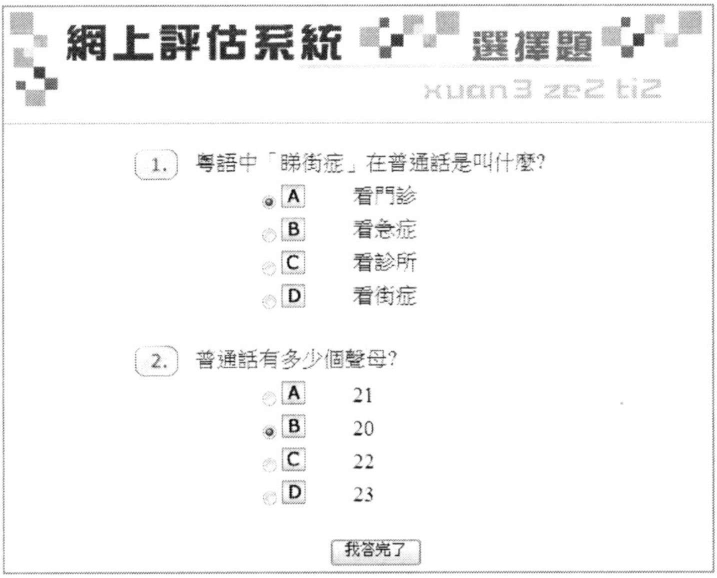

Fig. 3. Multiple Choice Question: before submission

4.1   Online Assessment System (OAS)

The OAS allows cyber teachers to set questions which will be stored in the question database. After submitting the answers, the system will check the answers and calculate the marks through question database. Then the marks will be stored in the marks database. The implementation of the OAS is shown in Fig. 2. Fig. 3 and 4 show the screen shots of different types of questions in OAS.

Fig. 4. Pinyin Translation Question

4.2   Learning Tools

There are four learning tools implemented in this system. They are character dictionary (zidian), phrase dictionary (cidian), Pinyin converter and Text-to-Pinyin Speech. Fig. 5 shows the implementation of a learning tool – character dictionary.

For character dictionary, when the user enters a Chinese character in the textbox and presses the submit button, a connection to the database is established. It will first go through the "zidian" table to search the desired word.   If the word is in the database, then the system will find the audio mp3 file for that word. This can be achieved by using the tone number of that word. For example, the word "好" has two pronunciations --- "hao3" or "hao4". The system will go to find the correct audio file for each pronunciation and pass the mp3 file address to the Flash MP3 player. When the user clicks the player, it will play the pronunciation.

When the audio files were found, the system will move to "cidian" table to find all phrases containing the searched word. We can use the Pinyin with tone number of the searched word to find those matched words (obtained previously) having the same tone number. Then, it randomly generates the correct vocabulary. Fig. 6 shows the searching result of the Chinese character "好".

For Text-To-Pinyin Speech, there will be a voice folder containing the pronunciation of Chinese characters. Each time when the learners type in the Chinese characters, the system will look for the Pinyin from the Pinyin database and displays the Pinyin

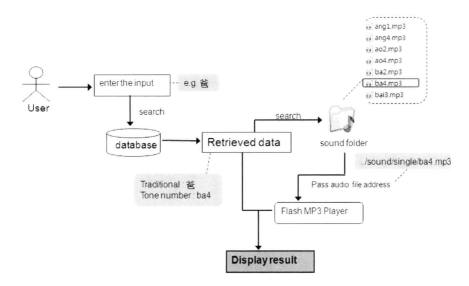

Fig. 5. The implementation of a learning tool – character dictionary (zidian)

Fig. 6. The search result of the word "好" in character dictionary

with correct tone marks, then it picks up the correct mp3 sound file to output the pronunciation.

In order to search the Pinyin and the audio mp3 file of each Chinese word, the inputted content will be first split into an array. For example, the content "今天, 我去了爬山。" will be split as follows:

After splitting, it needs to check whether the elements in the array are Chinese characters or not. If the element is a single Chinese character, the system will go through the "zidian" table to search the pinyin with tone mark of that character and output the Pinyin with tone mark and the character. If two or more elements are phrases after combination, the system will search another table called "cidian". After that, it will use the tone number of character /phrase to find the corresponding audio mp3 file. When all the addresses of audio files are collected, they will be sent to the Flash MP3 player. The player will play the pronunciation of the whole content. Fig. 7 shows the result of text to pinyin with spoken speech.

Fig. 7. The result of Text-To-Pinyin Speech

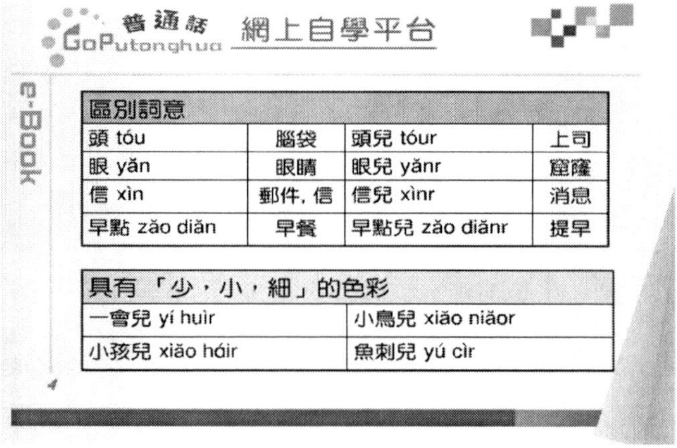

Fig. 8. A screen shot for e-book

4.3 Learning Materials

There are two types of learning materials available in the new online learning platform – e-book and lecture notes. The e-book contains a page turning effect when the user flips to the next page. The contents in the e-book are mainly in bulletin point format which makes users easy to read and memorize the contents. There is also zoom-in effect in e-book. Fig. 8 shows a screen shot of the e-book. The online lecture notes contain not only text, but also include multimedia elements. Most of the lecture notes include audio effect. When the user clicks the "Play" button, he or she can listen to the pronunciation of the words through the flash mp3 player. Fig. 9 shows a screen shot of the lecture notes.

第七課

普通話與廣州話的語法差異

每種語言都包括語音、辭彙和語法三大部份；普通話及廣州話也不例外。現代普通話的標準規定是：

語音方面：以北京話語音為標準音；
辭彙方面：以北方話為基礎方言；
語法方面：以典範的現代白話文著作為語法規範。

由以上可見，普通話與廣州話在語音和辭彙方面有顯著的差異，至於在語法上的差異則不如前兩者來得太明顯，然而，認識兩者之間在語法上的分別是在學習普通話過程中不可或缺的，因此必須認真對待。本課題會集中探討普通話與廣州話之間在語法上的對比與差異。

詞序上的分別

詞序就是指詞的先後次序。這裡的詞序並不是指在詞彙中，語素出現的先後次序，而是指在句式中詞類出現的先後次序。在普通話與廣東話之間經常出現在詞序上的差異，例如：

廣州話	普通話	
你食先，我等陣至吃	你先吃，我等一會兒再吃	▶ □ □
你講少兩句啦	你少說兩句吧	▶ □ □
聽日我要訓多D	明天我要多睡點兒	▶ □ □

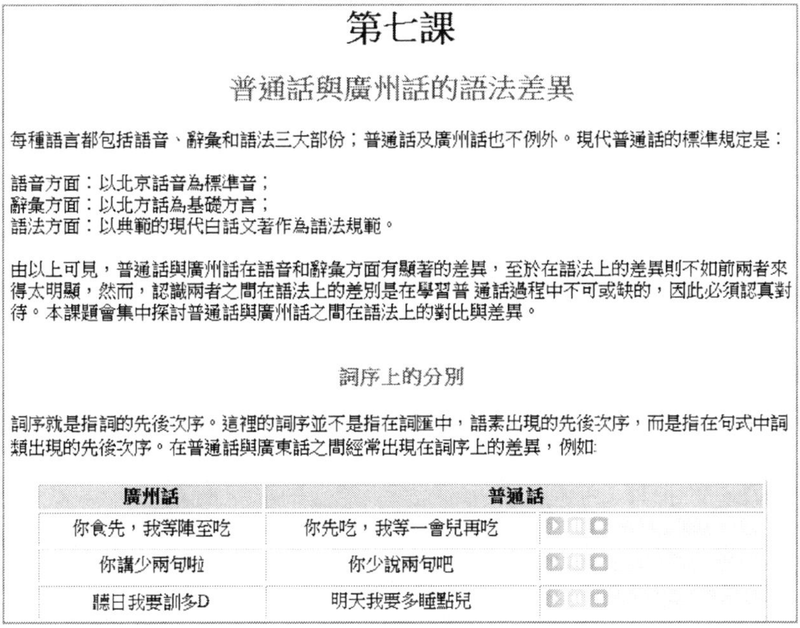

Fig. 9. A screen shot for lecture notes

線上老師

  黃老師

  陳老師

QQ離線

在線老師每天9:00 至 18:00為大家服務, 如在學習上遇有任何問題, 可向我們提問

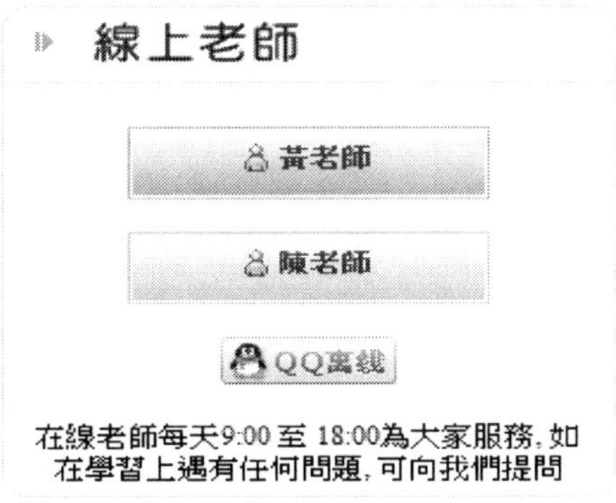

Fig. 10. Instant messaging

4.4 Communication Tools

Instant messaging and discussion forum are provided in communication tools. The new online platform uses Window Live Messenger to allow learners to have instant messaging with cyber teachers. Fig 10 shows a screenshot of instant messaging in GoPutonghua Self-learning Online Platform. It foments interactivity among learners and the cyber teachers. The learners can solve the questions quickly with the help of cyber teachers.

5 Discussion

In Mandarin, there are some rules of pronunciation. The tone of a word can be changed by the word placement. For example, the word "診所" (clinic) represents two characters with third tone distinction. If you pronounce both two characters in third tone, it is quite unnatural and slow in speed. In fact, the tone of the first word "診 "should be pronounced in second tone. However, this change will not affect its meaning. Note that, the examples listed below that has changed the tone marks are just used to show the correct tone when speaking. When writing Pinyin, although there is a change when speaking, the original tone marks are still written.

Rule 1 (Third Tone)
If a 3rd tone is followed by another 3rd tone, the first 3rd tone changes to a 2nd tone.

Examples:

你好 (hello): nǐ hǎo ➔ ní hǎo
保守 (conservative) : bǎo shǒu ➔ báo shǒu
好久 (a long time): hǎo jiǔ ➔ háo jiǔ

Rule 2 (The character "一")
The Chinese character "一" is pronounced in the first tone when it stands alone. But "一" is pronounced in 2nd tone when followed by a 4th tone.

Examples:

一個 (one): yī gè ➔ yí gè
一塊 (one piece): yī kuài ➔ yí kuài
一步 (one step): yī bù ➔ yí bù

Rule 3 (The character "不")
The Chinese character "不" is pronounced in the 4th tone when it stands alone but there is one situation where this changes. "不" is pronounced in 2nd tone when followed by a 4th tone.

Examples:

不變 (not change): bù biàn ➔ bú biàn
不會 (will not, cannot): bù huì ➔ bú huì
不錯 (not bad): bù cuò ➔ bú cuò

If we don't apply the above rules, the content entered by the user will be displayed one character by one character because it only searches the "character database". Also, the flash mp3 player will pronounce one character by one character which is slow in speed and not very natural. In order to make it more natural and increase the speed of pronunciation, one more database will be used that is "phrase dictionary". In addition, the n-gram algorithm will be applied to do the searching.

An n-gram is a sub-sequence of n items from a given sequence. N-grams are used in various areas of statistical natural language processing and genetic sequence analysis. The items in question can be characters, words or base pairs according to the application. For example, if the sequence of Chinese characters "研究生活動中心" uses a 2-gram(bigram) to do word segmentation, the results will be "研究", "究生", "生活", "活動", "動中", "中心". N-gram is determined by the size of N. So it will have unigram (n=1), bigram (n=2), trigram (n=3) and so on. The N-gram algorithm used for Text-To-Pinyin Speech is shown in the Fig. 11. Once a phrase is found in the cidian, the corresponding phrase mp3 file can be found from database, it makes the sound to be more natural.

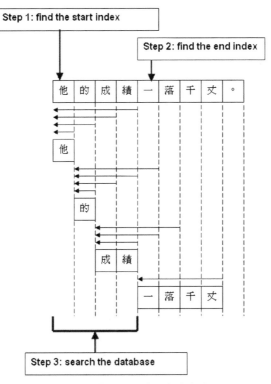

Fig. 11. The search result for using the N-gram algorithm

6   Evaluation of GoPutonghua Online Self-learning Platform

A questionnaire was designed to obtain views and opinions of the GoPutonghua Online Self-Learning Platform. The aim was to identify any areas that could be improved or changed in order to provide better services and resources to the self-learners. Respondents were also asked to rate various components of the platform based on two criteria: usefulness and quality. The total number of people invited to try the platform and fill in the questionnaires was 14, of which the majority of respondents were university students (57.14%), 14.29% were Putonghua teachers, 28.57% were working people.

The respondents were asked to rate the usefulness and quality of each of the components provided in the platform. Components that are high quality doesn't mean that are very useful, and components that are very useful doesn't mean that they are of high quality. Useful components are components that have a valuable purpose and are frequently utilized in learning. Quality components are components that have good graphic design, being free from defects, functioning properly and achieving high end-user satisfaction. Generally speaking, good components should achieve high usefulness and high quality. The results listed in Table 2 show that majority of components is of high usefulness which are over 80%. The most useful component is Text-To-Pinyin Speech (89.29%) while the lowest one is Pinyin Converter (69.64%). Concerning the quality of the platform, majority of components have values nearest to high which is over 70%. The highest quality component is e-Book (78.57%) while the lowest one is Pinyin Converter (60.71%). The result also shows that Text-To-Pinyin Speech has a great difference (21.43%) between its usefulness and quality.

Table 2. Comparison of usefulness and quality of components

	Usefulness	Quality
Lecture Notes	80.36%	75%
e-Book	80.36%	*78.57%*
Online Exercise	78.57%	73.21%
Character & Phrase Dictionary	87.50%	73.21%
Pinyin Converter	*69.64%*	*60.71%*
Text-To-Pinyin Speech	*89.29%*	67.86%
Multiple Choice	80.36%	71.43%
True or false	82.14%	66.07%
Listening	83.93%	73.21%
Translation	80.36%	69.64%
Fill in the blanks	78.57%	69.64%
Windows Live Messenger	83.93%	71.43%
Forum	82.14%	75%

Respondents were asked if they had any additional comments or suggestions regarding the platform components, in particular any additional components they would like to see in the platform. The number of responses to this question was 11 and the results are as follows:

1. *"The lecture notes could be more colorful. It is better not to use flash for the e-Book"*
2. *"It is better to press "enter" key to login in instead of pressing the "submit" button"*
3. *"There should an improvement in the quality of pictures.*
4. *"E-book can insert sound and video to enhance its function and effect.*
5. *"For true or false question, it is better to include explanation after submitting the answer. It is better for user to login to the forum without registering it again.*
6. *"It is better to have speaking test for the online assessment system.*
7. *"It is better to have speaking test in the online assessment system.*
8. *"Every word should have sound."*
9. *"It is suggested that to learn Putonghua from life, for example, the system can retrieve a news everyday from the Internet and provide pronunciation and Pinyin in order to attract users to learn Putonghua"*
10. *"E-book can insert sound"*
11. *"Navigation function of the forum is not obvious; there is no button to link to the index page. If the platform is put on the internet, the smoothness and the browsing speed will be affected by bandwidth"*

Respondents thought that users can use the "enter" key to login rather than pressing the "submit" button and the forum's navigation function is not clear. These can be improved in a short period of time so as to provide convenience to the users. Another comment was that the browsing speed may be affected by bandwidth. This can be solved by using the web hosting service as it is more reliable and faster. Other comments suggested inserting sound to e-Book and including speaking tests for the Online Assessment. These were seen as in need of expansion. Learning Putonghua from life through daily news is a new component to the platform. This was seen as in need of expansion and renovation.

Overall, respondents tended to rate the usefulness and quality of the platform as "high". There is also a fairly high percentage of respondents rate it as "very high". There were almost no respondents that rated it as "very low" and "low". To summarize, the results clearly identify that the overall usefulness (81.04%) is higher than the quality (72.1%). In order to minimize the difference between them, the quality of the platform was needed to be improved.

7 Conclusion

In this paper, an online learning platform "GoPutonghua" is proposed to allow self-learners to learn Putonghua online. The online platform contains components like learning materials, online exercises, online assessment, learning tools and communications tools. As compared to the existing online Putonghua platforms, the new learning platform includes more comprehensive functions which address the needs of learners. In order to produce more natural speech for the Text-To-Pinyin speech in the "Learning tools" of the platform, an N-gram algorithm is used to find phrases first in the dictionary. The evaluation results show that the users rated the overall usefulness as 81.04%; while the quality of the platform as 72.1%.

References

[1] Communication Tools, the Digital Education website,
     http://blogs.ubc.ca/clarkeetec565/communication-tools/
[2] E-assessment, http://en.wikipedia.org/wiki/E-assessment
[3] Yong, J.: Workflow-based e-Learning Platform. In: Ninth International Conference on
     Computer Supported Cooperative Work in Design, vol. 2 (2005)
[4] Ridgway, J., McCusker, S., Pead, D.: Literature Review of e-Assessment. Nesta Future
     Lab, Bristol, UK (2004)
[5] Rourke, L., Anderson, T.: Using peer teams to lead online discussions. Journal of
     Interactive Media en Education (2002), http://www-jime.open.ac.uk/2002/1/rourke-
     anderson-02-1.pdf
[6] TEENS Platform, http://teens.putonghuaonline.com/
[7] Trillo, R., Ilarri, S., López, J.R., Brisaboa, N.R.: Development of An Online
     Assessment System to Track the Performance of Students (2008),
     http://citeseerx.ist.psu.edu/viewdoc/
     download?doi=10.1.1.77.7210&rep=rep1&type=pdf
[8] Urdan, T.A., Weggen, C.C.: Towards Best Practices in Online Learning and Teaching
     in Higher Education. MERLOT Journal of Online Learning and Teaching 6 (2000)
[9] Le, W.P.: The Chinese University of Hong Kong,
     http://www.ilc.cuhk.edu.hk/Chinese/plw/
[10] What is an E-Learning Platform, Anyway?, Australian Flexible Learning Community
     website, http://community.flexiblelearning.net.au/
     TechnologiesforLearning/content/article_442.htm

Construction and Evaluation of a Blended Learning Platform for Higher Education

Lisa Beutelspacher and Wolfgang G. Stock

Heinrich-Heine-University Düsseldorf, Department of Information Science,
Universitätsstr. 1, D-40225 Düsseldorf, Germany
Lisa.Beutelspacher@uni-duesseldorf.de,
Stock@phil-fak.uni-duesseldorf.de

Abstract. The design of a platform for blended learning is dependent on the educational and didactic theories. We discuss behaviorism, cognitivism, and constructivism and the impact of these theories on the elements of learning platforms. We describe the construction of a learning platform (of the Dept. of Information Science at the University of Düsseldorf, Germany), developed from the results of the didactic theories. The InfoCenter consists of elements of face-to-face teaching, of multimedia mediation (text books, slides, classic texts, interactive videos, FAQ lists, video glossaries), of Web 2.0 tools (wikis, weblogs, social networks, social bookmarking and folksonomies) and of the use of a learning management system (with learning units and tests). The platform was evaluated by its users (university students) by means of SERVQUAL. According to the evaluation, students are satisfied with the InfoCenter and are willing to use it for their exam preparation.

Keywords: E-Learning, Blended Learning, Higher Education, Web 2.0, Didactic Theories.

1 Introduction

"With the emergence of Internet technologies, there has been an explosion of nontraditional learning opportunities during the past few years" [25, p. 299]. E-learning uses information technologies to disseminate and convey knowledge [49], [56]. The benefit of e-learning, according to Moriz [38], is the possibility of using multimedia content. Another important factor in terms of self-directed learning is place and time independence. Also, the flexible pace of learning plays a major role in successful learning. Each student can work through their courses individually without considering the progress of other students [38]. E-learning can also be a relief for teachers. For example, updating documents and courses that are available online is much easier and faster than updating printed material [49].

In addition to the benefits of e-learning there are also some disadvantages to be identified. According to Moriz [38], there is a lack of social interaction. Mandl & Kopp [32] show further disadvantages, such as the high resource and financial cost and the fact that some content is not suitable for a virtual presentation.

R. Kwan et al. (Eds.): ICT 2011, CCIS 177, pp. 109–122, 2011.
© Springer-Verlag Berlin Heidelberg 2011

For these reasons, so-called "blended learning" is at the center of attention. The concept of blended learning is based on the integration of classroom and e-learning phases [14], [15], [5]. Blended learning also means that the content is integrated in different media and methods [4]. The difficulty in developing a blended learning platform is an effective combination of different elements. It is important that the individual components in a blended learning platform be not only next to each other but also embedded and integrated in a social environment [32], [2]. The elements of a learning platform should incorporate all ways of communicating electronically: text, audio, static graphic and video [55].

This mixture of various e-learning elements and classroom phases at the university has been implemented by employees of the Department of Information Science at Heinrich-Heine University in Düsseldorf. In addition to printable teaching materials and short educational films, various Web 2.0 elements were integrated into the platform, which gave students the opportunity for collaborative work. In addition, interactive lecture recordings as well as learning control and learning items were created.

In this paper, we will discuss three Research Questions (RQs):

1st RQ: Which educational and didactic theories are important for blended learning?

2nd RQ: On the basis of the results of the educational and didactic theories, which elements should a blended learning platform employ?

3rd RQ: How will such a learning platform be evaluated by the students?

2 Didactic Theories

According to Moriz [38], e-learning and blended learning require an educational foundation. He identifies three main educational trends that are important for e-learning and blended learning: behaviorism, cognitivism and constructivism. As we shall see, these theories cannot be used to the same degree, as they employ very different approaches. However, it is important for the preparation of blended learning environments to deal with the various theories, so that their associated applications can be reasonably integrated into the platform [39].

2.1 Behaviorism

Representatives of behaviorism assume that learning consists of the linking of stimuli and reactions [50]. The classical conditioning [43] leads to the designated reflex. Reuter [47] highlights that, according to the behavioral learning theory, learners can only learn via reward and punishment. Here, however, rewards would be more effective because they reduce barriers to motivation and stress. Moriz [38] considers that a pure behavioristic foundation for blended learning is not very promising, as the passive memorization concentrates on the reproduction of specified learning content and the transferability of knowledge is neglected. Nevertheless, some important aspects of this theory can be applied to e-learning programs. Following Webb and Powis [57], Moriz [38] considers that the principle of behaviorism can be implemented by mediating and testing factual information. Here, a direct feedback would be important.

2.2 Cognitivism

In contrast to behaviorism, in cognitivism the learner can be seen as an individual [39]. External stimuli should be actively used [47]. The students should not be controlled by external stimuli, but turn them into knowledge. This increases the motivation of learners. Unlike behaviorism, cognitivism prizes not factual knowledge but a comprehensive problem-solving ability [39]. While designing educational software, it must be taken into account that not only memorized facts are requested, but the capacity to develop solution strategies will be encouraged [38].

2.3 Constructivism

The central thesis of constructivism is that "perception is construction and interpretation, [...] and objectivity, subject-independent thinking and understanding are impossible" [20, p. 868]. Representatives of constructivism believe that learning is an individual process and that each learner has his or her own way of learning [3]. From a constructivist perspective, learning in groups is especially important because it allows for an exchange between students and a change of perspectives [27]. According to Moriz [38] and Bruns & Gajewski [8], the following aspects of constructivism are important for blended learning:

- Learning must take place in authentic situations.
- The learner must be motivated so that they actively deal with the subject matter.
- The teacher encourages individual learning processes, but does not control them.
- The learner must be allowed to determine their time and place of learning.
- The curriculum must be presented from different perspectives and in different contexts.
- Learning should take place in groups.

For Höbarth [22], collaborative services are especially applicable with regard to constructivistic learning. This includes Web 2.0 services, which are described in detail below. Interactive videos also fulfill the specifications of this theory. Students can choose their own way of learning by deciding what information and topics they need.

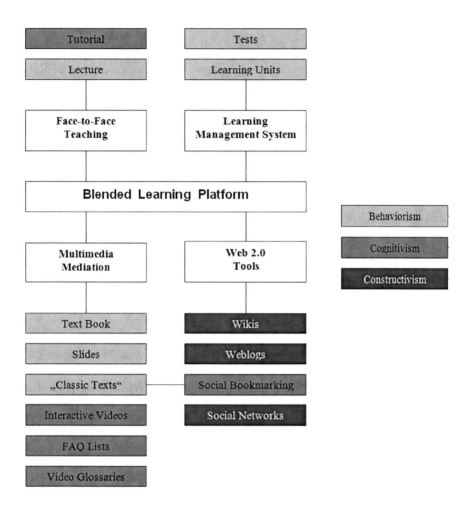

Fig. 1. Elements of the InfoCenter

3 Construction of the Learning Platform

The concept of blended learning has been implemented by Isabella Peters, Sonja Gust von Loh and Katrin Weller, of the Department of Information Science at Heinrich-Heine-University in Düsseldorf, Germany. The resulting learning platform "Info-Center" integrates various multimedia and collaborative services that allow students to repeat what they have learned, to ask questions and exchange information among themselves or with the teachers. It provides an ideal complement to classroom teaching, as themes and issues from the lecture can be taken up again and explained. The development of the platform has been implemented in seminars by the staff and students of the department of information science [45]. Through this cooperation, the students learn to handle information, prepare them for fellow students and make them searchable.

3.1 Concept

The InfoCenter has been included on the website of the Department of Information Science, so it is easily accessible for the students. Figure 1 shows all elements of the learning platform and the appropriate learning theories. The learning platform is designed so that students can choose their own time and place of learning individually. The wide range of different media and services and the interactive lecture recordings shall ensure that the students can choose their own learning path.

3.2 Interactive Video Lectures

Lecture recordings offer students the opportunity to become independent of time and place to watch a lecture [34], [36]. This may on the one hand be used for the repetition of a difficult and complex subject matter, but can also be of interest to students who have to reduce their presence at the university because of jobs or parenting [62].

Before the rise of the Internet, recording information via television or CD-ROM was characterized by a passive viewing by the user [30]. There were hardly any possibilities of intervening into the program or getting more background information. The Internet offers new opportunities for obtaining information that the user may also want to apply to videos [29]. He or she steps out of the role of a passive observer and wants to select information actively, to give or receive immediate feedback [30]. With the help of new formats and new software for video processing, it becomes possible to realize these wishes via so-called "interactive video" [62].

For these reasons, the idea of interactive videos has been included in the learning platform of information science. Interactivity is ensured through a clickable table of contents, by jumping directly to the topics the students are interested in and through the use of context-sensitive links to full texts and other important information. The recordings show not only the teachers but also students who can always ask questions during the lecture. This allows active discussions between students and teachers [6].

3.3 Web 2.0 Services

For Tsang [54, p. 575], the internet "provides a giant open-access 'virtual lab' for learners." In Web 2.0, users are not just readers, but may participate with little effort even in the creation and distribution of content [40]. Web 2.0 services such as blogs, wikis or social networks offer an easy and cost-effective way of online communication [10], [23], [61]. In Web 2.0, students are encouraged to generate their own content for other students [48]. Due to the easy handling of the collaborative services, it is possible to "teach" independently of time and place. The boundaries between teachers and learners become blurred. Both are the architects of the learning environment [24].

In the following, we will introduce the Web 2.0 services which were integrated into the learning platform of information science. The focus here is on collaborative content creation and development and on the communication between students using wikis, blogs, social bookmarking and social networking [13], [60]. According to Dahl and Vossen [12], the location of blog entries or articles in Web 2.0 is one of the most important factors in terms of e-learning. Therefore, the reasonable allocation of tags is to be noted in particular [12], [44].

3.3.1 Wikis

The use of a wiki requires only a little knowledge of the functionality and design of the World Wide Web [16]. Each user can create or change any content. Different priorities of students and discussions about difficult issues are integrated into one system. Wikis also allow one to link to websites and to embed multimedia objects [45]. This may cause a broad knowledge base that can be used by other students to search for information or discussion topics.

The students who were concerned with the creation of the wiki were faced with the task of designing a suitable structure and of populating the Wiki with initial information [45]. The main page of our wiki is divided into four areas. First, it gives general information about the curriculum. Here prospective students can find information about information science in general as well as about career opportunities or requirements. The help section contains, among other things, FAQs (Frequently Asked Questions), information about the Heinrich-Heine-University or the city of Düsseldorf. In the "formalities" section, important information about exam registration, term papers and study regulations have been assembled. The fourth area is the work area. This area provides collected information about information science topics. It also provides an overview of the courses and seminars in which the students worked on the wiki. Encyclopedia articles on selected topics help students to find specific information.

3.3.2 Weblogs

Weblogs (short: blogs) become increasingly important in blended learning [1], [35]. For writing a blog entry, no HTML knowledge is required, which makes participation easier. Blogs with education background, so-called Edublogs [1], are particularly useful for presenting research results and study-related issues [35]. Also, reviews of courses and internships can be easily applied to other students and interested parties. The comment feature allows one to make comments on each blog entry. This encourages discussion between the participants [1].

The Information Science Blog was established on the basis of the platform Wordpress [1]. Students and employees can present reports on their internship, experience, comment, get new research results or read up on current events [45]. Individual articles can be tagged, which makes them easier to retrieve. Tag Clouds facilitate additional browsing [12]. Moreover, it is possible to search not only for specific tags, but also for users or groups [45].

3.3.3 Social Bookmarking and Folksonomies

Social bookmarks are web bookmarks that can be created and developed collaboratively by users. Social bookmarking services like Delicious[2] or BibSonomy[3] are browser-based and users need no programming skills or additional software. The

---

[1] http://wordpress.com/
[2] http://www.delicious.com/
[3] http://www.bibsonomy.org/

literature can be accessed by using so-called "tags". These tags are not predetermined. All tags of an information service together form a folksonomy [44], [46], [52], [59]. This has the advantage that the vocabulary is not given by only a single indexer, but that a knowledge base is created with different vocabularies. Due to the collaborative content development, it is easier for students to find scientific works. Knowledge representation facilities can be improved via indexing [37]. Students can manage their bookmarks and references and make them available to other students [53]. In our platform, "classic texts" such as articles or conference proceedings were collected and tagged in BibSonomy. No registration is required for searching the literature. This is only necessary if the students themselves want to bookmark any literature. In a seminar, students tagged and included all cited references of an information science textbook in BibSonomy.

3.3.4 Social Networks

Social networks are platforms on which users can network with each other and form communities. Each user creates his or her own profile page with personal or (depending on platform) professional information that they can thus pass on to their virtual contacts [28]. In the private sector, these platforms have been around for several years, with great success. But social networking is gaining in importance in e-learning and blended learning as well [9], [11], [31]. Mason and Rennie [33] believe that the casual atmosphere in such networks is a good foundation for learning. It can help form learning groups, which meet independently of time and place and can discuss problems and difficulties. Another advantage of social networks, according to Mason and Rennie [33], is the option of students meeting virtually even before the start of a course.

The Department of Information Science has created its own Facebook[4] profile. Any Facebook user can become a "fan" of Information Science in Düsseldorf. On the profile page, the students can find updated information on the department and the discipline. As a fan of the profile it is possible to find other fans to contact. This creates a network of students and staff. As many students already know Facebook from their private lives, the environment is a familiar one, which allows for a relaxed working atmosphere.

3.4 Learning Management System

Important elements of blended learning platforms are Learning Management Systems, e.g. Moodle[5] or ILIAS[6] [21], [19]. The open-source system ILIAS (Integrated Learning, Information and Working System) allows teachers to include and create learning content and provide this to their students.

With the help of ILIAS learning items, students have the opportunity of revising and deepening the contents of a lecture. The learning items are, like the lecture, the accompanying text book [51] and corresponding films, divided into chapters, allowing for an easy navigation between topics. This approach follows the theory of

---

[4] http://www.facebook.com/
[5] http://www.moodle.de/
[6] http://www.ilias.de/

behaviorism. The learner absorbs factual knowledge in itself, with the aim of being able to reproduce it.

Behaviorism requires information to be queried periodically [39]. This is offered by the test function of ILIAS, which asks for students' current state of knowledge. The questions are closely related to the textbook, the lectures and the ILIAS learning items. As required by the behaviorist learning theory, students get their scores and the right solutions directly after responding to a question block.

3.5 Further Learning Material

Main topics of the lectures have been selected and filmed as video glossaries, which are hosted by YouTube[7]. These videos are organized in the form of a dialogue, where an employee takes on the role of the questioner, while another gives the answers. The videos are each about 3 minutes long, and explain the main facts of a topic.

In close cooperation with the examiner, typical exam questions were included in the learning platform. Students can get a picture of what they could expect in their oral exams. The answers are not given, in order to encourage students to solve the problem independently, as they would in an actual exam situation.

The reading of literature is very important for students so they can find their own interests and priorities. Therefore the InfoCenter provides links to articles and research literature for each topic.

The pre- and post-processing of lectures is important for the students' learning process. Here blended learning is of particular relevance. The InfoCenter provides the lecture slides, so that students are able to print out and learn from the slides. InfoCenter also provides summaries of each chapter in the book. These short summaries of a topic make it easier for students to get an overview of the curriculum.

4   Evaluation

4.1 Method

The learning platform was evaluated in the summer term 2009. The 19 participating students of information science were at the end of their second semester. For the evaluation, the SERVQUAL ("SERVice QUALity") method was applied. This is a questionnaire that works with two scales on each question [42]. On the one hand, SERVQUAL captures the expectations of the test persons of a service (in our case: the students' expectations of the learning platform) and, on the other hand, the specific experiences while using the service (with our learning platform). The two scales are important not only for the purposes of evaluation, but also to show the difference between the expectation value and the experience value. The participants had the opportunity of rating their expectations and experiences on a Likert-scale from 1 (worst) to 7 (best). All aspects of the learning platform were controlled, in order to identify strengths and weaknesses.

---

[7] http://www.youtube.com/

Table 1. Results of the evaluation of the blended learning platform

Scale	1	2	3	4	5	6	7
	Low rating					High rating	

Multimedia Mediation	Element	Expectation	Experience	Difference
	Video Lectures	5,89	5,67	-0,22
	Jump Lables in Video Lectures	6,11	6,00	-0,11
	Context Sensitive Links in Video Lectures	5,33	5,00	-0,33
	Textbook	6,06	5,78	-0,28
	Slides	6,39	5,56	-0,83
	FAQ Lists	6,56	6,56	0,00
	Video Glossaries	5,58	4,83	-0,75

Learning Management System	Element	Expectation	Experience	Difference
	Tests in ILIAS	5,56	5,67	0,11
	Learning Units in ILIAS	6,74	5,94	-0,80

Web 2.0 Tools	Element	Expectation	Experience	Difference
	Blog	4,00	3,82	-0,18
	Social Bookmarking	3,84	4,05	0,21
	Social Network	4,79	3,95	-0,84
	Wikis	5,63	5,53	-0,10

"Infocenter" in general	Are you planning to regularly use the learning platform for your test preparation?	What is your assessment of the usability?	Should other lectures be integrated into the platform?
	6,28	6,28	6,5

4.2 Results of the Evaluation

The evaluation results are shown in Table 1. Generally speaking, the expectations of students were very high, and were mostly fulfilled satisfactorily.

In the field of Multimedia Mediation, very large differences between the expectations of students and the actual experience of the InfoCenter can be observed. In particular, the experiences of the lecture slides differ by -0.83 in contrast to the expectations. Many students consider video lectures to be a useful complement to conventional teaching. The experiences of the lecture recordings of information science are lower than the expectations, but still satisfactory with a value of 5.67. The lower value may result from the fact that the videos are very long and exceed the attention span of many students. The rating of the context-sensitive links is very low. Here an appropriate approach would be to improve the description of links and to point out their relevance in order to increase the motivation of students. The use of typical test questions preparing students for the oral examination meets the expectations.

The clear questions of the tests and the immediate feedback from the students seem to raise motivation. The ILIAS learning modules have been rated relatively well, but do not meet the expectations. The reason for this may lie in the extent of the learning modules.

The students are very critical of the use of collaborative media for blended learning. A study by Klein et al. [26] found out that almost all students use Web 2.0 services. The most popular are Wikipedia, social networking and social media platforms like Facebook or YouTube [58], [18]. It seems to be difficult for the students to involve these services in the learning process. The worst results in terms of expectation and experience were found in social bookmarking. According to Freimanis & Dornstädter [18], only a quarter of German information science students know about social bookmarking. Although platforms such as YouTube and Facebook are fully exploited in the private sector, it is difficult for students to see those services as a part of their studies. The students have to be encouraged to integrate these platforms in their learning process.

Due to the wide range of offered learning materials, it is possible to address all types of learners. Students are thus able to select the one learning method that best fits their learning style and their personal information management. The fact that many students have to do with Web 2.0 services both in private and as part of their studies, there are few problems with using the learning platform, even if their use in the learning process is not sufficient so far.

Many students think that more courses need to be included in the InfoCenter. Here we must consider to what extent this can be rectified, keeping in mind the very high effort involved in preparing some of the materials. Creating the collective knowledge base is less expensive, because all students and staff can participate.

It is worth considering whether a better alignment of the individual materials may be promising [7]. Another important point that has been neglected is the publicity of the learning platform among the students. Although first-year students were made familiar with the InfoCenter via short training courses, these efforts should also be applied to older terms. This may motivate the students to participate in collaborative content generation.

5   Conclusion and Outlook

As it turns out, there are three educational theories that are suitable for use in blended learning platforms. First, there is behaviorism, which is marked by a passive memorization of facts. Here tests and traditional teaching media, such as textbooks or lecture slides can be offered. Cognitivism is also an important theory for blended learning. The problem-solving ability of students and the possibility of determining their own learning path is important. Elements that are offered for the implementation of this theory in particular are the presentation of typical exam questions and the interactive video, in which students choose their own way of learning. The third theory is constructivism. Especially important in this theory is group learning. Here the use of Web 2.0 elements such as blogs, wikis and social networks is very promising.

According to the evaluation, students are generally satisfied with the platform and are willing to use it regularly for their exam preparation. A majority of the respondents say that more courses should be integrated into the learning platform.

As the evaluation of the InfoCenter has shown, the platform needs to be adjusted in a couple of places. A particular difficulty that has occurred during the test phase is the acceptance among students, particularly with respect to Web 2.0 services. Furthermore, Ersoy [17] writes about his study results: "The results of the study revealed that students had positive perceptions about Web-based instruction and online instructor, while they were uncertain about their perceptions about online cooperative learning."

In further project steps, we will include more Web 2.0 services (such as microblogs via Twitter[8], serious games, virtual worlds and educational apps) into InfoCenter in order to measure the services' acceptance by their users.

Despite these problems with blended learning environments, Page et al. [41] suggest that the numerous advantages, including the ease of updating information as well as location and time independence, blended learning will be even more popular in the coming years.

Acknowledgement

Sonja Gust von Loh, Isabella Peters and Katrin Weller have played an important part in the construction of the InfoCenter learning platform. Paul Becker checked our English text. We would like to thank all of them.

References

1. Akbulut, Y., Kiyici, M.: Instructional Use of Weblogs. Turkish Online Journal of Distance Education 8(3), 6–15 (2007)
2. Akkoyunlu, B., Yilmaz-Soylu, M.: Development of a Scale on Learners' Views on Blended Learning and its Implementation Process. Internet and Higher Education 11, 26–32 (2008)
3. Alonso, F., López, G., Manrique, D., Viñes, J.M.: An Instructional Model for Web-based E-learning Education with a Blended Learning Process Approach. British Journal of Educational Technology 36(2), 217–235 (2005)
4. Arnold, P., Kilian, L., Thillosen, A., Zimmer, G.: E-Learning. Handbuch für Hochschulen und Bildungszentren. Didaktik, Organisation, Qualität. BW Bildung und Wissen, Nürnberg (2004)
5. Baelo, S.: Blended Learning and the European Higher Education Area: The Use of WebQuests. PortaLinguarum 13, 43–53 (2010)
6. Beutelspacher, L.: Interaktive Videos und Lernstandskontrollen in der Akademischen Lehre. Information – Wissenschaft und Praxis 61(8), 443–447 (2010)
7. Beutelspacher, L., Kessler, J.N., Klein, R.N.: Blended Learning in Academic Teaching – PresentState and Opportunities at the Heinrich-Heine-University Duesseldorf. In: Workshop Proceedings of the 18th International Conference on Computers in Education (2010)
8. Bruns, B., Gajewski, P.: Multimediales Lernen im Netz. Leitfaden für Entscheider und Planer. Springer, Berlin (2003)

---

[8] http://twitter.com

9. Caschera, M.C., D'Ulizia, A., Ferri, F., Grifoni, P.: An Advanced Multimodal Platform for Educational Social Networks. In: Meersman, R., Dillon, T., Herrero, P. (eds.) OTM 2010. LNCS, vol. 6428, pp. 339–348. Springer, Heidelberg (2010)
10. Chatti, M.A., Dahl, D., Jarke, M., Vossen, G.: Towards Web 2.0 Driven Learning Environments. In: Proceedings of the 4th International Conference of Web Information Systems and Technologies, pp. 370–375 (2008)
11. Colazza, L., Molinari, A., Villa, N.: Social Networks, Virtual Communities and Learning Management Systems. Towards an Integrated Environment. In: Proceedings of the 8th IASTED International Conference on Web-based Education, pp. 209–215 (2010)
12. Dahl, D., Vossen, G.: Evolution of Learning Folksonomies: Social Tagging in E-learning Repositories. International Journal of Technology Enhanced Learning 1(1-2), 35–46 (2008)
13. Dron, J.: Designing the Undesignable. Social Software and Control. Educational Technology and Society 10(3), 60–71 (2007)
14. Dziuban, C.D., Hartman, J.L., Moskal, P.D.: Blended Learning. EducauseCenter for Applied Research. Research Bulletin 7, 2–12 (2004)
15. Dziuban, C.D., Moskal, P.D., Hartman, J.L.: Higher Education, Blended Learning and the Generations: Knowledge is Power-no more. In: Bourne, J., Moore, J.C. (eds.) Elements of Quality Online Education: Engaging Communities, Sloan Center for Online Education, Needham (2005)
16. Ebersbach, A.: Wiki-Tools: Kooperation im Web. Springer, Berlin (2005)
17. Ersoy, H.: Blending Online Instruction with Traditional Instruction in the Programming Language Course: A Case Study. ODTÜ SosyalBilimlerEnstitüsü, Ankara (2003)
18. Freimanis, R., Dornstädter, R.: Informationskompetenz junger Information Professionals: Stand und Entwicklung. Information – Wissenschaft und Praxis 61(2), 123–128 (2010)
19. Georgouli, K., Skalkidis, I., Guerreiro, P.: A Framework for Adopting LMS to Introduce E-learning in a Traditional Course. Journal of Educational Technology&Society 11(2), 227–240 (2008)
20. Gerstenmaier, J., Mandl, H.: Wissenserwerb unter konstruktivistischer Perspektive. Zeitschrift für Pädagogik 41, 867–888 (1995)
21. Graf, S., List, B.: An Evaluation of Open Source E-learning Platforms Stressing Adaption Issues. In: 5th IEEE International Conference on Advanced Learning Technologies, pp. 163–165 (2005)
22. Höbarth, U.: Konstruktivistisches Lernen mit Moodle – Praktische Einsatzmöglichkeiten in Bildungsinstitutionen. Werner Hülsbusch, Boizenburg (2007)
23. Hohenstein, A., Wilbers, K. (eds.): Handbuch E-Learning. Deutscher Wirtschaftsdienst, Köln (2002)
24. Kerres, M.: Potenziale von Web 2.0 nutzen. In: Hohenstein, A., Wilbers, K. (eds.) Handbuch E-Learning, pp. 1–15. DWD, München (2006)
25. Kim, K.-J., Bonk, J.C., Teng, Y.-T.: The PresentState and Future Trends of Blended Learning in Workplace Learning Settings Across Five Countries. Asia Pacific Education Review 10, 299–308 (2009)
26. Klein, R.N., Beutelspacher, L., Hauk, K., Terp, C., Anuschewski, D., Zensen, C., Trkulja, V., Weller, K.: Informationskompetenz in Zeiten des Web 2.0. - Chancen und Herausforderungen im Umgang mit Social Software. Information – Wissenschaft und Praxis 60(3), 129–142 (2009)
27. Kundi, G.H., Nawaz, A.: From Objectivism to Social Constructivism: The Impact of Information and Communication Technologies (ICTs) on Higher Education. Journal of Science and Technology Education Research 1(2), 30–36 (2010)

28. Künzler, S., Iltgen, A.: Social Networking – Plattformen und Potenziale. GRIN, München (2008)
29. Lehner, F., Siegel, B.: Interaktive Videos – Überblick über den Stand der Entwicklung und Vergleich verfügbarer Autorentools. In: Kuhlen, R. (ed.) Information: Droge, Ware oder Commons? Wertschöpfungs- und Transformationsprozesse auf den Informationsmärkten. Proceedings des 11. Internationalen Symposiums für Informationswissenschaft (ISI 2009), Konstanz, Germany, pp. 363–377. Werner Hülsbusch, Boizenburg (2009)
30. Lehner, F., Siegel, B., Müller, C., Stephan, A.: Interaktive Videos und Hypervideos – Entwicklung, Technologien und Konzeption eines Authoring-Tools. Passauer Diskussionspapiere (Diskussionsbeitrag W-28-08) (2008)
31. Lim, T.: The Use of Facebook for Online Discussions Among Distance Learners. Turkish Online Journal of Distance Education 11(4), 72–81 (2010)
32. Mandl, H., Kopp, B.: Blended Learning: Forschungsfragen und Perspektiven (Forschungsbericht Nr. 182). Ludwig-Maximilians-Universität, München (2006)
33. Mason, R., Rennie, F.: E-learning and Social Networking Handbook: Resources for Higher Education. Routledge, Hampshire (2008)
34. Maxwell, K., Angehrn, A.A.: Lessons Learned from Deploying a Video-Based Web 2.0 Platform in an Executive Education Context. In: Lytras, M.D., Ordonez De Pablos, P., Avison, D., Sipior, J., Jin, Q., Leal, W., Uden, L., Thomas, M., Cervai, S., Horner, D. (eds.) ECH-EDUCATION 2010. Communications in Computer and Information Science, vol. 73, pp. 195–201. Springer, Heidelberg (2010)
35. McGee, P., Diaz, V.: Wikis and Podcasts and Blogs! Oh, My! What Is a Faculty Member Supposed to Do? Educause Review 42(5), 28–41 (2007)
36. Mertens, R., Krüger, A., Vornberger, O.: Einsatz von Vorlesungsaufzeichnungen. In: Hamborg, K.-C., Knaden, A. (eds.) Good Practice - Netzbasiertes Lehren und Lernen. Osnabrücker Beiträge zum medienbasierten Lernen, Band 1, pp. 79–92 (2004)
37. Moria, L.: WEB 2.0 Implications on Knowledge Management. Journal of Knowledge Management 13(1), 120–134 (2009)
38. Moriz, W.: Blended-Learning: Entwicklung, Gestaltung, Betreuung und Evaluation von E-Learningunterstütztem Unterricht. Books on Demand, Norderstedt (2008)
39. Ojstersek, N.: Betreuungskonzepte beim Blended Learning – Gestaltung und Organisation tutorieller Betreuung. Waxmann, Münster (2007)
40. O'Reilly, T.: What Is Web 2.0 - Design Patterns and Business Models for the Next Generation of Software (2005), http://oreilly.com/web2/archive/what-is-web-20.html
41. Page, T., Thorsteinsson, G., Niculescu, A.: A Blended Learning Approach to Enhancing Innovation. Studies in Informatics and Control 17(3), 297–311 (2008)
42. Parasuraman, A., Zeithaml, V.A., Berry, L.L.: SERVQUAL: A Multiple-item Scale for Measuring Consumer Perceptions of Service Quality. Journal of Retailing 64(1), 12–40 (1988)
43. Pavlov, I.P.: Conditioned Reflexes: An Investigation of the Physiological Activity of the Cerebral Cortex. Dover, New York (1960)
44. Peters, I.: Folksonomies: Indexing and Retrieval in Web 2.0. De Gruyter Saur, Berlin (2009)
45. Peters, I., Gust von Loh, S., Weller, K.: Multimediale und kollaborative Lehr- und Lernumgebungen in der akademischen Ausbildung. In: Kuhlen, R. (ed.) Information: Droge, Ware oder Commons? Wertschöpfungs- und Transformationsprozesse auf den Informationsmärkten. Proceedings des 11. Internationalen Symposiums für Informationswissenschaft (ISI 2009), Konstanz, Germany, pp. 363–377. Werner Hülsbusch, Boizenburg (2009)

46. Peters, I., Stock, W.G.: Folksonomy and Information Retrieval. In: Joining Research and Practice: Social Computing and Information Science. Proceedings of the 70th ASIS&T Annual Meeting, vol. 44, pp. 1510–1542 (2007)
47. Reuter, S.: Lehr- und Lerntheorien – Behaviorismus, Kognitivismus und Konstruktivismus. GRIN, München (2005)
48. Richardson, W.: Blogs, Wikis, Podcasts and other Powerful Web Tools for Classrooms. Corwin Press, Thousand Oaks (2006)
49. Ruiz, J.G., Mintzer, M.J., Leipzig, R.M.: The Impact of E-learning in Medical Education. Academic Medicine 81(3), 207–212 (2006)
50. Schröder, H.: Lernen, Lehren, Unterricht: Lernpsychologische und didaktische Grundlagen. Oldenbourg, München (2002)
51. Stock, W.G.: Information Retrieval: Informationen suchen und finden. Oldenbourg, München (2007)
52. Stock, W.G.: Folksonomies and Science Communication. A Mash-up of Professional Science Databases and Web 2.0 Services. Information Services & Use 27, 97–103 (2007)
53. Torniai, C., Jovanović, J., Gasević, D., Bateman, S., Hatala, M.: E-learning Meets the Social Semantic Web. In: Proceedings – The 8th IEEE International Conference on Advanced Learning Technologies, pp. 389–393 (2008)
54. Tsang, P.: Harnessing the Internet as a Virtual Lab. International Journal of Innovation and Learning 3(6), 575–592 (2006)
55. Tsang, P., Fong, J., Tse, S.: Using E-learning Platform in Open and Flexible Learning. In: Cheung, R., Lau, R., Li, Q. (eds.) New Horizon in Web-based Learning, pp. 214–224. World Scientific Publ, Singapore (2004)
56. Tsang, P., Kwan, R., Fox, R. (eds.): Enhancing Learning through Technology. World Scientific Publ., Singapore (2007)
57. Webb, J., Powis, C.: Teaching Information Skills: Theory and Practice. Facet, London (2004)
58. Weller, K., Dornstädter, R., Freimanis, R., Klein, R.N., Perez, M.: Social Software in Academia: Three Studies on Users' Acceptance of Web 2.0 Services. In: Proceedings of the 2nd Web Science Conference (WebSci 2010): Extending the Frontiers of Society On-Line, Raleigh, NC, US (2010)
59. Weller, K., Peters, I., Stock, W.G.: Folksonomy. The Collaborative Knowledge Organization System. In: Dumova, T., Fiordo, R. (eds.) Handbook of Research on Social Interaction Technologies and Collaborative Software: Concepts and Trends, pp. 132–146. Information Science Reference, Hershey (2010)
60. Wheeler, S.: Learning Space Mashups: Combining Web 2.0 Tools to Create Collaborative and Reflective Learning Spaces. Future Internet 1, 3–13 (2009)
61. Yau, J., Lam, J., Cheung, K.S.: A Review of e-Learning Platforms in the Age of e-Learning 2.0. In: Wang, F.L., Fong, J., Zhang, L., Lee, V.S.K. (eds.) ICHL 2009. LNCS, vol. 5685, pp. 208–217. Springer, Heidelberg (2009)
62. Zhang, D., Zhou, L., Briggs, R.O., Nunamaker Jr., J.F.: Instructional Video in E-learning: Assessing the Impact of Interactive Video on Learning Effectiveness. Information and Management 43, 15–27 (2006)

Development of Engineers' Social Competences in the Settings of Web 2.0 Platform

Malinka Ivanova

Technical University – Sofia, College of Energetics and Electronics, Blvd. Kl. Ohridski 8,
1000 Sofia, Bulgaria
m_ivanova@tu-sofia.bg

Abstract. Successful professional realization requires not only specific technical competences of engineers, but also suitable social behavior. In this paper the essential social competences for engineers are investigated taking into consideration the competences proposed in current research published in scientific papers and gathered opinion of students from Technical University – Sofia. The findings lead to creation of social competences research model including key social competences: communication, collaboration, networking, self-management, adaptability, English knowledge, leading and loyalty. The characteristics of Web 2.0 as a platform that could support competence development are summarized and a model for social competences development of engineers in Web 2.0 settings is proposed.

Keywords: Web 2.0, social competency, research social competences model, social competences development, engineers.

1 Introduction

Web 2.0 is related to emerged technologies and trends in the second generation of the web's presence. Every internet user can become a publisher, sharing knowledge or artifacts. Web based social networks are popular worldwide and collaboration online is used method for successful tasks doing. Open access to scientific information under limited licensing restrictions and to learning resources is freely available. From the technical aspect, the web becomes a platform based on open standards, where information and knowledge can be easier exchanged and managed. Applications and services can be combined in new context useful variations. The paradigm shift – the web allows authoring and development to occur right in communities and arise out of users own needs. Local ideas and approaches are presented and discussed with a potential world audience in networks expanding from local to global scale.

Web 2.0 is called "social web" and web-based applications "social software". It turned out that the understanding about social web and social software is different among researchers. Dourish considers that web and software are always social because they reflect on given meanings and understandings of society [1]. Webb writes that purpose of social software is only to propose possibility for dealing with groups or interactions between people [2]. Klamma et al. define social software as tools and environments facilitating activities in digital social networks [3].

R. Kwan et al. (Eds.): ICT 2011, CCIS 177, pp. 123–137, 2011.
© Springer-Verlag Berlin Heidelberg 2011

For the purposes of this research, the terms "social" web and software include the possibilities of technologies and web-based software applications to connect individuals or groups, who generate content, share digital identities, information and knowledge, collaborate, participate in networks or just benefit from the "collective intelligence".

The potential of the social dimension of web for sustainable development of engineering education and for competence development of engineers has yet evaluated. The evidences are presented in different research reports and case studies. Junior and Coutinho consider that nowadays engineers have to posses more competences to be prepared in multidisciplinary and transversal aspects [4]. They experiment with wiki for collaborative writing and conclude that the inclusion of wikis in the learning processes is a natural path that an engineer can take to learn in a society of knowledge. Podcasting implementation in engineering education to provide an innovative communication format for student engagement and involvement in educational topics, debates and developments is described in [5]. The authors talk about the benefit for skills development in podcasting technology and science communication. Marenzi et al. present the main functionalities of specially developed social-oriented integrated environment LearnWeb2.0 to support lifelong competence development of individuals [6]. They realize not only the possibility for collaborative searching, but also for storing and reusing the most successful queries for competence development.

As it seen Web 2.0 proposes a social-oriented atmosphere and conditions for personal and professional development of knowledge, skills and competences. At the other hand the global-driven market need new type engineers who are social self-effective persons and thus effective in their work and useful for a company. In such settings it is important to know which social competences engineers have to possess, how they can be achieved and how a social environment like Web 2.0 can facilitate this.

In the paper the key competences for contemporary engineers are examined and the focus is given on importance of social competences for personal and professional development. A competency research model is developed taking into consideration the current research published in scientific papers and gathered opinion of students from Technical University – Sofia. Several models for competences development are explored and one is proposed for adoption in the settings of the platform of Web 2.0.

2 Method

The raised research questions are: "Which social competences do the future engineers need to possess to be successful and self-efficient in their personal and professional development?" and "How Web 2.0 environment can support social competences development?" The answer of the first research question is received after investigation of: (1) competencies that are likely to be important to engineering work identified from a broad range of literature in the fields of engineering education, higher education, and European key competencies, (2) survey results, summarized according to opinion of 40 students (15 female/25 male with averaged age 21 years) in their third year of specialization in Computer Systems and Technologies in

Technical University - Sofia, bachelor degree. A list with selected social competences is prepared and it is proposed to students for voting in scale from 1 to 5 (1-a competency with the lowest priority, 5-a competency with the highest priority). The gathered results are used for creation of a social competences research model. The answer of the second research question is related to exploration of: (1) existing models for competences development, (2) functional characteristics of Web 2.0 that support achievements of concrete social competences according to a selected model for competences development.

3 Competences Definition

Competences are defined as a combination of knowledge, skills and attitudes appropriate to a given context. Key competences are considered those which all individuals need for personal fulfillment and development, active citizenship, social inclusion and employment [7].

There is confusion and debates concerning the definition of the terms "competence" and "competency". Several authors assume that there are no differences between these two terms and they are interchangeable in a concrete context. Others feel need to distinguish between them classifying them as input-based and output-based approaches [8]. A competency is defined in [9] as any kind of qualification or ability, both formal and informal, a person should have in order to fulfill a particular task or job. The term competence is used to measure the output of a learning process and can be described as a standard that should be reached in order to perform a task [10]. According to Moore, Cheng and Dainty the term competence is related to what people need to be able to do to perform a job well and the term competency is defined as the behavior(s) supporting an area of work.

Therefore, these definitions describe the term competence as an output-based approach focused on the demands of a certain job and the term competency as an input-based approach related to the behavior that is needed for performing the work or task.

In this work, the term *competency* is utilized to examine and identify the needed behavior of engineers, what they should able to perform for successful accomplishment of tasks.

4 Essential and New Competences of Engineers

The key competences' set for engineers in our knowledge-based and social-oriented society is broadly discussed and universities are striving to implement more flexible programs, making more investments in laboratories and equipments, in software products and simulations, eLearning strategies, promoting more mobility programs. Research reports and case studies describe the changes in world scenario concerning the political, economical and social aspects in national and globe scale and their influence on engineering education and engineers. The findings result in lists of essential and new competences that engineers have to posses to be effective in their personal and professional development. Several competences' lists are examined and summarized in Table 1.

Alstrup and Andersen investigate the competences of engineers working in the consulting business [11]. They argue that engineers need the ability to embrace complex and transdisciplinary solutions. The findings point that among the key competences that engineers and engineering education need address are: communication, dialogue, social intelligence, reflection and creativity.

The essential competences for software engineers are explored in [12] by Turley and Bieman. A list consisting of 38 competencies is prepared and divided in three categories: derived competences that are related to the behavior of engineers, self-describes competences concerning the skills, techniques, and attributes that engineers think are important for successful job performance and manager described competences. The first ten competences from the list in the category self-described are the following: perseverance, team oriented, knowledge, skills/techniques, thinking, communication, obtains necessary training/learning, driven by desire to contribute, desire to do/bias for action.

The generic engineering competencies for engineers graduating in Australia are researched by Male, Bush and Chapman [13]. Their study identifies 64 technical, nontechnical and attitudinal competencies that are from importance. Over 50% from the survey participants agree that critical engineering competences that support their well job doing are: communication, teamwork, self-management and problem solving.

Nowadays engineers work in multicultural and diverse global environments and among the competences facilitating and enhancing their personal and professional development are identifies: social responsibility, practice culturally appropriate relationship, leadership, team working, communication, ethical behavior, empathy, cultural competence, embrace philosophy as a pursuit of wisdom in a global context [14]. The authors Allan and Chisholm conclude that development of global and multicultural competences for engineers is an important task for educators to prepare effective young generation for successful professional development in our global and social oriented information society.

A comparative analysis of some engineering competencies distinguished and identified by several accreditation agencies of US, UK, Australia, Japan, and Singapore is done by Goel [15]. The author sees great similarities in the competency set identified by these accreditation agencies and among the core competences are selected: ability to apply knowledge, design skills, problem solving skills, technical competence, ability to work in multidisciplinary teams, communication skills, sensitivity towards global, societal, and environmental issues, sensitivity towards ethical and professional issues, and readiness for life-long learning.

This review shows that engineers must be competent not only in the specific technical field but also in a social aspect. Communication skills and team working are highly appreciated competences, also ability for fruitful dialogue, ability to experience and shape relationships, to interact with others, ability for development of social responsibility and solidarity, ability to make benefits from the "collective" intelligence", ability to be sensitive towards social problems.

Table 1. Key and New Competences of Engineers

Author/s	Key competences	Social competences
Alstrup and Andersen [1]	communication, dialogue, social intelligence, reflection and creativity	*communication, *dialogue, *social intelligence *team working *social responsibility *culturally appropriate *relationship, *empathy, *embrace philosophy as a pursuit of wisdom in a global context, *sensitivity towards global, societal, and environmental issues
Turley and Bieman [2]	perseverance, team oriented, knowledge, skills/techniques, thinking, communication, obtains necessary training/learning, driven by desire to contribute, desire to do/bias for action	
Male, Bush and Chapman [3]	communication, teamwork, self-management and problem solving	
Allan and Chisholm [4]	social responsibility, practice culturally appropriate relationship, leadership, team working, communication, ethical behavior, empathy, cultural competence, embrace philosophy as a pursuit of wisdom in a global context	
Goel [5]	ability to apply knowledge, design skills, problem solving skills, technical competence, ability to work in multidisciplinary teams, communication skills, sensitivity towards global, societal, and environmental issues, sensitivity towards ethical and professional issues, readiness for life-long learning	

5   Social Competences – Definition and Model

Social competences are also among key competences defined in the European Reference Framework [7] that cover all forms of behavior and equip individuals to participate in an effective and constructive way in social and working life. Other description of social competences is given by Archan and Tutschek who defined the social competency as the ability and willingness to cooperate, to interact with others responsibly and behave in a group and relationally oriented way [16]. Also, social competences are defined as skills needed to recruit and maintain satisfying and supportive relationships [17]. Social competencies are described as the behavior that one needs to have and needs to demonstrate to interact and cooperate with others and to build and sustain different relationships [18]. One competency research model applied to engineers from Philips Enabling Technology Group is presented in [18] and it includes shown in Figure 1 social competences: communication, collaboration, ability for realizing of social contacts, networking, adaptability and empathy.

This model is used as bases for further research the needed social competences of our undergraduate students in order to be prepared for working in national and international companies that require the context-based social behavior.

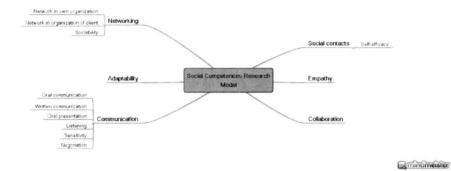

Fig. 1. Social (sub)-competencies of the competency research model

6 Survey and Result

For purposes of this survey, the list with generic competencies for engineers [13] is used for selection of these competences that are oriented to define and manage social behavior of engineers. They are supplemented with the essential social competences defined in [18] and identified in Table 1. The following rating of competences is applied: 5 – this competency is mandatory for an engineer, 1 – an engineer does not need this competency. The students' voting with scores 4 and 5 is converted in percents and it is summarized in Table 2 (female vote and male vote are presented in different columns).

Table 2. Students voting in percents

№	Competency	Short description	Female		Male	
			vote with 4 and 5	vote with 5	vote with 4 and 5	vote with 5
1	Written comm.	Communicating clearly and concisely in writing	87	47	80	60
2	Managing Comm.	Managing own communications	87	67	80	52
3	Create/maintain contacts	Create contacts using social media, other media or face-to-face	100	60	68	36
4	Self-management	Managing self social behavior	100	80	92	68
5	Verbal comm.	Using effective verbal communication	100	80	88	56
6	Teamwork	Working in teams, trusting and respecting other team members	87	87	96	76
7	English	Speaking and writing fluent English	93	53	80	60
8	Interdisciplinary skills	Interacting with people in diverse disciplines	67	27	56	8

Table 2. (*continued*)

9	Honesty	Demonstrating honesty - admitting one's mistakes, ect.	80	27	52	36
10	Managing	Managing projects/programs/ contracts/people	73	33	84	20
11	Graphical comm.	Using effective graphical communication – reading drawings	47	20	40	8
12	Flexibility/ad aptability	Being flexible/adaptable	80	47	88	56
13	Concern for others	Being concerned for the welfare of others in your organization	73	13	40	8
14	Negotiation	Negotiating, asserting, defending approaches, needs	60	13	60	24
15	Coordinating	Coordinating the work of others	73	33	56	28
16	Meeting skills	Chairing, participating constructively in meetings	80	47	64	32
17	Loyalty	Being loyal to your organization	67	60	84	60
18	Presenting	Presenting clearly and engagingly	67	27	56	20
19	Diversity skills	Interacting with people from diverse cultures/backgrounds	60	20	56	16
20	Networking	Networking - building/maintaining personal/organizational networks	87	67	72	36
21	Leading	Leading - gaining cooperation /motivating and inspiring others	67	27	84	52
22	Supervising	Supervising work/people	67	13	60	20
23	Embracing change	Trying new behavior, approaches, technology	93	53	84	52
24	Mentoring	Mentoring/coaching co-workers	67	13	44	16
25	Community	Being concerned for the welfare of the local, national and global communities	67	33	60	16

The results from Table 2 show that the key social competences according to students' vote with 4 and 5 scores are slightly different between female and male students (Table 3). The highest rated social competences that are the same in female and male students' lists are: teamwork, self-management, verbal communication, and embracing change. The highest vote with 5 marks the students give to the common social competences for male and female students: teamwork, self-management, managing communication, English knowledge (Table 4).

Table 3. Key social competences according to students' vote with 4 and 5 scores

№	Competency - Female		№	Competency - Male	
		vote with 4 and 5			
1	Create/maintain contacts	100	1	Teamwork	96
2	Self-management	100	2	Self-management	92
3	Verbal communication	100	3	Verbal communication	88
4	English	93	4	Flexibility/adaptability	88
5	Embracing change	93	5	Managing	84
6	Written communication	87	6	Loyalty	84
7	Managing communication	87	7	Leading	84
8	Teamwork	87	8	Embracing change	84
9	Networking	87			

Table 4. Key social competences according to students' vote with 5 scores

№	Competency - Female		№	Competency - Male	
		vote with 5			
1	Teamwork	87	1	Teamwork	76
2	Self-management	80	2	Self-management	68
3	Verbal communication	80	3	Written communication	60
4	Managing Communication	67	4	English	60
5	Networking	67	5	Loyalty	60
6	Create/maintain contacts	60	6	Verbal communication	56
7	Loyalty	60	7	Flexibility/adaptability	56
8	English	53	8	Managing Communication	52
9	Embracing change	53	9	Leading	52

The rating of all surveyed students regardless of their gender is summarized in the Table 5 and it stands the basis for the construction of research competency model (Figure 2). The main competences that influence on engineers social behavior are grouped in 8 categories: self-management, communication, collaboration, adaptability, networking, English knowledge, leading, and loyalty.

With the highest scores is the competency *self-management*. Students consider ability for self- management of their social behavior as very important, which gives the possibility for time control in tasks performing, for priorities defining of raised tasks, for achievement of output quality. Students believe that the self-management is the main factor for their self-efficiency, stimulation of motivation and insurance of balanced social life.

Communication can take different forms, but in this survey the main *communication* abilities are related to: *verbal communication* – abilities for giving instructions in an appropriate manner, asking for information, listening; *written communication* – writing technical documents, instructions, specifications, preparing technical news, email answering; *communication management*, including updating communication tools and channels.

The competency *collaboration* is included in the competency research model too, because it is rated by students as an important ability at: *team working* – abilities for respecting and trusting other members' opinion and sharing own ideas and results, reconcile the conflicts, ensuring the team cohesion; and *management* – ability to motivate, inspire, and encourage people.

Table 5. Social competences with highest rates given by all surveyed students

№	Competences vote with 5		№	Competences vote with 4 and 5	
1	Teamwork	80	1	Self-management	97
2	Self-management	74	2	Verbal communication	92.5
3	Verbal communication	65	3	Teamwork	92.5
4	Loyalty	60	4	Embracing change	87.5
5	Managing Communication	58	5	English	85
6	English	58	6	Flexibility/adaptability	85
7	Flexibility/adaptability	53	7	Loyalty	85
8	Embracing change	53	8	Written communication	82.5
			9	Managing Communication	82.5
			10	Create/maintain contacts	80
			11	Managing	80
			12	Networking	77.5
			13	Leading	77.5

Adaptability is the category consists of ability of engineers to be *flexible* and *adaptable* in complex social situations, changing behavior according to emerged uncertainty or ill-defined problems; and ability for *change embracing* trying new technologies, approaches, tasks, responsibilities and people management.

Networking is other important for our future engineers' competency that supports building and maintaining personal and professional networks, using them for questions asking, receiving of advices, applying knowledge and expertise of other colleagues and experts, taking advantages of "collective" intelligence. Networking is related also to ability for *contacts creation*/updating and relationships management.

English knowledge - speaking and writing fluent English is rated with high scores by 58% of surveyed students that indicating that if they want to work in multinational team or they want to implement innovative solutions in their organizations or just desire to follow the latest concepts and solutions in the engineering area they must know at least one foreign language.

It is surprising, but in this competency research model the competencies *leading* and *loyalty* are included because of high students' rating. They consider that abilities for recruiting team members, gaining cooperation, influencing and persuading others are among important social qualities. They believe that being loyal to a company, team and colleagues will open doors to certain choices and certain social behavior.

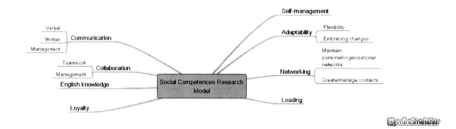

Fig. 2. Social competences research model

7   Models of Competences Development

A model for continues enhancement and development of an individual's or a group's competences is proposed in [19]. The authors described competences development as a lifecycle in five steps: (1) creation of a competence model through the identification of required job, (2) the assessment of existing competences and the needed competences for a specific job or task, (3) the gap analysis between existing competences and the required competences for a given job or task, (4) the definition of competence development programmes or units of programmes to minimize the identified gaps, (5) the continuous performance monitoring and assessment to confirm improvement.

Rogers' model for competence development in a learning network consists of four phases: aware, interested in, trying engaging, and actively involved and connected [20]. In the first phase, students *aware of* (1) relationship and connections among peers and (2) own opportunity for value-created involvement. In the second phase, students *interested in* (1) engaging in informal knowledge exchange and (2) revision of competence development objectives. In the third phase, they *are trying engagement* in individual or collaborative learning, in social network activities, in pro-active contribution of their own insights and expertise. In the last phase, they are *involved in* contribution of their own experiences and artifacts, and they are connected with other peers, educators and professionals.

Another model of competence development is presented in [21], which is composed from four stages: (1) a process of orientation, in which the learner determines which competences s/he wants to develop, (2) evidence collection, which shows the learner's current proficiency level, (3) assessment by others, (4) competence development activities to attain a higher proficiency level.

8   Characteristics of Web 2.0 in Support of Social Competences Development

In recent years the Web is constantly undergoing changes, becoming a borderless space for dynamic interactions among people with the same interests, giving the possibilities for contribution of everyone and for expression of the personal qualities.

Web 2.0 is explained through examples by Tim O'Reilly founder of O'Reilly Media who outlines a bunch of seven themes that he thinks are important characteristics of Web 2.0. They are basis for discussion bellow from the perspective of competence development [22].

(1)   *Web as a Platform* - In computing, the term "platform" is related to the full set of technologies, including hardware components and the hardware/software interface, software and application frameworks, operating systems, and runtime environments that allow a piece of software to run. The new generation of Web has begun utilizing these technologies, starting at the top of the set. Nowadays, one Web site can deliver the same, or better, functionality than the equivalent application on the desktop, e.g. functions of word processors, spreadsheets, audio/video/image editors, presentation packages, project management and visualization, etc. combining and aggregating content and services. Students take advantage of these sites utilizing them in different learning scenarios. Functions of such applications can be used to support an active role in development of social competences promoting authoring, interaction, networked communication, discussions, and offering the students community a range of pathways, modes, and styles of knowledge gathering.

(2)   *Harnessing Collective Intelligence* - The connections in the Web grow as a result of the collective activity of all web users and the structure of the Web is changing dynamically. This fact is called "network effect" and the term is applied to describe the increase in value to the existing users of a service in which there is some form of interaction with others, as more and more users start to use it. Each user therefore immediately becomes a member of a community with a low barrier to participate. Competences development can occur in specially or not specially created learning networks and it is seen as an activity that takes place in a social context. The social network approach holds that the behavior of an individual is affected by the kinds of relations, or technical ties, and networks more than by the norms and attributes that an individual possesses. Recently, many web sites benefit from a network effect: the number of contributions grows, more students turn to it as a source of information, the quality of information on the website improves and the authoring process is transparent. A wide range of social networks are formed building online communities of students, experts and professionals who share and examine the common interests and/or activities. The networked web influences on the performance of authoring, relationships creating, communication realizing, information receiving and give the possibilities for collaboration.

(3)   *Data as the Intel Inside* - We generate and make use of ever increasing amounts of data. Several companies orient their core competencies to database management and networking and develop the ability to collect and manage this data on an epic scale. This data is also made available to developers, who can recombine it in new ways. The web is mashable allowing a combination of separate, stand-alone technologies into a novel application or service. The power of mashups for competence development lies in the way they help new conclusions reaching or new relationships discerning by uniting large amounts of data in a manageable way.

Web 2.0 services enable access to data at an unprecedented scale, such as images (e. g. Flickr), bookmarks (e.g. Delicious), mapping data (e. g. Google Maps), but also indexed data, such as the Google search index. Many of the new search engines use the modular functionality of Web 2.0: mash together several services and add new features. Students use the found data as information sources in their learning process, and also as building blocks for creating new content mixing or mashup of existing one. Thus, Web 2.0 services employ different measures for increasing students' contributions and participations, for instance by visualizing data, aggregating from different sources, by making content accessible through RSS syndication and APIs.

(4)   *End of the Software Release Cycle* - Two things are behind this Web characteristic: software that is always in beta version and software that is treated as service. Software as a service is a software application delivery model by which a producer develops a web-based software application, and then hosts and operates that application over the Internet for use by its users. Often, users can be treated as co-developers of web-based applications and services participating in such process conscious or unconscious. The web-based software development is in "the perpetual beta" status in which the product is developed in the open, with new features slipstreamed in on a monthly, weekly, or even daily basis, instead to be realized early and often. Changes to services happen gradually. This is facilitated by the ability of Web applications to track the user's interaction with the service and thereby gathering data about interaction patterns that is nearly impossible to collect for desktop applications. However, it has an effect on students that use a specific service. One advantage of the "perpetual beta" is that the developers are usually open to suggestions from adaptors. They often set up developer discussion boards and use these to receive additional feedback. Working with software as a service can enhance the learning experience, supporting informal learning and the many-directional transfer of knowledge.

(5)   *Lightweight Programming Models* - Lightweight or simplified programming models facilitate the creation of "loosely coupled" systems, using syndication and remixing. Lightweight programming is programming based on a high level of accessibility for users and creators and on the idea of adaptation and change for improvement. Mashup and service-based approach allow students to discover, implement and manage suitable applications/services for solving an immediate, specific problem by blending externalities with existing content and services. Such an approach contributes to the social competence development giving the possibilities for improvement versions of resources, as well as sharing further knowledge about these resources, their use, and their interrelationships; community-based collaborations can be fostered, thanks to the culture of collaboration and to the "network effect".

(6)   *Software above the Level of a Single Device* - In order for web applications to compete in a world of constantly changing platforms, users need to cater to a wide variety of access points, including mobile, iPhone, PDA, laptop, etc., ensuring the access to Web2.0 and software above the level of a single device. Delivering of a ubiquitous access to information and knowledge at anytime and from anywhere utilizing mobile and other devices creates a flexible environment for different social competency realization. Research shows, that such a way of instant access leads to greater efficiencies and effectiveness in learning, increased individual support and opportunities for personal development, better methods of collaborating and communicating and greater exposure to technology.

(7)   *Rich User Experiences* - Web 2.0 involves several emerging technologies that allow students to move, beyond the page metaphor to deliver rich user experiences. Such technologies mean that users will no longer have their experiences

dictated to them, but will instead have as much power to define their own experiences, as they are comfortable exercising it. The breadth, richness, and flexibility provided by these technologies transforms the user interface beyond a dynamic UI to a full interactive audio-visual experience, with new, powerful ways for interacting with systems and one another still being explored.

It seems that the social nature of Web 2.0 has the potential and power to facilitate development of social characteristics of our students giving in their hands services, applications, open resources and programs for development of specific social personal and professional behavior.

9   A model for Social Competences Development of Engineers in Web 2.0 Settings

The presented in Figure 3 model for social competences development of engineers in Web 2.0 settings is created into considerations of the Social competences research model (Figure 2), main characteristics of Web 2.0 facilitating the formation of a given social behavior and the presented three models for competence development in section 7. The created model presents four steps for social competences development utilizing the platform of Web 2.0.

In the first step: *Occurrence of interests in the development of social competences*, the first relationships and connections are realized, the opportunity for value adding is seen and the need from appropriate social competences development is determined.

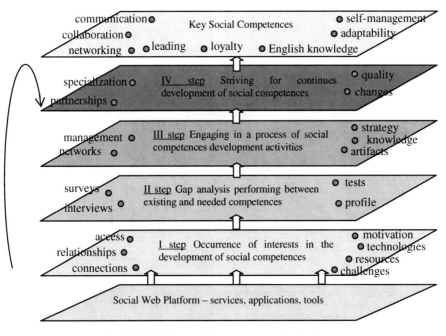

Fig. 3. Model for social competences development

In the second step a *gap analysis* between existing and needed social competences is performed using different tools like surveys, tests, interviews and a digital profile of a student is created.

In the third step: *Engagement in a process of social competences development activities* - the students are more actively involved in learning activities, participating and organizing networks, using "collective intelligence" and experts/peers knowledge to produce artifacts and connections, a strategy for a learning process is defined.

The fourth step is *Striving for continues development of social competences*, and it includes further specialization of existing social competences, or receiving new ones if the situation is changed with aim the quality to be achieved through formed social behavior.

10   Conclusion and Future Research Directions

In this work interesting results are achieved gathering the students' opinion about what kind of social competences they would like to posses in their future professional life. Social competences like communication, collaboration, networking and adaptability are among the competences with high priority. These competences are pointed by established engineers from Philips Enabling Technology Group [18] as very important for successful social behavior too. With the highest scores our students rate the ability for self-management of social activities. That means that they wish to know how to manage their behavior, what kind of tools to use and how to utilize a social environment like Web 2.0 to be successful persons in their career development. It would be great if universities propose to future engineers such courses introducing them to several concepts and best practices in social behavior. Other surprising social competences are leading and loyalty. English knowledge as a tool for communication in our global world is rated with high scores too. The performed investigation about key competences for engineers results in a social competences research model. The characteristics of Web 2.0 are discussed to provide knowledge how they can be used for realization of the four steps in created model for social competences development.

The work is bases for future research related to: (1) testing and evaluating the proposed models in prototyped Web 2.0 environment, (2) models refinement considering the real engineering practice.

References

1. Dourish, P.: Where the Action Is: The Foundations of Embodied Interaction. MIT Press, Cambridge (2001) ISBN 0-262-04196-0
2. Webb, M.: On social software consultancy (2004), http://interconnected.org/home/2004/04/28/on_social_software
3. Klamma, R., Spaniol, M., Cao, Y., Jarke, M.: Pattern-based cross media social network analysis for technology enhanced learning in europe. In: Nejdl, W., Tochtermann, K. (eds.) EC-TEL 2006. LNCS, vol. 4227, pp. 242–256. Springer, Heidelberg (2006)
4. Bottentuit Jr., J.B., Coutinho, C.P.: Collaborative Writing Tools in Engineering Education: challenges for knowledge management and sharing. In: V International Conference on Multimedia and Information and Communication Technologies in Education, Lisboa – Portugal. Proceedings of M-ICTE, vol. 2, pp. 1070–1074 (2009)

5. Alpay, E., Gulati, S.: Student-led Podcasting for Engineering Education, `http://www.sefi.be/wp-content/abstracts2009/Alpaystudentled.pdf`
6. Marenzi, I., Zerr, S., Abel, F., Nejdl, W.: Social sharing in LearnWeb2.0. International Journal Continuing Engineering Education and Life-Long Learning, `http://www.l3s.de/web/upload/documents/1/Social%20Sharing%20in%20LearnWeb2.0_.pdf`
7. European Commission: Report. Key Competences for Lifelong Learning: European Reference Framework (2007), `http://ec.europa.eu/dgs/education_culture/publ/pdf/ll-learning/keycomp_en.pdf`
8. Hoffmann, T.: The meanings of Competency. Journal of European Industrial Training 23(6), 275–285 (1999)
9. Competence Observatory User Manual (2007), `http://dspace.ou.nl/bitstream/1820/1117/1/User%20manual%20Competence%20Observatory%20w2003%20_3_.pdf`
10. Horton, S.: Introduction – the competency movement: its origins and impact on the publicsector. The International Journal of Public Sector Management 13(4), 306–318 (2000)
11. Alstrup, N.C., Andersen, C.O.: Beyond specialists and generalists. A case study of new competencies for engineers in the consulting business, `http://alone.dk/wp-content/uploads/2007/10/sefi-alstrup-ohm-58.pdf`
12. Turley, R.T., Bieman, J.M.: Identifying Essential Competencies of Software Engineers. In: ACM Conference on Computer Science, pp. 271–278 (1994)
13. Male, S.A., Bush, M.B., Chapman, E.S.: Identification of competencies required by engineers graduating in Australia, `http://aaee.com.au/conferences/AAEE2009/PDF/AUTHOR/AE090085.PDF`
14. Allan, M., Chisholm, C.U.: The Development of Competencies for Engineers within a Global Context, `http://www.engsc.ac.uk/downloads/scholarart/ee2008/p001-allan.pdf`
15. Goel, S.: Competency Focused Engineering Education with Reference to IT Related Disciplines: Is the Indian System Ready for Transformation? Journal of Information Technology Education 5 (2006), `http://jite.org/documents/Vol5/V5p027-052Goel88.pdf`
16. Archan, S., Tutschek, E.: Schlüsselqualifikationen: WievermittleichsieLehrlingen. InstitutfürBildungsforschung der Wirtschaft, Vienna (2002)
17. Mallinckrodt, B., Wei, M.: Attachment, social competencies, social support, and psychological distress. Journal of Counseling Psychology 52, 358–367 (2005)
18. Cramer, C., van der Zwaal, M.: Social and cognitive competencies in the semiconductor and medical device market (2006), `http://essay.utwente.nl/57722/1/scriptie_Cramer_van_der_Zwaal.pdf`
19. Sinnott, G.C., Madison, G.H., Pataki, G.E.: Competencies: Report of the Competencies Workgroup. Workforce and Succession Planning Work Groups. New York State Governot's Office of Employee Relations and the Department of Civil Service (2002), `http://www.cs.state.ny.us/successionplanning/workgroups/competencies/CompetenciesFinalReport.pdf`
20. Rogers, E.M.: Diffusion of innovations, 5th edn. Free Press, New York (2003)
21. Schoonenboom, J., Tattersall, C., Miao, Y., Stefanov, K., Aleksieva-Petrova, A.: A four-stage model for lifelong competence development. In: Proceedings of the 2nd TENCompetence Open Workshop, Manchester, UK, pp. 131–136 (2007)
22. O'Reilly, T.: What is Web 2.0. Design Patterns and Business Models for the Next Generation of Software, `http://oreilly.com/pub/a/web2/archive/what-is-web-20.html?page=1`

Students' Self-reported Assessment of E-Dictionaries

Yoko Hirata and Yoshihiro Hirata

Hokkai-Gakuen University
Sapporo, Japan
{hira,hirata}@eli.hokkai-s-u.ac.jp

Abstract. In recent years e-dictionaries have been getting enormously popular in Japan. A variety of small pocket electronic dictionaries (PEDs) are gaining popularity, especially among high school and university students. Dictionaries which are contained in personal digital assistants (PDAs), including the iPhone and cellular phones, have also been used by students. In addition to these handy pocket-sized tools, dictionaries are now available online, free of charge, created by publishers and educational institutions. Recently, computers have become accessible to the public in Japan, these online dictionaries have recognized as useful tools for students to study with. However, little research has been conducted regarding how students view these different kinds of e-dictionaries. This study examines students' perceptions of different types of e-dictionaries and looks at what they think about various effects of dictionary use in different educational situations. The results of this study suggest that advantages and disadvantages of e-dictionaries are perceived differently in different educational contexts. The findings also suggest some important implications regarding how instructors should encourage students to utilize these dictionaries in the classroom.

Keywords: evaluation, electronic dictionaries, language learning.

1 Introduction

Recently more and more Japanese university students use websites as various resources to accomplish tasks and assignments. When reading English websites, in particular, students are always required to use English dictionaries. These dictionaries can be divided into three types of media: paper dictionaries, pocket electronic dictionaries (henceforth PEDs), and online dictionaries [1]. Online dictionaries include not only those on desktop computers, but also those in mobile phones which are regarded to have great benefits of being readily usable [2]. The number of mobile phones users has been increased and, accordingly, various educational applications of mobile phones have been researched [3] [4]. The data for mobile phones used in Japan in 2003 show that approximately 55 million mobile phones are capable of browsing internet [5]. However, the dictionaries in mobile phones are not those frequently used by Japanese secondary and tertiary students. There are two major reasons why consulting dictionaries on a mobile phone is not an easy task for such students. First of all, many dictionary publishers have provided paid consulting systems, such as 'Pocket Eijiro'

R. Kwan et al. (Eds.): ICT 2011, CCIS 177, pp. 138–151, 2011.
© Springer-Verlag Berlin Heidelberg 2011

for mobile phone users [5]. Using this kind of fee-based service is a tremendous financial burden for students. Secondly, many mobile phones presently available still do not have traditional keyboards and even ones with small keypads are not convenient for users to consult dictionaries. Because of these limitations, desktop computers and PEDs are more widely used for consulting dictionaries than mobile phones. In secondary schools, in particular, PEDs are must-have items for students in preparation for taking the university admission test. The major reason for this is because PEDs are light-weight and portable 'with a large database of lexical entries from several dictionaries' [1]. On the contrary, in tertiary institutions, as students' use of the web has been dramatically increasing, many different types of online dictionaries have been gaining in popularity among students. This is because many institutions now provide computer facilities and online dictionaries are readily available for anyone for free of charge. Like PEDs, speed is also perceived as the main advantage of online dictionaries. These dictionary websites are, therefore, regarded as powerful language sources for language learners in second/foreign language acquisition [1]. Although this technology has been seen to enhance the students' learning, there are not many educators who understand the potential benefits of these e-dictionaries [6]. Despite the fact that there are various studies which focus on the comparison between the paper-based dictionaries and PEDs [7] [8], there is still little research addressing how different e-dictionaries can be best used for students to facilitate their learning. Because the dictionaries which are easy to use can allow students to have control over their learning [9], instructors should be aware of what kinds of dictionaries could be recommended to students and how they should be used in different educational situations.

2 Research Background

2.1 PEDs

As many Asian students do, almost all Japanese university students keep using PEDs as indispensable tools for their studies [9]. A study found that 88% of the 781 students surveyed were PED owners [8]. This students' preference of PEDs is due to the Japanese 'educational systems which put more emphasis on accuracy' [9]. There are various brands of PEDs available in Japan, for example, Casio, Seiko, and Sharp, and all of them contain at least three types of English dictionaries: English-Japanese bilingual, Japanese-English bilingual, and English monolingual. Many PEDs have the similar major features and some advantageous functions such as high-speed data retrieval and record keeping of the most recently looked-up entries [7]. PEDs also have the *jump* function which gets the user to change the dictionaries for cross referencing without losing the key word [10]. Another current common feature is the *voice* function which helps the user to check pronunciation. Other main features include a system that can identify the user's handwriting and voice [11] so that the user does not have to use the keyboards for input. In addition to these useful functions of dictionary consultation, the recent PEDs contain exercises, games, and even educational movies. Although PEDs with these various effective features are seen as a 'preferable alternative to paper dictionaries' [7], some instructors have a negative attitude towards the students' use of PEDs. A study indicates that there is a possibility that the speed and ease of PEDs is disadvantageous for learning vocabulary [9]. Another critical attitude towards PEDs includes the fact that these features are often created without thinking of users' actual preferences in different situations and some features are beyond the users' abilities to understand [1]. Although there is a study which shows that PEDs are not significantly different from paper-based dictionaries when students use them for acquiring vocabulary [7], studies on PEDs in language education are still relatively scarce and more in-depth research is needed.

2.2 Online English Dictionaries

The number of online English dictionaries has rapidly increased. Up until recently online dictionaries have been regarded mostly as supplementary resources for language learning. However, for Japanese students who have had a very limited exposure to authentic English in everyday life, online dictionaries have been well integrated into the classroom when reading English websites and the benefit of using these dictionaries is regarded to be of the utmost importance [12]. Other reasons also explain the increased use of online dictionaries in recent years. First of all, different types of online dictionaries have been developed for different types of users in various situations and they are easily accessible from almost everywhere. Students can easily consult them on the screen whenever they encounter an unknown word while reading online reading materials. Secondly, online dictionaries usually have major features which include a system with 'useful hyperlinks and speedy navigation' [1]. Because they are non-linear, the user can simultaneously consult idioms, phrasal verbs, and compound words, and get search results instantaneously. Thirdly, online dictionaries are suitable for any level of English because there are various kinds available to choose from. The dictionaries can also help the user look up definitions which are easy to understand and various examples in full sentences through several different dictionaries [11]. Despite these rather obvious benefits of using online dictionaries, there have been few studies which compare the different features the online dictionaries contain. In addition, not enough research has been conducted which examine online dictionaries from the perspective of Japanese students [11]. Investigating the positive and negative effects of using online dictionaries will help the student to make the most of them and the instructor to teach in a better way in the classroom.

3 Purpose of the Study

The purpose of this study was to examine Japanese university students' preferences of using different e-dictionaries in helping them accomplish different types of reading tasks. The focus was placed on the effectiveness of e-dictionaries viewed by individual students in different educational situations.

Research questions

1. How do students perceive two different types of e-dictionaries: PEDs and online dictionaries?

2. What are the relationships between the students' educational contexts and background, such as computer skills, and their perception of using different e-dictionaries?

Research hypotheses

1. The students will highly value PEDs rather than online dictionaries from every point of view.
2. The students, who are frequently reading English websites, will prefer using PEDs to online dictionaries and understand their effectiveness.

4 Methodology

4.1 The Setting and Student Profiles

The subjects of this study (n=30) were lower intermediate learners of English enrolled in a university English course. They consisted of 28 males and 2 females, who were full time students between the age of eighteen and twenty. The course was offered by the Department of Electronics and Information Engineering and it was a semester-long hybrid course which provided both a traditional face-to-face learning environment and an online environment. The course was held once a week for ninety minutes in a computer lab. The objective of this course was to help students develop their English skills. However, the emphasis was also placed on understanding how to use the navigational functions of web browsers and acquiring basic computer literacy. Although this was an English course, the course was conducted both in Japanese and English since the students' English communication skills were not high. Although the students were enrolled in the Department of Electronics and Information Engineering, the majority of them thought that they were not fully skilled in using computers. There were four students who stated that their computer skill was 'very low' and four students who stated that their computer skill was 'high'.

4.2 Procedures

The project described in this paper had two stages: searching for effective online dictionaries and evaluating the best of them. At the beginning of the first stage, the instructor explained the various uses of online English dictionaries in different contexts. This included a detailed introduction of online English dictionaries and their important features. Students were asked to examine some online English dictionaries as samples and to evaluate the quality and the appropriate use of the dictionaries for their own study. The criteria used for the evaluation at this stage were the measures for evaluating ESL/EFL materials [13]. The criteria were modified to fit the present study and were divided into three major sections: 'Navigability', 'Explanation & Examples', and 'Attractiveness'. These measures are seen as effective in that they provide students with a standard for evaluating websites [14]. On the second stage, the students were required to choose online English dictionaries on their own for their task and examine their preferences. The tasks included translating a paper-based textbook and computer-based text, as well as doing English exercises on the computer and in the textbook. If students didn't understand the meaning of the word or expressions even though they consulted a dictionary, they were asked to change to another dictionary to try to find more suitable meaning.

Some examples of online English dictionaries the students chose were as follows.

- http://www.yourdictionary.com/
- http://www.wordcentral.com/
- http://www.onelook.com/
- http://www.merriam-webster.com/
- http://dictionary.cambridge.org/
- http://www.ldoceonline.com/

A student's sample evaluation is shown below in Table 1, 2, and 3.

Table 1. A student's sample evaluation: Navigability

Navigability		Comments
Is everything clearly indicated? Easy to use? Are the icons easy to follow?	4	Examples which contained the key word and the usages are displayed without too much inconvenient scrolling.
Does the website link to other dictionaries, for example thesaurus, or language information? Is the dictionary based on large language sources?	4	This dictionary site is based on the database containing Webster's New World Law Dictionary, Science Dictionary, Webster's New World College Dictionary, Wall Street Words. It is convenient for me to choose what I want to consult directly from the websites.
Is the dictionary well organized? Does it produce audible pronunciation of the word? American English or British English? Does it help you notice the correct pronunciation of a word?	3	This dictionary has the spoken pronunciation function. I can check the pronunciation of the word and also repeat what I have heard. However, the voice is very artificial and I think it is ideal that I can slow down the speed of the voice to make it clearer for me.

The students' evaluation ranged from a simple, superficial explanation to comprehensive, detailed explanations. Although each major section was subdivided into three categories with each subsection worth 5 points, the point the students gave for each subsection was generally 3. After evaluating some online dictionaries, the students filled in the evaluation forms and submitted them to the instructor through a learning management system.

At the end of the course, the students were provided with a questionnaire which attempted to find out how the students perceive online dictionaries they consulted and a PED that they have. The questions in the questionnaire were based on the previous study examining students' attitudes to learning grammar with web- and book-based contexts [15]. Twenty six questions from the questionnaire referred to the evaluation based on the difference between the online dictionaries and the PEDs. Most of the questions had a 10-point Likert scale, with "1" representing "strongly disagree" and "10" representing "strongly agree". The points were totaled and averaged, and a standard deviation was also attained. The data is presented in this paper as mean ±SD.

Table 2. A student's sample evaluation: Explanation & Examples

Explanation & Examples		Comments
Is the definition or the meanings of the target word clearly shown? Are they written in plain English?	3	The definition and the meanings of the words I have consulted are easy to understand. But I had some problems understanding the meaning of some definitions, so that I had to consult another dictionary to make it clear.
Does it contain many useful explanations of how to use the word? Does it provide you with a variety of examples? Is it easy to find out common usage of the word or phrase and how it is used with other words?	3	Examples are abundant but the information of common usage of the word or phrase is insufficient. I have noticed that there are many over-simplified explanations for lower-level students like me.
Does it have idioms, phrasal verbs or sentences including the target word?	2	This dictionary does not contain many idioms nor phrasal verbs.

Table 3. A student's sample evaluation: Attractiveness

Attractiveness		Comments
Does the dictionary attract your interest? Is the dictionary interesting to explore?	4	Unlike my portable electronic dictionary, this online dictionary has a wide range of features. Although this dictionary doesn't have any activities for the users to test themselves on the key words, I am happy to use it more like a paper dictionary based on its large database.
Does the website contain attractive visuals? Does it have pictures or illustrations?	2	This dictionary doesn't have any attractive visuals. It doesn't have pictures or illustrations. Like a paper dictionary for advanced learners, this dictionary seems to be more suitable for students with high English proficiency levels.
Who is the intended reader? Is the word level clearly shown? Is it graded, for example, with stars, to show its frequency?	3	The intended reader is probably an advanced learner of English, because the definition of some key words I consulted contained difficult words that I didn't know. This dictionary wasn't graded with stars, either, so that I couldn't find out the frequency of the word.

Although, initially the students' computer levels were divided into four groups: 'very low', 'low', 'high', and 'very high', in the analysis, the levels of computer skills were divided into two groups: 'high' and 'low'. The different computer levels were compared by t-test with the results of the students' ratings based on the 26 questions mentioned above. In addition, the results of the students' ratings were analyzed by using Spearman's correlation to determine correlations between responses and significant factors underlying their responses. Correlation is significant at the .01 level (2-tailed).

5   Findings

The findings obtained by the questionnaire are shown below. As shown in Figure 1, with regard to the students' views on reading English websites, more than half of them (26 students) thought reading English websites was difficult. On the other hand, about half of the students (15 students) thought reading English websites was necessary. In addition, there was only one student who thought reading English websites was boring.

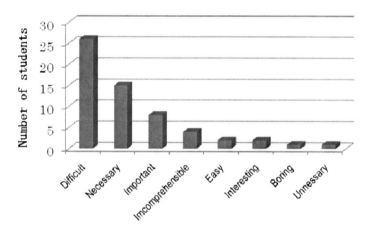

Fig. 1. Students' views on reading English websites

With regard to the frequency of reading English websites, almost 85% of students stated that they didn't read them even once a week. None of the students read English websites every day.

Table 4. Dictionaries used with a paper-based traditional textbook in a computer lab (%)

Dictionary types	Online	PEDs
Percentage of students	4.48	6.07

Table 4 and 5 show that the dictionary the students preferred to use when they read different types of texts. When they read paper-based textbook, approximately half of the students preferred online dictionaries and the other half prefer PEDs. When they read English websites, more than 93% of the students preferred online dictionaries. Table 6 and 7 show that the dictionary the students preferred to use when they take different types of examinations. In terms of the paper-based English examinations, approximately half of the students preferred online dictionaries and the other half preferred PEDs. In terms of the computer-based English examinations, more than 83% of the students preferred online dictionaries.

Table 5. Dictionaries used when students read English websites (%)

Dictionary types	Online	PEDs
Percentage of students	6.6	93.4

Table 6. Dictionaries used when students answer paper-based English exercises (%)

Dictionary types	Online	PEDs
Percentage of students	53.4	46.6

Table 7. Dictionaries used when students answer computer-based English exercises (%)

Dictionary types	Online	PEDs
Percentage of students	16.6	83.4

Table 8 and 9 show the students' view on online dictionaries and PEDs respectively. When compared with these Tables, it is clear that not many students thought that online dictionaries were appropriate to their English level. Averages (±SD) of these responses were 4.87 (±1.96) and 6.33 (±1.81) respectively. In addition, many students thought that PEDs were more user-friendly and easier-to-use than online dictionaries. With regard to language examples and usages and detailed instructions about them, the students highly valued online dictionaries. The students also highly valued online dictionaries in that they thought the dictionaries would help them understand the importance of learning English, and therefore, enjoy studying English. The Tables also show that the students thought that online dictionaries had simpler and clearer screen layout than the PEDs. The Average (±SD) of this response was 6.45 (±1.95).

Table 8. Students' view on online dictionaries

	Mean (SD)
1. The online dictionaries were appropriate to my English level.	4.87 (1.96)
2. The online dictionaries were appropriate to my study needs.	5.26 (1.98)
3. The online dictionaries provided me with various language examples and usages.	6.90 (1.78)
4. The online dictionaries helped me enjoy studying English.	6.10 (1.97)
5. The online dictionaries explained examples and usages in an easy way.	6.10 (1.81)
6. The online dictionaries gave me detailed instructions about examples and usages.	6.35 (1.78)
7. The online dictionaries helped me enhance the efficiency of my English study.	6.16 (2.21)
8. The online dictionaries helped me understand the importance of learning English.	6.00 (2.21)
9. The online dictionaries had a simple and clear screen layout.	6.45 (1.95)
10. The online dictionaries were easy to navigate.	5.84 (1.90)
11. The online dictionaries were user-friendly.	5.48 (2.43)
12. The online dictionaries were easier-to-use than PEDs.	5.39 (2.33)
13. The online dictionaries would help me improve my English proficiency level.	5.35 (2.04)

(N = 30).

The results of the t-test indicate that, with regard to the difference between the students who preferred online dictionaries and who preferred PEDs, the students, who preferred online dictionaries when taking paper-based exercises, thought that they contained various examples and usages, and therefore the dictionaries would help improve their English skills ($t = 2.20$, $t = 2.12$ respectively; $p < .05$). On the other hand, the students who preferred PEDs highly valued the usability of the PEDs when they consult paper-based textbooks, even if online dictionaries were available ($t = 2.06$, $p < .05$). In addition, the students, who preferred PEDs when reading English websites, thought that the screen layout of the PEDs was not suitable ($t = 2.96$,

$p < .05$). With regard to online dictionaries, the students who frequently read English websites thought the dictionaries were appropriate to their study needs and therefore the dictionaries helped them enhance the efficiency of their English study ($t = 2.53$, $t = 2.08$ respectively; $p < .05$). With regard to PEDs, the students who frequently read English websites thought the PEDs had a simple and clear screen layout, and also the PEDs helped them understand the importance of learning English and therefore enjoy studying English ($t = 2.59$, $t = 2.83$, $t = 3.00$ respectively; $p < .05$). The results of the t-test showed that there were no significant differences between the students' frequency of reading English websites and the rest of the questions.

Table 9. Students' view on PEDs

	Mean (SD)
1. The PEDs were appropriate to my English level.	6.33 (1.81)
2. The PEDs were appropriate to my study needs.	5.97 (1.71)
3. The PEDs provided me with various language examples and usages.	5.90 (1.92)
4. The PEDs helped me enjoy studying English.	5.97 (2.06)
5. The PEDs explained examples and usages in an easy way.	5.90 (2.01)
6. The PEDs gave me detailed instructions about examples and usages.	5.70 (1.91)
7. The PEDs helped me enhance the efficiency of my English study.	6.23 (1.50)
8. The PEDs helped me understand the importance of learning English.	5.60 (1.73)
9. The PEDs had a simple and clear screen layout.	4.90 (2.17)
10. The PEDs were easy to navigate.	5.87 (2.06)
11. The PEDs were user-friendly.	6.21 (1.78)
12. The PEDs were easier-to-use than online dictionaries.	6.24 (2.01)
13. The PEDs would help me improve my English proficiency level.	5.43 (1.52)

($N = 30$).

Table 10. Correlation between factors for using online dictionaries

Online dictionaries...	helped me enjoy studying English.	explained examples and usages in an easy way.	gave me detailed instructions about examples and usages.	helped me enhance the efficiency of my English study.	helped me understand the importance of learning English.
were appropriate to my study needs.	.697**	.627**	.482**	.695**	.691**
provided me with various language examples and usages.	.617**	.714**	.774**	.750**	.581**
explained examples and usages in an easy way.	.711**	1.00	.800**	.709**	.578**

*Notes: Correlation Matrix (N=30), **p < .01.*

Table 10 shows that there was a strong correlation (r < .8) between those who thought the online dictionaries explained examples and usages in an easy way and those who thought the online dictionaries gave them detailed instructions about examples and usages (r = .800, p < .01). There was a moderate correlation (r < .6) between those who thought the online dictionaries were appropriate to their study needs and those who thought the online dictionaries helped them enhance the efficiency of their English studies (r = .695, p < .01). The correlation of .691 was also significant between those who thought the online dictionaries were appropriate to their study needs and those who helped them understand the importance of learning English. There was a moderate correlation between those who thought the online dictionaries provided them various language examples and usages and those who thought the online dictionaries gave them detailed instructions about examples and usages (r = .774, p < .01). There was also a moderate correlation between those who thought the online dictionaries provided them various language examples and usages and those who thought the online dictionaries helped them enhance the efficiency of their English study (r = .750, p < .01).

In Table 11 below, there was a strong correlation between those who thought the online dictionaries were easier-to-use than PEDs and those who thought the online dictionaries were user-friendly (r = .850, p < .01). There was also a strong correlation between those who thought the online dictionaries were easier-to-use than PEDs and those who thought the online dictionaries would help them improve their English proficiency level (r = .823, p < .01).

The correlation of .739 was significant between those who thought the online dictionaries were user-friendly and those who thought the online dictionaries would help them improve their English proficiency level.

Table 11. Correlation between factors for using online dictionaries

Online dictionaries...	were easier-to-use than PEDs.	would help them improve their English proficiency level.
were user-friendly.	.850**	.739**
were easier-to-use than PEDs.	1.00	.823**

Notes: Correlation Matrix (N=30), **p < .01.

6 Discussion of Findings

Although the sample size of the present study was small, the findings revealed students' preferences of dictionary use in different contexts and their distinctive views on online dictionaries as compared with PEDs. The findings suggest that, although some students were totally new in consulting online dictionaries, the majority of students appeared to realize that these two different types of dictionaries had both advantages and disadvantages. This result is in accordance with a study by Chen [7]. In terms of the relationship between the educational situations where students were required to use the dictionaries and the students' preference of the dictionaries, there were several distinctive findings. First of all, when students engaged in the paper-based study, approximately half of the students preferred online dictionaries and the other half of the students preferred PEDs. However, when they engaged in computer-based study, the results indicated that the majority of students preferred online dictionaries. The findings also suggested that the students highly valued the various language examples and instructions provided by online dictionaries. They believed that these ample resources would help them choose the right meaning of the word and find synonyms or antonyms of a word [1], and, as a result, assist them with the improvement of their English skills.

Secondly, the results of the *t*-test indicated that the students who were accustomed to English websites thought that online dictionaries helped enhancing the efficiency of English study and, therefore, improving their English proficiency level. These students preferred online dictionaries whether they were doing paper-based or computer-based exercises. These results suggest that students' experiences using websites had an impact on the use of online dictionaries. It can readily be said that those who are not new in browsing websites benefit more from the use of these dictionaries. On the contrary, these students didn't deny the value of PEDs and stated that PEDs made them enjoy learning English as well. It is also important to note that the students who were accustomed to using PEDs thought that the screen layout of PEDs was not satisfactory while doing computer-based exercises. The findings also indicate that many students thought PEDs had less detailed information than online dictionaries. These results show that, as Chen suggested, 'a combined and complimentary use' of different types of dictionaries should be encouraged [7] depending on the situation where students use e-dictionaries.

Lastly, the findings revealed the students' problems of their inability to use online dictionaries efficiently. These students thought PEDs were more user-friendly and easier-to-use. User-friendliness seems to be the key factor to improve students' English levels. In addition, the findings suggest that choosing online dictionaries which are appropriate to their needs enables students to enhance the efficiency of their English study. These results suggest that the main cause of the problem appeared to be the students' lack of chance to be trained to find the right dictionaries from the websites. As the findings suggest, the evaluation of online dictionaries was one of the effective methods to develop students' awareness of how to choose the best dictionary for themselves. The criteria used in the evaluation in this study helped students assess the effectiveness of the dictionary they needed. This result is in accordance with the previous study [14]. Looking up a word or phrase in a dictionaries is basically a rather passive process, and in order to make this process more active, the students' self-reported assessment employed in this study, including the translation tasks and exercises, seemed to be a perfect tool to encourage students to make maximum use of various online dictionaries. So far, there are not many suggestions available concerning how to evaluate and choose effective online dictionaries for students when they try to accomplish different language tasks and examinations using online resources. The instructor should provide students with detailed dictionary instruction and guidance [7] and encourage them to make better use of various functions of online dictionaries.

7 Conclusions

This study examines how Japanese university students evaluate the usefulness of PEDs and online English dictionaries in different study contexts. The results reveal their opinions on advantages and disadvantages of these two types of dictionaries. Although online dictionaries are a rather new development, the findings indicate that online dictionaries can be as effective as PEDs and there are different roles to play in different educational contexts. The students' evaluation of dictionaries enhances their awareness of how to find a suitable dictionary for themselves and improve their reference skills. Although this study had some limitations concerning the small number of respondents, the results shed light on how e-dictionaries can be used to support their online learning.

Acknowledgement

This study was supported by a research grant provided by Hokkai-Gakuen.

References

1. Al-Jarf, R.: Teaching vocabulary to EFL college students online. CALL-EJ Online 8(2), 1–27 (2007)
2. Chen, Y.: Dictionary use and EFL learning. A contrastive study of pocket electronic dictionaries and paper dictionaries. International Journal of Lexicography 23(3), 275–306 (2010)
3. Cooker, L.: Self-Access Materials. In: Tomlinson, B. (ed.) English Language Learning Materials, pp. 100–132. Continuum, London (2008)

4. Hatanaka, Y.: Denshijisho Daikenkyuu [Detailed research on electronic dictionaries], http://homepage1.nifty.com/inshi/dic/edic.html (retrieved March 8, 2011)
5. Hirata, Y., Hirata, Y.: Students' evaluation of websites in hybrid language learning. In: Wang, F.L., Fong, J., Zhang, L., Lee, V.S.K. (eds.) ICHL 2009. LNCS, vol. 5685, pp. 186–196. Springer, Heidelberg (2009)
6. Houser, C., Thornton, P.: Poodle: A course management system for mobile phones. In: Proceedings of the Third IEEE Workshop on Wireless Technologies in Education, pp. 159–163 (2005)
7. Jarvis, H., Szymczyk, M.: Student views on learning grammar with web- and book-based materials. ELT Journal 64(1), 32–44 (2009)
8. Kukulska-Hulme, A., Shield, L.: An overview of mobile assisted language learning: From content delivery to supported collaboration and interaction. ReCall 20(3), 271–289 (2008)
9. Loucky, J.P.: Using computerized bilingual dictionaries to help maximize English vocabulary learning at Japanese colleges. CALICO Journal 23(1), 105–129 (2003)
10. Loucky, J.P.: Combining the benefits of electronic and online dictionaries with CALL Web sites to produce effective and enjoyable vocabulary and language learning lessons. Computer-Assisted Language Learning 18(5), 389–416 (2005)
11. McCarty, S.: Making mobile phone websites. In: Selected Proceedings of the Thirteenth Annual JALT CALL SIG Conference, pp. 65–70 (2008)
12. Morita, M.: Mobile based learning (MBL) in Japan. In: Proceedings of the First Conference on Creating, Connecting and Collaborating Through Computing (2003), http://ieeexplore.ieee.org/xpl/freeabs_all.jsp?tp=&arnumber=1222348&abstractAccess=no&userType=inst (retrieved April 25, 2011)
13. Okuyama, Y., Igarashi, H.: Think-aloud protocol on dictionary use by advanced learners of Japanese. The JALT CALL Journal 3(1-2), 45–58 (2007)
14. Stirling, J.: The portable electronic dictionary: faithful friend or faceless foe? (2003), http://www.elgweb.net/ped-article.html (retrieved February 20, 2011)
15. Weschler, R., Pitts, C.: An experiment using electronic dictionaries with EFL students (2000), http://iteslj.org/Articles/Weschler-ElectroDict.html (retrieved February 20, 2011)

Leveraging Low-Cost Mobile Technologies in Bangladesh: A Case Study of Innovative Practices for Teacher Professional Development and Communicative English Language Teaching

Christopher S. Walsh, Prithvi Shrestha, and Claire Hedges

The Open University, Faculty of Education and Language Studies,
Walton Hall, Milton Keynes MK7 6AA UK
{c.s.walsh,c.l.hedges}@open.ac.uk,
pns52@openmail.open.ac.uk

Abstract. Using mobile technologies, particularly mobile phones, for teacher professional development in developing economies is extremely rare. This article presents a case study of English in Action (EIA) and its use of mobile technologies that moves beyond documenting their functionality as ubiquitous handheld hardware to enhance and extend the reach of teaching and learning. It presents compelling evidence of an effective and innovative professional development intervention that simultaneously improves communicative English language teaching. We argue this large-scale intervention was significant in enhancing teachers' professional knowledge and presents important implications for using mobile phones in developing countries for teacher professional development and classroom-based English teaching and learning.

Keywords: English in Action (EIA), teacher professional development, Communicative Language Teaching (CLT), mobile phones.

1 Introduction

English in Action (EIA), a project designed to contribute to the growth of Bangladesh by providing English language as a tool for better access to the world economy, piloted a number of teacher professional development initiatives that have transformed English language teaching. EIA, through a collaborative international partnership, aims to assist 25 million people in Bangladesh improve their English language skills over 9 years (2008-2017). Originally requested by the government of Bangladesh and subsequently funded (£50 million) by the United Kingdom's Department for International development (DfID), it leverages mobile technologies within a programme of school-based teacher professional development to present new opportunities for teachers and pupils to acquire English to levels that enable them to participate more fully in economic and social opportunities. The project is led and managed by BMB Mott McDonald, the Open University (UK) and The British Broadcasting Corporation (BBC) World Service Trust. EIA also works collaboratively with local organisations

R. Kwan et al. (Eds.): ICT 2011, CCIS 177, pp. 152–166, 2011.
© Springer-Verlag Berlin Heidelberg 2011

including the Underprivileged Children's Educational Programme (UCEP) and Friends in Village Development Bangladesh (FIVDB).

In this paper we describe The Open University's involvement in EIA which centres around targeted ICT-enhanced teacher professional development and the introduction of a variety of audio resources, both through using handheld mobile technologies. We first used Apple's iPod Nano and Touch to pilot (2009-2010) the use of our audio and video teacher professional development training resources and audio resources aligned with Bangladesh's English language curriculum and textbooks used in government schools. Then as we are scaling up in 2011-2012, we are using low-cost mobile phones with preloaded teacher professional development content and audio classroom resources on secure digital (SD) cards. EIA has 3 stage approach to meet its primary objective of assisting 25 million Bangladeshis improve their communicative English language skills.

The first stage focused on developmental research (2008 – 2011) and was carried out with 700 teachers from government schools across 21 of Bangladesh's Upazillas (smaller than districts), as well as some 60 teachers from non-governmental organisations (NGOs). Two thirds of these teachers work in primary schools, one-third in secondary. 80% of all EIA project schools are in rural areas with limited or no access to electricity. The developmental research phase helped us determine the most effective, scalable and sustainable models of supported open and distance learning for English language teachers and the most appropriate forms of mobile technology to support this. The research focused on three key areas: the reach of the training provided (e.g. the extent of training, tools, and resources, and the numbers of teachers, pupils and schools participating), and the participants' perception and evaluation of that reach; the classroom practice of teachers and pupils participating in the project; and the English language competence of teachers and pupils in the project.

During the first phase, to better understand the unique context of Bangladesh, EIA also conducted six baseline studies[1] to identify the contexts in which the project was beginning. This included: large scale examinations of teachers' classroom practice; teachers' and pupils' competence in speaking and listening in English; pupils' and communities' attitudes and motivations towards English language learning; the materials and training programmes currently used in Bangladesh for teaching and learning English; and the communications technologies and power supplies used and/or available within schools and communities

EIA's second phase will focus on upscaling (2011 – 2014) where we are drawing on the research completed in Phase I and take the most cost effective model of teacher professional development and delivery of EIA's audio materials on mobile phones forward at scale. During phase two, the Open University will provide teacher professional development and mobile technology kits to at least 8-10,000 teachers from five national districts in Bangladesh. 80% of these teachers will come from rural schools.

EIA's third phase will focus on embedding (2014 – 2017) where the project will draw on Phases I and II and design teacher professional development programmes which will be available across Bangladesh through locally supported open and distance learning. EIA understands that the final phase programme will require Public

---

[1] To view the EIA's 6 Baseline Studies visit
http://www.eiabd.com/eia/index.php?option=com_content&view=article&id=160&Itemid=84

Private Partnership (PPP) to provide up to 100,000 teachers with mobile technology 'toolkits' that include audio, visual and print classroom resources and teacher professional development materials delivered through community networks and increasingly ubiquitous ICT access. It what follows we provide a review of the literature, EIA's evolving technology strategy and two case studies that illustrate our innovative use of mobile technologies for teacher professional development and improving teacher's communicative language teaching (CLT) practices in English. We then discuss the implications of these case studies for upscaling and embedding the project. We then put forth an argument for using mobile phones in developing countries for providing teacher professional development and improving classroom-based English teaching and learning.

2   Review of the Literature

Mobile technologies, particularly mobile phones, for teacher professional development and ELT teaching and learning are still an emerging field in developing countries. But, studies in developing and developed countries do offer evidence of mobile phones' impact across various global contexts in regards to the aforementioned fields as well as other areas of development. There are many remarkable case studies outside education that highlight the efficacy of mobile phones for entrepreneurial activity among women in Bangladesh (Aminuzzaman, Baldersheim, and Jamil, 2003; Sullivan, 2007); economic development in relation to microenterprises in Rwanda (Donner, 2007); social innovations in health in Tanzania (Mulgan, 2006) and India (Biswas, 2009); and activism (see www.mobileactive.org) in developing countries. Of key importance to EIA is leveraging the power of mobile phones, in similar ways, to provide effective teacher professional development in Bangladesh that concurrently improves teachers' English language fluency and communicative English language teaching practices to bring about increased student proficiency in communicative English. The literature review briefly outlines various global initiatives with mobile phones that provide a situating contextual background to EIA's ICT-enhanced programme of school-based teacher professional development using mobile phones. We then argue how our use of mobile phones presents new opportunities for teachers and pupils to acquire English to levels that enable them to participate more fully in economic and social opportunities.

2.1 Mobile Phones for Development

Mobile phones offer increased opportunities by providing more choice in when, where, and how teachers teach and how pupils learn. Largely, research on mobile phones in developing countries tends to provide anecdotal, rather than qualitative evidence of the technologies' impact on teaching and learning. Kaplan (2006) explores evidence that both supports and/or refutes the idea that fixed and mobile telephones is, or could be, an effective healthcare intervention in developing countries. Of importance to EIA is how Kaplan's study illustrates the ways mobile phones provide "the ability to create a multi-way interaction between patient and provider(s) and thus facilitate the dynamic nature of this relationship" (¶ 4). Orlov, Schoeni and

Chapuis (2006) present compelling evidence on how the wide adoption of the Java environment for mobile phones provides the opportunity to develop custom-made applications for educational purposes. Their study illustrates that when students have spare time, they can devote themselves to self-study without the need of a computer or books. Also relevant to EIA is Metcalfe's (2007) argument that oral technologies have more potential than is presently perceived, as being particularly useful for supporting oral communication through audio files played on mobile phones.

EIA's video and audio resources are designed to both provide professional development to teachers and help them and their pupils acquire English. The audio resources provide examples of near native speakers reading aloud part of the national textbook as well as additional dialogues, songs and poems directly related to primary textbook's lessons. As EIA scales up it will consider how Andersson and Hatakka (2010) used The Bangladesh Virtual Classroom (BVC) project (2005-2007) to design a methodology to deliver interactive distance courses to learners via mobile phones and TV. But unlike Andersson and Hatakka's project, EIA aims to design a programme that goes beyond using the mobile phones' functions for administrative purposes (student registration, attendance functions, etc.) and interactive purposes (e.g. self-quizzes and feedback systems). Rather it wants to build on and extend those aspects of the BVC project that used mobile phones, SMS and video recordings to create interactivity and provide teachers with the pedagogical knowledge needed to teach in more communicative ways with their students alongside and EIA's extensive range of corresponding print, visual, tactile and audio resources.

2.2 Mobile Phones for Teacher Professional Development

Technology-enhanced teacher-professional development on mobile phones in emerging economies, like Bangladesh, is a promising field whose applications are context specific and largely absent from the literature. While not about teacher professional development in the developing word, Walton et al (2005) describe a project in the USA which explored the potential for mobile technologies to give health students in the community access to learning resources. Students in the study placed great importance on accessing learning resources using mobile technologies, particularly PDAs, laptops, mobile phones and portable radios. Similarly, Kinsella (2009) describes open source software that allows large numbers of students to provide their lecturers access to instant feedback via SMS on the material presented in lectures to give them more persoanlised input over the direction of the lecture or ask questions on content that was unclear. Kennedy, Gray and Tse's (2008) study with medical students in Australia found mobile phone use was ubiquitous and that students did not always have access to a memory stick, a desktop computer and a broadband Internet connection. Their study found that the functionality of new generation mobile phones might be making these devices redundant (Wireless Healthcare Report 2007). EIA understands the relevance of these studies and as a result has field tested a number of mobile phones that provide all of the abilities of the iPod Nano and Touch but also offer increased opportunities for more target and innovative teacher professional development through SMS messaging and open distance learning models currently being designed as we scale up in phases II and III of the 9 year project.

2.3 Mobile Phones for ELT Teaching and Learning

There are very few examples of the use of mobile phones to teach English in developing countries in the research literature, but there are examples from developed countries. Salameh (2011) used an offline Flash-based prototype system for English language learning on mobile phones in Palestine. The system consists of ten Learning Objects (LO) constructed using a multimedia approach. Initial testing demonstrated the systems' efficiency of and students enjoyed using the software on their mobile phones to learn English. Cavus and Ibrahim's (2009) research explores the potential of learning new technical English language words using SMS to 1st-year undergraduate students in Cyprus. In another study, Thorton and Houser (2005) sent English vocabulary lessons at timed intervals to the mobile phones of 44 Japanese university students, hoping to promote regular study. Compared with students urged to regularly study identical materials on paper or via the Internet, students receiving mobile e-mail learned more. Their study reports that seventy-one percent of the subjects preferred receiving these lessons on their mobile phones rather than PCs. Ninety-three percent of these Japanese students also believed this was a valuable teaching method.

EIA's managing partner the BBC World Trust launched BBC Janala, a partner project that works with BBC Learning English. BBC Janala is a unique multiplatform project that harnesses multimedia technology to provide affordable English education to millions of people in Bangladesh and the wider international diaspora. BBC Janala offers an innovative way of learning English on mobile phones to the 50 million Bangladeshis who own mobile handsets. After viewing The BBC Janala TV show, they have the opportunity to dial up a series of three-minute-long English lessons for 3 taka (2.5 pence) each, which is less than the cost of a cup of tea at a roadside stall in Dhaka (The Times, 2009). By December 2009—a month after launching the initiative—they received over 750,000 calls.

EIA's use of mobile technologies to provide ICT-enhanced teacher professional development or "the trainer in your pocket" (Walsh, in press) is critically different to what is reported on in the literature. Not only did EIA focus on the potential of video and audio resources to train teachers, they also designed a range of audio resources that complement the national curriculum to assist teachers in changing their English teaching practice to make it more communicative. These were not stand-alone, rather they were embedded in a cyclical programme of targeted face-to-face and ICT enhanced professional development with comprehensive print-based activity guides by grade level (1 to 5) with visual (posters) and tactile (flash cards and figurines) resources. Next we turn to EIA technology strategy and illustrate the project through two case studies.

3 EIA's Technology Strategy

Criticisms of mobile technologies and/or ICT for development projects are that they fail to build on existing systems or work in a participatory way and therefore do not achieve local ownership. As EIA is currently preparing to scale up in the next phase, EIA's Technology strategy has identified possible local partners and is field testing mobile phone based technology kits to deliver audio files alongside supplementary print and visual resources to more than 10,000 teachers in Phase III. To ensure scalability, we are working towards a mobile phone based kit cost of no more than £60 (per teacher) for this phase (mobile phone, SD card and portable rechargeable speakers) and possibly as low as £15 for phase IV (using only an SD card on teachers' own mobile phones with portable rechargeable speakers). To inform the choice of the best kit, EIA is field testing a variety of mobile phone based portable media players and rechargeable speakers (that use the same battery as mobile phones) across two rural Upazillas (March-April 2011), looking at ease of use, performance in classroom contexts, durability and recharging. The goal is to assemble kits for distribution to teachers across the country, some with limited and/or no electricity. To that aim we are also piloting these kits with solar power chargers (one per school, 2 schools at £32 each).

EIA understands that mobile technologies, not yet available in Bangladesh, may offer new possibilities for helping children, young people and adults acquire English to levels that may give them increased economic and social opportunities. Additionally, the project is working collaboratively—through innovative teacher professional development—to locally contextualise the use of mobile technologies in ways that are truly sustainable. All of the options we have identified play video allowing for continuing ICT-enhanced teacher professional development.

EIA's strategy does not view information communication technologies (ICT) as simply software and hardware systems adopted by teachers, but rather they are powerful tools applied to human needs (educational and English language learning) within specific cultural contexts across a diverse country. EIA's technology strategy is incorporating these new mobile phone based resources alongside a programme of school-based teacher professional development to present new opportunities for teachers and pupils to acquire English to levels that enable them to participate more fully in economic and social opportunities. We examined existing classroom contexts in remote areas and have demonstrated the potential of using EIA's resources first on the iPod Nano and then on mobile phones with lightweight portable speakers. We present findings of both of these as case studies below. The case studies highlight how mobile technologies, as a tool, can change significantly classroom-based English learning and concurrently influence teacher to adopt CLT practices. EIA's technology strategy challenges current assumptions around the use of mobile technologies for development and communicative English language teaching. This is because we are not relying only on the network aspect of mobile phones, but rather that possibilities of incorporating them into large scale targeted teacher professional development with complementary audio, video and visual resources to improve English classroom teaching and learning in a developing economy.

EIA's technology strategy is also constantly driven and reflected on through research, monitoring and evaluation. EIA's research methods incorporate sociocultural anthropology and ethnography to help elucidate the cultural contexts of ICT use. Such methods also are clearly relevant to answering the question of what strategies or actions are most likely to result in the deployment of mobile technologies that will truly advance EIA's primary goals and remain sustainable after the project ends in 2017.

4   EIA's Case Studies

In order to explore the use of mobile technologies for teacher professional development, EIA launched its first pilot from February to March (2010) in six Upazillas across Bangladesh. Prior to this pilot, a pre-pilot was run from August 2009 with 32 secondary school teachers from schools run by a non-governmental organisation in Dhaka. This provided a test-bed for the main pilot. This pre-pilot indicated that mobile technologies (particularly MP3s) were effective in providing film and audio-based learning opportunities to English teachers who previously had limited/no access to this kind of professional development and support. The pilot was run with 200 teachers from 100 secondary schools and 400 teachers from 200 primary schools who were mostly from rural areas. Each teacher was paired with another teacher from the same school to promote collaborative learning, reflection and problem solving.

Each secondary teacher was given an iPod Touch with teacher professional development resources, while each primary teacher was provided with an iPod Nano (Apple) with the audio materials for classroom use. In addition, they were also given a portable speaker (LogiTech) that could be recharged (£60). Each participating school also received a large rechargeable Block Rocker speaker (£140), which a field testing proved to be too big and difficult to recharge in schools with no electricity. These mobile devices contained audio materials to enhance ELT classroom teaching as well as vod and podcasts for teacher professional development. Whilst the classroom resources were mainly audio-based, designed around the existing school curriculum and supported by print materials such as posters and flashcards, the teacher professional development materials contained audio and video materials modeled and/or focused certain techniques and pedagogical practices that incorporate CLT principles such as integration of language skills and grammar in context.

4.1   Pilot Test 1 (iPod Nano and Touch--2009-2010)

The first EIA pilot test was conducted with both primary and secondary school English teachers from across Bangladesh. For the pilot test, 21 Upazillas from six divisions were selected in consultation with the Government of Bangladesh. The teachers were from government schools and had almost never used any learning technologies in their classroom. However, 70% of these teachers reported that they had access to mobile phones (EIA Study 1a 2010). Assuming that these teachers would find the use of a media player such as an iPod relatively easy, for the pilot test, iPods were chosen over other mobile devices such as a basic MP3 player or a more sophisticated one such as iRiver. Although iPods were more expensive than other devices, iPods were used because they were simple to use and had more functionalities than others at the time.

Given that the project focused more on classroom materials for the primary sector which were mainly audio, iPod Nanos (8GB 4th Generation) were selected for this purpose. They could still display videos and pictures though the screen was small. The materials contained audio recordings of the existing English textbooks and a set of activities to supplement all units in the national textbook, *English in Action* for Grades 1 to 5. The materials were bilingual (i.e., both Bangla and English).

For the secondary sector, however, a second generation iPod Touch (8GB) was used. The secondary materials were different and they were aimed to enhance the teachers' professional development as well as their English language skills. But the materials also included audio recordings of 'listening' texts, dialogues, stories, poems and plays from the *English for Today* textbooks from Grades 6 to 10. The main teacher professional development materials were divided into 12 modules as shown in Table below:

Module	Key points
1. Active listening	• elicitation techniques • stages of a listening lesson
2. Choral dialogues	• scaffolding students • setting up pairwork
3. Listening and responding	• active involvement • different learning styles
4. Information gaps	• creating an information gap • authenticity
5. Pronunciation practice	• sounds, stress and rhythm • pronunciation models
6. Predictive listening	• elicitation techniques • creativity
7. Roleplay	• using dialogues • pairwork and groupwork
8. Songs for language practice	• automatisation • grammar integration
9. Using visuals	• classroom interaction • skills integration
10. Creative writing	• Personalization and creativity • stages of a writing lesson
11. Listening to the world	• real-life purposes • listening for gist/key points
12. Grammar games	• grammar integration • motivation

Each module contained a sequence of teacher development activities using print, audio and video. The print materials and the expository parts of the audio were in English, in order to provide language improvement, but the audio materials also featured conversations in Bangla. These features ensured that key ideas were reinforced through different media and languages. The video materials included real classroom lessons being conducted by Bangladeshi teachers in Bangladeshi classrooms. The bigger screen of the iPod Touch allowed the teachers to watch the videos which showed the implementation of the key principles discussed in each of the 12 modules.

4.1.1 Pilot Test Results

A number of research studies were carried out in order to explore the feasibility of the mobile devices used in the EIA project. These studies indicate that both primary and secondary teachers and students participating in the project found the use of mobile devices (i.e., iPods and portable speakers) an effective tool for learning English language and for teachers to both learn about and view CLT practices. These studies also suggest that there is an increasing use of English in the classroom both by the teacher and the students.

The study that concentrated on classroom experience of teachers and students showed that the mobile technology-enhanced ELT materials improved teachers' English and their confidence in using English in their lessons. For example, a primary teacher summed up the increasing use of English in English lessons in an interview like this (EIA Study 1b 2010):

> *Before [EIA] there was no difference... no distinction... the English class was the same as the Bangla class. If you walked in, you would not have been able to tell which was which.*

> *But now we can differentiate... we [the teacher and students] are speaking English much more now...*

> *...The students are using English with their families too, outside school... Their pronunciation has improved... they are using English confidently.*

On interview, the teachers also reported that the most useful ideas in supporting their learning and pedagogical changes back at school were either (1) the iPod and audio materials or (2) their project partner in school. Taken together, teachers saw these two components as being the core support for their school-based professional development.

Likewise, through a survey of almost 1700 students, they reported enjoying listening to the audio (iPod) and indicated this helped them learn English more effectively. The following student quotes reflect their positive attitudes towards the use of iPods in their classroom:

> *We like most to listen song and poem from the sound box... [Student 1]*

> *We like to hear the songs and rhymes of iPod which are easier and very helpful ... [Student 2]*

> *The IPod songs are very enjoyable... [Student 3]*

> *We like audio listening... [Student 4]*

> *I like to hear songs, rhymes and speaking from the iPod... [Student 5]*

EIA's research, monitoring and evaluation also suggested that the students enjoyed their English lesson because they were engaged in student-based or 'interesting' activities such as listening to songs and dialogues which they had no access to previously. Teachers confirmed this view when they reported that their students were more motivated to learn English as a result of the introduction of the new technologies and their shifted communicative English language teaching approach.

EIA's preliminary studies also indicated that there are significant future challenges to take into consideration as the project scales up in the next two phases. Often teachers from the rural schools reported that they had difficulty of recharging the speakers and their iPods, as the electricity supply across Bangladesh is intermittent. Classroom observations have also shown that some teachers are still struggling regarding the use of the iPod in terms of navigation. In particular, they seem to take a long to time to locate the material for their specific lesson (aligned with the national curriculum and textbook) when in the classroom. Even though they were trained to queue the device before class, some found this not possible for various reasons. As a result, some teachers may not use the device regularly.

4.2 Pilot Test 2 (Nokia, Maximus and SD Cards)

EIA understands, from their own research and that exists in the literature, that mobile technologies offer increased opportunities by providing more choice in when, where, and how teachers teach and how pupils learn (for example see Naismith et al., 2004). Unlike many other funded development projects specific to mobile phones and often driven on making the various technologies work to ensure learning happens and satisfies funding conditions in the present (SAIDE, 2008), EIA has been conceptualized to intentionally address issues of scale, embedding and quality for the present *and future* across rural and urban contexts. Budget constraints of 6000 BDT (per teacher or £60) mandated that EIA construct multiple kits to field test/pilot the use of technology in Phase II while also thinking about Phase III to continue improve the English language skills/proficiency of both students and teachers. EIA is piloting the kits and assess the viability of various mobile phones to determine which kit to implement in the forthcoming scale up to Phase III. The current kits are outlined below:

Kit Option 1:	Cost
Equipment: • Nokia C1-01 Mobile Phone (plays audio/video supported with SD card up to 32 GB) 　4GB midrange SD card 　Portable rechargeable speakers	**59£**
Kit Option 2:	
Equipment: • Maximus M45i Mobile Phone (plays audio/video supported with SD card up to 32 GB) • 4GB midrange SD card • Portable rechargeable speakers	**51£**
Kit Option 3:	
Equipment: • 8 GB SD card • Portable rechargeable Speakers • Teacher's own mobile phone	**28£**

During the field test (March to April 2011) there are 40 participating teachers from two Upazillas (Rangamati & Pengsha) as well as 5 teacher facilitators (trainers). Additionally we have recruited five teachers who have their own mobile phones that can support SD cards and five additional teachers who have never used EIA's materials before were also recruited and provided with Kit 1. 20 teachers (10 from each Upazilla) received Kit 1 (Nokia C1-01) and the other 20 received Kit 2 (Maximus). All teachers received a small portable rechargeable speaker that is chargeable with the Nokia phone battery.

To support the teachers EIA produced a one page instructional guide on where to find EIA materials on either the Nokia/Maximus mobile and how to use/recharge the portable speakers with each phone. All teachers also received a face-to-face induction session to introduce the new kits and we required them to return their iPod Nanos. Individual follow-up with the teachers was provided through phone calls twice a week and teachers were encouraged to call for assistance if they needed it. EIA also piloted a short message service (SMS) teacher professional development weekly over the 12 week testing period. In March visits were made to each Upazilla and 12 classroom lessons were videotaped to assess the teachers' use of the various Kits. Teachers were also briefly interviewed. In May, all of the teachers will come together in Dhaka for a Milestone workshop where we will also survey teachers' use of the kits and conduct individual and group interviews to determine which Kit will be used for 4000 teachers in Phase 3 of the project (January 2012).

5 Implications for Scaling Up in Phase II and III (2012-2017)

Over the next two phases of the EIA project, there is an exponential growth in the number of teachers it is planned to reach. This is shown in the table below, setting out the reach numbers according to the EIA project planning documents.

Item	2011 - 2014 target no. of Teachers	2014 - 2017 target no. of Teachers
Primary Teachers	7,500	90,000
Primary Schools	2,500	40,000
Secondary Teachers	5,000	12,000
Secondary Schools	2,500	6,000

5.1 Phase II Model

Teachers are provided with professional development resources and classroom resources through the mobile technologies set out above. The implications of operating at a scale of 10,000+ teachers are manifold, but may be seen to have three focal points. First, the professional development will take place in the school, not at remote off-school centres. Second, there will be extensive use of classroom activities, principally made available to teachers through mobile technologies, which have proven in the field tests to model good practice. Third, structured peer learning will support teacher development. A diagrammatic representation of EIA's for upscaling model is set out below:

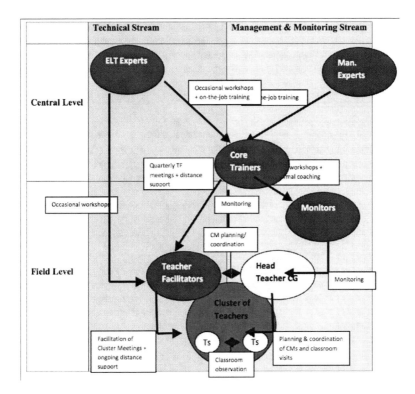

Its features can be described in relation to these three focal points. First, the place of learning is the school, which is made significantly more available and potentially powerful through mobile technologies. This is reinforced by setting up the coordination of the learning by a head teacher coordinating group. Second, teachers working in pairs in their schools explore and try out classroom activities, available through the mobile technologies supplemented by print texts, which model CLT techniques. In addition, participating teachers from nearby schools observe each others' lessons. Third, the teachers meet monthly in clusters of 30 teachers to follow a structured curriculum of professional development focused on classroom practice. Lead teachers, called Teacher Facilitators, guide these cluster meetings and are supported in doing so through intensive training by ELT experts and audio/visual materials available through mobile technologies.

5.2 Phase III Model

As EIA moves into phase III, increasing elements of the model will be taken over by existing Government of Bangladesh (GoB) structures, both in pre-service as well as in-service teacher training and support. This form of institutionalization is paramount to ensuring that both EIA's materials development/distribution and teacher development/support will become sustainable. In this phase, the mobile technology tools will be provided through forms of open distance leanring (ODL) and available to teachers and schools, with the EIA's resources made available through SD cards and/or the internet. EIA's vision in this regard is that:

- EIA approaches, methods and materials will be used in and fully integrated with the pre-service training taking place in Primary Teacher Training Institutes (PTIs) and Teacher Training Colleges (TTCs) in the country.
- EIA approaches, methods and materials, including the model of ongoing peer support, will become the GoB mechanism of continuous professional development for teachers (or in-service teacher training as it is currently called) as far as English as a subject is concerned, and will replace the current mechanisms of subject-based training. We view this as an effective way to provide sustainable continuous support that can stimulate ongoing reflection among teachers about using EIA methods, materials and techniques in the classroom after the project has officially ended.

Providing EIA's model of continuous professional development and distribution of audio, visual, tactile and print resources through GoB, will institutionalise those intrinsic elements of our model/project to provide the GoB its own mechanism for ongoing teacher support, while allowing new teachers to be trained on EIA methods through their pre-service training at the PTIs and TTCs. EIA considers this approach, now, to be the way forward towards project sustainability.

6 Conclusion

Largely, research on mobile technologies in emerging economies generally focuses only on the use of mobile phones and/or internet-based interventions. This research tends to provide anecdotal, rather than qualitative evidence of the technologies impact on teaching and learning (see SAIDE (2008) for examples from South Africa & ADB (2010) for examples from Asia & South East Asia). EIA is different as its mobile resources are primarily audio files designed to assist both teachers and pupils in acquiring English on low cost portable media players in its second and third phases.

EIA's wider technology strategy to meet EIA's goals is leveraging and use mobile phones as a strategic tool to (1) increase significantly the number of people able to communicate in English to levels that enable them to participate fully in economic and social activities and opportunities and (2) promote communicative language teaching (CLT) practices through ICT-enhanced teacher professional development interventions (alongside a face-to-face school-based programme of teacher professioal development) that have been tested and adapted in primary and secondary schools in regard to the lived realities and contexts within Upazillaa across Bangladesh. At the core of EIA's strategy are the following components:

- Access: Using ICTs to facilitate access to and sharing of relevant information, knowledge and resources.
- Voice/communication: Using ICTs to strengthen the English Communication teaching practices (pedagogical knowledge) of teachers as well as classroom-based learning of students.
- Networking: Using ICTs for networking and communication (in terms of teacher professional development) while fostering multi-stakeholder partnerships to achieve effects on a larger scale (i.e., upscaling).

The use of mobile phones in relationship to development is still relatively new and largely confined to university-based distance learning. In Bangladesh, Gronlund and Islam (2010) describe a low-cost, large-scale project working to improve distance education by means of a university-based student-centred interactive learning environment using video, mobile phones and SMS-based tools administered through a learning management system. Yet these forms of e-Learning largely rely on delivery through computers, rather than mobile devices. EIA's ICT-enhanced teacher professional development through the 'trainer in your pocket' stands out as both different and innovative, particularly in terms of how it is not constrained by the need for an internet connection or access to a computer.

A core component of EIA's planned school-based open learning model of professional development is working to build capacity among teachers themselves which explicitly addresses the human and teacher professional development impacts of the projects 9 year logistical framework. This is an example of using mobile technologies, particularly mobile phones, for development that ensures the stakeholders (teachers) are central to the process right from the beginning. EIA's framework although massive in scale (25 million individuals) leverages 'the trainer in your pocket' to facilitate grassroots innovation and achievement of localized community goals around improving/changing English education, thereby making it more communicative and student-centred. In this view, EIA's target is centred around human development strategies with mobile phones that provide ICT-enhanced professional development as complimentary, but essential as open distance learning strategy for development in emerging economies like Bangladesh.

References

1. Aminuzzaman, S., Baldersheim, H., Jamil, I.: Talking back! Empowerment and Mobile Phones in Rural Bangladesh: A study of the Village Phone Scheme of Grameen Bank. Contemporary South Asia. Asia. 12(3), 327–348 (2003)
2. Andersson, A., Hatakka, M.: Increasing Interactivity in Distance Educations: Case Studies Bangladesh and Sri Lanka. Information Technology for Development 16(1), 16–33 (2010)
3. Biswas, R., Joshi, A., Joshi, R., Kaufman, T., Peterson, C., Sturmberg, J.P., Maitra, A., Martin, C.M.: Revitalizing Primary Health Care and Family Medicine/PrimaryCare in India – Disruptive Innovation? J. of Evaluation in Clinical Practice 15, 873–880 (2009)
4. Cavus, N., Ibrahim, D.: m-Learning: An experiment in using SMS to supportlearning new English language words. British Journal of Educational Technology 40(1), 78–79 (2009)
5. Kaplan, W.A.: Can the ubiquitous power of mobile phones be used to improve health outcomes in developing countries? Globalization and Health,
   http://www.globalizationandhealth.com/content/2/1/9
6. Kennedy, G., Gray, K., Tse, J.: 'Net Generation' medical students: technological experiences of pre-clinical and clinical students. Medical Teacher 30, 10–16 (2008)
7. Kinsella, S.: Many to one: Using the mobile phone to interact with large classes. British Journal of Educational Technology 40(5), 956–958 (2009)
8. Donner, J.: The use of mobile phones by microentrepreneurs in Kigali, Rwanda: changes to social and business networks. Information Technologies and International Development 3(2), 3–19 (2007)
9. Metcalfe, M.: Development and Oral Technologies: View From Practice. Information Technology for Development 13(2), 199–204 (2007)
10. Mulgan, G.: The process of social innovation. Innovations 1(2), 145–162 (2006)

11. Blakely, R.: UK to teach English in Bangladesh via mobile. The Times (2009), `http://business.timesonline.co.uk/tol/business/industry_sect ors/telecoms/article6918153.ece`

12. Orlov, I., Schoeni, N., Chapuis, G.: Crystallography on mobile phones. J. of Applied Crystallography 39, 595–597 (2006)

13. Salameh, O.: A Multimedia Offline Cell Phone System For English Language Learning. International Arab J. of e-Technology 2(1), 44–48 (2011)

14. Sha, G.Q.: AI-based Chatterbots and Spoken English Teaching. J. Computer Assisted Learning 22(3), 197–268 (2009)

15. South African Institute for Education (SAIDE): Using Mobile Technology for Learner Support in Open Schooling, Project report for: Commonwealth of Learning (2008), `http://www.col.org/sitecollectiondocuments/mobile_technologi es_finalreport.pdf`

16. Sullivan, N.P.: Can You Hear Me Now? How Microloans and Cell Phones are Connectingthe World's Poor to the Global Economy. Jossey-Bass, San Francisco (2007)

17. Thorton, P., Houser, C.: Using mobile phones in English education in Japan. J. Computer Assisted Learning 21, 217–228 (2005)

18. Walton, G., Childs, S., Blenkinsopp, E.: Using mobile technologies to give healthstudents access to learning resources in the UK community setting. Health Information and Libraries Journal 22, 51–65 (2005)

Addressing Some Quality and Effectiveness Issues in E-Learning

Kin Chew Lim

Senior Lecturer and Research Fellow,
SIM University, Singapore
kclim@unisim.edu.sg

Abstract. E-learning has now been accepted and practised widely. However, many people are concerned about the quality and effectiveness of e-learning programmes. Invariably, they will be faced with questions like the following: Are the e-learning programmes meeting the learning objectives? Did the students like the e-learning? Did they learn what they were supposed to learn? Did they actually use the knowledge? How do we determine the quality of e-learning courses?

In an attempt to answer all the above questions, the author has taken the approach based on some current discussions and trends in the e-learning world. The author shared a few case studies in Singapore. In schools, much attention is placed on the use of sound pedagogical principles whenever e-learning programmes are rolled out. What about the effectiveness of e-training programmes like those for the policemen or the armed forces?

The author proposed a simple framework which can be used to measure the quality and effectiveness of e-learning programmes quickly.

Keywords: quality, effectiveness, activity, performance.

1 Introduction

In a recent project that the author was involved in, the client wanted to evaluate the quality and effectiveness of the e-learning courses in their organization. Specifically, the project entailed firstly, a thorough evaluation of e-learning features that support the pedagogical design of e-learning content and the instructional objectives. Secondly, the client wanted to have some measurable criteria for e-learning effectiveness. Thirdly, the client wanted to carry out an evaluation of the various teaching and learning domains, i.e. the facilitation, transference and retention of learning. Fourthly, the client also wanted to develop the key competencies of their learners, instructors and facilitators.

Increasingly, as e-learning becomes widely accepted everywhere, the author has observed that end-user organizations become more concerned about the quality and effectiveness of e-learning courses rather than evaluating cost and technology matters.

R. Kwan et al. (Eds.): ICT 2011, CCIS 177, pp. 167–176, 2011.

However, quality and effectiveness of e-learning are concepts and practices that are not so easy to define, specify and use. The purpose of this paper is to examine some of the issues and suggest some ways in which end-user organizations can adopt in order to evaluate the quality and effectiveness of e-learning courses.

In fact, there is "the need for a credible evaluation instrument to measure its effectiveness" as maintained by Allie Hodges of the University of Alabama [1].

2 E-learning Quality and Effectiveness

There are many definitions for "E-learning Quality". Claudio Dondi, President of the EFQUEL (European Foundation for E-Learning) and of SCIENTER (a non-profit organization, specializing in educational research & innovation) gave eight different sectoral approaches in the definition of quality in e-learning [2].

Another definition approach is taken by the European Observatory [3]:

"The predominant view is that quality relates to obtaining the best learning achievements (50%). Together with 'something that is excellent in performance' (19%), this primarily pedagogical understanding was more widespread than options related to best value for money or marketing."

The key points in such a definition approach are learning achievements and performance. These can constitute one way to define "effectiveness".

In an article [4], Ms Chua Hui Min, a reporter with the Business Times newspaper in Singapore, said:

"Effectiveness, rather than technology, is the key, and defining this is perhaps both the most difficult and important step in deciding how to invest in e-learning."

Although e-learning quality and effectiveness are intertwined, they need to be clarified so that specific tools can be recommended to attempt to quantify its influence and impact. It is more so in the corporate world as measurements must be developed in order to track the connections between learning, employee performance, and profitability [1].

The explanation on e-learning quality as given by the European Observatory is preferred by the author as it focuses on best learning achievement, excellence in performance and pedagogical understanding.

Similarly, it is pointless to try to define "e-learning effectiveness" strictly. Rather, the author has considered the explanations from a few authors [5]. The concept of "e-learning effectiveness" can be summarized as follows:

- Match between stated goals and achievement
- Doing the right things
- Different from "efficiency" (Efficiency means making the best use of the resources.)

- Based on evidence gathered through various procedures (e.g. inspection, observation, site visits, etc)
- Value-added process through quality assurance and accreditation review

The following diagram gives a simple visual representation of some possible performance measurements for e-learning.

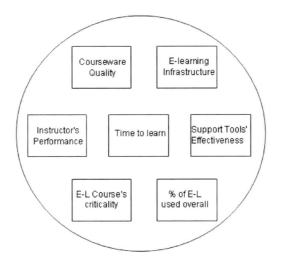

Fig. 1. Possible performance measurements for E-Learning

Jeffrey Berk [6] proposed the following criteria (performance measurements) to determine the effectiveness of e-learning courses:

- Instructor's performance
- Courseware quality
- Facility's conduciveness to e-learning
- Training vendor's customer service ratings (if using a vendor)
- Effectiveness of on-the-job support tools
- Effectiveness of learning (knowledge gain)
- Percentage of e-learning applied to job
- Time required for e-learning to impact job
- Percentage of time e-learning skills are used on the job
- Criticality of e-learning course to the programme

Effectiveness is something that is not absolute. Even in an organization, there will be different views on the effectiveness of e-learning. For example, in some organizational units, effectiveness is measured from an economic point of view.

Another organizational unit might measure it in terms of how much learning has been retained 3 months after the training has ended.

3   Some Examples of Quality and Effectiveness Initiatives

3.1   Quality Activities in Singapore Schools

Singapore schools have several quality activities. One initiative is called Quality and Excellence in Schools through Technology (edu.QUEST). This is a programme initiated by the Ministry of Education and it encourages teachers to learn about information and communication technology (ICT), provides them with project ideas, and connects them to other educators interested in sharing best practices. It also encourages teachers to be reflective practitioners by engaging them in action research.

The major challenge, according to Assoc. Prof. Tan Seng Chee, Head of the Learning Sciences and Technologies Department in the National Institute of Education of the Nanyang Technological University [15], "... is to encourage teachers to explore the various ways of using IT based on sound pedagogy. While it is relatively easy to learn a program, it is much harder to for a teacher to be convinced that alternative pedagogies will work [6]".

One example is as follows: students were asked to use the Internet to search for information. However, they were given only 15 minutes to discuss what they have found before they put up a PowerPoint presentation. They spent much of their time doing up the PowerPoint presentation.

In this scenario, one might ask, "What is more important? Discussing with your fellow students or spend more time practising your IT skills?" In the above scenario, the way the students use ICT neither transforms nor enhances the learning experience. The learning programme must address the crucial need of the students which in the above scenario is all about collaborative learning not practising more on using the PowerPoint software.

3.2   The SPOT-ON Projects in the SAFTI Military Institute (SAFTI MI)

Since 1997, the Ministry of Defence have adopted a Self-Paced On Time On Need (SPOT-ON) concept as the training philosophy for the Singapore Armed Forces. The SPOT-ON concept can now effectively incorporate online learning to further enhance the quality of training. SAFTI-MI capitalized on these advances in technology and have now launched many online learning programmes deliver training to their middle and senior level commanders before they join the residential phase of the courses. This initiative has greatly benefited the National Service officers in particular, as many of them have to travel overseas frequently. They can now study online anywhere and at any time before they come for the formal courses.

The SAFTI MI is also very particular about the quality and effectiveness of their online programmes. They have developed a Five-Ps management indicator to evaluate their online courses. The 5Ps stand for Purpose, Participants, Pedagogy, Process and Performance. The following table summarizes the explanations of the 5Ps:

Table 1. The 5Ps Management Indicator of the SAFTI Military Institute [7]

The Ps	Explanation
Purpose	Effect of e-Learning on meeting the organization's aim and course objectives
Players	Effect of e-Learning on the students and instructors
Pedagogy	Effect of e-Learning on adult education
Process	Effect of e-Learning on training system processes ranging from curriculum design to delivery
Performance	Quality of the end product

4   Proposed Quality and Effectiveness Model for the SIM University

Fig. 2 below is the proposed Quality and Effectiveness Model for e-learning courses in the SIM University:

This simple framework allows us to gauge quickly the effectiveness of the courseware and whether or not the e-learning course actually improves the student's learning.

Fig. 2. Proposed Quality & Effectiveness Model for UniSIM

5 Start with the Educational Considerations

In the evaluation framework, the author proposed starting the evaluation from the educational considerations. For example, the following eight educational considerations can be the foundation for an evaluation framework in an educational setting: outcomes-based, active learning, collaborative environment, student-centred approach, provision of learning styles, independent learning, feedback and reflection.

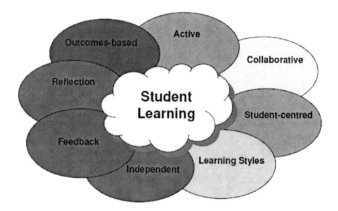

Fig. 3. Spectrum of educational considerations [8]

Based on these educational considerations, a quality criteria checklist can be developed quickly. Many other quality criteria (e.g. Prof. Merrill's 5-star rating for courseware [9], Brandon-Hall's Evaluation Criteria [10]) have been developed. However, these criteria might not be directly suitable for use in the end-user organization.

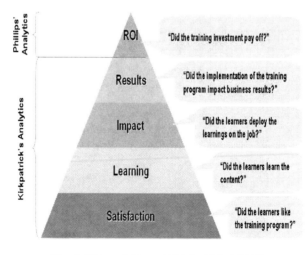

Fig. 4. Kirkpatrick's and Phillips' Model [11]

6 Kirkpatrick's Model

The other two levels in the Evaluation Framework are the first two levels in the Kirkpatrick's 4 or 5 Levels of Training Evaluation. The original model comprises only four levels. However, Dr. Jack Phillips added a fifth level called Return On Investment (ROI).

7 Example from SIM University

We have an e-learning course on the Principles of Graph Theory (MTH303e). This course has more than 80 topics. But with appropriate design and use of multimedia, the e-learning course can be engaging.

This course has been delivered to the January semester of 2010. Compared to this batch of students, the other batches in 2008 and 2009 did not have the e-learning course delivered to them. We then decided to do a quick evaluation on the quality and effectiveness of the e-learning course on the student's learning.

Based on our quality and effectiveness model, we first evaluated the courseware quality. Thereafter, we obtained the satisfaction feedback from the tutors. Finally, we obtained the test scores of students when they were doing their continuous assessments and their actual examination results.

An evaluation of the MTH303e course indicated that the courseware has been well designed; is easy to navigate; has enough quiz questions for practice and can engage the students effectively. However, there is just too much content.

In terms of the student satisfaction level, a survey indicated that the students valued the online quizzes which helped them to get better insights into their strengths and weaknesses in the Principles of Graph Theory. They did not think that using discussion forum would help them in their studies.

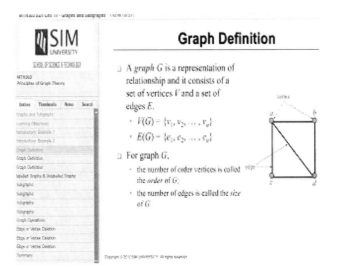

Fig. 5. Screenshot of the e-course on Principles of Graph Theory

In terms of their performance in their examinations, we compared the results of two groups of students. One student group studied using the e-learning course materials provided in our Blackboard Learning Management System (LMS). The second group did not or used little of the e-learning course materials in their study. The following two charts show the final overall performances of these two groups of students:

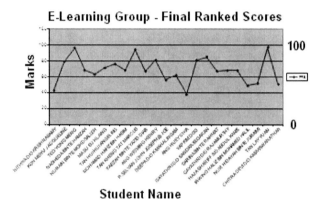
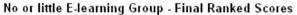
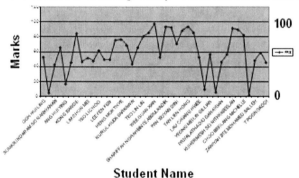

Fig. 6. Chart of E-Learning student group

Fig. 7. Chart of No or Little E-Learning student group

The average mark for the control group is 68.7 whilst the average mark for the non-control group is 59.8. There is a marked improvement of 8.9 marks.

8   Conclusion

Different organizations have different views about the quality and effectiveness of e-learning courses. For example, according to Claudio Dondi, President of EFQUEL

(European Foundation for QUality in E-Learning) [12] and of SCIENTER [13], if you come from the industry, then your quality view of e-learning would comprise items like conformance, interoperability, standardization, provision of scalable integrated learning services and product quality process. If you are in school education, you would be concerned about things like customer satisfaction, curricula integration, educational value and use of learning services, user-friendliness and usability of resources.

In the same way, there is no single definition for the effectiveness of e-learning courses. One view that can be adopted is on whether when some effectiveness parameters are being measured, the process can add value to the quality assurance.

The author has proposed a simple framework which allows educators and trainers to evaluate the quality and effectiveness of e-learning courses whether these are conducted in the school of in a corporate organization. This framework allows the quality of an e-learning course to be evaluated quickly. At the same time, the effectiveness of the e-learning course can be ascertained by taking the results of the learner's satisfaction survey and comparing the performance scores of the learner after he finishes an e-learning course. Other effectiveness performance measurements can be taken [6]. However, there needs to be a balance between taking more measurements versus the manpower and other resources needed to carry out the measurements.

References

1. Aptech's Lean Learning Wiki. (n.d.): Representation of Kirkpatrick's and Phillips' model of learning analytics showing level-wise measurement objectives,
   `http://leanlearning.wikispaces.com/file/view/LA_02.jpg/`
   `34068659/LA_02.jpg`
2. Berk, J.: Learning Measurement: It's Not How Much You Train, But How Well, The eLearning Developers' Journal (2003),
   `http://www.elearningguild.com/pdf/2/110303mgt-h%5B1%5D.pdf`
3. Brandon-Hall's Evaluation Criteria,
   `http://www.cognitivedesignsolutions.com/Instruction/`
   `TestingEvaluation.htm`
4. Chua, H. M.: Looking beyond cost savings in online learning. Business Times, Monday, BizIT Section (September 3, 2001)
5. Dondi, C.: Development of approaches to quality of eLearning at Universities and Enterprises level (2009),
   `http://www.elearningasia.net/_program/`
   `pdf_pt/%5BInvited%203-1%5DClaudio%20Dondi.pdf`
6. EFQUEL (European Foundation for QUality in E-Learning).: EFQUEL Presidents and Board of Directors (2010),
   `http://www.qualityfoundation.org/index.php?option=`
   `com_content&view=section&layout=blog&id=4&Itemid=135&lang=en`
7. European Quality Observatory, Quality in e-learning – use and dissemination of quality approaches in European e-learning (2005),
   `http://www2.trainingvillage.gr/etv/publication/download/`
   `panorama/5162_en.pdf`
8. Faculty of the Learning Sciences and Technologies Department, National Institute of Education of the Nanyang Technological University,
   `http://www.nie.edu.sg/learning-sciences-and-technologies/`
   `faculty`

9. Hawthorne, E., Tan, S.: Online Learning in Singapore Primary Schools: An Interview with Seng Chee Tan (2005), http://innovateonline.info/pdf/vol1_issue3/Online_Learning_in_Singapore_Primary_Schools-_An_Interview_with_Seng_Chee_Tan.pdf
10. Hodges, A.: A Literature Review on E-Learning and Its Effectiveness in Corporate Training Programs. The University of Alabama. Effectiveness of E-Learning (2008)
11. LTC Chan, A.: The SAFTI Experience in Using e-Learning to Complement Military Training (2002), http://www.cdtl.nus.edu.sg/link/mar2002/tech3.htm
12. Merrill, D.: 5-star instructional design rating for courseware, http://www.id2.usu.edu/5Star/FiveStarRating.PDF
13. Quality Research International, Analytic Quality Glossary – Effectiveness (2009), http://www.qualityresearchinternational.com/glossary/effectiveness.htm
14. SCIENTER. Claudio Dondi (2010), http://www.scienter.org/index.php/about/team/management/
15. Stephenson, J.E.: Educational Considerations for Blended Learning (2008), http://www.brunel.ac.uk/2812/entice1/BrunelUniEduConsiderationsv16.pdf

Peer Assessment Using Wiki to Enhance Their Mastery of the Chinese Language

Carole Chen[1], Kat Leung[2], and Gordon Maxwell[1]

[1] Caritas Francis Hsu College, Hong Kong
[2] Caritas Bianchi College of Careers, Hong Kong
{ychen,kleung,gmaxwell}@cihe.edu.hk

Abstract. This paper probes the responses of students to opportunities to participate in peer assessment in the context of Chinese language educational activities using the wiki-supported environment provided by a self-financing Hong Kong community college. Questionnaire items presented in anonymous format examined student willingness or reluctance to read peer essays and receive peer feedback, their preference for the type of feedback and the language used and their ideas or the desirability of using an on-line peer assessment system. Of the 25 questionnaire items given, all revealed positive levels of support for this on-line peer-based process. This finding was consistent despite some variation in the intensity of support within items. Perhaps most interestingly and educationally rewarding was the observation that the interactions generated by both assessor and assessed tended to deepen the quality of and interest in the learning process. The paper discusses the details of the questionnaire findings and concludes with some avenues for further work and suggestion for refinement of research protocols.

Keywords: Peer e-assessment, wiki-supported learning environment, Chinese language Learning.

1 Introduction

Though considerable number of overseas studies reported that Wiki could be a useful tool in supporting writing instruction and collaborative learning [1][2][3], Wiki so far has not been widely implemented in the Hong Kong education arena. In the past decade, only few attempts have been made to explore the learning effectiveness of Wiki in group projects and writing activities locally. Most of them were confined to the less accessible academic publications such as conference papers and dissertations by postgraduate students [4][5][6][7]. It is not surprising that to a large extent, the volume and depth of the related local works by no means can be compared to those of the non-Hong Kong literature. Another problem is that most of the extant local literature in the area of writing instruction using peer feedback was conducted in the context of face-to-face learning environment. Research on the use of e-feedback in the Hong Kong language classrooms is obviously an under-researched topic, not to mention the number of attempts specifically designed to contribute to the field of Chinese language education. Most importantly, the success of an emergent educational technology

R. Kwan et al. (Eds.): ICT 2011, CCIS 177, pp. 177–185, 2011.
© Springer-Verlag Berlin Heidelberg 2011

largely depends on the degree of which students accept and embrace it as a positive tool to provide them with meaningful learning experiences and opportunities.

In view of these considerations, an attempt is made to explore the potential use of Wiki as a collaborative learning medium for sub-degree students in the context of Chinese writing. Goals of the present study were to examine students' perceptions of: (a) the usefulness of a wiki-supported Chinese writing class, (b) their attitudes toward the process of online peer assessment, and (c) their choice of e-feedback type and language used. We envisaged that the present study will shed light on how Wiki and peer e-feedback can be best employed in a Chinese Writing class. It is hoped, too, that course designers and programme developers may use the research findings to better design, develop, and implement a Wiki-based programme/tutorials that promote positive attitudes toward collaborative writing in post-secondary Chinese language education.

The following paper begins with a review of the recent literature in the use of online peer feedback with special reference to instruction in writing, followed by the findings and analysis of a questionnaire study. Suggestions and recommendations for future research for refinement of research protocols are provided in the subsequent section.

2 Literature Review

A considerable amount of published work on the types of e-peer feedback and writing instruction have been done in the English as first / second / foreign language teaching and learning settings over the past decades. Most of the earlier research was conducted with technology designed neither for facilitating peer review or for responding to language writing tasks. In Liu and Sadler's study [8] eight freshmen university students were asked to comment on their writing partners' initial drafts of a journal assignment in an English composition class in which they were divided into 2 groups, each of which consisted of 4 students. The first group, the technology-enhanced group, used the commenting features in Word to perform peer review. The second group, the traditional commenting group, completed the same writing and reviewing activity using pen and paper in the classroom. It was found that the technology-enhanced group made more local alternative comments than the traditional commenting group. Though positive, the evaluative comments given by both groups were not revision-oriented in nature.

In the exploratory study by Guardado and Shi [9], 22 Japanese students from an English writing class in a western Canadian university were included to investigate their online peer feedback experiences. The Blackboard system was used to support the on-line peer feedback discussion. As reflected in the results, all the peer feedback collected included both positive and negative comments. Many negative comments were specifically revision-oriented.

Tseng and Tsai [10] addressed some aspects of e-peer feedback made by students using 184 high school students who were asked to comment and evaluate their fellow classmates' group projects in three rounds using an on-line peer assessment system in an anonymous manner. This study showed that suggestive feedback was helpful at the beginning of the peer assessment process and Reinforcing feedback was very useful in the development of student projects, while corrective feedback and feedback with lengthy explanation in a didactic tone had negative effects on students' project performance.

Some researchers on e-peer feedback have been inclined to analyze students' responses to peer writings drawn from the web-based systems which were specifically designed for peer reviewing. In research on the typology of student comments undertaken in two undergraduate and one graduate-level psychology courses, Cho et al. [11] found that directive and praise comments were the most frequent types of peer feedback made by the undergraduate students, whereas the graduate students tended to use more criticism explicitly than the undergraduate peers. In their study, both the undergraduate and graduate students conducted the peer reviewing activities in SWORD, a web-based system that participants were able to access from any internet-connected computer using standard Internet browsers.

Another study conducted by van den Berg [12] focused on analyzing the written peer feedback collected from two undergraduate and one graduate psychology courses at University of Pittsburgh. Again, the SWORD system was used by the participants to evaluate both qualitatively and quantitatively the draft academic essays of 6 other students. The finding showed that undergraduate students generated more praise comments than graduate students. On the other hand, graduate students produced more non-directive and criticism remarks than the undergraduate counterparts.

Van der Pol et al. [13] also studied the effect of using different media for commenting and interaction (Annotation system versus Blackboard) on the nature of comments produced by peer reviewers in the context of higher education. It was found that with the Blackboard discussion forum more evaluative comments were provided compared with the Annotation system. However, concrete suggestions were generated more often with the Annotation system.

3   Methodology

3.1 Setting and Participants

The study is part of a larger scale research on web-based peer assessment in Chinese language education conducted at a self-financing, post-secondary institute in Hong Kong. It is based on the data collected from 29 Hong Kong Chinese students who were studying in an Intensive training Programme (ITP) in Chinese Communication during the 2010-11 academic year. It is compulsory for all these students to attend the ITP programme because of their unsatisfactory performance in the HKCEE. They were in their Foundation year of the three-year Associate Degree when the study was conducted. Among the participants, the majority of them (65%) majored in Design and 35% of them majored in Business. Male students constituted 65.5% of the total sample, and the remaining 34.5% were female students. No more than 45% of the students had previous experience in providing and/or receiving online peer feedback in language course, while those who had participated in peer assessment prior the study, indicated that they had only been involved in similar practice once or twice before.

3.2 Procedure

The students were assigned to take part in online peer assessment via Wiki during the semester. The exercise was in anonymous format. A questionnaire survey was conducted to solicit students' perceptions and attitudes towards online peer review after the collaborative learning arrangement at the end of the semester.

The questionnaire comprised four sections. Part One consisted of 20 statements. A 5-point Likert scale format was employed to measure the extent to which the participants agreed or disagreed with a given statement. The response was coded as 5 for strongly agree, 4 for agree, 3 for neither agree nor disagree, 2 for disagree and 1 for strongly disagree and reported in means and standard deviations. On some occasions, percentage was used as a supplement.

The items in Part One were designed to reflect students' attitudes towards three main areas, including:

(1)   Reading and commenting on peer work (Item 1 to Item 5);
(2)   Providing and receiving peer feedback (Item 6 to Item 18);
(3)   The effect of anonymity on peer feedback (Item 19 and Item 20);

Part Two included 5 questions on participants' previous e-feedback experience in Chinese and/or English language studies.

In Part Three, three questions were designed to explore students' preferred types of peer feedback:

(1) Scope Dimension
     Scope dimension of a Chinese writing consists of content, organization, word choice and expression, sentence structure, punctuation, typo/misuse of Chinese character, format, length, and layout. Comments on content include those on the relevance of information, the clarity of the expression, and the logic of the argument, while those on organization include the ones on the inner consistency of the writing. Students were invited to choose one or more dimensions which they valued the most when receiving their classmates' comments.
(2) Affective language
     Affective language is classified in terms of praise, criticism, mitigation language, praise then criticism, and criticism then praise. Mitigation language is a kind of comment which provides compliment as well as criticism, and usually, compliment comes first.
(3) Function dimension
     It contains identifying errors and/or good points, offering corrections, and providing explanation of the errors and/or good points without offering a particular correction, and offering solutions to improve writing.

In Part Four, students were invited to provide their opinions of the pros and cons of using an online peer assessment system.

4   Analysis and Discussion

Data collected from the survey are analyzed in means and standard deviations (SD) for the items in Session One, and in numbers and percentages for questions in Session

Two, Three and Four, in order to reveal possible correlations between several variables and students' attitudes towards using online peer assessment system. The data is presented in Table 1, 2 and 3.

Table 1. Means and Standard Deviations for Part A of the Questionnaire (n=29)

Item	Questions asked	Mean$(\bar{x})$	SD
1	It is useful to read and comment on my classmates' work.	4.03	0.42
2	I would like to spend more time reviewing my classmates' work in the future.	3.66	0.55
3	Reviewing other students' work helps me organize my own writing better.	3.83	0.47
4	Reviewing other students' work give me ideas for my own writing.	3.93	0.59
5	My classmates probably found my comments useful.	3.69	0.60
6	I would prefer not to make comments on my classmates' writing.	2.93	0.84
7	It is difficult to comment on my classmates' writing.	2.92	1.00
8	I tell my classmate if I do not understand something they have written.	3.50	0.79
9	I tell my classmate if I like something they have written.	3.93	0.54
10	I have ever worried about hurting my classmate's feelings with my comments.	3.29	0.94
11	I enjoy commenting on my classmates' work.	3.55	0.63
12	I enjoy receiving my classmates' comments.	3.79	0.56
13	My classmates' comments help me when I revise my writing.	3.90	0.49
14	My classmates sometimes point out problems which I have not noticed.	4.03	0.57
15	I sometimes disagree with my classmate's comments.	3.69	0.60
16	It is not useful if my classmates only say good things about my writing.	3.07	1.00
17	My classmates' comments help me improve the organization of my writing.	3.86	0.44
18	My classmates' comments help me improve the language of my writing.	3.71	0.53
19	My comments will be the same no mater I know the writer's name or not.	3.86	0.79
20	My comments will be the same no matter my classmates know who made the comments or not.	3.83	0.85

4.1 Attitudes towards Reading and Reviewing Peer Work Online

There was a strong agreement that reading and commenting on others' writing online was a useful exercise both for themselves and for their fellow classmates in general (Item 1 $\bar{x}$ 4.03±0.42). The finding was echoed by the responses to Item 2 that most of the students were willing to spend more time reviewing classmates' writing in the future ($\bar{x}$ 3.66±0.55), and they were confident about the relevance of their comments on others' work (Item 5 $\bar{x}$ 3.69±0.60).

In addition, the responses to Items 3 and 4 demonstrated that most of the students considered reviewing others' work could help them either organize their own writing better or obtain more ideas or both (Item 3 $\bar{x}$ 3.87±0.47; Item 4 $\bar{x}$ 3.93±0.59). It was strengthened by their answers to the question in Part Four. Six students extended their affection towards the online peer assessment system with the reason that they could view and comment on others' work.

4.2   Attitudes towards Providing Feedback on the Web

Although most of the participants regarded reading and reviewing others' writing beneficial and they enjoyed the process of commenting others' work (Item 11 $\bar{x}$ 3.55 ±0.63), their attitudes towards providing feedback varied, according to the results from Item 6 ($\bar{x}$ 2.93±0.84) and Item 7($\bar{x}$ 2.92±1.00).

Table 2. Percentages for Item 6 and Item 7 in Part One

Item	Questions asked	Percentage of students (%)		
		in agreement	in disagreement	neutral
6	I would prefer not to make comments on my classmates' writing.	34.14	34.48	41.38
7	It is difficult to comment on my classmates' writing.	34.48	37.93	27.59

When responding to Item 6 'I would prefer not to make comments on my classmates' writing', 24.1% of the students agreed with the statement, 34.5% of them disagreed and 41.4% of them were neutral. A similar result was found in Item 7 about their self-esteem towards commenting on classmates' work: 34.5% of the students considered commenting on others' work difficult, 38% not difficult and 27.6% were neutral.

When the data from the two items were closely examined, it is interesting to find that 65.5% of the students chose the same score or scores of the same type (strongly agree and agree are considered of the same type, strongly disagree and disagree are considered of the same type) in Items 6 and 7. Among those who selected different types of score, 70% of them chose neutral in Item 6 and agree or disagree in Item 7, while 30% of them chose neutral in Item 7 and disagree in Item 6. It is reasonable to assume that students' willingness to provide feedback and their self-esteem towards providing comments were positively correlated.

Regarding the content of the comment, students agreed that they would tell their classmates if they did not understand something and if they liked what others have written (Item 8 $\bar{x}$ 3.50±0.79, Item 9 $\bar{x}$ 3.93±0.54). Nevertheless, 51.7% of the students indicated that they sometimes worried about hurting their classmates' feelings (Item 10 $\bar{x}$ 3.29±0.94).

4.3   Attitudes towards Receiving Feedback

The majority of the students enjoyed receiving comments from their classmates (Item 12 $\bar{x}$ 3.79±0.56), although they might not always agree with the comments by their classmates (Item 15 $\bar{x}$ 3.69±0.60). They agreed that peer feedback could help them to revise their compositions, and alert them to the problems they might not previously be aware of (Items 13 $\bar{x}$ 3.90±0.49; Item 14 $\bar{x}$ 4.03±0.57). They also agreed that their classmates' feedbacks could help to improve their composition structure and language (Item 17 $\bar{x}$ 3.86±0.44; Item 18 $\bar{x}$ 3.71±0.53).

Scope dimension. Data on this aspect revealed that students valued some of the scope dimensions higher than others. Comments on the contents of their writing were highly appreciated by the students (86.2%). Feedbacks about the structure (75.8%) and language expression (62.1%) were also valued highly. It was interesting to find that not many students cared for the format (24.1%) and punctuation (27.5%).

Table 3. Percentage of the Attitudes towards Scope Dimension of the Comments

Dimensions	Number	Percentage %
Content	25	86.21
Organization	22	75.86
Expression	18	62.07
Sentence	17	58.62
Punctuation	8	27.59
Typo/Character misuse	15	51.72
Format	7	24.14
Length	10	34.48
Layout	12	41.38
Others	0	0

As can be seen from an inspection of the data in Table 3, when the students were asked about the reasons of choosing such particular aspects, 18 of the total participants provided their opinions. Ten out of the 18 answers just revealed that the items they chose were more important or relevant than the other options; 2 of them provided specific answers, for example, 'good language expression could make the article easier to be understood', and 'a good writer should be able to use the least language to express the most ideas'.

Affective language. In Session Three, students voted overwhelmingly in favor of the comments in mitigation language (75.8%), followed by criticism (31%), praise (27.5%), praise then criticism (20.7%) and criticism then praise (17.2%). Some 58.6% of the students indicated that they expected comments which could point out the weaknesses of their writing while they needed some compliments to make themselves feel better.

The result was consistent with that from Item 16 ($\bar{x}$ 3.07±1.00). When responding to the statement 'It is not useful if my classmates only say good thing about my writing', 37.9% of them agreed with the statement, 37.9% disagreed and 24.1% were neutral.

The study showed that the students were willing to receive both praise and criticism, although they tended to give positive feedback rather than negative feedback in real practice (Leung et al, 2010).

Function dimension. On this aspect, students tended to receive the following comments in a descending order: offering solutions to improve the writing (65.5%), identification of errors (62.0%), explanation of the errors (51.7%), identification of good points (41.3%), explanation the good points (31.0%), and direct error correction (17.2%).

Compared with the findings in our previous research on the function dimensions of providing comments (Leung et al, 2010), what the students expected to receive and what they offered in practice were of the same order, that is, providing solutions, identification of problem/good point, and explanation.

4.4 Anonymity of Peer Feedback

In students' answers to Items 19 ($\bar{x}$ 3.86±0.79) and 20 ($\bar{x}$ 3.83±0.85), it was found that they might not adjust their comments if they know the writers' names or the writers were aware of reviewers.

4.5 Like or Dislike the Online Peer Assessment System

When students were encouraged to say why they were interested in using the web-based peer assessment system, 65.5% of them mentioned the convenience of using online system, while other advantages of using the system included 'the opportunity to review and comment on others' work', 'environmental friendly', and 'being able to learn from classmates' assignments'.

On the other hand, some students (34.4%) did not like the online system mainly because of technical inefficiency. Other reasons consisted of a small proportion of the total and included e.g.: 'not being familiar with others' writing topics' and 'not being able to increase the final mark'. It is, again, assumed that students' attitudes towards online peer assessment system were related, at least in part, to their IT efficiency.

5   Limitations of the Present Study

The study ran a risk of drawing a firm conclusion from what some might describe as a limited sample. More students will be involved the online peer assessment project and their perception will be collected in the near future in order to further strengthen theses findings.

6   Conclusion and Implications for Future Research

The present study demonstrated that students of post-secondary level in a self-financing institute tend to consider on-line peer assessment a beneficial practice in Chinese language learning. The system provides them a channel to review, comment and study from their classmates.

The data also strengthens our previous finding about students' commenting style and functional dimension of their comments. Mitigation language (i.e. compliment and then criticism) is again more acceptable than mere praise and mere criticism. Moreover, they expected and tended to provide feedback which could offer solutions to improve the writing or identify errors or explain errors.

The study revealed that self-esteem towards providing comments and computer efficiency were two relevant variables in studying students' behavior in online peer assessment. However, it is necessary to find out or confirm the correlation between the following pairs of variables, and determine which variables are the major ones in this kind of study.

(1) The positive correlation between the willingness to provide comments and the self-esteem towards providing comments;

(2) The negative correlation between language proficiency and the specificity of their comments; and

(3) The positive correlation between computer efficiency and the willingness to use online peer assessment system.

References

1. Rick, J., et al.: Collaborative Learning at Low Cost: CoWeb Use in English Composition. In: Proceedings of Computer Support for Collaborative Learning Conference, pp. 435–442 (2002) (retrieved February 3, 2009 from Google Scholar)

2. Forte, A., Bruckman, A.: From wikipedia to the classroom: Exploring online publication and learning. In: Proceedings of the 7th International Conference on Learning Sciences, Bloomington (2006) (retrieved January 30, 2009 from Google Scholar)

3. Chao, Y., Huang, C.: The Effectiveness of Computer-mediated Communication on Enhancing Writing Process and Writing Outcomes: The implementation of Blog and Wiki in the EFL Writing Class in Taiwan. In: Montgomerie, Seale, J. (eds.) Proceedings of World Conference on Educational Multimedia, Hypermedia and Telecommunications 2007, pp. 3463–3468 (2007)

4. Ma, W., Yuen, A.: Learning News Writing Using Emergent Collaborative Writing Technology Wiki. In: Fong, J., Wang, F.L. (eds.) Blended Learning, pp. 296–307 (2007)

5. Ma, W., Yuen, A.: A Qualitative Analysis on Collaborative learning Experience of Student Journalists Using Wiki. In: Fong, J., et al. (eds.) Hybrid Learning and Education, pp. 104–114 (2008)

6. Leung, K., Chan, M., Maxwell, G., Poon, T.: A Qualitative Analysis of Sub-degree students Commentary Styles and patterns in the context of Gender and Peer e-Feedback. In: Tsang, P., et al. (eds.) Hybrid Learning, pp. 149–159. Springer, New York (2010)

7. Leung, K., Maxwell, G., Chan, M., Wong, K.: Using Peer Feedback in a Wiki-supported Chinese Writing Class. In: 2010 International Conference on ICT in Teaching and Learning, Singapore (2010)

8. Liu, J., Sadler, R.W.: The effect and affect of peer review in electronic versus traditional modes on L2 writing. Journal of English for Academic Purposes 2, 193–227 (2003)

9. Guardado, M., Shi, L.: ESL student's experiences of online peer feedback. Computers and Composition 24, 443–461 (2007)

10. Tseng, S.C., Tsai, C.C.: On-line peer assessment and the role of the peer feedback: A study of high school computer course. Computers & Education 49, 1161–1174 (2007)

11. Cho, K., Schunn, C.D., Charney, D.: Commenting on writing: typology and perceived helpfulness of comments from novice peer reviewers and subject matter experts. Written Communication 23(3), 260–294 (2006)

12. van den Berg, I., Admirall, W.F., Pilot, A.: Designing student peer assessment in higher education: analysis of written and oral peer feedback. Teaching in Higher Education 11(2), 135–147 (2006)

13. van der Pol, J., van den Berg, B.A.M., Admirall, W.F., Simons, P.R.J.: The nature, reception, and use of online peer feedback in higher education. Computers & Education 51, 1804–1817 (2008)

E-Learning Design for Chinese Classifiers: Reclassification of Nouns for a Novel Approach

Helena Hong Gao

Nanyang Technological University
14 Nanyang Drive, HSS-03-05, Singapore 637332
helenagao@ntu.edu.sg

Abstract. Chinese classifiers are found to be a category that creates true challenges for second language learners of Chinese to grasp its meaning and use it easily. It is also found that even native speakers of Chinese may lose their competence in using classifiers appropriately after years of living in a non-Chinese speaking community. This paper presents a novel approach in the design of an e-learning tool for Chinese classifier learning and teaching. With this approach, Chinese noun categories are reclassified according to their associations with the types of classifiers. The design is based on both theoretical studies of Chinese classifiers and empirical studies of Chinese classifier acquisition by both children and adults. It allows users to use cognitive strategies to explore and learn with a bottom-up approach the associations of classifiers with nouns.

Keywords: e-learning tool, Chinese classifier, semantic features, agent based model.

1 Introduction

Noun classifiers are a typical feature of Chinese that distinguishes itself from many other languages. In simple terms, a classifier is a morpheme or word used to classify a noun according to its inherent semantic features. Noun classifiers in Chinese are obligatory as a category of its own and used to specify a noun when it is used with a determiner or a numeral. In other words, A Chinese classifier is never used independently. It must occur before a noun with a numeral (e.g. *yī* 'one', *sān* 'three', *wǔ* 'five') and/or a determiner (e.g. *zhè* 'this', *nèi* 'that'), or certain quantifiers (e.g., *jǐ* 'how many', *měi* 'every'). Such a combination is referred to as a classifier phrase.

However, the definition of Chinese classifiers is not a simple one. There are different types of classifiers in terms of their semantic functions. Some of them carry the unique features of the Chinese language; others are representative of the classifier languages, and yet all of them have the functions of measure words, which are of a universal category of all languages. Due to the complexity of classifier functions, different definitions and classifications have been found [1, 2, 3, 4, 5, 6, 7, 8, 9, 10]. However, generally speaking, classifiers refer to common properties of noun referents

R. Kwan et al. (Eds.): ICT 2011, CCIS 177, pp. 186–199, 2011.
© Springer-Verlag Berlin Heidelberg 2011

across domains and common relations of noun referents in the world, rather than to categories having to do solely with language-internal relations [11]. Some researchers take a functional approach and define Chinese classifiers based on their grammatical functions. For example, Chao [12] divides classifiers into nine categories. They are "classifiers or individual measures", "classifiers associated with v-o", "group measures", "partitive measures", "container measures", "temporary measures", "standard measures", "quasi-measures or autonomous measures", and "measures for verbs of action". From his classification we can see that he does not distinguish the concept of a classifier from that of a measure word. The advantage of such a classification is its inclusion of all the three types of classifiers mentioned above and being able to define them all as measure words, but the disadvantage is that those that are Chinese specific noun classifiers are all treated under the universal concept of measure words. This may be easy for learners to understand the grammatical functions of Chinese classifiers but the ontological nature of noun objects that classifiers are associated with is largely ignored.

In recent decades, researchers have started to take a cognitive approach to understand the links between nouns and classifiers and found it necessary to make a distinction between classifiers and measure words. For instance, Tai & Wang [13] state that "A classifier categorizes a class of nouns by picking out some salient perceptual properties, either physically or functionally based, which are permanently associated with entities named by the class of nouns; a measure word does not categorize but denotes the quantity of the entity named by a noun." This definition makes a clear distinction between a classifier and a measure word, which is believed to be helpful for second language learners to have a better understanding of the cognitive basis of a classifier system. This is because there are no measure words in English or other European languages that also function as classifiers in the same sense as Chinese classifiers do. A recent study done by Gao [14] has shown that Swedish adult learners of Chinese had a lower proficiency in classifier application than their general Chinese proficiency and that most of them were not aware of the difference between the concept of a classifier and that of a measure word. Another recent study done by Quek & Gao [15] shows that native speakers of Chinese tend to associate one noun with a number of classifiers based on their own perception and cognitive understanding of the shape and functions of the noun referent. We assume that this phenomenon would be mainly due to the fact that the cognitively based semantic properties of classifiers allow speakers to perceive and project the features of the associated noun objects from different angles or perspectives and that this phenomenon can be more distinctive in a Chinese speaking community where a number of Chinese dialects are spoken as well.

Other previous studies of classifiers include descriptive and experimental studies of classifier systems of natural languages. For example, some descriptive studies make typological surveys of classifier systems in different languages (e.g. [16, 17, 18]); others provide semantic analysis of classifiers and their associated nouns (e.g. 19, 20, 21]), and some also propose that there is an ontological base on which classifiers and nouns are associated with [22, 23, 24].

Experimental studies using computer technologies to apply findings of classifier knowledge to natural language processing (NLP) have provided a new approach for the semantic analysis of classifiers (e.g. [25], [26]) and for computer-assisted language learning (e.g. [27]). However, no e-learning systems developed so far are found to be able to guide learners to use the semantic properties to understand the links between classifiers and their associated nouns.

Yet, the emergence of computer-assisted language learning (CALL) provides language learners with a user-friendly and flexible e-learning tool. CALL incorporates technology into the language learning process and also applies itself across a broad spectrum of teaching styles, textbooks, and courses [28]. Its bi-directional and individualized features make it possible for learners to use it effectively to improve different aspects of language skills (e.g. [29], [30]).

My idea of designing the e-learning tool of Chinese classifiers is similar to that of CALL. Empirical studies have shown that classifier learning is a big challenge for second language learners of Chinese. My argument with regards to Chinese classifier acquisition is that cognitive strategies with a bottom-up approach are the key to the understanding of the complexity of classifier and noun associations. Therefore, the design of the e-learning tool has a focus on guiding learners to explore the cognitive foundations of classifier-noun relations. The e-learning system is implemented in the e-dictionary of classifiers, which is part of the design, to promote various ways of self-paced accelerated learning. It consists of a database of the decomposed semantic features of classifiers and their associated nouns. These well-defined unique and non-unique features will help learners take a cognitive approach to explore case by case the matched pairs of classifiers and nouns. Currently the e-dictionary has included 168 noun classifiers and 680 nouns, of which 80 classifiers and 560 nouns have been analysed and entered into the e-learning database. My aim is to define and include all Chinese classifiers and their associated nouns [1] and eventually link them to the e-learning system.

2　Multi-Categorization of Classifiers

In cognitive linguistics, categories are defined by groups of features and relationships within a same family. From this viewpoint, the occurrence of a noun with a particular classifier is dependent upon the categorical features of both nouns and classifiers. However, the internal semantic network of categories may be ambiguous due to historical and social factors, which make categorization dependent on not only noun referents' intrinsic properties but also their functional and human perceptual ones. In other words, classifier and noun associations encode as well human cognitive understandings of the real world entities. As a result, classifiers are found to be able to link nouns cross-categorically. That is, one single classifier can associate itself with a number of nouns from different noun categories and at the same time one single noun can be associated with not one but two classifiers. This multiple-categorization nature of classifiers complicates the classification of classifiers and nouns for the purpose of providing an effective learning strategy. It is also virtually impossible for linguists to build a meta-theory for a systematic organization of any clear logical classifier-noun

---

[1] Based on the 11 classifier dictionaries (see details in the References) consulted, the number of classifiers ranges from 143 to 422 and the number of associated nouns is from 388 to 8609. However, if we follow Tai and Wang's (1990) definition of classifiers, there are 178.

categories and thus hard for lexicographers to find an effective way to illustrate the semantic connections between classifiers and nouns. However, one thing we are clear about is that the main obstacles in classifier acquisition are that the inhabited meaning associations in the nature of classifiers are opaque and that the complex classifier associations with nouns have caused noun categorizations to be linguistically unconventional. Yet, from a cognitive viewpoint, these associations and categorizations can provide cognitive motivations to learners if we can provide a learning tool that allows them to pay attention to the pragmatic use of classifiers from a cognitive perspective.

3   Semantic Decomposition of Classifiers and Nouns

Table 1 is a demonstration of the semantic features of some most commonly used noun classifiers and their associated nouns. A total of 168 classifiers are collected and sorted out according to the number of noun categories each classifier is associated with. One special feature of this e-dictionary design is that the classifiers' associated nouns are grouped into categories based on the real-world entities as noun referents. Currently I have defined 11 categories and entered them in the e-dictionary. They are: "nature, humans & body parts", "animals", "vegetables & fruits", "man-made objects", "buildings", "clothing", "food", "furniture", "tools" and "vehicles". A hierarchy of noun classifiers is built up based on the number of the noun categories they enter into. For instance, the classifier *liàng* occurs only in the "vehicles" category, (e.g. car, lorry, bicycle, etc.) and thus it is ranked at the bottom in terms of complexity. Out of the 168 classifiers, 149 occur in fewer than 3 noun categories. The cognitive mapping between these 149 classifiers and their associated nouns are straightforward. Hence it is relatively easy for users to picture quickly how a classifier is associated with certain type(s) of nouns. For the rest of the 19 classifiers listed in Table 1, each occurs in at least 3 noun categories. At the current stage my work focuses on individual noun classifiers; the other types of classifiers will be added in the future when more people are involved in the project. In the e-learning part of the dictionary, I temporarily exclude the general classifier *gè* because pedagogically it is not a challenge and it is possibly among the first few classifiers that learners master in order to make grammatical phrases.

Through semantic decomposition, the cognitive mapping between a classifier and its associated nouns are revealed. Take the classifier *tiáo* for example. It is associated with nouns such as *rainbow, leg, snake, cucumber, road, scarf, potato chip, boat* and *necklace*, which are from 9 of the 11 noun categories listed in Table 1. Despite of the different categories they belong to, the 9 nouns share one same cognitive property – the shape of the noun referents, which we define as "longitudinal". This shows that the classifier *tiáo* is inhabited with this semantic feature as a cognitive basis on which speakers perceive it and link it to the nouns accordingly.

Similarly, the classifier *gēn* is used with the nouns such as *stick, bone, banana, pillar, sausage, needle* and *ribbon* that belong to 7 noun categories respectively. These nouns possess the same "longitudinal" feature as *tiáo*. This shows that extracting one same feature from *gēn and tiáo* is not helpful enough for learners to understand the differences between the two classifiers though classifying nouns into categories can constrain the cross-category interference to learners to some extent.

What needs to be carried out is to define each noun with a unique feature of its own, either from its lexical semantic meanings, pragmatic functions, or human perceptions. For instance, besides "longitudinal", "for walking" is added as a feature to *stick*, "a piece of human skeleton" to *bone*, "turns from green to yellow when ripe" to *banana*, "one end stuck to the ground" to *pillar*, etc. etc. until finally each noun is distinguished from other nouns that are associated with the same classifier. These definitions are the core part of the database for the e-learning tool linked to the e-dictionary.

Table 1. Classifiers sorted by the number of noun categories they are associated with

Classifier in Chinese	Classifier	No. of categories the classifier is associated with	Examples of nouns the classifier is associated with
条	tiáo	9 (nature, humans & body parts, animals, vegetables & fruits, buildings, clothing, food, vehicles, other man-made objects)	rainbow, leg, snake, cucumber, road, scarf, potato chip, boat, necklace
根	gēn	7 (nature, humans & body parts, vegetables & fruits, buildings, food, tools, other man-made objects)	stick, bone, banana, pillar, sausage, needle, ribbon
块	kuài	6 (nature, humans & body parts, clothing, food, tools, other man-made objects)	stone, scar, handkerchief, candy, eraser, soap
层	céng	5 (nature, humans & body parts, building, clothing, other man-made objects)	wave/fog, skin, building storey, curtain, paper
张	zhāng	5 (humans & body parts, food, furniture, tool, other man-made objects)	mouth, pancake, bed, bow, map
只	zhī	5 (humans & body parts, animal, clothing, vehicle, other man-made objects)	ear, tiger, sock, sailing boat, watch
粒	lì	4 (nature, vegetables & fruits, food, other man-made objects)	sand, cherry, rice, sleeping tablet
段	duàn	4 (nature, vegetables & fruits, building, other man-made objects)	wood, lotus root, city wall, iron wire
口	kǒu	4 (humans & body parts, animal, tools, other man-made objects)	person(people), pig, sword, well
面	miàn	4 (buildings, tools, furniture, other man-made objects)	wall, drum, mirror, flag
节	jié	4 (building, food, tool, vehicle)	chimney, sugarcane, battery, railway carriage
道	dào	3 (nature, humans & body parts, building)	lightening, eyebow, dam

Table 1. *(countinue)*

滴	dī	3 (nature, humans & body parts, other man-made objects)	water/rain, blood, ink
件	jiàn	3 (clothing, tools, other man-made objects)	shirt, (music) instrument, toy
把	bǎ	3 (furniture, tools, other man-made objects)	chair, knife, cello
截	jié	3 (nature, tools, other man-made objects)	rope, pencil, pipe
颗	kē	3 (nature, humans & body parts, other man-made objects)	star, tooth, artillery shell
片	piàn	3 (nature, food, other man-made objects)	leaf, loaf, tablet
枝	zhī	3 (nature, tools, other man-made objects)	rose, pen, arrow/rifle

4   Methodology

The database of the cognitive-based e-learning tool is designed with two types of words stored separately, one type being Chinese classifiers and the other Chinese nouns. A semantic decomposition method is used to classify and project the semantic features of nouns and classifiers on the basis of which their associations are made categorically. An agent-based model is applied for setting up the goal of making the e-learning tool select automatically classifier-noun associations as learners explore its functions to learn the different aspects of their associated semantic features. The method used in designing the e-learning tool makes it possible for its database to be used in its own as an e-dictionary of Chinese classifiers. It is easily accessed via an interface designed for quick learning.

The e-learning system has currently linked 11 classes of nouns (more will be linked later) with their associated classifiers. The feature-based classifications of nouns and the semantic decomposition of noun and classifier properties are able to show learners of Chinese the cognitive mapping of linguistic constructions. The proposed agent-based model utilizes the match between pseudo-binary-bit strings to indicate the probability of interactions between agents. It hence predicts how likely a classifier and a noun will occur in a classifier phrase.

4.1   Application of Cognitive Strategies in Noun Classifier Acquisition

In this section I will describe an approach that can enhance the practical use of the e-classifier dictionary. Developed in the software environment of FileMaker Pro 8.5 (see Fig.1), the dictionary is established on a database system. Categorical records created as data files are used to store the associated nouns. The records created so far include 11 categories of nouns described in Section 3. Such a categorization appears explicit, but its top-down approach fails to reveal the feature-based mapping between a classifier and its associated nouns. The objective of the e-learning approach, on the other hand, is to guide users to search for correct classifier and noun pairs by looking for the defined features of the noun referents, firstly from those broadly defined as "animacy", "shape", "size", "thickness", "length", "function", etc., then to those specific ones extracted from each particular noun referent.

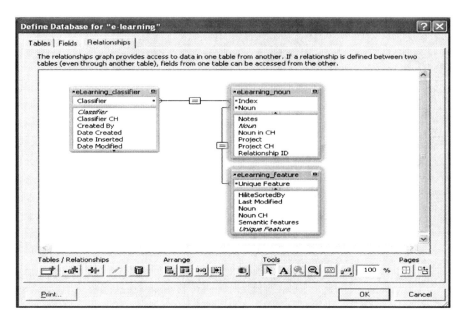

Fig. 1. A display of the database in the e-learning environment

With such a bottom-up approach, the e-dictionary allows users to learn the interrelated features of a classifier and its associated noun referents in a case-by-case fashion. In this way, learners can better understand the point that a classifier reflects the cognitive classification of its associated noun referents. Each individual record thus contains both general and specific information of a classifier and its associated nouns as data entries. The features decomposed from the noun referents are recorded as independent data entries linked to the e-learning tool. For instance, if a learner wants to know which classifier is the correct one for *boat*, he enters the word *boat*, finds its category as "vehicles", chooses its shape as "longitudinal" and then *tiáo* should automatically pop up because in this case *boat* is the only noun referent from the "vehicles" category (see Table 2). In other cases where there are two or more items that are featured as "longitudinal", the user will be guided to look for a more specific or unique feature with a few more clicks on the users' interface.

The e-learning environment in the dictionary also provides users the noun-classifier phrases that are commonly used but they may not be easy for learners to acquire. Take the noun classifier *zhī* for example. It is associated with noun referents that belong to "animals and body-parts" and "man-made objects", such as *bird*, *hand*, *pen*, etc. The unique perceptual features of these noun referents are identified but all are built into the e-learning system correspondingly so that users can click different categories in the interface to make particular associations as long as they have some general knowledge of the entities in terms of their functions and perceptual features.

Table 2. Examples of noun-classifier phrases of tiáo

English equivalent of Chinese classifier phrase	Classifier phrase in Chinese			Properties	
	numeral	classifier	noun	cognitive	intrinsic
a rainbow	yì	tiáo	cǎihóng	longitudinal	nature
a leg	yì	tiáo	tuǐ	longitudinal	human
a snake	yì	tiáo	shé	longitudinal	animal
a cucumber	yì	tiáo	huángguā	longitudinal	vegetable
a road	yì	tiáo	lù	longitudinal	building
a scarf	yì	tiáo	wéijīn	longitudinal	clothing
a potato chip	yì	tiáo	shǔtiáo	longitudinal	food
a boat	yì	tiáo	Chuán	longitudinal	vehicle
a rope	yì	tiáo	shéngzī	longitudinal	man-made tool
a necklace	yì	tiáo	xiàngliàn	longitudinal	jewelry

4.2   Implementation of An Agent-Based Model in Classifier E-learning

The e-learning tool linked to the classifier e-dictionary is targeted for automatic classifier-noun associations. By adopting an agent-based model [31], we [2] have developed a classifier-noun classifier network for users to learn step by step classifier phrases. Included in the prototype model would be nouns and classifiers, divided into two groups of agents. To design a semantic interface between the two types of agents in a computational perspective, a tag is attached to each agent. The tags are of opposite polarity, one to a noun, and another to a classifier. Each tag is a pseudo-binary-bit string of {0, 1, #}, where "#" is the "doesn't care" symbol. The position a symbol occupies in the string corresponds to a particular semantic feature of the agent, with "#" indicating that the corresponding feature is not critical for the formulation of the classifier phrase, even though the noun referent owns such a feature. When a noun agent meets a classifier agent, we line up the two tags and match the digits in one string with those in the other position by position. To report a match score at the end of this comparison, three match rules are listed as follows: (i) it scores 1 given there is a match between two "1"s or between two "0"s; (ii) it scores 0 given there is a match between a "1" and a "#" or a "0" and a "#" or between two "#"s; (iii) it scores -1 given there is a match between a "1" and a "0". The aggregate match score indicates the likeliness of a correct classifier phrase with the involved classifier and noun.

The first simple model is illustrated as follows. In this model each tag consists of 4 pseudo-binary bits. Out of the noun's many semantic features, we selectively

---

[2] Acknowledgements to Ni Wei, research student, for his contributions to the technical trials.

represent two of them: the first feature with the first two symbols, and the second with the last two. For example, a tag "1100" is assigned to the agent (noun) *leg* to represent the noun's features defined as "longitudinal" and "body-part" respectively. In this case, "longitudinal" might be considered as the most salient feature of *leg* with regards to the selection of a classifier. Hence, it is represented by "11". On the other hand, if "longitudinal" is by no means an external or internal feature of the associated noun referent, the symbols at the corresponding positions would be "00". Other possible combinations of symbols such as "01" and "10" are reserved for fuzzy states, which are associated with marginally accepted classifier phrases. Besides, the noun referent *leg* also has a "body-part" property listed, but it is not of primary importance for finding its classifier match. Therefore, it is represented by "##" at the last two string positions, rather than explicitly indicated by any of the four combinations mentioned above.

We assign the tags to classifier agents in a similar way. For instance, "11##" may be assigned to the classifier *tiáo*, due to the fact that *tiáo* often occurs in a classifier phrase with nouns defined as having "longitudinal" features. On the other hand, "##11" may be assigned to the noun classifier *zhī*, which is commonly applied to noun referents of body-part.

Regarding the agent's interaction with those agents of classifiers, when the tag "1100" of *leg* is compared with the tag "11##" of the agent *tiáo*, the match score is 1+1+0+0 = 2. In contrast, its match score with the tag "##11" of the agent *zhi* is reported as 0+0+0+0 = -2. The match score 2 indicates *tiao* is more likely to be linked to *leg*, and the match score -2 implies an undesirable match between *leg* and *zhī*. It is noteworthy, however, that if a user assigns "1111" to *leg*, they will obtain a match score of 2 (0+0+1+1) with *zhī*. They will hence conclude that, beside *tiáo*, *zhī* is another correct classifier for *leg*.

In addition, we include the defined features of nouns and classifiers as a group of interactive agents. Interactions between agents are controlled by tags and conditions defined with pseudo-binary bit strings. This group is designed to facilitate the learning process from learner's perspective. Let's take second language learners for example. First they may learn that *tiáo* is the correct classifier for *leg* because the noun referent of *leg* has the longitudinal attribute. Next, they tend to look for other nouns with the longitudinal feature, such as *necklace* and *snake*, and to verify whether *tiáo* is also the correct classifier for these nouns. By establishing the mapping between the defined features of nouns and classifiers, the agent-based model explicitly shows learners the possible connections between these groups of agents.

Among the semantic features, some are defined as unique features which distinguish their corresponding nouns from the rest in the nouns' group. For instance, we may define "chained jewel" as the unique feature of a necklace, and "limbless reptile, some of which produce venom" as that of a snake (see Fig. 2). We assign two kinds of tags respectively, one for non-unique feature agents and the other for unique feature agents. Each non-unique feature agent is attached with an adhesion tag [31]. When adhesion tags match, the corresponding agents group together – that is, they form aggregates. Thus, adhesion tags provide the possibility of forming multi-feature agent aggregates with individual unique feature agents.

To implement this feature, each unique semantic feature is attached with a two-segment tag: (i) the first segment plays the same role as the classifier/noun tag, which controls the agent's interaction with agents of other groups, i.e. nouns and noun classifiers; and (ii) the second segment functions simply as an adhesion tag. To decide whether to form a multi-feature agent aggregate, we can match a non-unique feature agent's adhesion tag and the second segment of a unique feature agent's tag. The match score is calculated in a similar way with that between noun's agents and classifier's agents. To simplify the discussion, we can state that adhesion only occurs between one unique feature agent and one or more non-unique feature agents. In other words, adhesion does not occur between either two unique feature agents or two non-unique feature agents.

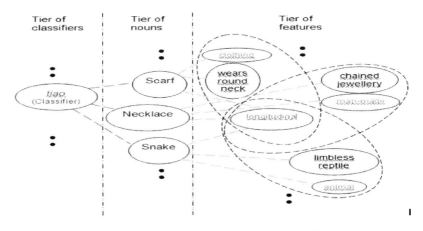

Fig. 2. Mapping among the tiers of classifiers, nouns, and defined features

To explicitly show the cognitive mapping between classifiers/nouns and their features, we use a collection of condition/action if-then rules [31]. In this model, both the condition and the action are linguistic variables, which are in turn represented by pseudo-binary-bit strings. The rules represent the interconnection among the agent group of classifiers, the agent group of nouns, and the group of defined features. For instance, the same noun classifier tiáo occurs in the classifier phrase yì tiáo xiànglián 'a necklace'. Let ①, ② and ③ respectively denote the features of "chained jewel", "man-made", and "longitudinal", where ① is the unique feature to identify the noun referent of necklace. As discussed earlier, the individual features ①, ②, and ③ can form a multi-feature agent aggregate, which we denote as ①②③. The if-then Rule 1 can be implemented as:

```
Rule 1: {If (①②③) Then (necklace)}.
```

Following the tag interaction approach discussed previously in this section, Rule 2 can be implemented to reflect the inter-agent communication between the noun and its classifier:

Rule 2: {If (necklace) Then (*tiáo*)}.

Based on these two rules, Rule 3 can be implemented as

Rule 3: {If (①②③) Then (*tiáo*)}.

Note that Rule 3 has the same input (condition) with Rule 1 and the same output (action) with Rule 2. Rule 1 outputs its action as a message, which is subsequently received by Rule 2 as its condition. This is an example of transitivity, a property of the rule-based network. The condition and action part in each of the three rules could also be exchanged to implement three inverse rules.

Now let's take the noun snake as another example. Given that ④ represents "animate" and ⑤ represents "limbless reptile, some of which produce venom", we can retrieve ③, ④, ⑤ from the features' group and form them as another multi-feature agent aggregate as ③④⑤. Here ⑤ is the unique feature of snake. We add another three if-then rules concerned with snake and tiáo as follows.

Rule 4: {If (③④⑤) Then (snake)};
Rule 5: {If (snake) Then (*tiáo*)};
Rule 6: {If (③④⑤) Then (*tiáo*)}.

So far only multi-feature agent aggregate, rather than single feature agents are used as conditions. It is also noteworthy that non-unique feature agents are incapable of interacting directly with noun agents or classifier agents, since their adhesion tags cannot be matched with the classifier/noun tags. The property of transitivity implies, however, that we can establish the mapping between nouns and non-unique feature agents indirectly. For example, we can represent the relation between the noun *necklace* and the unique feature agent ① "chained jewel" by Rule 7 as follows:

Rule 7: {If (necklace) Then (①)}

We also represent the relation between the noun *snake* and the unique feature agent ⑤ "limbless reptile, some of which produce venom" by Rule 8 as follows:

Rule 8: {If (snake) Then (⑤)}

Either ① or ⑤ is related with the non-unique feature agent ③ "longitudinal", which could be represented by Rules 9 & 10.

Rule 9: {If (⑦) Then (③)}
Rule 10: {If (⑤) Then (③)}

The mapping between *necklace/snake* and the non-unique feature agent ③ "longitudinal" could then be implemented by Rules 11 & 12.

Rule 11: {If (necklace) Then (③)}
Rule 12: {If (snake) Then (③)}

In Rules 11 and 12, the noun is taken as the input and its non-unique semantic feature as the output. By swapping the two kinds of agents' roles in the message-processing rules, we may inversely implement Rule 13 by taking the non-unique feature as the input and the noun as the output. If a user chooses ③ as the single input agent, two possible outputs pop up for his selection.

```
Rule 13: {If (③) Then (necklace or snake)}
```

More rules could be added in the classifier network by selecting different agents from the three groups, in a similar way as we implement Rules 1-13. With these rules set as conditions, the if-then rule-based network explicitly shows the cognitive mapping between the classifiers and their corresponding nouns. Learners will find out the association between the target words and their features that are essential for their classifier acquisition. So far we have tested the commonly used classifiers and their associated nouns selected from the e-dictionary and tried them within the agent-based model. The automatic matching is successful, though more pairs need to be tested.

5   Conclusion

This paper presents a feature-based approach in designing a classifier e-dictionary with an e-learning environment created for learners to use cognitive strategies to explore and learn the classifier and noun associations.

The current dictionary as a learning system is based on a database with classes of nouns (11 classes at present) and classifiers (168 added) that are stored as individual records. The records are not organized according to the lexical meanings of the words; instead, their classification schemes are built based on the noun referents' external or functional features. The objective of the design is to use such features to set up a classifier network that can automatically associate all possible nouns. A computer-based model with such a design is expected to show learners of Chinese the cognitive mapping of linguistic constructions. The proposed agent-based model utilizes the match between pseudo-binary-bit strings to indicate the probability of interactions between agents. It hence predicts how likely a classifier and a noun will occur in a classifier phrase. The relations among the agent groups are shown within the framework of the if-then rule-based network. Learners can explore case by case, within the e-learning environment, the classifier and noun associations and the defined features that the association is based on. A future task is to include the rest of the classifiers and all possible associated nouns. Linguistically, a challenge to carry out the task would be the definitions of the unique features of the nouns and classifiers that have fuzzy boundaries. Technically, the challenge would be the solution to making perfect matches of those cases where one classifier agent as input is expected to link a number of noun agents as output and demonstrate them effectively from users' perspective.

Acknowledgments. I would like to thank the editors, the two anonymous reviewers' valuable comments and suggestions on the earlier draft of this paper, research student, Ni Wei, for his assistance in testing the model, and Nanyang Technological University (NTU) for a grant to H. H. Gao for this research. A special thank-you note goes to Prof. John Holland for his inspirations and thought provocative questions raised in his series of lectures on language modeling delivered at the workshops organized by Santa Fe Institute, the Centre for the Study of Complex Systems at the University of Michigan, and Nanyang Technological University.

References

1. He, J.: The Prompt Understanding of Measure Words. Beijing Language & Culture University Press, Beijing (2003), 何杰《量词一点通》，北京; 北京语言文化大学出版社 (2003)
2. Yu, S.W., Zhu, X.F., Wang, H., Zhang, Y.Y.: The Grammatical Knowledge Base of Contemporary Chinese - A Complete Specification. Tsinghua University Press, Beijing (2003), 俞士汶，朱学锋，王惠, 张芸芸. 《现代汉语语法信息词典详解》. 北京：清华大学出版社，第2版 (2003)
3. Guo, X.Z.: Handbook of Modern Chinese Classifier Usage. Yuwen Press, Beijing (2002), 郭先诊《现代汉语量词用法手册》，北京：语文出版社 (2002)
4. Jiao, F.: Dictionary of Chinese Classifier. Chinese Teaching Press, Beijing (2001), 焦凡《汉英量词词典》，北京：华语教学出版社 (2001)
5. Lü, S.X.: Eight Hundred Words of Modern Chinese, 2nd edn. The Commercial Press, Beijing (1999), 吕叔湘《现代汉语八百词》（增订本），北京：商务印书馆(1999)
6. Jiao, F.: Learning Classifiers Through Pictures. Chinese Teaching Press, Beijing (1993), 焦凡《看图学量词》，北京：华语教学出版社(1993)
7. Yin, H.G.: Dictionary of Modern Chinese Commonly Used Classifiers. Shandong University Press, Jinan (1991), 殷焕光、何平《现代汉语常用量词词典》，济南：山东大学出版社(1991)
8. Liu, X.W., Deng, C.M.: Dictionary of Modern Chinese Noun Classifier Associations with Nouns. Zhejiang Education Press, Hongzhou (1989), 刘学武、邓崇谟《现代汉语名词量词搭配词典》，杭州：浙江教育出版社 (1989)
9. Chen, B.C.: Dictionary of Chinese Classifiers. Fujian People's Press, Fuzhou (1988), 陈保存等《汉语量词词典》，福州：福建人民出版社 (1988)
10. Guo, X.Z.: Handbook of Modern Chinese Classifiers. Zhongguo Peace Press, Beijing (1987), 郭先诊《现代汉语量词手册》，北京：中国和平出版社 (1987)
11. Lucy, J.A.: Language Diversity and Thought. Cambridge University Press, Cambridge (1992a)
12. Chao, Y.R.: A Grammar of Spoken Chinese. University of California Press, California (1968)
13. Tai, J.H.-Y., Wang, L.Q.: A Semantic Study of the Classifier Tiao. Journal of the Chinese Language Teachers Association 25.1, 35–56 (1990)
14. Gao, H.H.: A Study of Swedish Speakers' Learning of Chinese Noun Classifiers. Nordic Journal of Linguistics 33(2), 197–229 (2010)
15. Quek, S.L., Gao, H.H.: 马来西亚华语"一名多量"的认知基础之实证研究, 第十二届漢語詞彙語義學研討會論文集, An Experimental Investigation of the Cognitive Basis of Malaysian Chinese Speakers' Association of One Noun with Multiple Classifiers. In: Proceedings of 12th Chinese Lexical Semantics Workshop, pp. 232–243 (2011)
16. Allan, K.: Classifiers. Language 53(2), 285–311 (1977)
17. Allan, K.: Classifiers. Language 53(2), 285–311 (1977)
18. Lyons, J.: Semantics. Cambridge University Press, Cambridge (1977)
19. Goddard, C.: Semantic Analysis: A Practical Introduction. Oxford University Press, Oxford (1998)

20. Downing, P.: Pragmatic and Semantic Constraints on Numeral Quantifier Position in Japanese. Linguistics 29, 65–93 (1993)
21. Huang, C.-R., Ahrens, K.: Individuals, Kinds and Events: Classifier Coercion of Nouns. Language Sciences 25, 353–373 (2003)
22. Matsumoto, Y.: Japanese Numeral Classifiers: A Study of Semantic Categories and Lexical Organization. Linguistics 31(4), 667–713 (1993)
23. Sowa, J.F.: Knowledge Representation. Brooks Cole Publishing Co., Pacific Grove (2000)
24. Philpot, A.G., Fleischman, M., Hovy, E.H.: Semi-automatic Construction of A General Purposeontology. Paper Presented at the International Lisp Conference, New York, pp. 1–8 (2003)
25. Nichols, E., Bond, F., Flickinger, D.: Robust Ontology Acquisition from Machine-Readable Dictionaries. Paper Presented at the 19th International Joint Conference on Artificial Intelligence, Edinburgh, pp. 1111–1116 (2005)
26. Nirenburg, S., Raskin, V.: Ontological Semantics. MIT Press, Cambridge (2004)
27. Hwang, S., Yoon, A.-S., Kwon, H.-C.: Semantic Representation of Korean Numeral Classifier and Its Ontology Building for HLT Applications. Language Resources and Evaluation 42, 151–172 (2008)
28. Guo, H., Zhong, H.-Y.: Chinese Classifier Assignment Using SVMs. Paper presented at the 4th SIGHAN Workshop on Chinese Language Processing, Jeju Island, pp. 25–31 (2005)
29. Donaldson, R.P., Haggstrom, M.A.: Changing Language Education Through CALL. Routledge, New York (2006)
30. Mallon, A.: ELingua Latina: Designing a Classical-Language E-Learning Resource. Computer Assisted Language Learning 19(4), 373–387 (2006)
31. Chang, Y.-C., Chang, J.S., Chen, H.-J., Liou, H.-C.: An Automatic Collocation Writing Assistant for Taiwanese EFL Learners: A Case of Corpus-based NLP Technology. Computer Assisted Language Learning 21(3), 283–299 (2008)
32. Holland, J.H.: Hidden Order: How Adaption Builds Complexity. Addison-Wesley, Reading (1995)

Using a Conversational Framework in Mobile Game Based Learning - Assessment and Evaluation

Faranak Fotouhi-Ghazvini[1,2], Rae Earnshaw[1], David Robison[1], Ali Moeini[3],
and Peter Excell[4]

[1] School of Informatics, Computing and Media, University of Bradford, UK
[2] Dept of Software Engineering, University of Qom, Iran
[3] University of Tehran, Informatics Center, 286 Keshavarz Blvd., Tehran, Iran
[4] Centre for Applied Internet Research, Glyndŵr University, Wrexham, UK
Faranak_fotouhi@hotmail.com

Abstract. Mobile language learning games usually only focus on spelling or out of context meaning for the entire dictionary, ignoring the role of an authentic environment. 'Detective Alavi' is an educational mobile game that provides a shared space for students to work collaboratively towards language learning in a narrative rich environment. This game motivates and preserves a conversation between learners and their teachers, and also between learners and learners, whilst being immersed in the story of the game. A seamless self-assessment scoring system in the game structure provides a less dominating environment for students to expose their weaknesses, and at the same time assists students to judge what skills they have learned and how much. This game has produced improvement in different cognitive processes and a deeper level of learning during the collaborative game play.

Keywords: Mobile Learning, Mobile Games, Game Based Learning, Conversational Framework, Educational Assessment, Self-Assessment.

1 Introduction

In this article we propose a new approach to develop a conversational framework for educational games. Mobile learning provides teachers, experts and students with a unique opportunity to have a degree of presence in a number of different physical locations. Whenever the learner raises questions which cannot immediately be answered by the virtual world, then teachers and experts provide supplementary information to assist the learners, and allow teachers and learners to attain a shared understanding. Laullilard [1 and 2] has proposed a psycho-pedagogical framework for education that clearly defines the role and responsibilities of the teacher, the learners and the peers. In the first version of her model she uses Pask [3] conversation theory to represent her model. Pask believed that learning is basically a conversation between different knowledge systems (i.e. students, teacher and computers), where the system converses with itself and reflects on its actions and converses with other systems to share a description of the world. Pask believed learning is not to "transmit knowledge", rather, they provoke participants into becoming informed of each other's "informings" [3]. Pask made a distinction

R. Kwan et al. (Eds.): ICT 2011, CCIS 177, pp. 200–213, 2011.
© Springer-Verlag Berlin Heidelberg 2011

between knowledge of "knowing why" (cognitive, conceptual knowledge) and "knowing how" (procedural, performance knowledge)' [3]. Laullilard [2] constructed her first version of a conversational framework based on learning as a conversation. The framework had two levels of action and description. In action learners converse with each other while they are experimenting or doing practical work. In the description level, they discuss what happened in the action level, they ask questions such as "why did that happen?", "what does this mean?", and they offer re-explanation of theories and by means of justification and rationalization. Then she proposes a second version of the conversational framework [1] where she combines her representation of learning as conversation with other important pedagogical theories. She extracts all the important features of instructionism, social learning, constructionism, and collaborative learning, where each is emphasizing a particular aspect of learning. She classified learning into two levels of '(1) the discursive, articulating and discussing theory, ideas, concepts, and forms of representation; and (2) the experiential, acting on the world, experimenting and practicing on goal-oriented tasks' [1]. The teacher is added to the framework as an important element in formal learning. Teachers and learners converse with each other with 'repeated iterative interaction on both levels' [1]. The two levels connect with each other when the learners reflect on feedback received from teachers and other peers at a conceptual level or a practical level; teachers also reflect on the learner's actions and adapt the practice environment accordingly.

2   A Conversation Framework for the Detective Alavi Mobile Game

The Detective game is a vocabulary learning program using a technical context to help the Iranian students to use focused, goal oriented and effective learning approach to learn vocabularies related to computer's 'Central processing Unit'. The game can access a rich instruction set and provides continuous cognitive assessment, where a reasonable amount of time is spent on each word such as its meaning, spelling and form. Moreover it uses Laullilard [1] conversational framework in a natural, simple manner while players converse with real experts and virtual characters throughout the game. A series of puzzles are used to deliberately assess different aspects of vocabulary, while taking advantage of the communicative nature of implicit learning. The game strategies make the best possible use of implicit and explicit processes to achieve specific learning goals while learners consciously apply metacognitive strategies in acquiring new vocabularies. Figure 1 displays the main character of the game, 'Detective Alavi', while searching for clues to help players to solve a cryptogram. A clear sequence of dialogues was planned amongst virtual game characters according to the progress of cognitive processes to help students in their analytic journey. Progressing from one cognitive development to the next and increasing the complexity of the levels benefits the individual in their intellectual growth and matures and deepens their thought process [4]. The dialogues were accessible only in hierarchal order. This 'linearization' was set as a starting goal for solving each puzzle and for students to stay in the right track while having a free form of conversation. At the start solving puzzles could be extracted and inferred directly from the dialogues but gradually limited information could be found in the dialogues. Students need to analyse, compare and make choice from studying and discussing different resources and collaborate with each other and the teacher.

Puzzles and mini games were designed using QR tags printed on pieces of paper. These visual tags contain information that could be accessed via a mobile phone camera using the 'Camera' option the game's option menu (see Figure 1). QR codes are two dimensional bar codes that are read on camera phones using QR reader software. Once they are accessed, they allow players to complete an action. QR codes launch and redirect a phone's browser to an embedded URL, or initiate a phone call, or send an SMS or simply present some text. This technique helps the learners to collect data from puzzles and transfer them to their own game virtual space for further analysis. These tags can also activate access to mobile space and cyberspace, and act as a dynamic hub for accessing further help and learning resources.

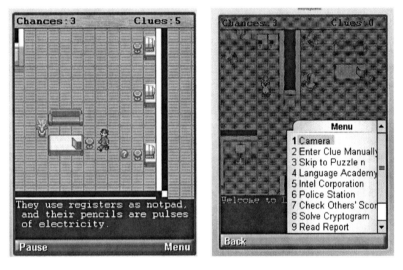

Fig. 1. (a) Print screens from the Detective Alavi's Main Play Environment (b) Detective Game's Option menu

There are different clues distributed in QR puzzles to solve a cryptogram. At different stages during the game play, the player is asked to find the necessary clue. The player captures the clues by the camera and then the player uses 'check clues' option to check if he/she has captured the right clue (see Figure 2).

The puzzles were flexible, and the teacher could easily change the puzzles and produce new QR tags. There was both flexibility in content and connections, and challenges were provided by both virtual and real space information. Teachers had a game framework that they could easily customise without needing technical knowledge. It met the teacher's needs by motivating and assessing students continuously. Teacher could use the skills that were familiar to her like managing discussions and guiding students to customise the game framework for the classroom.

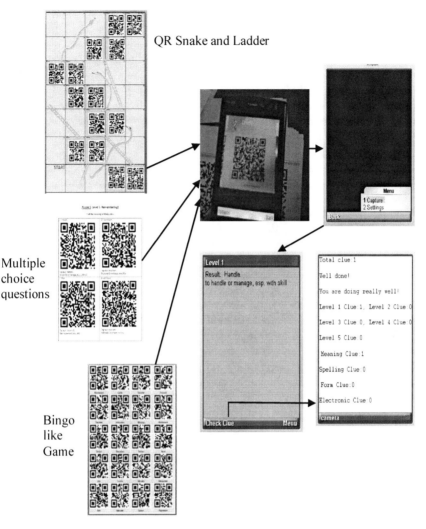

Fig. 2. The process of capturing a clue

Distance experts were encouraged to take part in students' discussion whenever called. This was carried out by pointing out the problem, providing interesting examples and posing provoking questions within the story's theme. They encouraged students to learn from each other and did not give the answers directly. At the same time they kept the conversations short and to the point because the game was still part of the classroom space.

3 Game's Assessment

Similar to any educational programs educational games' incorporation in education requires assessment and evaluation. Thirteen students from the third year of

Computing Engineering in an Iranian university were selected. At first the electronic concepts of the computer's central processing unit was taught in English via a comprehension in normal classroom. Then a test was taken to investigate students' knowledge of technical vocabulary, considering 'vocabulary meaning', 'spelling', 'word form' and 'electronic knowledge' in English. These skills were examined at different cognitive levels; the questions were designed according to the Bloom' taxonomy of learning objectives. After this, the participants took part in playing the 'Detective Alavi's game that were intended for improving the students' technical vocabulary within the boundary of the previously taught comprehension. The game sessions lasted 2 hours for six weeks during November to December 2010. The game was played privately in a classroom. The teacher integrated the game as part of a lesson, letting students play one level of the game at each session for them to become familiar with the CPU structure, its functions and key technical vocabularies. Puzzles were printed by the teacher and supplied to the students. Students were typically free to move around, as long as they did not exceed a 10 metre distance between their devices (to ensure Bluetooth wireless communication stays connected).The game play was also extended to the different rooms of the university building with computer rooms. Puzzles were distributed throughout the building in different locations in each room. During the execution, rooms were chosen to show as close a resemblance to a room in the CPU complex's virtual space as possible, with a label such as 'Level 2-Room 2'. Puzzles were hidden in different locations in each room. Players could find them using guidance from the virtual space's characters. People from the real world such as university staff and other students could also become part of the game, making conversation with the players or providing extra assistance. Players needed to note that in this mode the Bluetooth connection of the game will be lost when they became more than 10 metres apart. When the game sessions' period ended, a post-test was taken by the students. It was then analysed to see whether there had been any differences between the pre-test scores and the post-test scores. The paired t-test was used to compare and analyse each student's pre and post- test. Some students developed more and others improved less. But on average there was a substantial improvement.

Detective Game has improved different skills. The 'Electronic Skill' by 53.25%, the 'Word Meaning Skill' by 34.8%, the 'Word Form skill' by 24.69% and the 'Spelling Skill' by 19.23%. The two-tailed P value for all skills was 0.000 which was less than 0.05. This difference was considered to be statistically significant.

The detective Game has improved the students' reporting skills gradually during level 1 to 5. It has increased the 'Reporting skill' at level 1 by 1.53%, at level 2 by 10.76%, at level 3 by 32.30%, at level 4 by 41.53% and at level 5 by 61.53%. The two-tailed P value in level 1 and 2 were 0.337and 0.068 which were more than 0.05. At these two level students still lacked the necessary reporting skills. At level 3, 4 and 5 the two-tailed P value was .000 which was less than 0.05 which means a statistically significant improvement on reporting skill.

This game has improved all cognitive processes. It has increased the 'Remembering' cognitive process by 43.58%, the 'Understanding' cognitive process by 21.97%, the 'Applying' cognitive process by 30.76%, the 'Analysis' cognitive process by 20.51% and the 'Evaluation' cognitive process by 56.15%. This improvement was especially evident when the students utilized the game for the critical thinking in level 5. The improvement was lower in level 2, 3 and 4 that they more focused on spelling or word forms. This game was more suitable to improve student's electronic skills and word meaning skills by encouraging them to think deeply and collaborate with their peers and teachers. However the two-tailed P value at all levels was .000 and less than 0.05 which means a statistically significant improvement has took place at all levels.

All students (denoted by Sts) experienced an increase in their test results. The rise in the test scores amongst different groups was Group 1 (St 1, 2, 3 and 4) by 32.19%, Group 2 (St 5, 6 and 7) by 37.28% , Group 3 (St 8, 9 and 10) by 22.87% and Group 4 (St 11, 12 and 13) by 32.19%. The more advanced students helped students with lower language skills to improve. If the team scored higher in the game as a group, they achieved higher test results compared to the groups with a lower gaming score.

The Pearson correlation test was performed regarding the students' game score with their post test results. The correlation coefficient was 0.731 which was positive and it indicated that there is a direct relationship between the total game score and the test result. The relationship was strong because it was more than 70 % of its possible value (i.e. the coefficient maximum value is 1 or -1). The game scoring that was achieved in the game play appears to be an important predictor of the students' individual test results. Our sample accurately reflects the relationship between the game scoring and the students' results from which the sample was drawn (labelled as Sig. (2-tailed)). The probability value was 0.004 which was well below the conventional threshold of $p < .05$. Thus, our hypothesis was supported.

4   Students' Learning Processes during the Classroom Observations

Students have been normally passive and quiet in English classes and rarely engaged in discussions. When the game sessions first started students felt reluctant to work collaboratively but gradually they succeeded in integrating the appropriate skills with the aid of game narrative, graphics, QR puzzles, distance experts and their teacher.

4.1   Remembering Level

Their communication at level 1 was in monologue form where each member spoke their ideas by remembering important vocabularies, recognising and listing embedded facts. They retrieved and searched for further information in the game's virtual space with the help of the on-site teacher. Signs of 'surface level processing' were present in some learners where they only focused on guessing the right answer or asking the teacher for the answer. However the teacher encouraged them to further research the game environment to make them think further by exploring the full capacity of the game. The following dialogues are extracted from students' conversations in level 1:

St1: Ms what does 'manipulate' mean in Farsi? (Asking the on-site teacher)

Teacher: You have already seen this word!

St2: I remember the word 'manipulate' from puzzle one. I am sure A is the wrong answer.

St3: Just by looking at the answers it tells you which one is correct! I go for option C (surface level processing)

St3: Oh it is wrong!

Teacher: Why do you think option C was wrong?

St1: Ms what is 'binary system'? I can't find it in the 'Language Academy'! (asking the on-site teacher).

Teacher: Try 'Intel Corporation'!

St1: No I can't find it there.

Teacher: Let's see we can find it by trying this link; you have to go to the camera and take a shot of this QR code.

St3: Oh camera failed!

Teacher: Let me try, don't shake your hands, it needs good exposure to light..., now it is opening the website.

St2: I have never worked with mobile web...

Teacher: It is not much different; this is how it works.....

St1: Here it says: 'Binary system is ....'.

St2: Oh I know it is our 'dodoi (in farsi) 0 and 1 system!

4.2   Understanding Level

In level 2 the on-site teacher has stepped in and acted as a member of the group, and she encouraged students to talk to each other by asking questions. Students practiced the meaning and spelling of the vocabularies. However when they were asked to choose the correct order of operation in the CPU Complex in puzzle 9, most conversations were evoked. They became involved in explaining, interpreting, summarising, paraphrasing and classifying the facts. The following dialogues are extracted from students' conversations in level 2:

St1: I can't fully understand 'when it finds a μop ready to process, the unit executes it'.

Teacher: Can you help us with this sentence St2?

St2: In other words the 'dispatch/execute unit' temporarily stores the results of executions.

St3: Execution of microoperations....

Teacher: So you are saying that......

4.3 Applying Level

In level 3, communication gradually turned into dialogue and students managed to maintain a group conversation. A Bingo like game was incorporated which required deducing the correct vocabularies' synonyms. They also had to choose an option which associated the appropriate processors components to their correspondence operations. At this stage they used the game resources automatically. They shared concepts and opinions by exchanging ideas, asking questions, giving the correct direction, encouraging or supporting each other, elaborating other member's explanations, relating to the previously learned materials and using the tables and diagrams.   The following dialogues are extracted from students' conversations in level 3:

St2: How we have to approach this puzzle?

St1: Let's see what the Dr Athlon has to tell us....

St3: We work through this logically; he provided us with this diagram...The decoder converts instruction to macrobytes.

St2: And Mr 'Register' explained how the ROB manages the execution and management of macrobytes,

St3: Well done!

St2: But what about FPU 3D?

St3: I don't know! But let's keep working!

St1: I think it has something to so with multimedia,

St3: Sounds right!

St1: I suggest we hold off making a decision until we have examined all our options. If we look at this link we visited last week we will get a better idea.

St2 – Let's see what we have missed?

4.4 Analysing Level

In level 4, Students practiced the word forms through a QR board game. Then they utilized tables from different processors' specifications to discover processors' capabilities. Their dialogue turned into comparing, organising and deconstructing information from different resources to help them analyse different problems. The following dialogues are extracted from students' conversations in level 4:

St1: Ms is it possible to tell us a brief history of the microprocessor? (Asking the on-site teacher)

Teacher: You can ask the Intel CPU's expert by making a phone call!

St1: Let's call the 'Intel' expert to give us a brief history of the microprocessors.

St3: What is the actual question here?

St2: We want to know about clock speed and MIPS.

St2: Could you please tell us more about the clock speed and MIPS... (talking)

'Intel' expert: Dr Intel suggests if you look at the table, you can compare 8088, 80386 and 80486 MIPS values...

St1: Let's see what are our facts?

St3: 80286's value is 1.

St2: Why did you make this choice?

St3: 3 and 4 are too big!

4.5 Evaluating Level

Finally in level 5, students made decisions based on in-depth reflection, criticism and assessment about word forms and complex CPU operations. The communication became dialectic where they started to manage cognitive conflicts by criticising and evaluating each other's ideas, integrating different opinions and participating in debates and enquiries.   Students expressed their views, listened to others, asked relevant questions purposefully and judged group's understanding. The following dialogues are extracted from the students' conversations in level 5:

St3: Let's get moving! Detective Alavi really needs this clue! Do you know how Quad compares with dual?

St2: Let's call the expert to clarify the advantages and disadvantages of Quad and dual core.

St1: Ringing CPU expert.....talking......Is it possible for you explain to us how the quad core of say 2.5ghz perform better than a dual core of 2.8ghz?

Expert: 'Professor Speedfast' has told me that you will notice quite an improved performance on a quad, especially if the software is adapted to using it.

St3: But the dual core has the higher clock speed!

Expert: In Dr Athlon's opinion, Quad core uses resources more efficiently switching between threads and processes.

St2: Does she think we will ever see more than 2.8 GHz?

Expert: No, she says it is about cooling, not overheating the cores.

St2: Future is multicore, isn't it true?

St3: But now it is debatable!

St2: Still I suggest to Professor 'Multicore' if he wants to modernise the CPU complex, it is better to buy Quad core, things change quickly.

Expert: I will pass on your message!

St1: I understand 4 cores, is doing 4 things at the same time. 1 core does one thing at a time. If we have a program written for 1 core surely this must execute faster in quad core?

Expert: Professor Multicore thinks it causes massive problem, each core wants to execute part of the problem, they all get kind of confused! ….(laughing not giving the answer) this is as far as I can help you guys! Mr Inspection is calling me! Bye for now!

St1: We can try the first link; it is about the 'Intel Core 2'.

St1: The website has all the technical stuff about the dual code, but not giving anything on two CPU's comparison.

St2: Here it says….

St1: It is kind of confusing! We can't compare them just on one or two factors.
……

A deep level of understanding was present in levels 3, 4 and 5 when students worked on the puzzle with more provocative questions that examined the students' applying, analysing and evaluating power. In these challenges students made plans to solve problems, used diagrams, suggested ideas, connected ideas logically, used their past experiences and changed or refined their opinion in the process. QR word search and board games seemed to create a more cheerful and relaxed environment. Conversations drifted to more general dialogues which represented the social development processes rather than cognitive ones. It benefited the students' bonding rather than deep processing. During the game sessions the learners appeared to be constantly moving in and out of reality and blurring the distinction between real and virtual. The game virtual space and the experts at a distance maintained the fantasy aspect of the game, while the websites and their previous educational or life experiences brought them back to reality. This periodic experience of realism and fantasy helped the game play to maintain the necessary control and the flow of learning in an authentic, meaningful and contextual environment.

5 Self-assessment

In the game environments players might develop wrong intuitions by haphazardly diving in the game. They do not know when their hypothesis is correct and when it should be discarded. The presence of some kind of assessment appears to be necessary. However direct surveillance of students' work could inhibit their intrinsic motivation and reduce their sense of control. Adding a self-assessment system in game scoring could assists students to evaluate their own actions in a non-controlling environment. On the other hand, teachers need to use a continuous assessment to supply them with consistent, accurate and useful information on students' knowledge. In normal classroom assessments, the results are collected too late and they are only used for student's grading. During the teaching sessions teachers have no idea if students have actually learned. The end of term results, often are disappointing to teachers and there is a large gap between what is taught with what is learned. Thus the teachers and they have little or no influence on the learning process and cannot remedy the student's gap in knowledge because they have no real-time information about this.

Self-assessment in the game was in the form of scores, skills gained and cognitive progress. Figure below shows how players could check their progress during the game. They can choose 'Skill-Score-Cognition' option from the game's main menu.

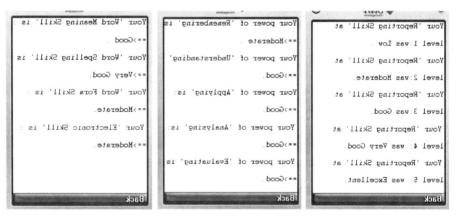

Fig. 3. (a) Skills' progress screen (b) cognitive progress screen (c) reporting progress

There are different kinds of clues that were included in each game level. Clues were categorized according to the type of skill gained during solving puzzles; 'meaning', 'spelling', 'form', 'electronic'.

Each game level targets a separate cognitive level of Bloom's learning objective taxonomy of *remembering, understanding, applying, analysis and evaluating cognitive progress* [4]. The total number of clues in each level provides the specific level's degree of strength, the table below shows the process of score allocation and corresponding feedback.

Writing restructures knowledge [5], improves thinking by making ideas explicit and contributes to critical thinking [6]. At the end of each game level the 'Read Report' item could be selected from the game menu which represents bloom's sixth level of cognitive progress i.e. *'Creating'*. This option involves students' writing a report of all their game experiences according to the game's learning objectives and a description of each clue. A list of 'learning objectives is presented from the main menu's 'Learning Objectives' item. The actual account of each learning object is narrated by dialogues that are carried out amongst the virtual characters and between teachers and students. When the players select the 'Read Report' a phone call is activated to a teacher at distance and a secret code will be provided according to the players' broadness in understanding of the topic. These codes represents any of six feedbacks : 'very low', 'low', 'moderate', 'good', 'very good' and 'excellent'. Each feedback assigns its specific gain in 'Reporting Skill'.

6   Game's Self-assessment User Experiences

In Detective game, the teacher believed to be empowered in examining at any stage during the game: (a) how students were responding to the learning environment? (b) how students were doing at initial or intermediate stages? (c) what were the students' current abilities or gaps in knowledge? (d) how to help students with early appropriate feedbacks? (e) how to improve next level of game and provide more information on skills that were yet unsatisfactory (f) to build an on-going communication loop to students providing them with appropriate feedback (g) to save time on collecting the responses and analysing them. Self-assessment had also assisted students to discover their weaknesses and strengths continuously during the learning session anonymously in a stress free environment. They were encouraged to take the responsibility to work on correcting themselves and adjusting themselves to the syllabus standards. The on-site teacher has observed the following statements usually when students checked their progress:

I think our 'spelling' is good!

We seem to be confused about the meaning of technical words.

I think it is necessary to improve our electronic knowledge. It is useful to visit this web site.

We need to learn more about the word 'form'. We have to play that board game again.

I am going to spend more time studying word meanings.

Look! Our analysis power has increased!

The self-assessment increased the metacognition behaviours amongst the learners. Students monitored and evaluated their progress towards certain educational goals regularly. They also planned specific steps and strategies to improve their weaknesses, correcting their cognitive process and enhancing their performance. The use of metacognition strategies by the students has been mentioned by many researchers as an important variable during thinking processes [8 and 9]. Halpern [10] has mentioned the metacognition process as a crucial element during the critical thinking.

7   Detective Alavi's Cost Efficiency versus Conventional Method

For a class of 30 students the cost of Detective game is 251552 Rials (15.2 GBP). If the students use university's WiFi the price decreases to 123552 Rials (7.46 GBP) for a group of 30 students. These costs compared to the cost of lecturers that often travel from Tehran (capital city) to smaller cities is very small. Lecturers have to travel by plane which a return ticket costs 72.53 GBP, and they normally charge the university 40% more than normal lecturers. Detective Alavi when using GPRS is 80% more cost effective than normal lectures and when using WiFi is 90% more efficient.

8   Discussions and Conclusion

In constructive learning, the learner constructs knowledge by discovery and enquiry [11], [12] and [13]. Direct instruction is not acceptable; however students need some instruction at the beginning. They have to slowly build up knowledge and be able to experiment with their ideas in real world. On the other hand, if the learner has difficulties with a problem, it is more effective to provide some direct instruction rather than allow the learner to waste valuable time by trial and error. This mode of learning often results in covering only a small amount of content, which makes it difficult to address the extensive curriculum of formal education.

The Conversational framework combines different modes of learning into one overall learning approach. Considering the unique nature of mobile learning we have designed the game's architecture using the conversational framework. To begin with students were unable to fully implement the constructivist philosophy of the conversational learning. Students focused on the content of virtual character's dialogues and approached puzzles as a memory task. They depended on teacher's authority and required explicit approval to move to the next task. However as the game sessions continued, students started sharing the authority with the teacher and mediating their own learning. This new authority transformed to a shared responsibility, fully exploring the potentials of the game, paying attention to the material and having active role on their learning. A continuous interaction between students, teachers, context and the learning material was shaped. This interaction was in conversation format and in its most productive nature led to a shared point of view over the curriculum objectives that were embedded in the game story.

On the other hand constructivists pay less attention to standard evaluations and their belief is students themselves must judge if they have learned [11] and [13].

Only careful analysis of the student's work will determine how much they have actually learned and what the next step in their education should be. In our game the essence of meta-cognition (i.e. self-monitoring and evaluation) was planned, which has been realized. The game fully implemented the hierarchy of learning objectives in the game structure.   The cognitive process hierarchy was implemented fully and sequentially using five game levels.   This structure motivated students to master the basic level first and take part in assessment and evaluation. *The game* challenges stimulated the recall of prior knowledge by new challenges referring back to things learned in previous levels. This enhanced retention and transfer of knowledge, challenges were graduated initially could be handled individually to the final performance level needing collaborative work.

References

1. Laurillard, D.: Rethinking University Teaching: A Framework for the Effective Use of Educational Technology. Routledge, London (1993)
2. Laurillard, D.: The pedagogical challenges to collaborative technologies. Computer-Supported Collaborative Learning 4(1), 5–20 (2009)
3. Scott, B.: Gordon Pask's Conversation Theory: A Domain Independent Constructivist Model of Human Knowing. Foundations of Science 6(4), 343–360 (2001)
4. Anderson, L.W., Krathwohl, D.R. (eds.): A taxonomy for learning, teaching and assessing: A revision of Bloom's Taxonomy of educational objectives, Complete edition. Longman, New York (2001)
5. Marzano, R.J.: Fostering thinking across the curriculum through knowledge restructuring. Journal of Reading 34/7, 518–525 (1991)
6. Langer, J.A., Applebee, A.N.: How writing shapes thinking: a study of teaching and learning. NCTE Research Report no. 22. Urbana, IL: National Council of Teachers of English (1987)
7. Facione, P.A.: Critical thinking: A statement of expert consensus for purposes of educational assessment and instruction—executive summary of the delphi report. California Academic Press, Millbrae (1990)
8. Luckey, G.M.: Critical thinking in colleges and universities: A model. In: Fasko, D. (ed.) Critical Thinking and Reasoning, pp. 253–271. Hampton Press, Cresskill (2003)
9. Swartz, R.: Infusing critical and creative thinking into instruction in high school classrooms. In: Fasko, D. (ed.) Critical thinking and reasoning, pp. 293–310. Hampton Press, Cresskill (2003)
10. Halpern, D.F.: Teaching for critical thinking: helping college students develop the skills and dispositions of a teaching critical thinking for transfer across domains: dispositions, skills, structure training, and metacognitive monitoring. The American Psychologist 53, 449–455 (1998)
11. Piaget, J.: Adaptation and Intelligence. University of Chicago Press, London (1980)
12. Bruner, J.S.: The course of cognitive growth. The American Psychologist 19(1), 1–15 (1964)
13. Papert, S.: Mindstorms. Children, Computers and Powerful Ideas. Basic books, New York (1980)

Knowledge, Skills, Competencies: A Model for Mathematics E-Learning

Giovannina Albano

DIEII - Dipartimento di Ingegneria Elettronica e Ingegneria Informatica,
Università di Salerno, via Ponte don Melillo,
84084 Fisciano (SA), Italy
galbano@unisa.it

Abstract. This work concerns modelling competence in mathematics in e-learning environment. Competence is something complex, which goes further the cognitive level, but involves meta-cognitive and non-cognitive factors. Anyway it requires the students to master knowledge and skills, at first, and some measurable abilities, defined as competencies. We present a model that, exploiting the innovative technological features of the platform IWT, aims at defining a personalised learning experience allowing the students to build up their competence in mathematics.

Keywords: mathematics learning, knowledge, skill, competence, competency, e-learning.

1 Introduction

This paper is framed in the areas of e-learning and mathematics education. We assume that integrating research outcomes in both areas is of paramount importance. The effort of the author has been devoted to exploit the technological potential of e-learning based on the domain-specific results from research in mathematics education, in order to model competence in mathematics in an e-learning environment. Competence is something complex, which goes beyond the cognitive level, but involves meta-cognitive and non-cognitive factors. Anyway it requires the students to master knowledge and skills, at first, and some measurable abilities we are going to see in details in section 2.2.

There is a general agreement on the importance of mastering mathematics: everyone needs to use mathematics in his or her personal life, in the workplace, and in further learning. In the same way , it is well known that effectiveness of the teaching/learning process requires personalization, as different students have different styles, needs, preferences, attitudes.

Through the chapter we focus on the definition of a model apt to generate personalized learning experiences allowing the students to master not only pieces of knowledge or skills, but to handle competencies in mathematics. To this aim, first of all we are going to define what are knowledge, skills and competencies in mathematics. From the technological point of view, we refer to the e-learning platforms we have used, which is named IWT (Intelligent Web Teacher). It is

R. Kwan et al. (Eds.): ICT 2011, CCIS 177, pp. 214–225, 2011.

equipped with features of LCMS (Learning Content Management System), adaptive learning system and allows the definition of personalized and collaborative teaching/learning experiences by means of the explicit representation of the knowledge and the use of techniques and tools of Web 2.0.

To begin with, in sections 2 and 3, we give an overview of the theoretical framework as well as the technological one.

Section 4 describes a model for mathematics learning. It is based on a multi-level graph representation of the domain, distinguishing the knowledge, the skill and the competence levels. Then the description of the work-flow needed o generate a tailored learning experience is given.

Finally, section 5 wraps up and explores some opportunities for future research.

2 Theoretical Framework

Mathematical literacy is concerned with "the capacity of students to analyse, reason and communicate effectively as they pose, solve and interpret mathematical problems in a variety of situations" [1]. Commonly speaking, this requires the students to become *competent* in mathematics. From the educational viewpoint, what does it means? And which are the teaching implications?

Many authors [2], [3], [4], [5], [6] have tried to explain what competence in mathematics is. All of them agree that it is something complex and dynamic, which is based on basic notions and procedures (knowledge and skills), but it goes beyond cognitive factors. Meta-cognitive and non-cognitive factors are strongly involved, such as awareness of own cognitive resources and of the thinking processes, self-regulation capabilities, for the former [7], and attitude, acceptance of the stimulus to use own knowing, desire and will to integrate it *in itinere* when necessary, for the latter [3].

2.1 Knowledge and Skills

Mathematical competence is not something "to be taught", rather it is a long-term goal for the teaching/learning process. Anyway it requires, as pre-requisites, mathematics domain's knowledge of declarative-propositional type, that is *knowledge* ("to know"), and of procedural type, that is *skill* ("to know how"). Note that both of them are equally important. Given a problem, first of all knowledge allows us to understand and analyze it, then it provides us the required theory, rationale and background to formulate and validate theoretical approaches in order to tackle the problem. Anyway, knowledge alone is not sufficient to solve the problem without procedural skills. The latter produce practical results and consequences, they make concrete our theoretical thoughts and reasoning. At the same time, skills without knowledge may lead to perform correct procedures starting from wrong data, thus producing senseless results.

According to the above distinction, we can try to list some basic requirements as shown in the following table:

Table 1. Classification of the main types of mathematical content

Content's type	Knowledge	Skill
Definition	Statement	Procedural/computational practice, if applicable
Theorem	Statement	Procedural/computational practice
Theorem	Proof	Procedural/computational practice
Algorithm		Performance of the algorithm
Example/counterexample	Description	
Exercise		Computational skills
Problems		Solving standard problems

Each content may have just theoretical interest, thus it represents just *knowledge*, or be a procedure, that is just *skill*, or have both theoretical and practical counterparts.

For instance, consider the concept of "rank" of a matrix and its definition as the greatest order of any non-zero minor in the matrix (the order of a minor being the size of the square sub-matrix of which it is the determinant). We can apply this as a procedure to compute the rank. The Kronecker theorem gives a more effective way of computing it, , which corresponds to a procedure, but knowing the proof of the theorem adds nothing to skills. On the other hand, the proof of the Gram-Schmidt theorem, stating the existence of an orthonormal basis for an Euclidian vector space of finite dimension, gives a constructive method to compute such a basis. Similarly the definition of the echelon form of a matrix is completely distinct from the techniques able to reduce a matrix in echelon form (Gauss' algorithm).

We can say that knowledge can be seen as factual information or content about a given topic or area, which can be stored, retrieved and autonomously elaborated by the learner during the learning process. We can say that knowledge represents "factual mathematics". On the other hand skills can be associated to what Skemp [8] called "instrumental mathematics" which is characterised by formulas, to keep in mind, exercises, products, and which corresponds to "instrumental comprehension", which means to be able to practice rules, without knowing why.

2.2 Competence and Competencies

According to Niss [5], *"possessing mathematical competence means having knowledge of, understanding, doing and using mathematics and having a well-founded opinion about it, in a variety of situations and contexts where mathematics plays or can play a role"*. In order to make more factual the notion of mathematical competence, we can consider a mathematical competency as a clearly recognizable distinct major constituent in mathematical competence [5]. Niss has distinguished eight characteristic cognitive mathematical competencies, which also PISA 2009 [8] refers to. The following table lists them, grouped in two cluster [5]:

Table 2. Clusters related to cognitive mathematical competencies

The ability to ask and answer questions in and with mathematics	*The ability to deal with mathematical language and tools*
Mathematical thinking competency	Representation competency
Problem handling competency	Symbols and formalism competency
Modelling competency	Communication competency
Reasoning competency	Tools and aids competency

Let us see them in more details.

Mathematical thinking competency includes understanding and handling of scope and limitations of a given concepts, abstracting and generalizing results, posing questions and knowing the kinds of answers, distinguishing between different sorts of mathematical statements (theorems, conjectures, definitions, conditional and quantified statements, etc.).

Problem handling competency includes investigating and formulating pure/applied and closed/open mathematical problems and solving such kinds of problems, in various ways.

Modelling competency includes analyzing, validating, performing in given contexts, monitoring existing models.

Reasoning competency includes understanding the logic of a proof or of a counterexample, proving statements, following and assessing others' reasoning.

Representation competency includes distinguishing different kinds of representations of mathematical entities, understanding the relations between different representation of the same object, transforming representations – treatment and conversion [10].

Symbols and formalism competency includes understanding and handling symbolic and formal language, translating back and forth between symbolic language and verbal language.

Communication competency includes understanding others' mathematical texts and expressing oneself about mathematical contents, in different semiotic representation systems and registers[1] [11].

Tools and aids competency includes knowing and reflectively using different tools and aids for mathematical activity.

As seen, competencies correspond to relational mathematics [8], which consists in reasoning, thinking, problems, processes; which is reflected by "relational comprehension", which is to be aware of connections and reasons.

---

[1] A register is defined as a linguistic variety according to use, i.e., the linguistic means developed to express meanings related to some context and goals.

Note that to acquire competence as well as competencies requires the students to be involved in didactical and adidactical situations[2] [12] where the students accept to be active actor building their *knowing* instead of passive repeater of what have learnt.

3 Technological Framework

From the technological point of view, in this paper we refer to the platform IWT (Intelligent Web Teacher)), we have used in our practices. It is a distance learning platform, realized at the Italian Pole of Excellence on Learning & Knowledge, equipped with features of LCMS, adaptive learning system and allowing the definition of personalized and collaborative teaching/learning experiences by means of the explicit representation of knowledge and the use of techniques and tools of Web 2.0. Due to the presence of three models (Didactic, Student, Knowledge), IWT allows the student to reach the learning objectives defined by delivering a personalised course which takes into account his/her specific needs, previous knowledge, preferred learning styles, didactical model more suitable to the knowledge at stake and to the mental model (then engagement) of the learner. Let us briefly describe the three models.

The Knowledge Model (KM) is able to represent in an intelligible manner for the computer the information associated to the available didactic material. It makes use of: 1) ontologies, that allow to formalise cognitive domains through the definition of concepts and relations between the concepts, 2) learning objects (LOs), that are defined as "any digital resource that can be reused to support learning" [13], 3) metadata, that are descriptive information and allow to tag each LO in order to associate it to one or more concepts defined in an ontology.

The Learner Model (LM) is able to catch (automatically) the previous knowledge and the knowledge the learners little by little acquire during his/her learning and the learning preferences (seen as cognitive abilities and perceptive capabilities) shown with regard to important pedagogical parameters such as: media, didactic approach, interaction level, semantic density, etc. The model is composed of three elements: a Cognitive State, a set of Learning Preferences and a set of Evolution Rules.

The Didactic Model (DM) defines the optimal modalities of knowledge transfer to the students on the basis of the domain (formalised in the KM) and to the characteristics of the involved student (formalised in the LM). Through this model

---

[2] In an environment which has been organized for the purpose of learning a special subject, we can talk about an adidactical situation, when the didactical intention is no longer explicit. The teacher suggests an activity without declaring the purpose of it; the student is well-aware that all activities in the classroom are meant to build up new knowledge, but in this case she/he does not know exactly what she/he is going to learn. If she/he decides to participate, accepting to get implicated, then she/he frees her/himself from "contract" constraints and participates in an adidactical activity. In this case, the teacher is just a spectator, that is to say, she/he is not explicitly implicated in the knowledge management. We talk about didactical situation when the specific didactic objective of the teacher is explicit since the beginning: the teacher openly informs her/his students about the knowledge content that is at issue in that moment.

IWT can personalise the didactic experience on the basis of the previous knowledge of the single learners and of their learning preferences.

Let us now briefly described how IWT is able to generate a tailored unit of learning, taking advantages of the previous models [14], [15], [16]. When student access to the course the first time, IWT is able to automatically generate for each student the best possible learning path according to the information available in the student model, to the course specifications and to the LOs available in the repository. At first the ontology is used to create the list of the concepts needed to reach the target concept of the course. Then the information of the student model is used to update this list according to the cognitive state and to choose the more suitable LOs according to the learner preferences. The choice is made possible taking the LOs whose metadata better matches with the learner preferences data. Moreover the platform is able to dynamically update the learning path according to the outcomes of the intermediate tests.

The described approach to personalisation, which is more 'teacher-centered' rather than 'learner-centred' as the flow of the LOs is predefined and determined by the platform (that is the teacher/instructor), is combined with a non-linear approach, which allows the learners to navigate among the various alternative resources available and to select and also to create their own preferred ones.

4   Modelling Mathematics Learning

In the following we are going to extend the IWT Knowledge Model in order to distinguish mathematical knowledge, skills and competencies and then take them into consideration for defining and setting up tailored learning experiences.

4.1 Domain Representation

A rough domain formalisation could consist in teaching according to "fundamental nodes". With this term we refer to "those fundamental concepts which occur in various places of a discipline and then have structural and knowledge procreative value" [17]. Teaching by fundamental nodes means "to weave a conceptual map, strategic and logic, fine and smart", where each concept actually is the goal of a complex system with mesh and anyway no concept stands completely alone and each of them is part of a relations' web rather than being single "conceptual object" [3].

Let us consider an example choosing the topic "Matrices". We can take the following as fundamental nodes: Matrix definition, Operations with matrices, Determinant, Rank, Echelon matrix, Inverse matrix. A conceptual map could be the one shown in the Fig. 1, where the edges describe the links existing among various nodes, which can be of different kind: from those purely relational – for instance, the need of the concept of determinant in order to define the rank – to the instrumental ones – such as the use of the echelon matrices to compute the inverse of a given matrix.

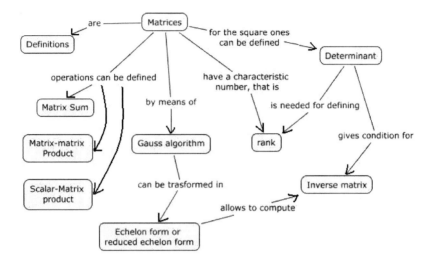

Fig. 1. This shows an example of conceptual map for the topic "Matrices"

Thus the relations appeared in the map of Fig. 1 have intersection with both knowledge and skill levels, as well as with relational and instrumental mathematics.

We wish to manage the previous map using the ontologies in IWT and the corresponding implemented relations, that are "HasPart", "IsRequiredBy" and "SuggestedOrder". We want to consider a multi-level graph representation: an ontology related to the fundamental nodes (corresponding to the use of ontology at the present in IWT, as shown in Fig. 2), an ontology related to the knowledge, an ontology related to the skills. All these should help students in mastering knowledge and skills which are pre-requisites to be involved in learning activities aimed at acquiring competencies (corresponding to the conceptual map in Fig. 1).

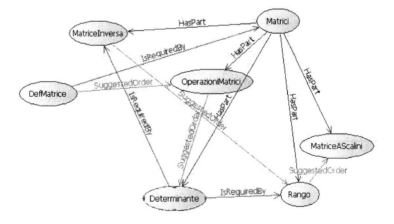

Fig. 2. This shows an example of "fundamental nodes" for the topic "Matrices"

The idea that the fundamental nodes actually are the goals of a relations' web let us to consider each of them as "root" of a further graph (ontology), where the levels of knowledge, skill and competency are made explicit.

- Knowledge level: here we consider nodes corresponding to definitions, theorems, examples, and so on (see table 1); Fig. 3 schematises the possible typologies of nodes and the connecting edges represent possible relations among various typologies, some of them mandatory, in some sense (designed as continuous lines) and some others optional (designed as discontinuous lines): for instance, given a definition of a mathematical entity, some characterizing properties can be proved, thus a link with one or more theorems is foreseen, and at the same time some examples or counterexamples can or cannot be generated.

Knowledge level

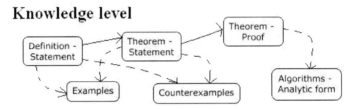

Fig. 3. Generic ontology at knowledge level

- Skill level: here we consider nodes corresponding basically to computational methods and standard solving problem capabilities (see Table 1); Fig. 4 outlines the possible typologies of nodes and the connecting edges representing possible relations among various typologies are designed with discontinuous lines to indicate that they can or cannot concur to the reached skill: for instance solving standard procedure requires one or more "elementary" calculation capabilities.

Skill level

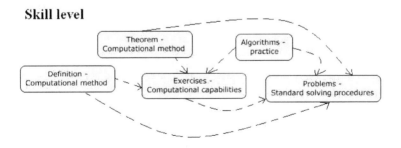

Fig. 4. Generic ontology at skill level

- Competency level: here we take into account the eight clusters described in section 2.2 and the possible links among them. Note that the given classification does not correspond to the separation of the clusters: it is evident that they are closely connected and some differences are actually very fine. This means that it is quite impossible to focus on just one competency. Fig. 5 schematises the eight clusters. The links can concern the whole cluster or some specific items, depending on the domain topic. The figure shows just some examples of linked items.

Competency level

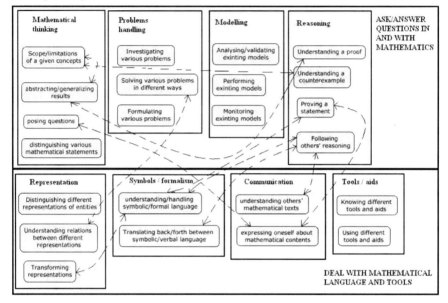

Fig. 5. Generic ontology at competency level

4.2 The Creation of a Personalised Learning Experience

First of all, the domain expert has to represent the domain by means of ontologies where fundamental nodes are roots of corresponding knowledge nodes as well as skills nodes. Further he has to specialize the competencies related to those nodes.

Now let us see which are the steps needed to define a personalised learning experience. The teacher has to define the learning goals of the learning experience. This is made by various choices:

a) The target concepts among the fundamental nodes;
b) The typologies at Knowledge level, if desired;
c) The typologies at Skill level, if desired;
d) The typologies at Competency level, if desired.

Each choice corresponds to the generation of a personalised learning experience, differing one from one other with respect to the global learning goal, as we are going to describe:

1) Aim at making students able to master knowledge and/or skills:
   given the target concepts, the ontology of the fundamental nodes allows to create the list of the concepts needed to reach them. For each node of this list, a corresponding list at Knowledge and/or Skill levels is generated, according to the chosen typologies. Then a further list comes from the join of the latter ones, according to the fundamental concepts order. Now the information stored in the Student Model are used to update the list according to the student cognitive state and to choice the best LOs according to the student preferences, as described in section 3.

2) Aim at making students able to master competencies:
   as seen in section 2.2, competencies stand cross wisely along all the mathematical domain, so they are not linked to specific knowledge or skill. Anyway, it has been proved [14] that students' success in performing activities related to competencies are strongly influenced by the level of their mastering of knowledge and skills involved in the activities. Thus, given competency typologies (at macro or micro level) some learning activities can be setting up, according to some templates. These latter specify the methodology and the tools or services required. Then the concepts from Knowledge and/or Skill levels to be involved have to be fixed. The concepts will be assumed as and target concepts of a personalised course, generated according to the procedure described in 1) and it will be the pre-requisite for the learning activity. The templates can be equipped with material related to the implementation of the general methodology referred to specific knowledge and skills, that can be re-used.

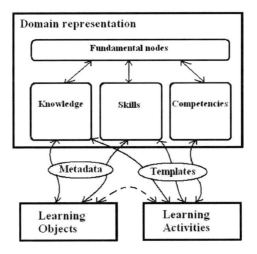

Fig. 6. Model of learning experience generation

5 Future Trends

In this paper we have proposed a model for tailored learning experience generation, taking into consideration knowledge, skill and competency levels in mathematics learning and taking advantages from the Knowledge Model of the platform IWT. The model foresees to design ontologies for the cited three levels concerned the chosen domain. The ones related to the first two levels should be used according to the current generation of cognitive-based personalised unit of learning, consisting in the delivery of suitable LOs. The third one should be used to generate learning activities aimed at students' mastering of some competencies.
We plan to go further on this way, along two main directions:

- definition of details for implementation of learning activities and interconnection with the unit of learning needed as pre-requisites;
- definition of assessment procedures for competencies according to the requirements of PISA [9], both in closed and open form [14], [18].

References

1. OECD: Learning for tomorrow's world. First results from PISA 2003 (2004), from the World Wide Web, http://www.oecd.org/dataoecd/1/60/34002216.pdf (retrieved January 28, 2011)
2. Weinert, F.: Concept of competence: a conceptual clarification. In: Rychen, D., Salgenik, L. (eds.) Defining and Electing Key Competencies. Hogrefe & Huber Publishers, Seattle (2001)
3. D'Amore, B.: La complessità dell'educazione e della costruzione dei saperi. Riforma e didattica 4, 35–40 (2000)
4. Godino, J.: Competencia y comprensión matemática:¿Qué son y cómo se consiguen? Uno. 29, 9–19 (2002)
5. Niss, M.: Mathematical competencies and the learning of mathematics: The Danish KOM project. In: Gagatsis, A., Papastavridis, S. (eds.) 3rd Mediterranean Conference on Mathematical Education, January 3-5, pp. 115–124. Hellenic Mathematical Society, Athens (2003)
6. Niss, M.: The Danish KOM project and possible consequences for teacher education. Cuadernos de Investigacion y Formacion en Education Matematica 6(9), 13–24 (2011)
7. Zan, R.: A metacognitive intervention in Mathematics at University level. International Journal Math. Educ. Sci. Technol. 31, 1 (2000)
8. Skemp, R.: Relational understanding and instrumental understanding. Mathematics Teaching 77, 20–26 (1976)
9. OECD: PISA 2009 Assessment Framework - Key Competencies in Reading, Mathematics and Science, from the World Wide Web, http://www.oecd.org/dataoecd/11/40/44455820.pdf (retrieved January 28, 2011)
10. Duval, R.: The Cognitive Analysis of Problems of Comprehension in the Learning of Mathematics. Educational Studies in Mathematics 61(1), 103–131 (2006)
11. Ferrari, P.L.: Abstraction in mathematics. Phil. Trans. R. Soc. Lond. B 358, 1225–1230 (2003)

12. Brousseau, G.: Theory of Didactical Situations in Mathematics. Kluwer Academics Publisher, Dordrecht (1997)
13. Wiley, D.A.: Connecting learning objects to instructional design theory: A definition, a metaphor, and a taxonomy. In: Wiley, D.A. (ed.) The Instructional Use of Learning Objects: Online Version (2000), from the World Wide Web
    `http://reusability.org/read/chapters/wiley`
    (retrieved February 18, 2010)
14. Albano, G.: Mathematics education: teaching and learning opportunities in blended learning. In: Juan, A., Huertas, A., Trenholm, S., Steegmann, C. (eds.) Teaching Mathematics Online: Emergent Technologies and Methodologies (in press, 2011)
15. Albano, G., Gaeta, M., Ritrovato, P.: IWT: an innovative solution for AGS e-Learning model. International Journal of Knowledge and Learning 3(2/3), 209–224 (2007)
16. Gaeta, M., Orciuoli, F., Ritrovato, P.: Advanced Ontology Management System for Personalised e-Learning. Knowledge-Based Systems– Special Issue on AI and Blended Learning 22, 292–301 (2009)
17. Arzarello, F., Robutti, O.: Matematica. La Scuola, Brescia (2002)
18. Albano, G., Ferrari, P.L.: Integrating technology and research in mathematics education: the case of e-learning. In: Peñalvo, G. (ed.) Advances in E-Learning: Experiences and Methodologies, pp. 132–148 (2008)

Building an Effective Online Learning Community: An Ethnographic Study

Ken Eustace

Centre for Research in Complex Systems
School of Computing & Mathematics
Charles Sturt University
keustace@csu.edu.au

Abstract. What happens when a group of co-learners engage in a continuous lifelong learning community in the context of rapid changes in both the use of ICT in learning and the curriculum?

A rare longitudinal ethnographic-action research study over 15 years has provided interpretive practice opportunities through analysis of rich data into building and sustaining a learning community. The study has involved a process of evaluating adult educational interaction and efficacy with rapid changes in ICT and curriculum models and theories associated with online learning and teaching.

Border Studies is a non-traditional, lifelong learning community that was built and sustained over a period of fifteen years. As a result of the ethnographic action research cycles a RITA model for enabling effective online learning networks is proposed for action by the reader.

Keywords: Action research, associate practice, conventional and complementary education, curriculum action, curriculum model, deep learning experiences, educational value, ethnography, e-learning environments, hypothesis, improvisation, learning journey as interpretive practice, learning moments, metaphor, narrative, peer dialogue, peer review.

1 Introduction

By the mid 1990's the need for a university teacher to study changing practises to teaching and learning due to the emergence of new technologies and dynamic online learning communities, such as the Paideia MA degree was in strong demand.

The focus of this research was an investigation into how postgraduate e-learning participants can be guided to provide their own effective conditions for peer discourse and deep learning opportunities using the Internet for situated adult learning (Lave & Wenger , 1991), especially for adult learners seeking alternative pathways to traditional learning and research (Knowles, 1984). The study followed a learning journey, beginning with the entering experiences of the teacher-researcher as an information technology lecturer and then following research stages of literature search, questions, action and reflection and various social learning contexts according to Vygotsky (1978), Bandura (1977; 1997; 2002).

R. Kwan et al. (Eds.): ICT 2011, CCIS 177, pp. 226–242, 2011.
© Springer-Verlag Berlin Heidelberg 2011

The Impetus for a Longitudinal Study

An invitation was made to build and adapt a user-centred e-learning environment to support the learning process of participants in an online Master of Arts degree at Paideia, one of the first of its kind as a virtual or online university. The research would be longitudinal and examine changes to the ICT e-learning environment, the curriculum design or model and the influences of a user-centred design of the e-learning environment change upon the learner, the teacher and the institution.

As Nolan & Weiss (2002) concluded, in order to understand how each online community is a learning community, they suggested that knowing the history and descriptive features described in this study, allow educators to determine the various learning interactions that are needed for: "initiation, maintenance, and indeed success." while Hiltz (1999) supported the use of online learning as being effective, rather than a source of "digital diploma mills".

2 Research Design

The research design was an interpretive learning journey (Symington, 2003) using a mixed methodology of ethnography (Forester, 1992; Williamson 2000) and action research (Kemmis & McTaggart, 1988). This hybrid approach was a cyclic, three-stage longitudinal study using ethnographic and complementary action research methods, used often in education research.   While some e-learning environment developers were building cyber worlds based upon openness, other individuals and groups were busy building their own private cyber worlds. Habermas (1987) supported the openness approach in his theory of communicative action and suggested that: *"free and open communication leads to a free and open society."*

The study had three distinct stages, concerned with design and development of an ICT-based, flexible curriculum for deep learning experiences, through dialogue with peers and guided by use of a focus group (Kreuger & Casey, 2000).

Each stage of the research follows a reflective pattern of interpretive practice, leading to a revised plan, identified by a title and questions leading to further actions, observation and reflection in the next stage, (Griffin, 1998) according to the iterative Deakin model of the action research process, as outlined by Kemmis and McTaggart (1988). There was a clear intention or planning stage before each action as an *intention-plan-act-review* cycle or spiral for activation by the teacher-researcher and the focus group. The Deakin Model was modified to fit its re-conception to online learning and teaching studies as shown in Figure 1.

Discussion group data was used by the researcher to describe the learning community discourse and to analyse events and processes about educational value, deep learning theories, conventional and complementary education e-learning curricula, that can be quickly evaluated and assimilated into the researcher's own teaching practice.

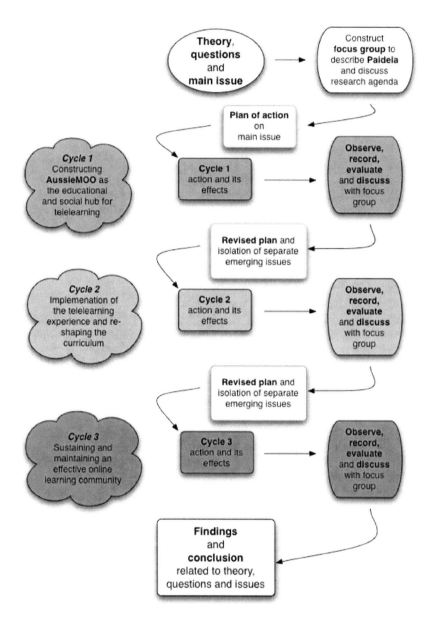

Fig. 1. Re-conceiving an action research model to a study of e-learning

3 Findings and Discussion

The findings are concerned with changes in practice and policy through theory development as user-centred e-learning environment design was tightly coupled with curriculum modelling as defined by learning theories such as social constructivism. In the context of the internationalisation of higher education, the research findings on this longitudinal study of adult learners, which began at Paideia, with those leaners seeking alternatives to conventional higher education, became a broader learning journey into the teacher-researcher's own teaching practice with information and communications technologies.

During this study several "change agents" were identified among the participants as being the introduction of new media, focus group impact on the curriculum model and learner needs and behaviours. The influence of those change agents on the professional practices of others in online learning community was observed and analysed, during each action research cycle.

The study into effective online learning communities and the ways that e-learning environments create new curriculum dynamics in e-learning required conscious and regular examination of who we are, who we talk to, what we talk about, and how we talk about it. This mattered in any teaching and learning interaction at all levels as institutions seek to integrate new ICT to support student interaction and collaborative learning as seen by use of Web 2.0 tools such as blogs, wikis and vodcasts, as providing engaging environments for learning. (Beldarrain, 2006).

This section examines the findings according to each of the three ethnographic action research cycles. The initial baseline field study question was centred on developing an open source e-learning environment that would be both efficient and effective as a scaffold (Rada, 1998) for a wide range of learning paradigms such as problem-based peer learning within the Master of Arts degree.

The findings focus on three main agents of change as:

1. The ICT environment for e-learning and its features
2. Participant behaviour and actions (the role play and interaction WITH the curriculum model and peers THROUGH the e-learning environment)
3. Curriculum design and modelling

First Ethnographic Action Research Cycle (AR1): Baseline Study

From the original discussion about how to build and sustain on online learning environment for Paideia and its Master of Arts program, the focus group had decided upon a summative key question for the initial baseline investigation by the teacher-researcher as he studied in the MA program. This was an alternative to a completely open ended ethnography with a grounded approach, but supported exploration and discovery.

Key Question

Can an ethnographic action research study of changes in innovation, culture and practice over time with the user-centred design and development of the e-learning environment provide the guidelines to build and sustain an effective online learning community?

When the teacher-researcher became the first Australian to be conferred an MA degree from a Virtual university, it made an impact at a time when higher education was finding it way with the new medium. The conferring of a Master of Arts degree from a virtual university like Paideia in 1995 as witnessed by so many qualified educators, was evidence that the learning community was effective with its curriculum agenda as a developing learning community and online university. Headlines like "Virtual university confers MA" captured media attention as most higher education institutions in the Commonwealth of Learning were now on track to explore, adopt and develop the virtual operation.

It was a major finding that showed that a user-centred e-learning environment like AussieMOO had not only built and sustained a learning community but had a good record of completion among candidates.

The AR1 baseline study of participants in the MA had examined the types of e-learning environments that best supported the peer-based collaborative research and learning culture in the Paideia programme. Using open source Web software, each e-learning tool was developed using the user centred design approach.

Each time that changes were made to the e-learning environment, its impact on the educational value for participants (their research and learning practices,) the evolving curriculum model and the host institution were evaluated.

The changing ICT media required participants to develop efficacy with each new ICT tool quickly in order to maintain the desired level of interaction. This would occur five times during the length of the study, with two changes in this Cycle near its beginning. The first big change in ICT was moving participants from attending weekly or monthly teleconferences towards using online chat and e-mail forum applications. Synchronous Internet applications like Internet Relay Chat (IRC) and the asynchronous use of e-mail for posting and sharing messages prior to later Web-based applications were the early tools for learning online. User-centred design was limited to access via an IRC client to an IRC channel called GlobalNt channel and e-mail access via membership of the Paideia-L LISTSERV service.

The second big change came quickly. Rather than have interaction spread over separate tools, the user-centred drive was a single tool with all features, leading to the selection of a LamdaMOO server at Charles Sturt University called AussieMOO over IRC and LISTERV. As a form of social virtual reality, the MOO technology would dominate online learning for some years until Web applications, computers and Internet bandwidth all improved, resulting in tools such as Second Life.

Since AussieMOO already had a prototype social and education Hub, meeting rooms were setup for Paideia participants, MOO clients or Java applets were used to connect via telnet and the system already had chat and internal mail forums. This time the efficacy required participants to have a login name, password, and a persona. This persona was an online identity or profile to design and manage as your avatar. The level of immersion, design and interaction included virtual world building inside the MOO. The level of efficacy required to be a participant was arranged in a player hierarchy so participants were rewarded for building competence inside a MOO, in addition to their weekly course work.

AussieMOO was a big hit and its use spread wider to other higher education course in the USA and Switzerland in particular. The way that the MOO environment handled group dialogue, deep learning experiences and the development of *information technology literacy standards* led to a popularity that still remains today.

Table 1. Primary findings for AR1

ICT environment	Participant behaviour/actions	Curriculum model change
Education and social hub with novelties and dialogue framework.	Motivating student use with sense of place and feelings of belonging.	Peer learning process via dialogue and ePortfolio writing.
Avatar profile and role play and feedback support from Wizard staff.	Identity and profile management as a team member.	New standards for ICT literacy through shared dialogue and the "written conversation".
User-centred design, programming and virtual world building as a classroom.	Enhancing experience, user control and satisfaction.	Concept of learning spaces with social constructivist approach.
Text-based interface via several Telnet clients options allows for all interaction captured as re-usable text.	Collaborative writing and ePortfolio editing made easy though a single interface.	Continuous peer assessment via regular evaluation of dialogue contribution and the ePortfolio.
Tutorial help for new users, map screens for navigation and a sign tool for dialogue control.	Participants build their own learning objects and spaces with a simple Object-oriented language.	Self-efficacy with ICT developed as part of the philosophical "box" curriculum model.

The primary findings for AR1 as the baseline study are listed in Table 1. AR1 demonstrated that the user centred e-learning environment design using open source software products provided greater user involvement, rapid prototype building and feedback among participants. Its flexible approach aligned with the action research. Enhancing the user interface via split windows for a Web client, Text editor and a MOO client was an influential user-centred design feature.

The new wave of online collaboration helped to develop the "art of the written conversation" as collaborative writing, portfolio assessment and the conversational framework behind the learning process had improved the learning experience.

Changes to the ICT e-learning environment influenced the curriculum model, the professional practice of participants and the educational value of the new experience.

The philosophical box curriculum model in Figure 2 was a dialogue intensive model for putting knowledge into action by participants. This baseline model was directed by a curriculum agenda for using participant's sources of knowledge and using existing knowledge and perspectives for building new knowledge as validated through dialogue as opportunities for action and development of a personal portfolio (a pre-cursor to a blog in the pre-Web 2.0 era). The dynamic drivers of dialogue were not only the metaphors, narratives, hypotheses, theory, policy, practices and life experiences but also the opportunities of dialogue as provided by the ICT e-learning environment such as AussieMOO.

The curriculum model for each action research cycle 1

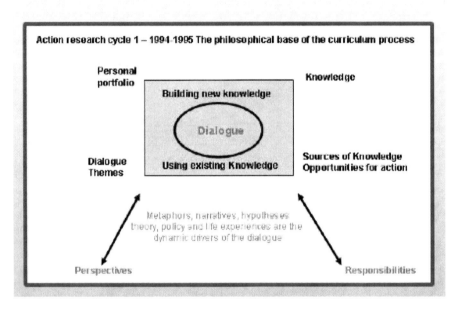

Fig. 2. AR1 baseline curriculum model

Second Ethnographic Action Research Cycle (AR2)

A revised plan for action research cycle 2, where the key field study question became: *How can the e-learning environment and the curriculum model be developed and sustained for growth and development?*

The focus group also considered the influence of allowing the user-centred e-learning environment design upon curriculum modelling, teaching, learning and research paradigms at Paideia and the feedback loop provided by those paradigms on the design. This approach of examining interrelationships meant that AussieMOO was adapted and developed to holistically support sustainable learning communities.

Figure 3 illustrates the H-model for operation over seven realms in the pattern of a letter 'H' with all six realms passing through the core realm 0, described as critical analysis of all sources of knowledge.

During AR2 the community was busy working on the design until disagreement on the course to take on future directions with the user interface. On one side were the original Wizards seeking to conserve what they had started and on the other side were the newer educational Wizards seeking to use a Web browser interface. This "cultural crisis" would be the most serious challenge to the sustainability of the learning community, but an agreement was made to make a new e-learning environment for those seeking the change. The primary findings of this stage are listed in Table 2. Apart from the cultural crisis, other changes of the curricula were also pending.

The terms *adjacent* and *complementary* education were used to describe the operation of the new curriculum model, with learning taking place adjacent or nearby to the learner and any new online learning paradigm was described as *complementing rather than competing* with traditional methods.

Hiltz (1999) was concerned about the negative image of online courses in the media, however the participants in this study found that regular contact in e-learning environments provided a positive set of outcomes for a small group, practising collaborative learning and discussion via a *sources>knowledge>intent>actions* framework, which Mason (2001); Gongla & Rizzuto (2001) and McAfee et al (2001) helped to define and map at the core of the curriculum model.

The curriculum model for each action research cycle 2

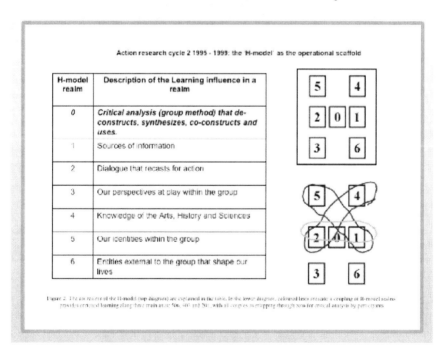

Fig. 3. AR2 curriculum model

Development of an Adjacent Schools curriculum model using the H model goes one step further and includes curriculum operations leading to the emergence of the online schools:

1. original Paideia and its structured 'box' model approach;
2. School for Journeys as a place for documenting a learning journey and
3. School for Projects using project-based learning and growth through a personal or professional project or thesis.

The H-model had transformed the global MA degree into a wider Adjacent Schools curriculum model with several pathways and new ways to operate, as shown briefly in Table 3.

Table 2. Primary findings table for AR2 on AussieMOO and curriculum development

ICT environment	Participant behaviour/actions	Curriculum model change
Virtual classrooms added to the main welcome screen map.	User-centred virtual world design and growth of topology at AussieMOO with extended building as a "multi-function" polis.	Recognition of the educational value and accreditation of Paideia with the support of the Commonwealth of Learning was halted by political problems surrounding a global award.
An e-learning environment must be able to support the curriculum process and curriculum modelling.	With rapid growth and change, tension builds and a "cultural divide" develops between programmers and educators among the Wizards at AussieMOO.	Curriculum modelling led to development of a complementary education model working alongside the traditional adult learning approaches. AR2 resulted in an adjacent and complementary learning paradigm.
Wizard staff use feedback and research to develop support for new users with "training" at first login via the Tutorial Caverns	Wizard staff act as scaffold and win acclaim in supporting participant ICT efficacy via the Tutorial Caverns	An Adjacent Schools curriculum model, using the H model for curriculum operations and the emergence of two other online schools: one for Journeys and the other for Projects provided more learning mode options or pathways.

Paidiea: Now We are Three

Participants were now able to move among several pathways in learning. The original Paideia and its curriculum model was retained but under the Adjacent Schools model, the operation presented three modes of learning style, with participants able to operate in one, two or all three at various times.

Table 3. The learning pathway with the adjacent schools

ADJACENT SCHOOLS		
PAIDEIA The original **Paideia** retaining at its core, the philosophical box model and the global MA degree and other research up to PhD level.	**SCHOOL FOR JOURNEYS** Using the H-model, this school supports documentation of a learning journey.	**SCHOOL FOR PROJECTS** Using the H-model, this school supports projects and project-based learning and growth, ranging from personal projects, professional projects, collaborative academic writing or a thesis.

Third Ethnographic Action Research Cycle (AR)

A revised plan for action research cycle 3, largely impacted by the cultural crisis at AussieMOO in July 1999, shaped the key field study questions for AR3:

What ICT management policies and teaching techniques support collaborative learning interaction and workflow?

The focus group also sought to consider the impact of a MOO-based e-learning environment support upon the curriculum process, curriculum modelling and the ongoing desire of systems integration with other ICT tools for e-learning or migration to a new media platform. The Web 2.0 era was approaching, so the final stage with all change agents created an environment with changes moving at a rapid pace as described in Table 4. Despite the amount of change it was a period of effective learning and recruitment.

ICT management and teaching techniques supported learner interaction, collaboration, learning and workflow. By 2005 this lengthy process of negotiation, interviews and discussion led to the final **Border Studies curriculum model** as shown in Figure 4.

The three schools from AR2 were now operating under a single umbrella as the learning community settled into a single integrated e-learning environment at the Border Studies MOODLE site at http://borderstudiesassociates.net/. The MOODLE had many of the features of MOO and ZOPE and the training and development in future was now in a simpler, single realm for the learning community.

Figure 4 has two diagrams, The main model at the top has the ICT learning environment at the centre with all interaction pathways mapped to included learner development, learning material (objects) and learning theories. The model includes a second diagram to explain the way that associates works as peers in practice engaged in a conversational framework as proposed by Laurillard (2002).

Table 4. Primary findings table for the final cycle - AR3

ICT environment	Participant behaviour/actions	Curriculum model change
The education Wizards leave AussieMOO and form Learning Communities MOO or LC_MOO and K9. The new environments helped to sustain the learning community and support a new level of ownership and interaction.	The rules of engagement. The "cultural divide" between programmer and educator Wizards led to increased policy development and planning for copyright, intellectual property issues and for the management of player interactions.	Interaction management is now part of the curriculum model. The School for Projects becomes the School on Borders.
A new integrated environment with LC_MOO as the main site, K9 as a "sandpit" for training new members, while a ZOPE site was used for content management of learning materials and the COREblog engine. Live Web MOO simulcasts are trialled.	Participants exchange roles and the shared experiences as "associates in practice". The ePortfolio becomes the Online Learning Record (OLR) approach as a blog schema. The OLR schema was adapted from Syverson's Learning Record Online (Syverson, 1995).	The Border Studies model focused on the borders between the personal, knowledge, our intentions, our organizational roles, our actions and our inquiries into how and what you know, why and with whom you intend to act on what you know and where and when you act accordingly.
Training and use of log recorders was a new interface feature, which improved the "conversational framework".	Participants used log recorders to make their own data collection of all online dialogue for review and analysis. The improvisation approach to learning is welcomed by participants.	The learning journey with peers as interpretive research into learning and teaching. Self-directed and group-directed learning as peer learning driven by theory and adopted into practice.
The Border Studies ICT migrates towards Web 2.0 tools. MOODLE for content management, blogs and forums, replaces ZOPE and COREblog	The asymptotic nature of multiple disciplines as asymptotic education e.g. computer science can learn from sociology and music.	Border Studies curriculum model evolves, fostering improvisation and asymptotic aspects as "associates in practice".
Web 2.0 and the Social media become the final ICT setting for the e-learning environment through use of MOODLE, TokBox, Skype and Yammer.	Dialogue seen as an "international rhapsody" using the metaphors from music education.	Improved interaction management across the integrated e-learning environment as a result of change agents in this cycle.

The teacher and the student were now roles that each participant can role-play on demand and not be a position fixed on any one individual. As an effective online learning community, the participants were **Associates in Practice**.

The curriculum model for each action research cycle 3

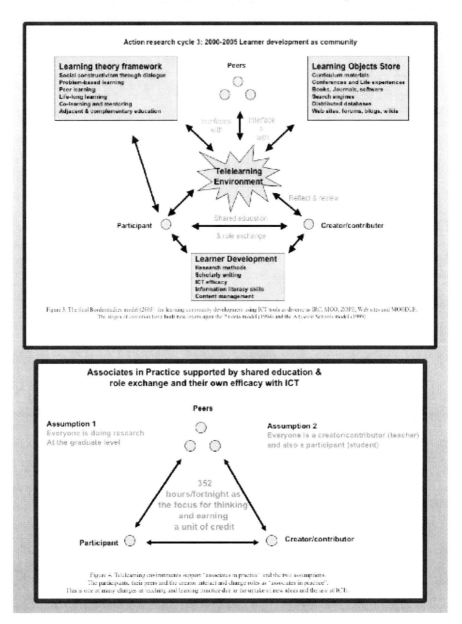

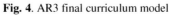

Fig. 4. AR3 final curriculum model

4 Conclusion

This interpretive research is not solely about outcomes -- it's about the ritual of communion between the participants in the group and their collective expression, unconcealment and discovery of information *in-the-moment* (**learning moments**). It is about the liberation of the individual learner from traditional hierarchical student-teacher relationships - a liberation that empowers participants to learn in a unique, unrepeatable and real-time engagement as associates in practice.

Events and processes about educational value, deep learning theories, conventional and complementary education, e-learning curricula, were quickly evaluated and assimilated into the teacher-researcher's own teaching practice. The learning journey as interpretive research has been presented and such research is fundamental to self-evaluation of teaching and complements the development of a teaching portfolio as professional development.

Building an online learning community and seeking instructional improvement by including learning theories such as problem-based learning can be a tapestry that weaves together new technology, individual learning styles, developmental learning programs, inter-institutional collaboration, rapid and participative curriculum change and new instructional methods for e-learning is a challenging task.

This learning journey went beyond the frontiers established by most Australian universities dealing with the distance learning environment and its various modalities. From the beginning, creating the virtual classroom environment at AussieMOO with a university that was virtual in properties helped develop learning as well as fostering a sense of community based soundly on personal interaction.

Peer dialogue provided the mechanism for deep learning experiences of educational value as well as forging rapid curriculum change and the shift to a system of student management/responsibility of learning, using problem-based learning, project-based learning, peer review and reflective practise. The results also revealed the Adjacent Schools e-learning scaffold to be a useful place for a wide range of educational research in participant observation and testing of e-learning ideas, independent to the institutional view.

As the project closed, more effective conditions for learning existed using the popular ICT learning environments under Web 2.0 (MOODLE) and the rise of social media (Yammer) where many of the key informers still work to sustain the learning community as Border Studies Associates with the original Paideia school at the core.

In an early search of the literature, it was found that little attention had been paid to the online teachers' role in students' learning during an online class session. Many began by taking conventional teaching to the online only to discover that more opportunities to support learning theories and complement the conventional.

The teacher-researcher had completed a learning journey which initially involved confirmation of his views about teaching and learning practices on the Internet in general, followed by the development of a tentative framework at Paideia which provided participants with strategies for facilitating learning, the testing and refinement of this framework over several action research cycles.

As an ICT educator, the teacher-researcher's journey had developed a deeper understanding of participants' expectations and attitudes to online learning and about building and sustaining an effective learning community or community of practice,

Such understanding can change over time due to self-efficacy and the introduction of new media environments and other innovation. The teacher-researcher' own skills and attitudes are developed in tandem with understanding more about teaching and learning using e-learning environments.

RITA Model and the Social/Situational Cycle of Change

Curriculum model building in each cycle of the research was used to explain the dynamics of the programme of study and its stage of development within each ICT e-learning environment change.

Reflective analysis led to the proposed **RITA** model for enabling others to go forward with developing online learning networks. RITA is a simple acronym for the high-level concepts of *Relevance, Involvement, Technology* and *Acceptance* and the model (Figure 5) is proposed to show how all the theories and actions act together as enablers on building and sustaining an effective online learning community. The enablers have transformed learning communities into the wider development of continuous or lifelong action in amorphous personal learning networks.

Table 5. RITA curriculum model enablers for successful online learning networks

RITA enabling concept	Description	Example
RELEVANCE	Learning is supported in a social setting through alliances and trust building stages that are situated in context for adding meaning and relevance to adult learners.	Project or problem based learning situation at work or for promotion in future. This can be as an individual or as part of a team.
INVOLVEMENT	Learning supports continuous dialogue, reflective action, improvisation, self-expression and interpretive practice situated in context.	Co-learning in the moment together from multiple disciplines.
TECHOLOGY	Enabling self-efficacy with ICT and acceptance of ICT as part of the learning agenda.	Social learning and interface mobility across platforms and types of social media.
ACCEPTANCE	Recognition by peers and others in your situation or Profession.	Any holistic community of practice where members operate as associates in sharing roles and responsibilities.

Bandura (2002) and Wenger (1999) had described communities of practice and the reciprocal relation between the environment and self, with personal, social and socio-environmental influences, now taken to a new level with personal learning networks. Learning was defined as a process that had four learning theories with four different orientations and can include both formal and informal learning connections (Bull et al, 2008).

Similar to the Border Studies approach, there is the behaviourist, the cognitive, the humanistic or the **social/situational**, which by adding the time and space dimension to the approach, overlaps with the modern development of social networks and social media in learning.

Building and sustaining an effective online learning community takes time and effort by all participants and is built upon four key **enabling concepts** working at a cognitive level as described in Table 5.

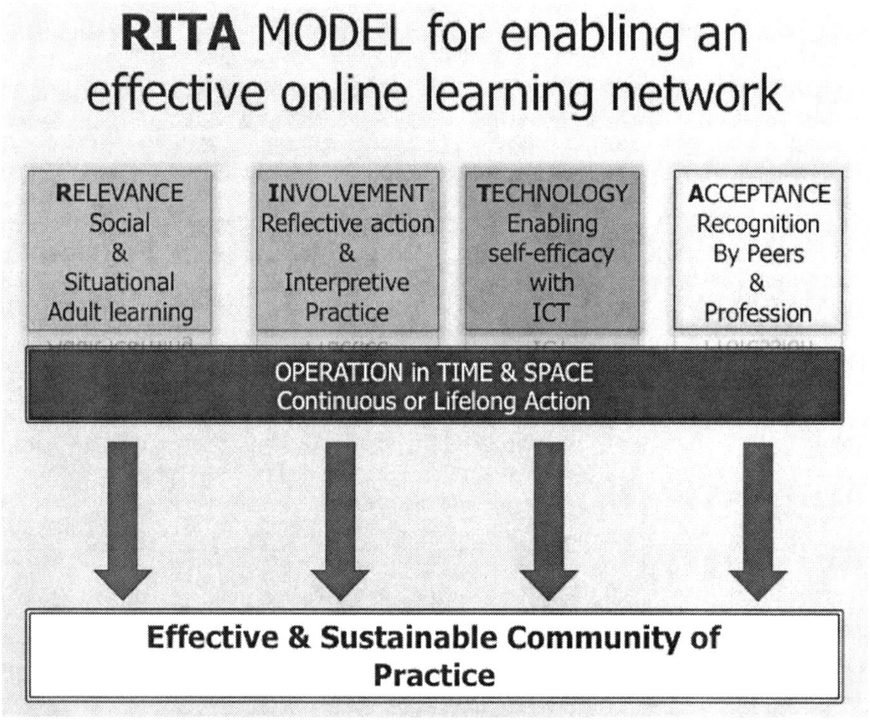

RITA MODEL for enabling an effective online learning network

RELEVANCE Social & Situational Adult learning	INVOLVEMENT Reflective action & Interpretive Practice	TECHNOLOGY Enabling self-efficacy with ICT	ACCEPTANCE Recognition By Peers & Profession

OPERATION in TIME & SPACE
Continuous or Lifelong Action

⬇   ⬇   ⬇   ⬇

Effective & Sustainable Community of Practice

Fig. 5. RITA: a model for enabling online learning networks

To build and sustain an online learning community or community of practice like Paideia/BorderStudies since 1995 required weaving together the stages of development of the e-learning environment, use of appropriate learning theories, changing curriculum models and self-efficacy with online learning and participant action.

Such integrated longitudinal development is part of the process of building and sustaining an effective social learning network today. As a result, educators or those self-organised learners seeking to build their own social learning networks for their semester or trimester or similar short courses may not achieve a desired level of efficiency and sustainability in such a limited time frame. Operation in time and space is needed to develop group processes, alliances and trust.

The path to an effective and sustainable learning network is at the program or degree level over several years or at the personal level for life. This research showed that online learning communities can be sustained beyond course boundaries or borders and grow further into a lifelong learning journey for participants.

The words of T S Eliot (1962) still ring true for all educators who embark on a learning journey as interpretive researchers into their own teaching practice:

We shall not cease from exploration
And the end of all our exploring
Will be to arrive where we started
And know the place for the first time.
T S Eliot 'LITTLE GIDDING' (No. 4 of 'Four Quartets')

References

1. Bandura, A.: Social Learning Theory. Prentice Hall, Englewood Cliffs (1977)
2. Bandura, A.: Self efficacy: The exercise of control. W. H. Freeman, New York (1997)
3. Bandura, A.: Social cognitive theory of mass communications. In: Bryant, J., Zillman, D. (eds.) Media Effects: Advances in Theory and Research, 2nd edn., pp. 121–153. Erlbaum, Hillsdale (2002)
4. Beldarrain, Y.: Distance Education Trends: Integrating New Technologies to Foster Student Interaction and Collaboration. Distance Education 27(2), 139–153 (2006)
5. Bull, G., Thompson, A., Searson, M., Garofalo, J., Park, J., Young, C., Lee, J.: Connecting Informal and Formal Learning: Experiences in the Age of Participatory Media. Contemporary Issues in Technology and Teacher Education 8(2), 100–107 (2008)
6. Eliot, T.S.: The complete poems and plays, pp. 1909–1950. Harcourt, Brace & World, New York (1962)
7. Forester, J.: Critical ethnography: on fieldwork in anHabermasian way. In: Alvesson, M., Willmott, H. (eds.) Critical Management Studies, pp. 46–65. Sage Publications, London (1992)
8. Griffin, J.M.: School museum integrated learning experiences in science: a learning journey. PhD thesis, University of Technology, Sydney (1998)
9. Habermas, J.: The Theory of Communicative Action (translated by Thomas McCarthy). Reason and the Rationalisation of Society, vol. 1. Heineman, London (1987)
10. Hiltz, S.R.: Online Courses as Effective Learning Environments or "Digital Diploma Mills": The Importance of Collaborative Learning (1999), http://web.njit.edu/~hiltz/MontrealRoxanneNature.ppt
11. Johnson, D.: The use of learning theories in the design of a work-based learning course at Masters level. Innovations in Educational Training International 37(4), 129–133 (2000)
12. Kellogg, K.: Learning communities. ERIC Clearinghouse on Higher Education, ERIC Document Reproduction No. ED 430 512 (1999)
13. Kemmis, S., McTaggart, R.: The Action Research Planner, 3rd edn. Deakin University, Geelong (1998)
14. Knowles, M.S.: The Adult Learner: A Neglected Species, 3rd edn. Gulf, Houston (1984)
15. Koszalka, T.A., Ganesan, R.: Designing online courses: a taxonomy to guide strategic use of features available in course management systems (CMS) in distance education. Distance Education 25(2), 243–256 (2004)

16. Laurillard, D.: Rethinking University Teaching: A conversational framework for the effective use of learning technologies, 2nd edn., p. 143. Routledge Falmer, London and New York (2002)
17. Kreuger, R.A., Casey, M.A.: Focus Groups: A Practical Guide for Applied Research, 3rd edn. Sage, Thousand Oaks (2000)
18. Lave, J., Wenger, E.: Situated Learning. Legitimate peripheral participation. University of Cambridge Press, Cambridge (1991)
19. McAfee, M., Eustace, K., Sherman, S.: Cyber participation study at SFSU: conventional and complementary higher education. In: Seventh IFIP World Conference on Computers in Education, WCCE 2001, Copenhagen, Denmark (2001)
20. Mason, R.: New Models for Delivering Lifelong Learning. In: Tschang, T., Della Senta, T. (eds.) Access to Knowledge. New Information Technologies and the Emergence of the Virtual University. Elsevier Science, Amsterdam (2001)
21. Nolan, J., Weiss, J.: Learning Cyberspace: An Educational View of Virtual Community. In: Renninger, A., Shumar, W. (eds.) Building Virtual Communities: Learning and Change in Cyberspace. Cambridge UP, Cambridge (2002)
22. Rada, R.: Efficiency and effectiveness in computer-supported peer-peer learning. Computers Educ. 30(3-4), 137–146 (1998)
23. Symington, D.: The learning journey as research. In: Thesis Writing Workshop. Charles Sturt University, Bathurst (2003)
24. Syverson, M.A.: Student evaluation using the Learning Record Online (1995), http://www.cwrl.utexas.edu/syverson/olr/evaluation.html
25. Vygotsky, L.S.: Mind in Society. Harvard University Press, Cambridge (1978)
26. Wenger, E.: Communities of Practice: Learning, Meaning and Identity. Cambridge University Press, New York (1998)
27. Williamson, K., et al.: Research methods for students and professionals: information management and systems. Centre for Information Studies, Charles Sturt University, Wagga Wagga, NSW, Australia (2000)

Constructing of ePortfolios with Mobile Phones and Web 2.0

Selena Chan

Christchurch Polytechnic Institute of Technology
PO Box 540, Christchurch 8140, New Zealand
Selena.Chan@cpit.ac.nz

Abstract. This paper provides rationalisation, description and evaluation of a project using mobile phones and web 2.0 sites to collate eportfolios. The paper will firstly provide a brief introduction to the context in which the project has been carried out. An overview of what has taken place in mlearning, eportfolios and web 2.0 that is relevant to this project will then be discussed. Reports on the various parts of the project, findings and results then follow. The paper concludes with a summary of the future work on mlearning pedagogy.

Keywords: eportfolios, Web 2.0, mlearning, workplace learning.

1   Introduction

CPIT is one of nineteen institutes of technology in New Zealand (NZ). It is the largest polytechnic in the South Island and offers a variety of courses and programmes leading to local and national certificates, diplomas and degrees. In this paper, a project undertaken to assist baking apprentices is reported.

Applied vocational qualifications for trades-based occupations involve completion of competency- based standards overseen by the New Zealand Qualifications Authority (NZQA). Individual components encompassing trade skills and knowledge components are prescribed in National Certificates. In many trades, the majority of the learning and assessments towards the attainment of National Certificates are undertaken in the workplace. However, many workplaces are work production orientated and apprentice completion rates are affected by delays in the completion of assessment requirements (Chan, 2003). Therefore, this project has been a pragmatic solution towards providing apprentices with the tools to gather evidence of skill and knowledge acquisition in the workplace using mobile phones, owned by a majority of apprentices. The project provided for an alternative method for apprentices to complete on-job assessment through collation of an eportfolio and completion of a challenge test.

2   Profile of Young Apprentice Learners

Preliminary student profile surveys of apprentice learners reveal most as young (between ages 16 to 20), male, recently re-sited from their nuclear family residence

R. Kwan et al. (Eds.): ICT 2011, CCIS 177, pp. 243–253, 2011.

and in their first or second year of paid employment. All the apprentices who participated in the various trials and pilots for the mlearning project owned a mobile phone. In the main, first year apprentices just beginning work owned basic mobile phones capable of text messaging and voice calling. Third and fourth year apprentices owned smart phones capable of web surfing. Therefore, the apprentices participating in this project example young learners having their learning styles reshaped by rapid advances in information technology. (Dede, 2005) These emerging learning styles include fluency in multiple media and simulation-based virtual settings, communal learning involving diverse, tacit, situated experiences and a balance between experiential learning, guided mentoring and collective reflection. The current cohorts of apprentices are now situated in the generation Y grouping of people born between 1982 and 2000. Generation Ys are different not only with respect to their age but are shaped by the economic, social and political conditions and experiences they have grown up with (McCrindle, 2003). Although young people could be characterised as being 'digital natives (Prensky, 2001), work on this project has revealed young apprentices evidence a continuum of digital literacy skills. Hence, the majority of the apprentices participating in the project were significantly proficient in the use of mobile phones. However, up to 25% were not equally confident or competent with the skills required to work with desktop computer-based software. Of these 25%, the majority had poor keyboard skills, were unfamiliar with the concept of 'folders' to archive evidence, had surface orientations to using search engines and were unfamiliar with desk-top based computing jargon.

Following on from the above, the concept of using mobile phones to collect evidence of workplace acquired skills and application of knowledge to practice was proposed.

3   The CPIT Project

The CPIT mlearning project consists of several distinct parts. Each section of the project was organized to meet specific learning outcomes. The sections of the project include the following:-

- Course content for knowledge-based competency standards are delivered to apprentices on hard copy.
- These theory courses are supported using mobile phones via voice and text messaging / short message service (SMS) (Chan, 2005).
- All formative / summative assessments for theory courses and the written part of workplace-based competencies are delivered and answers collected via SMS.
- Evidence gathering to form eportfolios using mobile phone to take photos or videos and posted on photo collation applications on the web.
- Collation and reflection on eportfolio is completed when apprentices attend their yearly block courses at CPIT.
- Eportfolios are collated and shared on social networking/Web 2.0 sites.

Therefore, the two major strands of the project are the

1)   provision of distance learning and support via mobile phones and
2)   use of mobile phones to gather and collate evidence of workplace-based skill
       and knowledge acquisition into eportfolios.   This second strand is described in
       this paper.

4   Mobile Phone Generated ePortfolios

Eportfolios are a tool for digitally storing evidence of learners' skill and knowledge
acquisition. They can be used to collect evidence to support competency-based
assessment in the form of artefacts including photos, video clips, audio snippets and
text files. These artefacts can then be collated and used to showcase learners'
achievement and for formative or summative assessments.

The use of mobile phones to gather evidence of workplace-based skills acquisition
was originally premised on apprentices collecting the photos, videos or text and
sending these to multi-media social sharing sites including flickr and youtube. Our
trials then advanced to using metacafe for storing mobile phone generated videos.
Eventually, many social networking sites provided the facility to directly post photos
or videos directly from a mobile phone. Eventually, social networking sites like vox,
multiply and bebo were used to archive and collate ePortfolio artefacts..

4.1   Making Use of ePortfolios

In a literature review of ePortfolios (Butler, 2006), advantages of deploying
eportfolios to support student learning include:

*   efficiency with regards to searching, retrieving information, manipulating and
        organising. This reduces effort and time needed to maintain the ePortfolio.
*   Possibly more comprehensive and rigorous as an assessment approach.
*   Able to support multimedia.
*   Cost effective to distribute.
*   Easy to share with other stakeholders including peers, teachers, parents,
        employers and others.
*   A showcase for the creator of the ePortfolio including access to a global
        audience if the ePortfolio is web-based.

An important precept of the project reported in this paper, was to adopt Love,
McKean and Gathercool's (2004) advise to move eportfolios beyond 'scrapbook' and
curriculum vitae type arrangements towards using portfolios as web folios as
authentic and authoritative artefacts, linked to standards or other descriptors of skill,
knowledge or dispositional development. This means a range of learning evidence
needs to be collected, reflected on, selected and collated to form eportfolios
showcasing the transformation of apprentices as they develop as trade workers.

4.2   Using Social Networking Sites

An article by O' Reilly (2005) provides a good introduction to what is Web 2.0. Web 2.0 emphasises the use of the web as a platform for 'social software'. Content hosted on various Web 2.0 applications is user generated. For educators, blogs and wikis are the most common examples of Web 2.0 applications. Files archived on Web 2.0 applications are stored on the servers of the companies providing these applications. Ubiquitous internet access to Web 2.0 sites is therefore possible.

Many of the apprentices participating in the trials described in this paper were familiar with social networking websites. A gradual increase in the number of apprentices who maintained their own social networking sites was measured over the 5 years of the project's life. At the start, 60% of apprentices utilised their own social networking sites for the purposes of networking with peers and family. Apprentices' familiarity with the structure, layout and navigation around social networking sites aided the implementation of the 'mobile phone eportfolio' concept.

4.3   'Cloud Computing' and Mobile Learning

The advent of 'cloud computing', with the ability to access digital media stored on remote servers, has increased options available for mobile learning (Corbeil & Valdes-Corbeil, 2007). This means the use of mobile phones to collect just-in-time, authentic and valid evidence of learning is enabled. Apprentices are able to collect photo, video or audio evidence, upload the evidence to a web-based archive and recover and collate the evidence when eportfolio compilation was required.

4.4   Using Social Networking Sites for Collating ePortfolios

Research participants' evaluation of three social networking sites concluded that user friendliness was the most important criteria for selecting a social networking site to use for eportfolio construction. Other criteria used to evaluate social networking sites include:

- ease of access via mobile phones,
- minimal costs and all of the Web 2.0 sites evaluated were free
- simplicity with uploading, archiving and tagging multimedia evidence; and
- suitability of the sites for collating evidence into eportfolios.

The three main social networking sites evaluated for this project are vox (unfortunately no longer available), multiply and bebo. Vox was a social networking site. It was chosen as it had a collation tool that allowed simple aggregation of various artefacts into one or more consolidated folders. This provided for a natural way to compile eportfolios, categorized either as 'product' folders or as 'audience-focused' folders.

Although Multiply was mainly a blogging site, aspects of social networking were also available. Multiply was chosen as it provided an audio blogging tool, important as a means for gathering non-text-based evidence of apprentices' descriptions of product or bakery production evidence in the form of photos and videos.

Bebo was also evaluated as it is one of the most popular social networking sites amongst New Zealand youth, with two thirds of secondary school children registered (Heyday, 2010). However, the project found reluctance amongst apprentices for using Bebo as they preferred to keep Bebo mainly as a personal social networking site. Bebo was accessed by their peers and maintaining a professional eportfolio was seen to not be of interest to peers.

Each of the above social networking sites was supplemented by other Web 2.0 sites. Some apprentices used other means of collating their work. In particular, a site which provided the facility to caption photos proved to be popular. Two sites comic life and comiq were evaluated. Both proved to be easy to use. Captioning of photos was a good way to provide descriptions of baking processes. Captioning encouraged apprentices to provide short text descriptions, leading for some, to more extensive postings on their social networking sites, to describe their learning.

The New Zealand developed open source eportfolio platform, Mahara, was also evaluated in the last iteration of the project. Apprentices found more time was required to learn how to use Mahara but appreciated the structure and layout of the platform, as being more aligned towards compilation of an eportfolio.

4.5   Multimedia and Multiliteracies

One major advantage of utilising mobile phones is the various means by which multimodal (audio, visual) and multimedia (voice recordings, photos, videos and text) could be collected. Many trade apprentices choose a vocational tertiary education route due to perceived lack of achievement with academic (i.e. mainly text-based) learning (Vaughan, Roberts & Gardiner, 2006; Williams, 2008). Therefore, the opportunity to collect and collate evidence of learning in the form of non-text-based media, provides for a wider range of multiliteracies (New London Group, 1996) to be recognised.

4.6   Compiling mPortfolios

The project evolved through several phases as social networking sites developed and matured, mobile phone capabilities increased and the cost of mobile web access lowered.   Figure 1 provides an overview of the final iteration of the project.

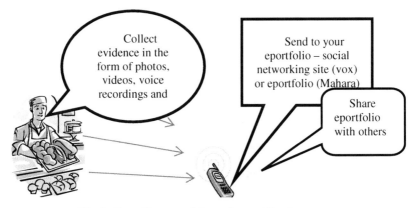

Fig. 1. Compiling eportfolios using mobile phones

In general, the process is as follows:

1)   Collection of evidence, usually in the form of photos, short video clips, audio files describing products or processes, text descriptions and 'comic strips' using photos with embedded comments.
2)   Archiving of all the above artifacts on a social networking site.
3)   Reflecting on the artifacts and collating these into evidence folders of skill acquisition and application of knowledge.
4)   Disseminating these evidence portfolios to workplace supervisor for validation and then to course tutors for assessment.
5)   Adjusting evidence portfolio based on feedback obtained from tutor.
6)   Presenting the evidence as a final eportfolio for summative assessment. From this eportfolio, items are selected and apprentices complete a challenge test to product the products selected. The accomplishment of the challenge test completes summative assessment and completion of an integrated range of competency-based standards.

4.7   Mlearning Pedagogy

The main premise of the projects described in this paper, is to encourage students to not only receive information but to also participate in the creation of knowledge. Hence, mobile technology may be seen as an enabler of a constructive learning process. Mobile phones are used to collect evidence of skill attainment and also as a means by which to access and share eportfolio content with employers, friends and family. Consequently, the mobility of the hardware, provides opportunity to collect evidence of learning on a just-in-time, as it occurs scenario, leading to the collection of 'authentic assessment' (Gipps, 2002) artefacts.   The process of eportfolio collation provides opportunities for reflection on the validity of the artefacts accumulated. Selection of artefacts to showcase on eportfolios requires students to match artefacts to required learning outcomes, and display an understanding of assessment requirements. These learning processes further engage learners into constructing deep learning of the skills and knowledge associated with learning a trade, and becoming bakers (Chan, 2011).

5   Evaluation of the Project

The various iterations of the project were evaluated via student feedback using formative evaluation guidelines based on an eclectic-mixed-methods-pragmatic paradigm. Formative evaluations are evaluations carried out to examine the learners' or users' experiences and acceptance of an 'instructional product's' usability. Findings derived from participants self-reporting provide authentic data through responses to written questionnaires, interviews, or thinking aloud (Reeves & Hedberg, 2003). In this project, structured questionnaires and focus groups were used to evaluate the various processes and platforms used in the projects.

6   Findings

Data garnered was then studied, both from an evaluative and a constructive-interpretive perspective.

6.1   Evaluative findings

These findings were used to improve iterations of the project. The main objective of this part of the project was to derive guidelines to inform the construction of mobile phone generated eportfolios. The guidelines include:

Importance of 'user-friendliness'
Apprentices only engaged if the process was user-friendly. The process was required to be intuitive, efficient and cost effective. In general, using mobile phones to gather photos, videos and audio clips was achieved easily. During the first iteration of the project, uploading evidence to social networking sites was challenging. However, as social networking sites became more mobile-centric, the process of uploading, and in some cases collating eportfolios using mobile phones was simplified.

A review of the term 'digital natives'
The term 'digital natives' (Prensky, 2001) has come into common usage as a term to describe young peoples' familiarity with current information and communications technology (ICT). It is based on a presumption that ICT skills of all young people born after 1985 are more extensive than 'digital immigrants' born before 1985. However, this study has revealed a large subset of young people, born after 1985, who are differently ICT literate. Their ICT skills are distinct from the norm perceived by the mainstream population.

Apprentices in this study were extremely skilled in the use of mobile phones and many maintained social networking sites using desktop computers. There is also an age based 'digital divide' with young people owning mobile hardware (mobile phones, game consoles, mp3 players) instead of desktop computers or laptops. This different set of information literacy skills privilege young people towards participation in the forthcoming mobile computing revolution and pre-dispose them to different ways of thinking and learning (Brown, 2002). Further investigation on how young people utilise mobile technology and how this can be used to enhance learning opportunities is a research area ready for further intensive exploration and analysis.

Non-dependence on specific mobile phone operating systems
Throughout the life of the project, apprentices used their own personal phones to collect evidence. If they had a phone capable of accessing the internet, the phones were used to collate and view the eportfolios. A wide range of ever evolving phone models and mobile phone operating systems meant it was difficult to institute a common structure for eportfolio construction. However, the need to accommodate the wide range of mobile phones used by apprentices provided the project team with on-going opportunities to learn more about mobile learning provision. The project found it important to provide apprentices with the means to evaluate the match between the

mobile phone they owned with the type of social networking site chosen to compile their eportfolio.

Possibility to move to a fully mobile phone eportfolio
Work on mobile learning continues. The current iteration of the mlearning projects revolve around the sole construction of eportfolios using mobile phones. This means the evidence is collected using the mobile phone and emailed directly to mobile web sites constructed as eportfolio showcases. The need to use desktop computers for the process is removed. In addition, the launch of a mobile learning engine (MLE) plug-in for Moodle provides impetus for work on delivering courses currently accessible on desktop computers using mobile phones or other mobile devices including mp3 players (exampled by the Apple iPod Touch), game consoles capable of WiFi browsing (including the play station portable (PSPII) and the Nintendo DS), netbooks and net tablets (exampled by the iPad). These devices are owned by many young people and the provision and evaluation of learning content, activities and interaction via mobile devices continues.

6.2   Constructive-Interpretive Findings

This aspect was analysed through adopting the underlying premises of vocational/ occupational identity formation (Chan, 2011).

Need to re-frame competency based assessments with more holistic descriptors
This paper does not undertake a comprehensive evaluation of the benefits or otherwise of competency based assessments. However, competency based assessments by virtue of their structure are often focused on the assessment of individual skills as opposed to more holistic assessment structures based on recognising capability (Robertson, Harford, Strickland; Simons & Harris, 2000). The use of eportfolios, especially with regard to the pedagogical direction and organisation in this project, proposes a more holistic method for the aggregation of evidence of skills acquisition (Gipps, 2002). In particular, the facility to closely match the visual vernacular preference of young people by accepting the use of multimedia evidence, engages young people more deeply in the process of eportfolio creation. This enhanced intrinsic motivation may lead to better assessment completion outcomes.

The construction of ubiquitous knowledge
Peng, Su, Chou and Tsai (2009) propose the concept of using mobile tools and the availability of 'cloud computing' to provide learners with the opportunity to not only access but create knowledge while 'un-tethered'. Therefore, this project provides one possible approach towards providing workplace based learners, in this case trades apprentices, with the opportunity to contribute their learning, ideas and innovations into their wider industry community of practice. Many apprentices will eventually become leaders in their industry. Therefore providing and encouraging digital skills attainment during apprenticeship training may lead to better understanding and utilisation of the future affordances provided by mobile tools and cloud computing to further knowledge in their respective industries. Exposure to the use of social networking sites beyond their original leisure and lifestyle objectives through the introduction of social networking professional eportfolios provides examples and models for young people to further investigate.

7   Discussion and Implications

From the above findings, several implications for practice have been derived. These include the following.

Participative Research

Technology over the course of the project, in particular, the capabilities of mobile phones to connect with Web 2.0 sites, meant that each iteration of the project, required modification of the types of sites used and adaptation of assessment guidelines for assessing the portfolios. Much of the information on worthwhile Web 2.0 sites to use and proposed techniques to construct eportfolios was contributed to by the apprentices. Therefore, as the project progressed, elements of participative research became much more widespread.

Moving Assessments beyond Competency

As discussed in the above section, there is a need to recognise the importance of 'authentic' assessments, implying a close match between how skills, knowledge and dispositions are applied to real-world environments and the way in which learners' skills, knowledge and dispositions are assessed. Therefore, in many vocational trades, the prevalence of written reports and tests to assess practical skills and dispositions, needs to be re-evaluated. Eportfolios may be one method to collect evidence of learning. Learning activities that create opportunities for the generation of evidence need to also be structured, so that authentic evidence is collected of learners' journeys.

Social Networking Sites to Re-engage Reluctant Learners

For apprentices, extrinsic motivation through the need to complete qualifications does not always yield dividends. This is evidenced by low bakery apprentice completion rates (Mahoney, 2009). Workplace learning with its inherent challenges (Billett, 2001) and workplace assessment issues (Cornford, 1998; Robertson et al, 2000), contribute considerable barriers towards the completion of assessment requirements. A combination of social agency in the form of resilience and conscientious action on the part of individual apprentices; and support from a workplace cognisant of the learning needs of novices to the trade are pre-requisites to ensuring that apprentices engage with workplace learning (Chan, 2008).

Therefore, there are significant advantages, in the form of intrinsic motivations for the learner, in employing social networking sites for the collation of eportfolios. These sites are generally familiar territory to young people. The added dividends of using social networking sites include ease of access not only for the apprentices but also by friends, colleagues and family; an increase in 'traditional' information technology skills; a greater awareness of assessment requirements including aspects of validity, sufficiency and authenticity of evidence; improved confidence in the use of the mobile phone for gathering photos, videos, voice recordings and text fragments; and better opportunities to obtain formative feedback from assessors and peers as the process of eportfolio compilation proceeds.

In addition to the above, the resulting eportfolio provides for a more streamlined approach to the workplace assessment process. The majority of the workload involved with workplace assessments is now transferred from bakery supervisors to the apprentices. Off-job training providers complete the final verification and judgements on the evidence presented in the eportfolios along with the results of a summative practical assessment. This process improves completion rates for apprentices of unit standards required for award of National Certificate qualifications.

Opportunities to Research Workplace-Based Skill Attainment and Identity Formation

The original objective of the CPIT mobile generated eportfolios was to provide an avenue for workplace based skill acquisition to be recognised. However, the aspect of eportfolios as narratives of vocational identity formation also occurred. This makes available a tool for the collection of user generated, ethnographical evidence for the study of identity formation. This area of research is now further enhanced by the ubiquity of ownership of mobile phones coupled with ready access to social networking sites and the mobility of the mobile phone. Currently, even low-end mobile phones include still and video camera capabilities along with direct accessibility to social networking sites including facebook, tweeter and bebo.

Social networking sites, by virtue of their structural framework, encourage the generation of user-generated multimedia entries. The sites also promote user-friendly networking capabilities. This further enhances opportunities for sites to be shared either with a close group of friends or with anyone able to access the internet.

8   Conclusion

The on-going projects have produced many results, some of which have exceeded our expectations. In particular, there was deep engagement in the eportfolio evidence collection and collation process. This engagement by students, who are often difficult to motivate with regards to providing evidence of their skill acquisition for the purposes of assessment, has been both heartening and re-affirming. The project has also led to the construction of a diverse range of digital stories that inform workplace and off-job assessors, the researcher, apprentices, their families and their workplace personnel, about how young people become bakers.

Acknowledgment

The work reported in this paper was supported in part by a grant from the CPIT Foundation.

References

1. Billett, S.: Learning at work: workplace affordances and individual engagement. Journal of Workplace Learning 13(5), 209–214 (2001)
2. Brown, J.S.: Growing up digital: How the web changes work, education and the say people learn. US Distance Learning Association Journal 16(2) (2002)

3. Butler, P.: A review of the Literature on Portfolios and Electronic Portfolios. A report for the eCDF ePortfolio Project. Massey University, College of Education, Palmerston North, New Zealand (2006)
4. Chan, S.: Becoming a Baker:-Factors Contributing to the Successful Completion of National Certificate in Food Production - Baking (level 4) by Apprentices in the New Zealand Baking Industry. Thesis presented in partial fulfilment of Master in Education (Adult Education). Massey University (2003)
5. Chan, S.: Trialling eTXT for mlearning formative assessments. Report completed as part of paper to complete the Graduate Certificate in Applied eLearning convened by Manukau Institute of Technology (2005)
6. Chan, S.: Belonging, becoming and being: The role of apprenticeship. In: ITF 5th Vocational Education Research Forum, Te Papa, Wellington (2008)
7. Chan, S.: Becoming a baker: Using mobile phones to compile eportfolios. In: Pachler, N., Pimmer, C., Seipold, J. (eds.) Work-based Mobile Learning: Concepts and Cases; A Handbook for Academics and Practitioners, pp. 91–115. Peter Lang, Oxford (2011)
8. Corbeil, J.R., Valdes-Corbeil, M.E.: Are you ready for mobile learning? Educause Quarterly 30(2), 51–58 (2007)
9. Cornford, I., Gunn, D.: Work-based learning of commercial cookery apprentices in the New South Wales hospitality industry. Journal of Vocational Education and Training 50(4), 549–567 (1998)
10. Gipps, C.: Sociocultural perspectives on assessment. In: Wells, G., Claxton, G. (eds.) Learning for Life in the 21st Century: Sociocultural Perspectives on the Future of Education, pp. 73–84. Blackwell Publishers, Malden (2002)
11. Heyday: Friend request accepted. In: Down to the wire: The story of New Zealand's internet (2007), http://downtothewire.co.nz/2007/ (2010)
12. Love, D., McKean, G., Gathercool, P.: Portfolios to webfolios and beyond: Levels of maturation. Educause Quarterly (2), 24–27 (2004)
13. Mahoney, P.: Modern apprenticeships: completion analysis. Ministry of Education, New Zealand (2009)
14. New London Group: A pedagogy of multiliteracies: Designing social futures. Harvard Educational Review 66(1), 60–92 (1996)
15. O'Reilly, T.: What is Web 2.0? Design patterns and business models for the next generation of software (2005), http://oreilly.com/web2/archive/what-is-web-20.html
16. Peng, H., Su, Y., Chou, C., Tsai, C.: Ubiquitous knowledge construction: Mobile learning redefined and a conceptual network. Innovations in Education and Teaching International 46(2), 171–183 (2009)
17. Prensky, M.: Digital natives, digital immigrants. On the Horizon 9(5) (2001)
18. Reeves, T., Hedberg, J.: Interactive learning systems evaluation. Education Technology Publications, Englewood Cliffs (2003)
19. Robertson, I., Harford, M., Strickland, A., Simons, M., Harris, R.: Learning and assessment issues in apprenticeships and traineeships. In: AVETRA Conference Report (2000)
20. Vaughan, K., Roberts, J., Gardiner, B.: Young people producing careers and identities: A first report from the pathways and prospects project. New Zealand Council for Educational Research, Wellington, New Zealand (2006)
21. Williams, B.T.: Tomorrow will not be like today: literacy and identity in a world of multiliteracies. Journal of Adolescent and Adult Literacy 51(8), 682–686 (2008)

University Students' Informal Learning Practices Using Facebook: Help or Hindrance?

Rebecca Vivian

University of South Australia, School of Education
Rebecca.Vivian@unisa.edu.au

Facebook (FB) has gained worldwide popularity and Higher Education Institutions have an interest in the Social Network Site's (SNSs) potential to support student learning and peer networking. This research paper reports on the findings from one online discussion group with 15 students from the University of South Australia about their preferences, experiences and use of FB for informal learning. This research found that students accessed and used FB in different ways. FB was used for informal learning via the use of status updates, private messaging, instant chat, tagging and FB 'groups'. Students in the group often viewed FB as a source of procrastination; however, some students felt the benefits of FB to support their learning outweighed the issue of the SNS as a distraction. Some students reported that they increased their use of FB during assessment periods and a number of students used 'SNS self-control' practices that inhibited or reduced their use of FB.

Keywords: Facebook, informal learning, social network site, university, student.

1 Literature

Since *Facebook* (FB) was created by Mark Zuckerberg and fellow co-founders in February 2004, the popular social network site (SNS) has since gained worldwide popularity and currently hosts over 500 million active users. The fundamental core of the user experience is the person's *Home Page* and user *Profile*. The Home Page consists of applications such as a *News Feed*, which feeds the users' friend's status updates and activity. The user profile consists of photos, user information and a *Wall* in which the user can post status updates and have friends post on their Wall. Other applications within the site include the ability to private message, instant chat, poke, create groups, pages, and events as well as the ability to share photos, videos and links. To maintain consistency with FB's terminology, this paper will also use the term *application* to describe these aspects within FB. Due to the vast array of FB applications and the growing number of users worldwide, such a site draws interest from Higher Education Institutions (HEIs) and its potential for teaching and learning.

R. Kwan et al. (Eds.): ICT 2011, CCIS 177, pp. 254–267, 2011.
© Springer-Verlag Berlin Heidelberg 2011

1.1   University Student Use of Facebook

FB use by university students in Australia has grown rapidly within the past few years. In 2006, an Australian study of first year student use of technologies, conducted by Kennedy and colleagues (2008, p. 115), found that at the time only 23.8% of incoming students used SNSs; 62.9% whom of which had never used a SNS. In 2010 a survey of 812 undergraduate and graduate students at the University of South Australia (UniSA) found that 91.1% of those students were active users of FB (Wood, Barnes, Vivian, Scutter & Stokes-Thompson 2010; Vivian & Barnes 2010). FB was also identified as the most preferred SNS by the students. Some 54.7% of students reported using the site, on average, seven times per day, 17.5% on average once a day and 13.1% three times a week (Vivian & Barnes 2010, p. 1009). This use is consistent with findings from other research studies (Ellison et al 2008; Mazman & Usluel 2010; Pempek et al 2008; Steinfield et al 2008), whereby they found students to be incorporating the site into their daily routine. Student access to FB has been found to occur both on- and off-campus. Fitzgibbon and Prior (2010, p. 30) found that 63% of UK first year students were accessing SNSs whilst on campus and the authors proposed that there is a shift in the blend of face-to-face and online socialising while on campus. It has been suggested that (Barkhuus & Tashiro 2010) FB is a technology that suits the nomadic lifestyle of university student due to the accessible nature of FB via computer and mobile technologies. Such accessibility has allowed students the ability to connect with their networks and organize 'ad-hoc' social gatherings on an off- campus (Barkhuus & Tashiro 2010), thus possibly changing the nature of university student socialization on and off-campus.

1.2   Motivations of Facebook Use

Research has identified the primary use of FB by users is to maintain existing offline relationships (Ellison et al 2008; Mazman & Usluel 2010; Pempek et al 2008). To investigate what motivates continued use of FB, Lin and Lu (2011, p. 1152) used networked externalities and motivational theory to survey 402 Taiwanese FB users. They found that the most influential reason for continued use was enjoyment of the site, followed by the number of peers one has, and usefulness. This was similar in a study by Mazman and Usluel (2010, p. 450) who discovered FB adoption to have 'a significant positive relationship with usefulness, ease of use, social influence, facilitating conditions and community identity'. Although these findings are not specific to student motivations, it would be important for research to consider these and student motivations in regards to student use of FB for informal learning.

Another exploration of motivations for technology use in the literature is the notion of *media stickiness*, coined by Huysman et al (2003). This was recognised by Geer and Barnes (2006) in their research of teacher technology use. They found that despite the range of ICTs available, individuals would continue to use the ICTs that they were familiar with. It might be that students choose FB because that is the communication method they are familiar with, therefore investigations as to why students select some technologies over others is required.

An issue that has been raised in the media is the 'addictive' nature of SNS. There is research that links mobile phone use with dependence, and one of the listed symptoms was found to be productivity loss (Leung 2007). As FB is becoming a significant part of student communication and daily life, in conjunction with the ease of access to FB via mobile technologies, it is important to investigate if students are dependent on SNSs or if SNSs have an impact on student study habits or productivity.

1.3   Informal Learning and Facebook

In an effort to engage students entering HEIs, academics and practitioners are interested in the potential that new technologies, like SNSs have for teaching and learning practice. In order to understand how to use these technologies to support formal learning in a way that is natural and engaging for university students, research could explore how students use the technology for informal learning. *Informal learning* can be described as learning that is outside of the classroom, which is often unstructured and unintentional (Knapper & Cropley 2000, p. 12). It is said that good teaching is not only about teaching students *what* to learn, but also about teaching students *how* to learn (Weinstein & Mayer 1983). Therefore, investigating student informal learning practices may be one way that research can inform students about successful learning practices with new technologies. Taking into consideration the frequent use of FB by a majority of university students today, and that they are using FB for informal learning, it is imperative that research investigates informal learning practices with the SNS so that students can be informed about how to effectively learn with the technology.

Despite assumptions that university students are 'tech-savvy', studies have identified that student use of various technologies are not uniform across the cohort (Conole et al 2008; Kennedy et al 2008; Vivian & Barnes 2010; Wood et al 2010). Conole et al (2008) found that students were selecting technologies that complimented the way they preferred to learn. SNSs have the potential to compliment collaboration and there is evidence that students are using SNSs for informal learning (Selwyn 2009; Madge et al 2009; Mazman & Usluel 2010; Vivian & Barnes 2010). Students with a collaborative learning preference have been found to use SNSs more frequently for informal learning (Vivian & Barnes 2010), suggesting that SNSs may be useful for educational collaboration, group work or discussions. Selwyn (2009, p. 161) identified five themes that emerged from education-related interaction on student FB Walls: '(1) recounting and reflecting on the university experience; (2) exchange of practical information; (3) exchange of academic information; (4) displays of supplication and/or disengagement; and (5) 'banter''. Madge et al (2009) found that as the academic year progressed, so did education-related activity on the FB Walls of British students. This activity included organising study groups, for revision and coursework queries. In a study by Kirschner and Karpinski (2010) student FB users had lower GPAs and were found to spend fewer hours studying than non-FB users. Some 26.2% (n=104) of students claimed they perceived FB had an impact of their academic performance; 74.3% of these were negative responses relating to FB being a distraction, source of procrastination and reason for poor time-management (Kirschner & Karpinski 2010, p. 23). The positive responses in the study related to the ability of students to form study groups, network and to provide and receive support. Students have demonstrated here that they recognise the potential issues of FB, and it would be of interest for practitioners, researchers and students to see if those students employ self-management strategies to reduce FB as a distraction and increase their self-control towards FB whilst studying.

2   Research Methodology

This paper reports on the findings from one discussion group that forms part of a larger PhD project that investigates student use of SNSs. The PhD project involved a pre- and post-survey along with observation of student FB 'Wall' activity. The results from this discussion group aim to provide the researcher with qualitative data that allows a deeper insight into student use of FB for informal learning, which frequency scales cannot provide alone. The discussion explored what FB applications students were using and the benefits and disadvantages of FB for informal learning and communication with peers. The research was approved by the UniSA Human Research Ethics Committee prior to commencement.

The project involved students (undergraduate and graduate) at UniSA. Students already involved in the researcher's PhD FB observation research, were invited to participate in an online discussion group about their use of FB. The online discussion group was advertised to these 'FB friends' via status updates and a closed, private FB event. Consent forms and information letters were published on the researcher's FB profile with the use of the *Notes* application. Students were provided with a link to the information and, if interested, to privately message the researcher with consent to participate. Of the 110 students who were invited, 15 gave their consent to participate in the online discussion group. There were 13 females and 2 males. The majority of participants were from the Division of Education, Arts, and Social Sciences (EAS; 7), and the Division of Health Sciences (HS; 6), with 1 student being from the Division of Information Technology, Engineering and Environment (ITEE), and 1 from the Division of Business (BUE). Six students were in their first year of study at university, five in their second year, and three in their third year. One participant was a Masters student. To ensure anonymity all student names have been changed.

The researcher created a closed-private FB Group to which 23 questions were posted prior to participants joining the Group Page. The online discussion was held in December 2010. Once students provided their consent, they were invited by the researcher to the group, and were able to begin responding to the questions. The discussion was conducted in an asynchronous manner and students were allowed two weeks to provide their responses. Students did not have to answer all questions if they did not feel comfortable doing so. The researcher used the qualitative software NVivo 8 to analyse key themes that emerged from the discussion.

3 Results

3.1 Student Access to Facebook

Students were asked to describe their access to FB. On the whole, students varied in terms of how often they accessed the site. On average, about 9 of the 15 students said they access the site throughout their day. In many cases it appeared to be habitual; students reported that they would check their FB account at key points of their day. One recurring sequence was morning and evening or, as in one case, a student said they checked their FB every morning before they got out of bed on their mobile. Students were also reporting that in conjunction with a habitual 'checking', they would check it randomly throughout the day, or whenever they had access to a computer. Sometimes students voiced that they felt they check the site too often, as one student had said: *"I access Facebook a bit too much"* (Dave, Masters, male, EAS student). However, use was found to vary and is not always consistent according to one student who said *"… there are days where I don't log on at all, and others where I'm on all day"* (Linda, 1st year, female, HS student).

On average, about two students reported accessing FB daily, three students estimated accessing FB every few days and nine of the other students reported checking their site at intervals or constantly throughout the day. It was those who reported to access the site constantly throughout the day, who appeared to be constantly FB *checking* their site for recent notifications and updates rather than merely accessing the site.

When asked how much engaged time students devote to spending on the FB site, estimations ranged from "[f]*or a few minutes to check and respond to things*" (Sue, 2nd year, female ITEE student) to "[t]*ime dedicated to Facebook… constant*" (Dave, Masters, male EAS student). Once again the specific use of the site varied between individual students.

Students reported that they were accessing FB on their personal computers, laptops, university computers and/or mobile phones. Some students used a combination of any (e.g. laptop and mobile phone). Those who were able to access FB with their mobile phone reported checking it more constantly throughout their day. This was also emphasized by students mentioning they could receive notifications on their mobile phone about when they received FB messages and could access the SNS anywhere or when bored. Those who used personal computers to access FB said that they would access it at certain times, such as morning and night, because this was most likely when they would be at home.

3.2 Student Use of Facebook for Informal Learning

The general consensus was that students were definitely using FB for informal learning; to discuss coursework, assignments, revise, share information and provide support or to merely vent. One student exclaimed a repetitive *'yes yes yes yes yes yes yes yes yes yes…'* to emphasise the fact that they are using the site to support their learning. Students were using FB for discussing a range of educational topics, as mentioned by Danielle (1st year, female, HS) who said: *'Yes absolutely I discuss uni course content, what lecturers will cover in tests and exams, questions that I can't work out and matters that need clarifying'*. Kate, a first year, EAS, female student also said: *'I frequently do to discuss questions that I have relating to assignments, or sometimes a concept I might not understand... to discuss outcomes.'*

One student associated FB use for informal learning as being similar to sitting in the library and working at a table with a group of peers; because they are able to ask a question and chat whenever they feel like it. This notion of feeling like they can instantly access friends was mentioned throughout the focus group discussion. Although the students are not physically together, it appears the site provides some sense of working together within a space, due to peer availability, albeit that online.

The university provides discussion boards for some courses and classes, and some of the focus group students mentioned using the university Moodle forums. However, students had mentioned that students had also created their own FB Groups to use in conjunction with the university forum. Students reported that they were using the FB Group to discuss coursework, exams and assignments. Some of the course pages mentioned were a Sustainable Environments Group, an Occupational Therapy Group and a other groups that revolved around social events and welcoming new students. Reasons students reported to be using these FB groups over university created groups were related to accessibility;

'Most of my subject have a moodle site. I don't really post anything on it but I will check it every now and then... If I need to ask a question though I'll just post it on my FB coz im more likely to have it open already and I have enough uni friends... that can answer' (Carly, 1st year, female, HS).

And the safety of asking questions within their friend network;

'I try to use the Uni site for anything that I think will be of use to the whole student group and use Facebook for things that I think I would be embarrassed to ask on the forum such as basic chem' (Lanie, 2nd year, female, HS).

Of the 15 students who responded to this question, four rejected the idea that they use FB for informal learning. One male (Tom, 3rd year, EAS), said that he often adds university group members to FB, but rarely do they talk, not even to discuss group work. One other female responded by saying: *'I avoid discussions about assignments online. If I do use it, I adjust the privacy to allow only specific people to see my comment'* (Sue, 2nd year, female, ITEE).

Another female student (2nd year, EAS), said that she does not use FB for informal learning, and hypothesizes that this may be due to the lack of university peers on the site or because she has not been 'imaginative' with the technology. Jess, a 1st year EAS student described that she uses FB in a 'solitary' fashion rather than for discussion about assignments. It must be noted here that perhaps these students are using FB as a means of progress reporting, or emotional support, but are not specifically using it for discussions with peers for coursework.

3.3 Purpose for Selecting Facebook as an Informal Learning Communication Method

The researcher categorized reasons as to why students within the focus group reported using FB to communicate with their university peers and for educational conversations. These themes have been summarised into a table below, with an explanation, or example as to why that was a given reason.

Table 1. A summary of themes as to why students use FB as a communication medium for informal learning and communication with peers

Reason	Explanation
Affordable	• Cheap communication (alternative to paying for mobile texts). • Able to communicate to many for an affordable price.
Habitual	• For clarification; to quickly chat with friends online (via minimization of the browser window, or access of a mobile). • Know that their peers will check FB frequently and they check the site regularly themselves. • To notify peers to check email; as they think they will check FB first. • Notifications allow for students to be notified of FB activity.
Features	• Easy to communicate as a group. • Useful features with the ability to share links, share pictures and have discussions. • Easy to use the features.
Availability	• Access to the site is possible at any time of day and night. • Instant Chat application is useful for urgent responses because peers are usually online. Can use it to quickly clarify with peers. • Peers are usually available or online.
Accessibility	• Can access anywhere/anytime on a mobile phone or laptop. • FB is often running in the background of student activities and during study time. • Peers are accessible.
Networking	• Can ask questions within a comfortable network of peers without feeling embarrassed. • Ability to communicate to a wide network; there is a higher chance of response to a question. • Someone is always online. • "Less intrusive" communication method. • To contact peers for whom they do not have a mobile number. • To organize class enrollment and events or meetings.

3.4 Facebook Applications Used for Informal Learning

Students were asked which FB applications they used for communication with peers in regards to coursework and assignments. Below is a table that features the specific FB application and how students reported to be using the application.

Table 2. A summary of the FB applications that students reported using for informal learning and their reasoning

Facebook Application	Student Reported Usage
Status Updates	• For general enquiries and to ask questions. • To ignite discussions about an assignment. • To seek help. • To list key topics before exams as a self-revision and checklist tool.
Wall Posts (to a friend's wall)	• To organize group sessions. • To hold revision discussions. • To ask a question.
Private Messages	• For private and useful information. • For small group work, or to arrange face-to-face meetings. • For when the information exceeds a standard post or status update length. • To migrate conversations about coursework to a private space for those who contribute.
Commenting	• As a response to a friend's conversation or question.
Sharing Links	• To share with Friends who will find the link useful.
Instant Chat	• To talk with those who are personally closer (conversation goes between university related and personal). • To chat with university friends whilst doing an assignment (to answer and ask questions). • To quickly clarify an assignment question with someone online. • To check university results. • Create a university grouping and be available to only those people who are online in chat.
Group Pages	• To discuss course assignments • For particular courses, programs or assignments. • To keep discussions in a private environment. • To organize events, meetings or accommodation.
Tagging (via Wall Post or Status Update)	• To tag certain people to get their attention. • To begin a discussion about coursework. • To have a discussion with those in a study group.
Events	• To organize study sessions and social events.

3.5   Student Access to Facebook during Study

Students were found to be using FB for informal learning, however they reported that FB was at times distracting to their studies. In order to determine if students believed that their FB use changed throughout the university semester, students were asked to discuss their use of FB whilst studying and during assessment periods. They were also asked about self-control during study and to reveal if they set themselves limitations in order to control FB access during these times. All but one student responded to the questions relating to this topic. During analysis of the discussion, the researcher was able to allocate students into one of three distinct categories: *'Open Access'*, *'Limited Access'* and *'No Access'* based on their individual responses to their use of FB during study time.

Table 3. A summary of student responses as to whether they use self-control to FB use during studying and during exam and assignment periods

Open Access
Dave, Masters, male, EAS
Has FB open all the time whilst working on assignments.
"..my peers might post tips about the assignment... help them with any questions... to check where everyone is up to (a form of motivation)".
Kylie, 3rd year, female, EAS
"...keep Facebook open while doing assignments so I can ask online friends questions and vice versa". Uses FB as a study 'break'.
Linda, 1st year, female, HS
"I usually have it open, as I like to be able to communicate with uni friends". Increases FB use during exam and assignment periods.
Carly, 1st year, female, HS
"Hmm I have it open and as much as I hate to admit it, it probably hinders my learning more than it helps...". *"Probably should* [limit use] *but I don't"*. Conversations increase around exam and assignment periods. Reports that conversations are usually about procrastination, and reporting assignment progress.
Lanie, 2nd year, female, HS
"I leave facebook running and I use it as a useful distraction". Likes having FB always open during study time, as others are instantly accessible.
Restricted Access
Kate, 1st year, female, EAS
Will log-in to FB to have a 'break': *"[I]f I am doing an assignment or stuck in a rut with my study I find it good to distract myself for a few minutes to re-group my thoughts or ask class mates how they are going"*.
Sarah, 1st year, female, HS
"I try [to limit use].. *but we did some really good revision via Facebook... and actually it really helped"*.
Anna, 2nd year, female, HS
"this [FB] *hinders my study. I generally try to avoid opening FB until I have completed what I need to"*. Communication with peers is minimal unless it is exam or assignment periods.
Tara, 3rd year, female, BUE
During exam time; limit FB access to morning and bedtime. The 'App' is deleted off the mobile phone to restrict access. *"During assignments I check it as a reward after various 'milestones' in my writing"*.

Table 3. (*continued*)

Danielle, 2nd year, female, HS FB use is increased during exam periods because needing to ask peers questions. Will generally try to keep away during study, but will log in for a 'break'.
Sue, 2nd year, female, ITEE Does not keep FB open while studying; *"that's too tempting"*. *"I sign in briefly as a distraction when studying... but I keep it very brief"*. Logs-out each time so that she cannot easily open FB.
Deb, 2nd year, EAS Not a big user of FB, but will not restrict access all together. *'I have found it to be encouraging for me when I read of friends or aquaintances struggling or struggle myself and we all support each other and then share the successes as well as the commiseraions!'*
No Access
Jess, 1st year, female, EAS During exam time restricts access: *"For good/productive study I need to have facebook closed"*.
Tom, 3rd year, male, EAS Reports that he does not use FB to discuss coursework. *"I get my girlfriend or someone to change my password until the workload is over"*.

Students within *'Open Access'* revealed that they had allowed themselves unlimited access to FB during exam and assignment time, as well as whilst studying. Students within this group generally reported benefits associated with having FB open permanently during study, such as: instant access to university peers, the ability to participate in and view conversations about university topics and assignments they are working on, and the ability to view peers' progress, via status updates and conversations.

Students within the *'Restricted Access'* group employed particular *SNS self-control strategies* to limit their use of FB whilst studying or during assignment and exam periods. These strategies included: having to log out of the site so that they need to sign back in with a password, deleting mobile phone 'Apps' and closing FB until tasks were completed. These strategies were employed to enhance self-control and reduce ability to procrastinate on the site. Students within this group often reported using FB as a reward for studying, and would log in to the site when feeling stuck, needing to seek help, or to have a 'break'. Students would not entirely sever FB use during study times. They acknowledged the benefits of the site, as described by those in the *'Open Access'* group, however found that to enhance their concentration and productivity they needed to restrict their access and not allow it to constantly run in the background.

Students who were within the *'No Access'* group identified that they do not use FB whilst studying and employ strategies that restrict their access for long periods of time. They did not reveal that they would log-in to FB to communicate with peers during study. One student reported that they do not use FB to discuss university work at all. Therefore, perhaps those students who do not see FB as an effective means to communicate with peers may restrict their access altogether, because they do not see the need, or benefit in the site for informal learning.

3.6 Perceived Disadvantages and Advantages of Facebook for Informal Learning

Perceived disadvantages of FB were often related to the SNS as being a source of procrastination and a distraction. This view also permeated through many of the responses to other questions. One student had said '*the definition of procrastination is facebook*' (Nicole, 1st year, female, EAS). A student reasoned that FB was a distraction because '[i]*t can be difficult to be disciplined about facebook use as it's always "there" while I am doing uni assignments*' (Jess, 1st year, female, HS). The advantage of FB as being accessible also appears to be a hindrance at times.

Issues of knowledge privacy were raised. Dave, an EAS Masters student, said that most university discussions are public for all friends to see, although, at times him and his friends, express concern for those who take their information without contributing. Therefore, often their conversations will move to the Private Message application on FB to include only those who are primary contributors.

Despite students viewing FB as a distraction they still perceived there to be benefits, and as reported in table 3 above, despite feeling FB is a distraction, there were still students who allowed themselves to access the site whilst studying because of the benefits. As one student put it; '[i]*t can be a huge distraction for me... I still love it*' (Danielle, 2nd year, female, HS).

The benefits of FB use for informal learning related to accessibility, availability of peers and the ability to communicate with university peers using the various site applications. As was voiced by two students who said that '*It makes the course much fuller, richer in depth etc... it's a fantastic way to collaborate*' (Lanie, 2nd year, female, HS) and that FB is '*useful to communicate with each other outside of contact hours*' (Anna, 2nd year, female, HS).

Two students expressed that they felt their use of FB for informal learning had assisted them in achieving additional assignment marks, as one student had said: '*I believe my grade has gone up significantly by working with others through Facebook*' (Lanie, 2nd year, female HS). Sarah (1st year, HS) also felt similarly, as she said; '*I think it's taken a lot of stress out of our course and also helped me get a few extra marks on assignments through brain storming with peers*'. However, whether assignment grades were actually influenced by FB use is beyond the scope of this paper.

4 Discussion

The results from this online discussion group confirm that the majority of university students within this particular group are using FB for informal learning and are using a range of particular FB applications to do so. Similar to existing research, these interactions included discussions of coursework, revision, sharing information and providing support, or to vent (Selwyn 2009; Madge et al 2009). There were variations in how often and when students accessed FB, and how long they were engaged with the site. Although a large percentage of students are reporting to be using FB, we cannot assume that all students use the site in the same way, just as is cautioned against by research (Conole et al 2008; Kennedy et al 2008; Wood et al 2010; Vivian & Barnes 2010). However it was evident, within this discussion group, that students did have a somewhat habitual nature of accessing FB throughout their day or week depending on factors, such as access to computers, daily routine, or whether they could access FB on their mobile phones. Those students who had access to FB on their mobile phones often mentioned that they can check it anytime, anywhere. These students appeared to be constantly '*FB checking*' rather than just *accessing*. This constant access to sites like FB ignites interesting possibilities for mobile learning and student participation. Like the research has discovered, this access is occurring both on- and off-campus (Fitzgibbon & Prior 2010), and the accessible nature of FB appears to lend itself to the lifestyle of students and their ability to network with peers anytime (Barkhuus & Tashiro 2010).

Many of the students in the discussion believed there were benefits to using FB for informal learning. The researcher acknowledges that students would be using other forms and/or a combination of communication for education-related purposes. Factors that influenced why students chose FB as a communication method included the SNS being an *affordable* technology, as being part of their *habitual* activities, as *useful* and familiar, as having benefits in terms of *availability* and *accessibility*, as well as the *networking* capabilities. These themes that emerged are similar to the motivations identified by other studies (Lin & Lu 2011; Mazman & Usluel 2010).

Despite the availability of university forums for course discussions, it was reported students had created student-initiated FB Groups that they would use for coursework discussion. How exclusive these FB Groups are, is unknown. It would appear to have benefits for those who are within the friendship networks; however for students that fall outside of this network, they may not be invited. Some students reported that they used these FB Pages to ask a question, or choose to use their profile pages to post a status update or question to a friend's Wall, instead of their university forum. This was found to be because FB is viewed as a safe place to ask questions, as well as it being easily accessible because they often had FB already open whilst studying. Perhaps the notion of 'media stickiness' (Huysman et al 2003) and their familiarity and preference of using FB over a Moodle forum influenced their decision. Or it could possibly be attributed to the space being outside of the academic-eye. Research should further investigate student reasoning for choosing to conduct discussions in student-initiated FB pages, over formal university forums.

Some students felt that they spend more time on FB than they should. Like the literature, this research found that some students did feel that FB use had an impact on their grades or productivity (Kirschner & Karpinski 2010). Students perceived FB to be a source of procrastination and a distraction. Students were found to have different levels of access to FB whilst studying: *Open Access*, *Restricted Access* and *No Access*. In an effort to reduce access and FB as a source of distraction, during study, students reported to employ a range of *SNS self-control strategies*, such as changing passwords, physically logging out of the site, and setting study goals. Despite these negative aspects, students still perceived FB to be a valuable technology for informal learning. Some students believed the benefits outweighed the negative; therefore they allowed themselves *Open Access* whilst studying. In some cases, FB access was identified as a motivational reward for productive study.

4.1 Limitations

The results reported are the perceived use of FB by the university students in the group, and therefore, may not reflect actual usage. The researcher made it known to students that they did not have to answer all of the questions, and the researcher acknowledges that not all participants contributed to every question. Where this paper refers to 'university students', it refers to those 15 students within the focus group of this research. The researchers recognize that generalizations cannot be made based on the small number of students involved in the discussion group. Similarly, claims based on demographical data are not possible due to the small number of participants. The views expressed by these individuals are those from one university in South Australia, and these may not be the shared views of university students from other HEIs. Further research could use qualitative analysis to determine if these perspectives are the same or similar for other university students.

4.2 Conclusions and Implications for Future Research

This research has identified that students are using FB and various FB applications for informal learning. Although FB is popular, students do not use the SNS in the same way. These student differences may pose implications if FB is to be employed for formal learning purposes. Future research could explore demographical differences between students. It was evident that some students felt FB is a distraction to their studies. If HEIs are to use FB for formal learning, considerations need to be made about the site being a distraction. As was identified in the literature, good teaching practice also takes into account teaching students *how* to learn. Research should endeavor to explore FB dependence and if student learning strategies are effective in managing self-control of FB use. Research should continue to explore effective learning practices so that research can inform students how to learn with emerging technologies. It is important that HEIs do not become static in terms of teaching students how to learn, and this is ever more important considering the role that technologies like FB appear to be playing in student informal learning practices.

References

1. Barkhuus, L., Tashiro, J.: Student Socialization in the Age of Facebook. In: Proceedings of the 28th International Conference on Human Factors in Computing Systems, CHI 2010, ACM, Atlanta (2010)
2. Conole, G., de Laat, M., Dillon, T., Darby, J.: 'Disruptive Technologies', 'Pedagogical Innovation': What's new? Findings from an In-Depth Study of Students' Use and Perception of Technology. Computers & Education 50(2), 511–524 (2008)
3. Ellison, N., Steinfield, C., Lampe, C.: The Benefits of Facebook "Friends": Social Capital and College Students' Use of Online Social Network Sites. Journal of CMC 12(4), 1143–1168 (2007)
4. Fitzgibbon, K., Prior, J.: The Changing Nature of Students' Social Experience Within University. Journal of Applied Research in Higher Education 2(1), 25–32 (2010)

5. Geer, R., Barnes, A.: Media Stickiness and Cognitive Imprinting: Inertia and Creativity in Cooperative Work and Learning with ICTs. International Federation for Information Processing 210, 55–64 (2006), http://www.springerlink.com/content/d9327285845v1613/fulltext.pdf
6. Kennedy, G., Judd, T., Churchward, A., Gray, K., Krause, K.L.: First year students' experiences with technology: Are they really digital natives? Australasian Journal of Educational Technology 24(1), 122 (2008)
7. Kirschner, P., Karpinski, A.: Facebook and academic performance. Computers in Human Behaviour 26(6), 1237–1245 (2010)
8. Knapper, C., Cropley, A.: Lifelong Learning in Higher Education, 3rd edn. Kogan Page, London (2000)
9. Leung, L.: Leisure Boredom, Sensation Seeking, Self-esteem, Addiction Symptoms and Patterns of Mobile Phone Use. In: Konijin, E., Tanis, M., Utz, S., Linden, A. (eds.) Mediated Interpersonal Communication. Department of Communication Science, Free University Amsterdam (2007), http://www.com.cuhk.edu.hk/cuccr/en/pdf/mp9-CMC.pdf
10. Lin, K.-Y., Lu, H.: Why People Use Social Networking Sites: An Empirical Study Integrating Network Externalities and Motivation Theory. Journal of Computers in Human Behaviour 27(3), 1152–1161 (2011)
11. Madge, C., Meek, J., Wellens, J., Hooley, T.: Facebook, Social Integration and Informal Learning at University: 'It Is More for Socialising and Talking to Friends About Work than for Actually Doing Work'. Learning, Media and Technology 34(2), 141–155 (2009)
12. Mazman, S., Usluel, Y.: Modeling Educational Usage of Facebook. Computers and Education 55(2), 444–453 (2010)
13. Pempek, T., Yermolayeva, Y., Calvert, S.: The College Students' Social Networking Experiences on Facebook. Journal of Applied Developmental Psychology 30(3), 227–238 (2009), http://www.sciencedirect.com/science/article/B6W52-4VBWPCV-1/2/f07127b3fecff05694e0ed4808a50f0c
14. Selwyn, N.: Faceworking: Exploring Students' Educational-Related Use of Facebook. Learning, Media and Technology 32(2), 157–174 (2010), http://pdfserve.informaworld.com/474623_731196606_912649395.pdf
15. Steinfield, C., Ellison, N., Lampe, C.: Social Capital, Self-Esteem, and Use of Online Social Network Sites: A Longitudinal Analysis. Journal of Applied Developmental Psychology 29(6), 434–445 (2008)
16. Vivian, R., Barnes, A.: Social Networking: From Living Technology to Learning Technology? In: Steel, C.H., Keppell, M.J., Gerbic, P., Housego, S. (eds.) Curriculum, Technology & Transformation for an unknown Future, Proceedings Ascilite Sydney 2010, pp. 1007–1019 (2010), http://ascilite.org.au/conferences/sydney10/procs/Vivian-full.pdf
17. Weinstein, C., Mayer, R.: The teaching of learning strategies. Innovation Abstracts 5(32), 4 (1983), http://eric.ed.gov/PDFS/ED237180.pdf
18. Wood, D., Barnes, A., Vivian, R., Scutter, S., Stokes-Thompson: The Future May have Arrived, but Engagement with ICTs is Not Equal Among Our Diverse "Net Gen" Learners. In: Steel, C.H., Keppell, M.J., Gerbic, P., Housego, S. (eds.) Curriculum, Technology & Transformation for an unknown Future. Proceedings Ascilite Sydney 2010, pp. 1107–1118 (2010), http://ascilite.org.au/conferences/sydney10/procs/Wood2-full.pdf

Piloting Lecture Capture:
An Experience Sharing from a Hong Kong University

Keng T. Tan[*], Eva Wong, and Theresa Kwong

Centre for Holistic Teaching and Learning,
Hong Kong Baptist University, Kowloon Tong, Kowloon, Hong Kong SAR
{alfredt,evawong,theresa}@hkbu.edu.hk
http://chtl.hkbu.edu.hk

Abstract. This paper reports on valuable experience gathered from a pilot project that deployed lecture capture as a student engaging e-learning tool at Hong Kong Baptist University. The paper presents the planning of the pilot project and how it was deployed. Furthermore, user satisfaction, and user perception on the use of lecture capture as an effective and efficient e-learning technology are presented. Based on these findings, some valuable lessons can be learned and shared with other institutions. Finally, while this paper only presents the findings from credit bearing academic courses across a number of different academic teaching faculties at HKBU, these findings are also applicable for non-credit bearing courses.

Keywords: lecture capture, pilot project planning and deployment.

1 Introduction

The pilot project, conducted during the second academic semester of 2010-2011, sought to introduce the use of lecture capture as a student engaging e-learning tool at Hong Kong Baptist University (HKBU). This paper focuses on the experiences learned from the pilot project for credit bearing academic courses represented from a number of different academic teaching faculties at HKBU.

The pilot targeted credit bearing academic courses in the Department of Physics (PHYS1XXX - a general physics level 2 course for first year undergraduates), Department of Communication (ORGC1XXX - a core public speaking course for all undergraduate students for the School of Communication), Academy of Visual Arts (VA2XXX - a second year undergraduate course on handicrafts and craft works), School of Business (MGNT7XXX - an elective course for the Master of Business Administration (MBA) program), Language Centre (LANG7XXX - a core unit in a Master of English program) and the Library (IT1XXX - a first year undergraduate course on information management technology). The use of lecture capture in these courses varied from recordings of brief instructional sessions, e.g. in IT1XXX, to elaborate recordings of both lectures and lab experiments, e.g. in PHYS1XXX. These

---

[*] Corresponding author.

R. Kwan et al. (Eds.): ICT 2011, CCIS 177, pp. 268–279, 2011.
© Springer-Verlag Berlin Heidelberg 2011

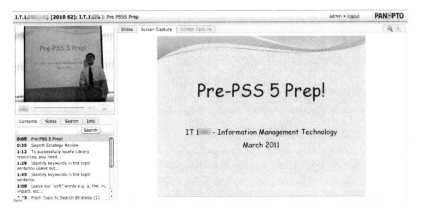

Fig. 1. A recording of the librarian and an introduction session in the course IT1XXX

Fig. 2. A recording of the lecturer and an experiment setup in the course PHYS1XXX

Fig. 3. A recording of a student presentation in the course ORGC1XXX

are illustrated in Figures 1 and 2.The lecture capture technology was also used to record student work, e.g. in ORGC1XXX. This is illustrated in Figure 3.The aim was to capture all audio, video and projected on-screen content (PowerPoint slides, screen captures and digital visualizer output - if any) of the presenter and publish the recorded content on the HKBU e-Learning platform - Moodle 1.9.10 (a.k.a BU eLearning platform).

2   The Context of the Pilot Project

The project was initiated by the Centre for Holistic Teaching and Learning (CHTL) at HKBU as part of an introduction to student engaging teaching and learning activities leveraged on e-learning technologies. Prior to this introduction, there were only sporadic and occasional uses of video recording of teaching or seminar events at HKBU. These were usually re-broadcast via the HKBUTV channel (which is an on-campus TV channel) and/or the HKBUTube (which is a video on demand system - similar to YouTube, hosted by the HKBU Library). Nonetheless, no system was available to capture, all audio, video and projected on-screen content (PowerPoint slides, screen captures and digital visualizer output - if any) of the presenter, and publish the recorded content on the HKBU e-Learning platform. Thus, this pilot project introduced such an e-learning technology to fill this gap.

Whilst there are a number of lecture capture technologies available, it was decided that the piloted lecture capture technology must be economical, scalable, flexible and centrally administrable such that on successful completion of the pilot project, the e-learning technology could be easily deployed across the institution comprising 8000 full time students.

Key requirements for the lecture capture system identified from the onset of the pilot project were as follow:

- to capture all audio, video and projected on-screen content (PowerPoint slides, screen captures and digital visualizer output - if any) of the presenter;
- to be flexibly deployable across the campus without the need for retrofitting into existing classrooms, thus, minimizing both cost of deployment and allowing for a greater ubiquity of this e-learning campus wide;
- to be centrally administered such that simultaneous recordings at different venues on campus can be scheduled and monitored. This is a necessity for an enterprise level deployment of lecture capture, otherwise, it would be too human resource intensive and not viable for any campus wide deployment, and
- to produce content that can be automatically published onto the BU eLearning platform.

With the above requirements in mind, a two month user trial of two competing lecture capture products currently available in the market, namely Echo360 and Panopto, was undertaken. While both are very compelling lecture capture systems in their own right (both meeting the above requirements), the pilot project was limited to the Panopto lecture capture system for the following reasons:

- Panopto is a total software based solution that can be run even from a laptop (both Macs and Windows environment are supported), thus, allowing better flexibility in maximizing the deployment of the pilot project.
- Panopto supports up to 8 recorded input sources (on paper at least, but in practice, 6 inputs are a more realistic outcome), thus allowing a greater flexibility in possible deployment of the pilot project.
- Being a software solution, Panopto is much more cost effective for both the pilot project and for future campus wide deployment.

The drawback of using Panopto is the fact that there is no immediate technical support from the supplier within the time zone as all support is based in the United States (A minimum13 hour time difference).

3   The Pilot Project Plan

A 10 pilot Panopto license setup was purchased to enable deployment across the HKBU campus. 5 teaching academic units and the HKBU library took up a license for their use in teaching and learning. The remaining 4 licenses were used to support co-curricular programs and staff professional development workshops.

The following protocols were applied for the participating pioneer lecturers:

- They must use the lecture capture in their teaching and learning activities.
- They must allow the research team to act as "teaching assistants" in their BU eLearning platform course rooms, so that technical assistance was available when needed for deployment of the recordings to their students.
- They must permit user evaluation studies, and compile case studies, on their use and on student use of the lecture capture technology.

A team of 5 support staff supported the pioneer lecturers, and a team of student helpers assisted them in their use of the lecture capture technology. Training lessons were given to the lecturers to enable them to have a better understanding of the technology. Furthermore, both software and hardware support was provided to each lecturer. Both online and in person assistance are also provided to troubleshoot any concerns voiced by the pioneer lecturers. The idea behind this comprehensive support package was to guarantee that these pioneers could fully test and try out the lecture capture technology for its true effective and efficient use as a student engaging teaching and learning tool, and not be bogged down by the technology. This was especially important given the short duration of the pilot.

4   The Different Pedagogies Used in the Pilot Project

The literature [1-3] points to a diversified use of lecture capture technologies across pedagogical practice. The pedagogical approach for each course in the pilot project is presented in Table 1.

Table 1. Approaches to lecture capture

Course	Major pedagogical use of lecture capture
IT1XXX	Lecture captured recordings are used to supplement actual face to face instructions.
LANG7XXX	Lecture captured recordings are released to students after the actual class allowing for student revision and review of the lecture they attended.
MGNT7XXX	Lecture captured recordings are used both for student revision and for self-review of their class presentations.
PHYS1XXX	Lecture captured recordings are used for student revision, together with laboratory experiments associated with in-class lectures; and for recording final projects wherein they are working in groups to present their experiments.
VA2XXX	Lecture captured recordings are used for student revision, together with close-ups of hand-craft works associated with in-class lectures, and for their project presentation.
ORGC1XXX	Lecture capture recordings of student public speaking presentations for self-improvement and assessment.

4.1   Rationale behind Pedagogical Use of Lecture Capture in IT1XXX

Although IT1XXX is a full credit bearing course for the first year cohorts of students in the Faculty of Science, the information literacy sessions from the library are only one part of the actual course and there are 30 groups of first year students receiving these instructions simultaneously. Thus, in order to manage the total workload and the face-to-face contact between the limited library staff with a growing students population (especially in view of the coming double cohorts in academic year 2012-2013), it is envisioned that teaching and learning must leverage on e-learning technologies, such as lecture captures.

4.2   Rationale behind Pedagogical Use of Lecture Capture in LANG7XXX

LANG7XXX is a credit bearing course in a postgraduate Master program in English. Lecture capture is used to better support the students' learning, especially for their after class revisions as most of the students are non-native English speakers. It is hoped that with the availability of such e-learning technology to further assist students to recap their lessons after class, students will have a much better learning experience.

4.3   Rationale behind Pedagogical Use of Lecture Capture in MGNT7XXX

MGNT7XXX is also a credit bearing course in a postgraduate Master in Business Administration (MBA) program. It is also both an elective course and a course in managing organizational change, thus, the lecturer found it very topical to introduce an actual change in her way of conducting lectures by also using the facility of lecture captures. In this course, the lecture capture system is also used to record the student's project presentations so that they can review and improve on their own performances.

4.4   Rationale behind Pedagogical Use of Lecture Capture in PHYS1XXX

The lecturer in PHYS1XXX has always used video recordings of laboratory experiments to supplement his lecture on physics fundamentals for first year undergraduate students. The students have also found that such multimedia supplements to the lectures helpful to their understanding of the subject at hand. Nonetheless, in the past, there was no recording of the class lectures together with the laboratory experiments. Thus, for this pilot project, the lecturer hoped that the lecture capture system would provide a more 'rounded' experience for his students in PHYS1XXX.

4.5   Rationale behind Pedagogical Use of Lecture Capture in VA2XXX

The credit bearing course VA2XXX is an undergraduate course offered in the Academy of Visual Arts at HKBU. In this course, students are required to learn the skills in creating a number different handicraft arts. In the past, students were only given in-class demonstrations on each skill and written notes on how to create such handicrafts, so that they can practice at home. This is often less than ideal as students may forget what they have seen in the class and the written notes are not helpful for all the students. Thus, the lecturer hoped that by providing lectured captured recordings for her lectures, together with a detailed recording of how to create each handicraft, students would have a more wholesome 'notes' to go back to and be better equipped to practice these skills at home. Obviously, with Panopto being a software based solution, students can also record their own work to share with their peers. An example of such a recording on how to create a handicraft is presented in Figure 4.

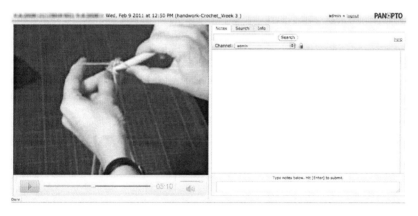

Fig. 4. A recording on how to crochet in the course VA2XXX

4.6   Rationale behind Pedagogical Use of Lecture Capture in ORGC1XXX

ORGC1XXX is an undergraduate credit bearing course on public speaking offered by the School of Communication at HKBU. The very nature of this course required each student to be able to present and practice their own public speaking skills. In the past, students were asked to present to their peers in the class, while the audience was asked to comment on the performance of each presenter on the spot. Obviously this is less than ideal as students in the audience are often reluctant to share critical comments amidst their peers. Furthermore, often students in the audience are more pre-occupied with getting ready for their own presentation and may not be focused on providing useful comments to the presentation at hand. Finally, without a recording of the actual presentation, it is rather difficult for a student to make good reflective use of the feedback from the lecturer on the performance. The lecturer of ORGC1XXX welcomed the functionality provided by the lecture capture system, wherein students can easily and quickly revise and reflect on their own performances and comment on the performances of their peers. An example of such a recording of a student's public speaking performance is presented in Figure 3.

5 Instructor Feedback

In order to gauge the effective and efficient use of lecture capture for teaching and learning, two groups of MBA students conducted user evaluation studies on both the pioneer lecturers and their students, respectively. The MBA students conducted a focus interview [4] with the pioneer lecturers. Their findings are as follow.

The expectations of the lecturers on the lecture capture system are:

- Ability to observe and improve their teaching mannerisms/appearance.
- Ability to do close-ups for demonstrations.
- Ability to pre-record the materials for teaching.
- Ability to refresh their memories for a new semester.
- Ability to give feedback to students after class.

From the focus interview, it was revealed that the lecturers found the lecture capture system addressed most of their expectations. One lecturer commented, "It lived up to my expectations. We got an email from the student asking about when it will be uploaded. ... Observe myself and I saw that there were mannerism that I could avoid."

Another lecturer commented that "it is much clearer than any other method for providing information after the fact. It is a medium that the generation that the students are using. They take a book and dust it off, and the language is very difficult for every tech. It's a big step forward from trying to get diagrammatic pictures. Nothing better than showing them." While on the same issue, another commented "We do a lot of presentations in class so we rely on a lot of demonstrations in class. The biggest problem is I have to do close ups. The video framing is tight. The USB chord and the size of the camera. Most of the time the demo goes unnoticed even when it is not really taped right. Many times if the connection goes out, you have to reboot and restart the lecture."

On using it to pre-record materials for teaching, one lecturer commented "You can add more to it after the class. A reading to refresh their memory before they come into class. For example, a five minute Panopto to assign material before class. They liked this a lot better than a reading. It got them the content they needed to have. If you have to add after. You can do so for their reference."

On assisting the students in learning after class, one lecturer commented "The students language skills are a handicap. This doesn't mean they are not genius but it is a factor. They sometimes day dream and don't understand what's going on. This way they can go back and really pick up more."

In fact, having participated, the pilot project dispelled some fears these pioneer lecturers may have had with the use of such e-learning technology. For example, there was a common concern about student absenteeism that might follow after the availability of lecture captured recordings. Nonetheless, some of the lecturers have pleasantly found that this is not the case. For example, one lecturer commented "I have not noticed any effect on the student attendance. In fact, I think this benefits latecomers. Many times they have to be late."

On the worries the pioneer lecturers may have, their chief concern is the stability of the technology and the availability of technical support (i.e. student helpers) after the pilot project. In fact, one lecturer commented "If I could work with the support team I would. Where do I find the time? In my ideal world I would. But if I can't manage it in a professional way I won't."

Another observation from the lecturers' focus interview is that the lecture capture technology is not suitable for all types of classes and teaching activities. In fact, one lecturer said, "...I stay where I am the whole lecture. They have to be aware that it doesn't work for every subject. That they have to rethink for what subjects they are using it for."

Overall it can be said that the pioneer lecturers had a positive experience within the pilot project and are most likely to adopt the Panopto lecture capture technology in the campus wide deployment, once some identified issues are resolved.

6 Student Feedback

While one group of MBA students studied the user experience for lecturers, the other group conducted their study on the student population within the given credit bearing courses in the pilot project. They only conducted their study on 4 of the 6 credit bearing courses piloting the lecture capture technology. The reason behind this was the fact that the course IT1XXX only used lecture capture in one part of the course, and consequently this did not represent a comprehensive student experience in the course. And for the course MGNT7XXX, because the MBA students themselves were students in the course this may bias the results of the study.

The findings on student experience with the lecture capture technology varied significantly depending on the course. From a data set of 88 students completed questionnaires, there were 62 valid replies, representing a response rate of about 70%. A summary of their findings is presented in Table 2.

Table 2. Student perceptions and usage patterns in selected credit bearing courses used in the pilot project

Course Code	Value added	Student usage	Interaction
LANG7XXX	No	No	No
PHYS1XXX	No	No	No
VA2XXX	Yes	No	No
ORGC1XXX	Yes	Yes	Yes

The descriptions of the labels in Table 2 are as follow:

- **Value added:** This is a measure of whether the student found the availability of lecture captured recordings added any value to learning of the subject in the course.
- **Student usage:** This is a measure whether the student actually reviewed the lecture captured recordings provided by their lecturers.
- **Interaction:** This is a measure whether the student interacted with their peers with regard to the use of lecture capture in their course.

From the study [5] of the MBA students, it was found that only students in two courses (VA2XXX and ORGC1XXX) think that the lecture capture technology was helpful, adding a significant amount of value to their learning experience. In the course PHYS1XXX, students did not consider that the capture would help them to pass the course or to gain a good grade from review of the lectures. In the course LANG7XXX, the students did not think that the lecture capture technology gave any added value compared to reviewing hard copies of the slides.

It was revealed that 30% the 62 valid student responses claimed that they had never used the lecture capture technology and 57% revealed that they only used it once a week. This was mostly attributed to the lack of communication from the lecturers to the students on the availability of the lecture capture and how to utilize them in their learning.

Students in the course ORGC1XXX were particularly enthusiastic about the possibility of seeing the performance of their peers. Furthermore, they had the opportunity to share knowledge and be inspired by best practice within the class. The lecture capture technology perfectly matched the needs of the students in this course.

Recording viewing statistics data for the pilot project is presented in Figure 5.

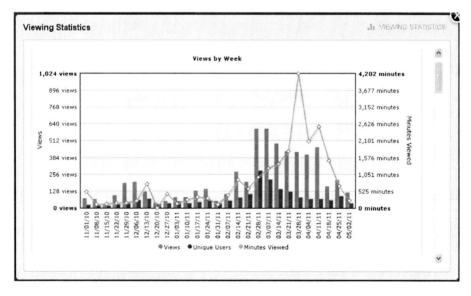

Fig. 5. A snapshot of user viewing statistics

From the statistics presented in Figure 5 it is interesting to observe that:

1. While the number of user views (the 'light green' bar) rose slightly in the beginning of the semester, the peak came towards the end of the teaching semester.
2. The number of unique viewers (the 'dark green' bar) was consistent from the beginning of the semester but peaked for a couple of weeks towards the lower half of the teaching semester.
3. The total viewing time (the 'orange line') follows the trend of the number of user views (i.e. as in observation 1) but with a delay in its peak relative to the number of unique viewers.

What is more interesting is the fact that findings were consistent with similar findings at other institutions. For example, in personal sharing from a sister institution in Hong Kong, similar trend of user usage of lecture capture was also observed at their institution.

Further information from the participants indicated:

1. Not all students subscribed to the use of lecture capture recordings. Those who prefer to use them will adopt these as part of their learning materials, while those who don't, will most likely not bother to logon to the system to view the recordings. Furthermore, unless there is perceived or real value in their viewing of the recordings, often the initial buzz in the student viewing will die off as the semester progresses. This finding correlates well with our observations in the initial (i.e. the first half of the teaching semester) trends of the viewing statistics data from our pilot project.
2. Across a couple of weeks in the second half of the teaching semester, both the courses ORGC1XXX and VA2XXX were requiring their students to post their own recordings as assignments for the respective course, wherein both self and peer assessments of these postings were conducted during these weeks. This would explain the sudden jump in the number of unique viewers accessing the system and the associated number of user views. Nonetheless, the total viewing time of such assessment activities did not increase significantly as these activities are often short episodes of student's viewing of each other's submission.
3. Finally, at the last few weeks of the teaching semester, while the number of unique viewers approximately returned to the pre-assignments-submission level, both the number of user views and their total viewing time were still very high. This can be explained by the use of the lecture capture recordings by those students, who preferred to use the system, for revisions of their lessons before their final examinations. Again, this is consistent with findings from other institutions.

7 Lessons Learned

The key lessons are:

1. While lecture capture can be a value adding technology, it is not suitable for all courses and all forms of teaching and learning activities. Furthermore, not

all students will subscribe to the use of such technology. Effective and efficient deployment of lecture capture must be targeted to areas where it can truly add value to the learning and teaching of the students. This is evident both from the pioneer lecturers' remarks and from observing the feedbacks from the students. While in some courses, even when the lecturer thinks lecture capture is suitable for teaching and learning, students are not engaged if they do not see value to their learning.

2. For better adoption of the lecture capture technology, it must be deployed in such a way that the technology is transparent to the lecturer (i.e. no technical setup on their part, just walk in and teach) and students must be trained on how to best use the lecture captured recordings. It is best if there are support groups for both segments of users - lecturers and students. This is evident from the comments from both the pioneer lectures and their students. Lecturers are more receptive of the technology if their concerns on technical support can be alleviated and students tend to use lecture capture more if they are aware of how they can use the system better as value added learning. The drive for adoption of such e-learning technology must be done from both fronts - lecturers and students. Lecturers need to be informed on what they can achieve with the technology and what they can expect from it, while students need to be informed of their availability and encouraged to use these as a tool to assist their own learning.

8   Future of the Pilot Project and Conclusion

To date the outcome of the pilot project is positive with some room for improvement. Thus, it is likelier than not that lecture capture will be part of the e-learning facilities to be available at HKBU campus wide in the near future. In that deployment it will be necessary to plan for a more technology transparent deployment, with education of both the teaching academics and the student users to be an utmost priority. Case studies based on current pioneering users will serve as a good starting point.

Acknowledgments. The authors especially thank Professor Dayle Smith and her class of MBA students for gathering and compiling the data on the preliminary users' satisfaction, the users' perception on the use of lecture capture as an effective and efficient e-learning technology. Special thanks also to the pioneer lecturers who participated in the pilot project. This pilot project is never possible without the hard work of the IT team at CHTL.

References

1. Davis, S., Connolly, A., Linfield, E.: Lecture capture: making the most of face-to-face learning. J. Engineering Education 4(2), 4–13 (2009)
2. Veeramani, R., Bradley, S.: Insights Regarding Undergraduate Preference for Lecture Capture, University of Wisconsin Madison E-Business Institute, September 23 (2008)

3. Martyn, M.A.: Engaging Lecture Capture: Lights, Camera Interaction! EDUCAUSE Quarterly 32(4) (2009)
4. Hui, W., Lui, Y., Norton-Torres, E., Zackrisson, E.: Panopto: A platform for enhanced teaching and learning, MNGT7070 project report (2011)
5. Chan, K., Morra, G.M., Persson, A., Tech, R.: Managing Change: Panopto, MNGT7070 project report (2011)

Generation of Hypertext for Web-Based Learning Based on Wikification

Andrew Kwok-Fai Lui, Vanessa Sin-Chun Ng, Eddy K.M. Tsang, and Alex C.H. Ho

School of Science and Technology, The Open University of Hong Kong
{alui,scng,s1011965,s1024743}@ouhk.edu.hk

Abstract. This paper presents a preliminary study into the conversion of plain text documents into hypertext for web-based learning. The novelty of this approach is the generation of two types of hyperlinks: links to Wikipedia article for exploratory learning, and self-referencing links for elaboration and references. Hyperlink generation is based on two rounds of wikification. The first round wikifies a set of source documents so that the wikified source documents can be semantically compared to Wikipedia articles using existing link-based measure techniques. The second round of wikification then evaluates each hyperlink in the wikified source documents and checks if there is a semantically related source document for replacing the current target Wikipedia article. While preliminary evaluation of a prototype implementation seemed feasible, relatively few self-referencing links could be generated using a test set of course text.

Keywords: web-based learning, hypertext generation, wikification, wikipedia.

1 Introduction

A hypertext medium offers readers a number of advantages such as providing non-linear navigation for seeking related information, creating opportunities for exploring new knowledge, and even facilitating the generation of new knowledge. The set up of hyperlinks between documents allows the continued expansion of hypertext as exemplified by the World Wide Web. Hyperlink is made up of text anchor in the source document and the location of the target document, and the target documents of the hyperlinks are believed to be useful for explanation, reference, or further exploration. Hypertext authoring involves careful consideration of the overall objectives, the needs of readers, and the relevance of target documents.

Authoring of hypertext learning materials has meant a lot of hard work for adopters of web-based learning. The conversion of existing course notes into electronic form is the relatively easier part. The hard part is to transform the linear electronic course notes into hypertext made up of non-linear set of linked documents. The original text has to be manually inspected, segmented, reorganized, and hyperlinked. The demand to make consistent and systematic decisions about the location of hyperlink, the anchor-text, and the target of hyperlink is often too much for individual instructors. Since the early adoption days of web-based learning, automatic construction of

R. Kwan et al. (Eds.): ICT 2011, CCIS 177, pp. 280–290, 2011.
© Springer-Verlag Berlin Heidelberg 2011

hypertexts has attracted some attention. The majority of notable previous attempts is based on text mining and information retrieval techniques.

This paper describes an approach of automatic conversion of plain course texts into hypertexts based on wikification. Wikification is a recent area of research that studies automatically enriching a piece of text with links to the online encyclopaedia Wikipedia [5][6]. The approach supports both generation of self-referencing links for self-contained study and Wikipedia links for exploratory study. Logically segmented plain texts are first wikified by adding anchors linking to specific pages in the Wikipedia. The wikified text segments are then considered as a virtual extension to the Wikipedia. The wikification process is repeated only this time the wikified text segments are also considered as potential targets of hyperlinks. The resulting hypertexts can therefore contain self-referencing hyperlinks as well as links to Wikipedia.

2 Background

Web-based learning offers a number of technological features that are relevant to educators [6]: (1) hypertext provides effective organization and ready access to vast amount of information; (2) communication medium offers opportuities for interaction and collaboration; (3) authoring tools enable everyone to create content and make available to others; (4) web-based learning environments integrate instructional activities into one delivery medium that now typically contains content management, student management, discussion forums and even weblogs. The first feature is arguably the most demanding on the effort of instructors. The development of a new hypertext based course needs a great deal of design, planning, and organization, and the level of complexity exceeds that of a traditional course. Conversion from existing course text into hypertext makes more economical sense, especially if lots of time and effort have been spent on writing the orignal course text.

2.1 Quality and Types of Hyperlinks

Hypertexts are conduicive to learning if the quality of hyerlinks are satisfactory. There should be a specific purpose for each hyperlink. Hypertext authors should ensure that the set of hyperlinks would fulfil the overall learning objectives. Instructionally, hyperlinks can be classified as structural links (ie. connect to another unit of hypertext), reference links (ie. direct to the source of the content), and associative links (leads to related concepts) [1]. The set up of associative links is more effort intensive because it requires deeper understanding of semantic relations [11]. The nature of hypertext suits the style of exploratory learning particularly well. The variety and complexity offered by hyperlinks enhances the motivation in an autonomous exploration of knowledge [9]. For examples, reference links help to elaborate anchor texts for a better understanding of a document, and associative links offer related topics to satisfy a curious mind.

2.2 Quantity of Hyperlinks in Hypertext

Hypertext based exploratory learning relies on sufficient amount of hyperlinks in a document. The so-called learning impasses describes the undesirable situation that a lack of hyperlinks restricts opportunities to find elaborations, references, and further topics to study [9]. Such a document represents a dead-end and a hinderance to the effectiveness of exploratory learning. Clearly adding more hyperlinks to the document can resolve the problem but there is a consideration related to the cost of expertise and time. An alternative approach is to exploit the intelligence of the mass and allow learners to contribute hyperlinks. The Free-Hyperlinks environment, for example, provides learners to create and share new hyperlinks in a web 2.0 collaborative manner [10].

2.3 Automatic Generation of Hypertext

Automatically adding hyperlinks to text documents is an inexpensive approach to generate useful hypertext for web-based learning. The Dynamic Medical Handbook Project was one of the first attempts of its kind [3]. A fulltext medical handbook was converted into hypertext in four steps: (1) partioning the handbook into text units based on its intrinsic hierarchical structure; (2) extracting the first words of each text unit as anchor texts; (3) adding structural hyperlinks between hierarchically related text units; and (4) indexing sematically related text units based on an essentially a bags-of-words statistical approach. Setting up links between text units in a hypertext requires a way to estimate the semantic relation of the text content. Most subsequent work in this area recognized this bascially as a text mining process of selecting anchor texts and hyperlink targets [2][11].

2.4 Wikification

Wikification is a related research area that investigates hyperlinking existing text to relevant articles in Wikipedia. Using Wikipedia as the target of hyperlnking should give educators and learners higher confidence about the content quality. Wikipedia is more than an online collaborative encyclopeadia as perceived by general public. Medelyan et. al. [4] listed a number of other perspectives of Wikipedia, including a huge corpus, a multi-lingual thesaurus, a semi-structured database, an ontology, a scale-free small-world type of network structure. Most significant to automatic hypertext generation is perhaps its semantic richness for many text mining processes. In general a wikification process involves link detection phase and disambiguation phase, which is virtually the same involved in hypertext generation from plain text. The link detection phase decides if a term should be turned into an anchor for a hyperlink. The disambiguation phase decides the most relevant target Wikipedia article for a hyperlink anchor which may have several meanings. For a wikification system called Wikify, Mihalcea & Csomai [5] proposed the use of an atribute called link probability to idenify anchor texts, which is the probability of a term used as an anchor in Wikipedia. To disambiguate the target for a hyperlink, Wikify relied on a classifier based on a text anchor's nearby terms and their part-of-speech. The classifier is trained with examples extracted from Wikipedia with reasonably good accuracy. The promising performance of a machine learning approach prompted Milne & Witten [6] to treat link detection also as a classification problem. The features used to predict if a term should be tuned into a hyperlink anchor include link probability, relatedness of the term to the surrounding context, generality of the term, and the location of term in the article. Using the examples in Wikipedia as the gold standard, the performance of the link detector was found to achieve 74% in precision and in recall.

3 Methodology

This section describes Hyperizer, an automatic text to hypertext converter. Text is assumed to be a set of paritioned course learning materials such as lecture notes, tutorial notes, technical manual in plain text format. Compared to earlier systems, Hyperizer is able to (1) generate links to Wikipedia articles for further explanation and exploration, and (2) generate self-referencing links for elaboration and references. The novelty of Hyperizer lies in the central role played by wikification in the generation of both types of hyperlinks.

Setting up self-referencing links between a set of text documents invariably needs a reliable way to work out the semantic relatedness between two text documents and between a term and a text document. Milne & Witten [7] developed a Wikipedia Link Based Measure that estimates the semantic similarity of two Wikipedia articles by comparing their sets of incoming or outgoing links. According to the evaluation done by Medelyan et. al. [4], the algorithm achieved a respectable 0.69 correlation on a gold standard test set and it was found to be the best among the algorithms that do not rely on deep text analysis. This algorithm can be applied on any text documents after they have been wikified. Wikification adds links to the text documents and enables the evaluation fo their semantic relatedness.

Hyperizer performs two rounds of wikification on a set of source text documents (see Fig. 1 and Fig. 2). The first round converts the text documents into hypertext documents. The added links all lead to a Wikipedia article. Hyperizer uses a machine learning approach based on the algorithm proposed by Milne & Witten to wikify the documents [6]. A full set of Wikipedia articles are needed in the training and also in the consideration of the targets of the hyperlinks. The significance of the first round of wikification is that the set of wikified documents can be regarded as Wikipedia articles for the rest of the processing. In the second round of wikification, the set of newly wikified documents has joined the existing Wikipedia articles to become potential targets for hyperlinks.

The following will describe the design of a prototype implementation of Hyperize, and will also demonstrate the conversion of a Chinese History course into a hypertext course. This version of Hyperize is designed to process Chinese text and a dump of Chinese Wikipedia is used as the corpus for training Hyperize. The techniques employed in Hyperize, however, are mostly language independent.

The wikification process of Hyperizer is based on the link detection and disambiguation algorithms proposed in [6]. The following gives a summary for each of the two algorithms. Readers may refer to the original paper for the details.

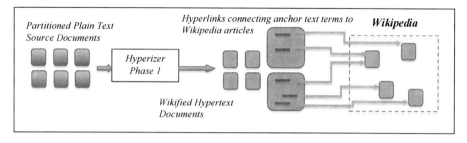

Fig. 1. Phase 1 of Hyperizer: source documents are wikified

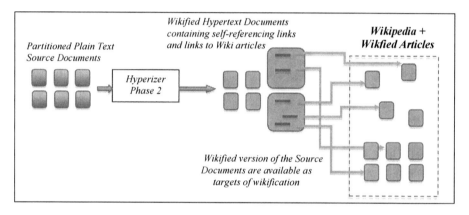

Fig. 2. Phase 2 of Hyperizer: wikified source documents after phase 1 are now considered as part of the extended Wikipedia for another round of wikification

3.1 Wikification: Disambiguation

Disambiguation algorithm is discussed first because it is part of the link detection algorithm [6]. The objective of disambiguation is to select the target Wikipedia article that matches the context of an anchor text term. For example, the term Liverpool can refer to the England city or the Premier League soccer team depending on the context of the source article. A classifer is built that evaluates the most likely target Wikipedia article. The classifier is to be trained with examples extracted from Wikipedia. There are three features used in the classifier:

- Prior probability of the link between an anchor text and a target Wikipedia article. This is obtained by mining the Wikipedia. For example, in the Chinese Wikipedia version used in the experiment, 21% of anchor text '利物浦' (Liverpool) is linked to the city's article and 79% is linked to the soccer team's article.
- Relatedness of the anchor text to the theme of the source document. This is estimated by comparing the semantic relatedness of the anchor text and the other anchor texts in the source article. The comparison is based on the Link Based Measure described in [7].
- Quality of the Relatedness feature. The reliability of the Relatedness feature depends on whether there is a central theme in the source document. This feature

estimates the cohesiveness of the theme in the source document by mutually comparing the semantic relatedness of all anchor texts.

3.2 Wikification: Link Detection

The objective of link detection is to identify the text terms for conversion into hyperlink anchors. A characteristic in the algorithm of Milne & Witten [6] is to consider only the text terms that have been used as anchor text in Wikipedia. Mining the Wikipedia can extract a table of anchor text terms. This characteristic is important for wikifying Chinese text because the problem of word segmentation can be circumvented. Chinese text has no natural boundary and most text processing operations begin with word segmentation that split up the text into terms. For example, this Chinese string "中國中古史是從秦、漢這兩個統一王朝開始的" (The ancient history of China began from the period of the unified dynasties of Qin and Han) is to be split up into terms such as "中國 中古史 是 從 秦、漢 這 兩個 統一 王 朝 開始 的". In the link detection algorithm, word segmentation, which is not always highly reliable, is not needed. Instead, the table of anchor text terms is used to extract all occurrences of anchor text terms in the source document, and each of these is a potential hyperlink anchor.

Similar to the disambiguation algorithm, a classifier is used to determine if an occurrence of an anchor text term should be converted to hyperlink anchor. The classifier is to be trained with examples extracted from Wikipedia. There are eight features used in this classifier:

- Probability of the anchor text actually used as a hyperlink anchor.
- Relatedness of the anchor text to the theme of the source document. This feature is the same as the one used in the disambiguation algorithm.
- Confidence of the disambiguation classifier when applied to this anchor text.
- Generality of the anchor text mined from the category information in Wikipedia.
- Frequency of the anchor text in the source document.
- The Location of the First Occurrence, the Last Occurrence, and the Distribution of the anchor text in the source document.

3.4 Hyperizer: Conversion to Self-reference Links

The wikified documents $Ws1$, $Ws2$, …, Wsn generated by the first phase of Hyperizer contain new hyperlinks to Wikipedia articles. They can be semantically compared to Wikipedia articles and each other. The second phase of Hyperizer then redirects some of the new hyperlinks from a Wikipedia article to one of the wikified source documents.

The algorithm is described below:

1.   For each wikified source document Wsi, consider every new hyperlink connecting to a Wikipedia article.

1.1 For a hyperlink Linkj in source document Wsi connecting to a Wikipedia article WKj

1.1.1 Evaluate the semantic relatedness of the article WKj with every wikified source document Ws1, Ws2, ..., Wsn. Find out the wikified source document Wshigh with the highest semantic relatedness.

1.1.2 If the highest semantic relatedness is greater than a threshold SemT, change the target of the hyperlink Linkj to the wikified source document Wshigh.

The algorithm considers only the hyperlinks generated by the first phase for efficiency reason.

4 Results

A prototype system of Hyperizer has been implemented for the evaluation of the algorithms. The system is implemented with Java and WEKA, the open-source machine-learning library (http://www.cs.waikato.ac.nz/ml/weka/).

4.1 Data Set

An article dump of Chinese Wikipedia released on 25 December 2009 has been downloaded (http://dumps.wikimedia.org/). The dump contains 593,003 articles, of which 303,341 are proper articles, 231,458 are re-direction pages, and 57,215 are category pages. Efficient handling of such a gigantic structured corpus requires processing tools, such as the Wikipedia API [12]. The pre-processing stage extracts sets of useful information from the Wikipedia dump, such frequency of anchor text terms, hyperlinks of every article, categories of article, etc. These extracted information sets are placed in a database for efficient query and access.

4.2 Wikification: Disambiguation

An experiment was carried out to investigate the performance of our implementation of the disambiguation algorithm trained with the Chinese Wikipedia dump. The training set contains 1,000 randomly chosen articles and the test set contains another 1,000 random articles. All articles selected have length between 1,000 to 2,000 Chinese characters. Hyperlinks found in lists are removed because they are less relevant to the aim of Hyperizer.

Table 1 below shows the performance of our implementation. The classification algorithm used was the C4.5 decision tree algorithm. The results showed are comparable with the performance reported in [6]. Chinese anchor text probably has fewer senses and the disambiguation classifier should find it less challenging. In the calculation of the feature Relatedness, Milne & Witten [6] used at most 30 anchors to represent the theme of the document. An experiment was carried out and found that relaxing the limit would not improve the performance.

4.3 Wikification: Link Detection

Another experiment was carried out to evaluate the performance of the link detection algorithm trained with the Chinese Wikipedia dump. Link detection is considerably more challenging than disambiguation. Deciding the creation of a hyperlink requires more considerations than choosing a target Wikipedia article between a few possibilities. The training set contains 100,000 examples and the testing set contains another 100,000 examples selected from Wikipedia articles.

Table 1. Performance of our implementation of the disambiguation algorithm

	Precision	Recall	F-Measure
C4.5 (Chinese Wikipedia)	98.3%	98.3%	98.3%
C4.5 (Chinese Wikipedia) limited to 30 anchors in calculating Relatedness	98.3%	98.3%	98.3%
C4.5 (English Wikipedia) disambiguation algorithm (Milne & Witten 2008a)	96.8%	96.5%	96.6%

Table 2 below shows the performance of our implementation. Using the Chinese Wikipedia as the corpus seems to produce poorer precision. Changing the classification algorithm to support vector machine gave a bit of improvement. The overall performance is comparable to Milne & Witten in [6].

Table 2. Performance of our implementation of the link detection algorithm

	Precision	Recall	F-Measure
C4.5 (Chinese Wikipedia)	71.2%	78.0%	74.4%
Support Vector Machine (Chinese Wikipedia)	73.7%	74.3%	74.0%
C4.5 (English Wikipedia) link detection algorithm (Milne & Witten 2008a)	77.6%	72.2%	74.8%

4.4 Hyperizer: Conversion to Self-reference Links

A set of source plain text documents was prepared for this experiment. The document set comes from a course in Chinese History. This theme is one of the most popular topics in Chinese Wikipedia and so wikification should produce an interesting lot of hyperlinks. The document set was first manually partitioned into thirty-six documents, each of size from around two thousand words to over five thousand words. The titles of some of the partitioned documents include 秦興起及統一過程 (The Rise and Unification of Qin), 秦始皇的統治政策 (The Rule and Policy of Emperor Qinshihuang), 秦朝的覆亡 (The Fall of Qin Dynasty), 秦亡原因 (Reasons of the Fall of Qin), and 漢初對秦政的因革 (Reform of Qin Ruling Style in Early Han). This granularity is comparable to a typical overview article in the Wikipedia. For example, the article on "秦朝" (Chin Dynasty) has approximately 4,600 words.

The following illustrates the operation of Hyperizer with the test document set. Fig 3 (top) shows a segment of text from the document 秦亡原因 (Reasons of the Fall of Qin) and the bottom shows all the anchor text terms (underlined) found in the segment.

秦始皇在政治上所作的改革，無疑是劃時代的，應該肯定他在這方面的功績。可是
秦始皇在政治上的極權表現，卻削減了在當時本來帶有進步意義的政制改革的作用
。在「丞相、大臣皆受成事，倚辦於上」，「天下之事無小大，皆決於上」
（《史記‧秦始皇本紀》）的政治情況下，任何完善的政治
規劃，都不可能確保發揮其應有的效用。

秦始皇在政治上所作的改革，無疑是劃時代的，應該肯定他在這方面的功績。可是
秦始皇在政治上的極權表現，卻削減了在當時本來帶有進步意義的政制改革的作用
。在「丞相、大臣皆受成事，倚辦於上」，「天下之事無小大，皆決於上」
（《史記‧秦始皇本紀》）的政治情況下，任何完善的政治 規劃，都不可能確保
發揮其應有的效用。

Fig. 3. An example text segment and the anchor text terms found

After the first round of wikification, only some of the anchor text terms were converted into hyperlinks (see Fig 4). Table 3 lists the target Wikipedia article of each hyperlink.

秦始皇在政治上所作的改革，無疑是劃時代的，應該肯定他在這方面的
功績。可是秦始皇在政治上的極權表現，卻削減了在當時本來帶有進步
意義的政制改革的作用。在「丞相、大臣皆受成事，倚辦於上」，「天
下之事無小大，皆決於上」（《史記‧秦始皇本紀》）的政治情況下，
任何完善的政治規劃，都不可能確保發揮其應有的效用。

Fig. 4. The wikified version of the text segment

Table 3. Hyperlinks and their target Wikipedia article generated by first round wikification

Anchor Text Term	Target Wikipedia Article (Chinese)	Corresponding Article in English Wikipedia
秦始皇 (QinShiHuang)	秦始皇 (QinShiHuang)	Qin Shi Huang
丞相 (Premier)	宰相 (Premier)	Chancellor
史記 (Ancient History)	史記 (Ancient History)	Records of the Grand Historian
秦(Qin)	秦朝 (Qin Dynasty)	Qin Dynasty

秦始皇在政治上所作的改革，無疑是劃時代的，應該肯定他在這方面的
功績。可是秦始皇在政治上的極權表現，卻削減了在當時本來帶有進步
意義的政制改革的作用。在「丞相、大臣皆受成事，倚辦於上」，「天
下之事無小大，皆決於上」（《史記‧秦始皇本紀》）的政治情況下，
任何完善的政治規劃，都不可能確保發揮其應有的效用。

Fig. 5. A self-reference link has replaced a hyperlink to Wikipedia (highlighted in HTML)

In the second round of wikification, the target Wikipedia page of each hyperlink was used to semantically compare to all the thirty-six wikified source documents. The source document with the highest link measure and over the threshold was chosen as a self-reference link. Only one in four hyperlinks was replaced (see Fig. 5). In fact, this was the only self-referencing link converted by Hyperizer in the whole document. While there was a successful conversion, the conversion rate was however rather disappointing.

5 Conclusion

This paper reports a preliminary study into the topic of the conversion of a set of plain text documents into hypertext for web-based learning. A prototype implementation called Hyperizer was design for the purpose, and it was developed as a proof of concept. Unlike earlier work in this problem, Hyperizer can generate links to both Wikipedia articles and within the original text documents. The former type of links enhances exploratory learning while the latter type provides references and elaboration to learners.

The key idea of Hyperizer is to first wikify the set of source documents, so that these wikified source documents can be semantically compared to Wikipedia articles using current semantic comparison techniques.

The evaluation showed that the wikification algorithms developed by Milne & Witten [6] performed equally well when they were using Chinese Wikipedia as the training corpus. The link detection algorithm scored slightly lower precision on Chinese Wikipedia but the overall performance was still comparable.

Finally, the experiment on Hyperizer illustrated that the feasibility of the approach seemed positive. However, the conversion rate from Wikipedia hyperlink to self-referencing link looked very low. One possible reason is that only hyperlinks were considered in the semantic comparison between the wikified documents and Wikipedia articles. There are often too few hyperlinks generated by the first round of wikification. A solution to evaluate in future work would be to consider all anchor text terms. The target Wikipedia articles of these anchor text terms could be estimated with the disambiguation algorithm.

References

1. Agosti, M., Crestani, F., Melucci, M.: On the use of information retrieval techniques for the automatic construction of hypertext. Information Processing and Management 33, 133–144 (1997)
2. Crestani, F., Melucci, M.: Automatic construction of hypertexts for self-referencing: the Hyper-Textbook project. Information Systems 28, 769–790 (2003)
3. Frisse, M.F.: Searching for Information in a Medical Handbook. Communications of the ACM 31(7), 880–886 (1988)
4. Medelyan, O., Milnea, D., Legga, C., Witten, I.H.: Mining meaning from Wikipedia. International Journal of Human-Computer Studies 67(9), 716–754 (2009)
5. Mihalcea, R., Csomai, A.: Wikify! Linking Documents to Encyclopedic Knowledge. In: Proceedings of the 16th ACM Conference on Information and Knowledge Management, CIKM 2007, Lisbon, Portugal, November 6-8, vol. 8, pp. 233–241 (2007)
6. Milne, D., Witten, I.H.: An effective, low-cost measure of semantic relatedness obtained from Wikipedia links. In: Proceedings of the AAAI 2008 Workshop on Wikipedia and Artificial Intelligence (WIKIAI 2008), Chicago, IL (2008)

7. Milne, D., Witten, I.H.: Learning to Link with Wikipedia. In: Proceedings of CIKM, pp. 509–518. ACM, New York (2008)
8. Mioduser, D., Nachmias, R., Lahav, O., Oren, A.: Web-based learning environments: current pedagogical and technological state. Journal of Research on Computing in Education 33(1), 55–76 (2000)
9. Mitsuhara, H., Ochi, Y., Kanenishi, K., Yano, Y.: Adaptive Web-based Learning System with Free-hyperlink Environment for Circumventing Exploration Impasse Caused by Hyperlink Shortage. The Journal of Information and Systems in Education 1(1), 109–118 (2002)
10. Mitsuhara, H., Ochi, Y., Kanenishi, K., Yano, Y.: An Adaptive Web-based Learning System with a Free-Hyperlink Environment. In: Proc. of Workshop on Adaptive Systems for Web-based Education, pp. 13–26 (2002)
11. Yang, H.C., Lee, C.H.: A text mining approach for automatic construction of hypertexts. Expert Systems with Applications 29, 723–734 (2005)
12. Zesch, T., Gurevych, I., Mühlhäuser, M.: Analyzing and Accessing Wikipedia as a Lexical Semantic Resource. In: Data Structures for Linguistic Resources and Applications, pp. 197–205 (2007)

The Impact of E-Learning in University Education: An Empirical Analysis in a Classroom Teaching Context

José Albors-Garrigos[1], María-del-Val Segarra-Oña[1],
and José Carlos Ramos-Carrasco[2]

[1] Universidad Politecnica de Valencia, Depto. Org. Empresas
Camino Vera, s.n., 46022 Valencia, Spain
[2] Avanzalis Knowledg Associates
Paseo de Gracia, 12, 1°
08007 Barcelona, Spain
{Jalbors,maseo}@doe.upv.es

Abstract. The goal of this chapter is to analyze the impact of e-learning technologies and tools as a support for teacher-led courses in the performance (efficiency) of teaching as well as in the learner's acceptance. It also aims at analyzing and determining the moderating factors which have an influence on the process. The paper is based on the data which has been accumulated during an academic year at a large Spanish university offering 2500 courses (with support of e learning) and employing 1800 professors.

Keywords: e learning supporting teacher led courses, e learning facilitators.

1 Introduction

This paper will try to answer various research questions. Is e-learning an effective tool as a support in traditional face-to-face classrooms? What are the moderating factors which influence e-learning adoption by teachers? Do e-learning tools have a positive impact on learning performance and student satisfaction? If so, what are the most promising tools? Does e-learning facilitate networked learning?

The paper presents the impact of e-learning as a support for traditional teaching activities. The paper will present the results of the analysis of e-learning data for an academic year at the Universidad Politecnica de Valencia (UPV). It will cross-reference the results of e-learning with the course performance and student satisfaction surveys at the UPV.

The paper has been organized as follows. A first section deals with the background and state of the art. Following the various e learning platforms for university support are described and their dissemination discussed. A third section examines whether e-learning efficiency in higher education can be measured. The fourth section describes the research methodology. Subsequently, the results are analyzed and discussed and, finally, the conclusions of the research are presented.

R. Kwan et al. (Eds.): ICT 2011, CCIS 177, pp. 291–304, 2011.

2   Background

The relationship between IT and learning has been studied by Leidner and Jarvenpaa (1995) and been associated with the principal learning schools and model theories. Figure 1 relates both schools and theories with the main IT-based learning models and tools. According to these authors IT based learning contributes, not only to the creation of knowledge by learners but to its sharing and dissemination as well. Its contribution to knowledge experience is low but it can provide a certain degree of context realism. Additionally, it provides opportunities for sharing and group work.

Additionally, other authors have highlighted the utilisation of e-learning and the use of Internet technologies, with its broad array of learning tools, for enhancing the learner knowledge and performance. These authors support the evidence that these tools have an impact on the effectiveness and acceptance of e-learning within the medical education community, especially when combined with traditional teacher-guided activities in a blended-learning educational experience (Ruiz et al, 2006).

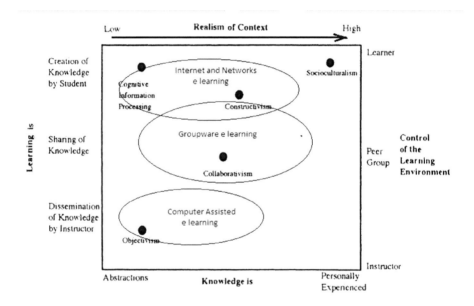

Fig. 1. IT-based e-learning models and tools (based on Leidner and Jarvenpaa, 1995)

Various studies have consistently demonstrated the satisfaction of students with e-learning methods. Learner satisfaction rates increase with e-learning usage as compared to traditional learning, together with a perceived ease of use and access, navigation, interactivity, and user friendly interface design. Interestingly, students do not see e-learning as replacing traditional teacher-led instruction but as a complement to it, forming part of a blended-learning strategy (Gibbons and Fairweather, 2000; Chumley-Jones et al, 2002). Its comparison and complementarity with classroom education has been also reviewed (Bernard et al, 2004; Letterie, 2003) as well as its constant and wide expansion (Martínez and Gallego, 2007).

On the other hand, little has been done to understand why, despite the crucial role e-learning plays in current education methods, many users discontinue their online-learning after their initial experience (Martínez and Gallego, 2007; Marshall and Mitchell, 2003, De la Cruz, 2005, Liaw, 2008). However, as has been demonstrated, e-learning technologies represent a good opportunity to ensure faster and higher development trends (Campanella et al, 2008).

Sun et al. (2008) studied six factors affecting a user's e-learning satisfaction within a wide range of factors that include learners, instructors, courses, technology, design, and environment aspects. They found that learner computer anxiety, instructor attitude toward e-learning, e-learning course flexibility, e-learning course quality, perceived usefulness, perceived ease of use, and diversity in assessments are the critical factors affecting a learner's perceived satisfaction.

Marshall and Mitchell (2003) studied the main problems found when introducing an e-learning system. In their opinion, in most situations, a personalized system is needed for each situation. Despite these findings, they propose a general model composed of six basic steps, the so called E-*learning Maturity Model* (see Figure 2), where the levels are not concerned with how the particular tasks are done, but rather with how well the process is performed and controlled.

Level	Focus
5: Optimising	Continual improvement in all aspects of the e-Learning process
4: Managed	Ensuring the quality of both the e-learning resources and student learning outcomes
3: Defined	Defined process for development and support of e-Learning
2: Planned	Clear and measurable objectives for e-learning projects
1: Initial	Ad-hoc processes
0: Not performed	Not done at all

Fig. 2. E-learning Maturity Model (source Marshall and Mitchell, (2003)

Littlejohn et al. (2006) identified twelve key characteristics, as shown in Figure 3, of learning resources that may promote changes in e-learning practice. These authors not only identified what types of resources are effective in the e-learning process, but conclude that what is most important is their use in context (Littlejohn et al., 2006, Littlejohn and McGill, 2004).

Many companies and universities are using e-learning systems to provide improved results but there are still various problems and barriers related to e-learning activities that require solutions (Cook et al., 2009, Campanella, et al, 2008, Littlejohn et al., 2006). It is especially relevant to show academic institutions how to improve learner satisfaction and further strengthen their e-learning implementation (Sun et al., 2008).

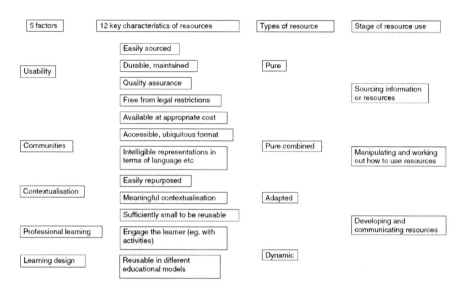

Fig. 3. Factors likely to have a positive influence on the use of a resource (source Littlejohn et al, 2006)

3   Open Course Platforms

Several universities have adopted e-learning platforms following the ICT dynamism (Correa and Paredes, 2009). Higher education institutions are involved in this *new technologies* movement which requires a complex blend of technological, pedagogical and organizational components (McPherson and Nunest, 2008).

On the other hand, there are some universities such as the Open University (UK) and the Universitat Oberta de Cataluyna (UOC, Spain) that have only e-learning platforms, that don't need to change their resources and are not suffering an adaptation process (Sclater, 2008).

Staff training courses, which try to prevent some of the main problems detected, are a common tool in several universities (see Figure 4), (Littlejohn, 2006, Mahdizadeh, 2008, Cook, 2009).

The financial effort to develop an e-learning platform is considerable, involving changes in pedagogic methods, communication methods, technological processes, and skills development. (Sclater, 2008). Therefore, the evaluation of the model and the evidence that the e-learning experience is fulfilling all the goals becomes crucial for the institution as well as for the learners involved.

According to Babo and Acevedo (2009) the most widely- used platforms in universities are Moodle, Blackboard, Webct and Sakai (see Figure 5). Graf and List (2005) have evaluated nine open-learning platforms: ATutor, Dokeos, dotLRN (based on OpenACS), ILIAS, LON-CAPA, Moodle, OpenUSS (Freestyle-learning), Sakai, and Spaghettilearning of which Sakai and Moodle are currently the most popular. These platforms were evaluated according to eight categories: communication tools, learning objects, management of user data, usability, adaptation, technical aspects,

University	Course name	Page link
University of Wisconsin	ADA statement-E-learning evaluation teaching course	http://www.uwstout.edu/static/pr ofdev/elearning/syllabus.html
University of Georgia	E-learning evaluation syllabus	http://www.coe.uga.edu/syllabus/ edit/EDIT_8350_ReevesT_FA0 8.pdf
The UNC School of Education	e-Learning for Educators - Designing a Virtual Field Trip: Online course syllabus	http://www.learnnc.org/lp/pages/ 6501
Free University of Berlin	Using e-learning for social sciences: practical lessons from the	www.elearningeuropa.info/files/ media/media11894.pdf

Fig. 4. E-learning staff courses (source authors)

administration, and course management. These categories included several subcategories which were utilised in a survey to evaluate the platforms. Moodle dominated the evaluation by achieving the best value five times. The strengths of Moodle were the realization of communication tools, and the creation and administration of learning objects. Sakai was penalized since it had not been fully developed at that time; today it has a community of 200 worldwide university users and developers. Moodle clearly has a wider extension with 50.000 users and a broader user profile, including various types of learning centres. In Spain, only 3 universities utilise Sakai while Moodle has more than thirty users.

4   Measure of E-Learning Efficiency in Higher Education

In this new context, the profiles of professors of higher education should change, especially with the expectation that education researchers will become more interdisciplinary, maintaining awareness of the topics, frameworks, and techniques that characterize related research in other disciplines; openness to sharing and learning from research outside their domains; and collective reflection on their practices (Greenhow et al., 2010). Despite the crucial importance of this issue, little research has been found concerning best practices and teacher characteristics which would facilitate e-learning processes in universities.

Campanella et al. (2008) analysed the e-learning platforms in Italian universities, studying 49 universities and using an evaluation model that considered five general aspects: system parameters, administration facilities, interaction support, teacher services, and learner services, comparing the Learning Management Systems (LMSs) adopted by each centre, but without considering learner or teacher abilities or competences.

In this respect, though learning processes have evolved from the post-industrial to an information technology and knowledge era, younger individuals, born after the 1980s, also labelled *digital natives*, learn in a different manner than older people. This digital divide has had a clear impact on the e-learning evolution (Prenski, 2001).

New environments, tools, and information input will have a stronger and more frequent impact. The amount of information available to human being, thanks to the Internet, would have been considered science fiction twenty years ago, and it increases exponentially every year. Instantaneity has arrived through search engines

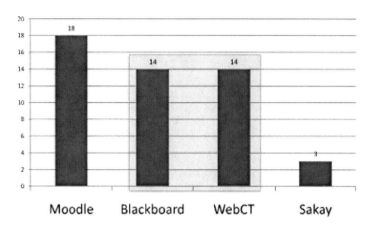

Fig. 5. utilisation of Open-course platforms as learning, management systems (Source Babo and Acevedo, 2009)

such as Google and repositories such as Wikipedia (Sharples 2000). The question on which we focussed deals with these aspects, and attempts to unlock understanding of the way a professor´s profile determinants: age, knowledge background or academic seniority, affect the teaching-learning process in e-learning environments.

On the other hand, several authors have analysed the main problems that institutions have to deal with when implementing e-learning platforms (Martínez and Gallego, 2007; Marshall and Mitchell, 2003, De la Cruz, 2005, Liaw, 2008, Campanella et al, 2008, Sun et al., 2008), but we have not yet found any reference to subject efficiency and student valorisation when comparing e-learning and classical classroom teaching.

5   Research Methodology

5.1   Objectives and Research Hypotheses

The study is the result of the collaboration between researchers and the UPV IT department leaders. The research hypotheses were:

H1. E-learning requires a new context for learning.
H2. The digital divide is a barrier for e-learning development and, therefore, it will be influenced by the generation differences of professors and their context (age, knowledge background or academic seniority).
H3. E-learning has a positive effect on learning impact and efficiency.

5.2   Data

Five years ago the UPV adopted the Sakai platform and some models of Open Course Ware to develop their e learning platform model denominated *Poliformat* as an e-learning support of physical attendance education. The analysis used is based on the data considering the results of 300[1] courses and relates the utilisation of various *Poliformat* tools by professors with their teaching efficiency ratios as well as with the student satisfaction reports for each subject. A number of moderating variables have been taken into account such as: professor age, status and seniority, subject area knowledge, course level (undergraduate, post graduate or life long learning) and other context factors. The analysis has been based on the UPV database corresponding to the 2008-09 academic year.

The data has been selected for the 288 courses, of which there was detailed information about the professor's profile and subject circumstances. Furthermore, the analysis took into account the results of the survey carried out during 2008 achieving responses from 315 teachers (out of 2600) and 432 students (out of 36.012).

6   Survey and Data Analysis Results

6.1   Survey Results

The majority of courses running at the UPV (97.5 %) are based on classroom learning methodology with e-learning acting as a support tool while only 2.5 % are partially based on online courses.

The first part of the survey addressed the opinions of the university students and faculty on the usefulness of e-learning tools. The replies have been summarized in Figure 6. The first block of six questions deals with the experience of students and staff with e-learning tools (social networks, SMS, news/ RSS, multimedia and websites), and their evaluation of their usefulness. The first outstanding result is that students have clearly had more experience with e-learning tools (approximately, an average 75 %) than their professors (an average of 50%). Among the students, SMS, websites and web tests are popular while the relevance of social networks must be emphasized. These results show a clear digital divide between students and faculty.

On the other hand, the second part of the survey addressed the use of the open course Poliformat platform and tools. Here the differences between students and faculty are lower since this platform was initiated five years ago by the university and various programs have been offered to motivate students and professors to its utilisation as well as reinforcement of its utilisation for academic evaluation. Still, students do find Poliformat more useful than their professors. PDAs, messages and calendars are more popular among students than faculty. Finally, though Google docs and blogs are less popular among students, these tools are found more useful by the students that by their professors. We could conclude here that although Poliformat is, in general, used by the faculty, students find it more useful and therefore, there would be more potential for the tools if the faculty would extend their usage.

Figure 7 shows the results of the survey concerning the opinions of students and faculty on the impact of e-learning tools. It shows that a majority of professors (approximately 70%) think that e-learning tools clearly contribute to improving teaching. Curiously, the opinions of students differ slightly, but that could be

---

[1] There are 2500 courses in the database but only 300 register one sole professor and his/her characteristics (age, seniority) can therefore be identified.

attributed to the fact that the teaching orientation of the professor is not completely changed by e-learning. The opinions related to learning are slightly different with 88 % of students believe that e-learning contributes to improved learning while this opinion is held by approximately 73% of the faculty members. Again this could be a result of the expectations of the generations within the digital divide proposed by Prenski (2001).

Teaching efficiency seems to be improved by e-learning tools and this opinion, again, is more strongly held by students than professors. The students are more accustomed to digital media and therefore, these tools are better adapted to their culture. The same applies to improving communication, though again, with some restrictions since digital tools cannot substitute for physical communication.

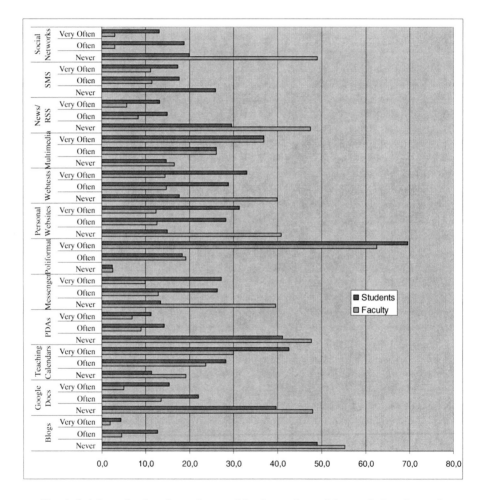

Fig. 6. Opinions of university students and faculty on the usefulness of e-learning tools

Finally, and this is an outstanding conclusion, there are large differences between students and faculty regarding the role of e-learning for improving team work. These results coincide with the previous analysis related to the opinions on the usefulness of e-learning tools as regarding social networks. Previous research has shown certain reluctance within the academic context to social networking (Albors and Ramos, 2008).

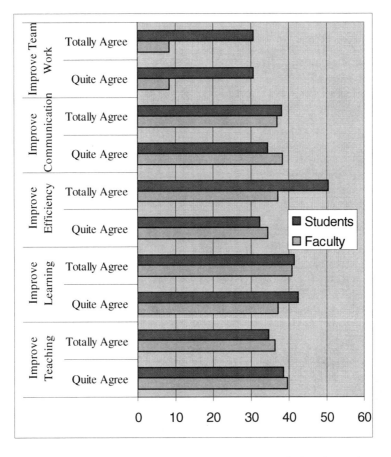

Fig. 7. Opinions of students and faculty on the impact of e-learning tools

6.3   Database Analysis Results

As has been pointed out, the researchers have had access to a database of 2500 subjects which were taught with the support of *Poliformat*. Of these, only 310 were selected since individual professors were identified as the one responsible for the subject and therefore their profile could be analysed. Though meaningful data were lost, it would have been a very complex task to identify groups by professors and filter all the relevant data. That exercise has been left for future research.

Table 1 shows the data that was taken into account in the analysis. It has to be mentioned that for our purposes the utilisation of electronic learning tools was an independent variable while teaching excellence (student satisfaction) and teaching efficiency, measuring learning indirectly, were dependent variables. The rest of the variables: e-learning training, professor age, professor category, seniority, subject type and number of registered students have been considered moderating factors.

Table 1. Utilised data and associated variables for the analysis

Variable	Meaning
Teachexcel	Results of student annual evaluation of faculty (range 1-10)
Training	Number of courses followed by faculty on e -learning
Age	Age of the Professor
Subj. Type	1: IT Engineering and Science; 2: Engineering; 3: Social sciences and Arts
Teach Categ	Professor Category: from 4, Full Professor to 1, Jr. Associate Prof.
Seniority	Years in the category
Efficiency	% of students passing the subject in the first call
Utilelteach	Utilisation of Poliformat tools (by number)
Matriculados	Number of registered students in the course

A first factor analysis has grouped these variables as shown in Table 2 with an explained variance of 70.7%. Thus, both independent and dependent variables have been grouped in component 2 while the moderating factors have been included in components 1, 3 and 4. Subject Type always has a negative sign, which is explained by the fact that IT subjects are taught by faculty with a background in digital learning while the highest number (3), assigned to liberal arts and social sciences subjects, signifies an opposite behaviour.

Table 2. Rotated components matrix

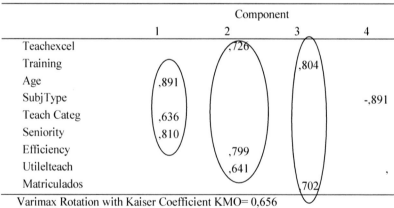

	Component			
	1	2	3	4
Teachexcel		,726		
Training			,804	
Age	,891			
SubjType				-,891
Teach Categ	,636			
Seniority	,810			
Efficiency		,799		
Utilelteach		,641		
Matriculados			,702	

Varimax Rotation with Kaiser Coefficient KMO= 0,656
Variance explained 70, 7 %.

A correlation exercise showed that Age is positively correlated with Professor Category and Seniority, which is logical. It is not, however, correlated with any dependent variable. Teaching Excellence is positively correlated with e-Learning training, Efficiency and e-Learning utilisation but negatively with Subject type.

When trying to build a regression model that could explain both teaching excellence and efficiency, the following models were obtained.

Table 3. Regression model explaining Teaching Excellence

Model	Standardized Coefficients	Sig.
	Beta	
(Constant)		,000
Utilelteach	,289	,000
Efficiency	,175	,005
SubjType	-,157	,009

$R^2 = 0,451$.

The model shown in Table 3 indicates that Teaching Excellence (student satisfaction) can be explained by the grade of utilization of e-learning tools, the efficiency of the subject taught and the subject type, favouring subjects in the area of IT and engineering.

On the other hand, the model shown in Table 4 indicates that teaching efficiency can be explained by the grade of utilization of e-learning tools, the student satisfaction level and the subject type, favouring subjects in the area of IT and engineering. Additionally, the teaching category appears as an influencing factor.

Table 4. Regression model explaining Teaching Efficiency

Model	Standarized Coefficients	Sig.
(Constant)		,000
Utilelteach	,378	,000
SubjType	-,277	,000
Teachexcel	,158	,007
TeachCateg	,151	,007

$R^2 = 0,327$.

Finally, and following the Baron and Kenny (1986) paradigm for mediating variables, the authors built a model which could explain the utilisation of e-learning tools. The model shown in Table 5 indicates that the utilisation of e-learning tools can be explained by Training in e-learning tools, the number of students registered in the subject, the professor's category and the subject type, favouring subjects in the area of IT. It is interesting to note that seniority appears as a negative factor in explaining the digital divide.

Table 5. Regression model explaining utilisation of e-learning tools

Model	Standarized Coefficients	Sig.
(Constant)		,957
Training	,220	,000
SubjType	,239	,000
Matriculados	,153	,010
Seniority	-,129	,021

$R^2 = 0,319$.

7   Conclusions

It was possible to validate H1 partially since e-learning seems to develop at a higher level in a context where information and communication technologies prevail, and training facilitates a new background for e-learning.

There was insufficient evidence to validate H2. The digital divide seems to be a barrier for e-learning development and, therefore, will be influenced by the difference in the generations of the professors and their context (age, knowledge background or academic seniority). Though the mediating model showed seniority as a barrier for utilization of e-learning tools, the sample composition, excessively composed of senior professors did not provide sufficient information in this direction.

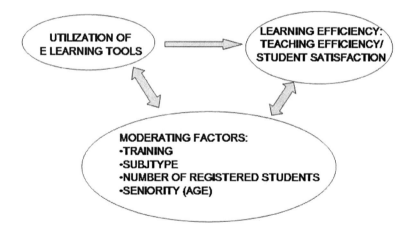

Fig. 8. Construct explaining impact of e-learning on higher teaching and the moderating factors influencing it

Finally it has been demonstrated that e-learning has a positive effect in the learning impact and teaching efficiency, thus providing evidence for validating H3.

It has to be mentioned that e-learning seems to provide support for those courses with a higher number of students registered by facilitating communication between professor and students.

Figure 8 shows the construct that was built from the research findings.

The utilisation of e-learning tools has a positive effect on learning efficiency as explained by student satisfaction and teaching efficiency. A number of moderating factors such as training in e-learning, context of IT, the number of registered students, have been found that somehow facilitates or motivates students and professors to take advantage of the e-learning tools. Finally, the research pointed out that seniority appears as a barrier for the utilization of e-learning tools. Further research should analyse more deeply the characteristics of this apparent digital divide.

Acknowledgements

The authors would like to thank the Vice Dean of the Universidad Politecnica de Valencia for making the data available that made this research possible.

The language revision of this paper was funded by the Universidad Politecnica de Valencia.

References

Albors, J., Ramos, J.C., Hervas, J.L.: New Learning Network Paradigms: Communities of Objectives, Crowd-sourcing, Wikis and Open Source. International Journal of Information Management 28, 194–202 (2008)

Babo, R., Acevedo, A.: Learning management systems usage on higher education. Paper Presented at 13th IBIMA Conference, Marraketch, Morocco, pp. 221–232 (November 2009)

Baron, R.M., Kenny, D.A.: The moderator-mediator variable distinction in social psychological research: Conceptual, strategic and statistical considerations. Journal of Personality and Social Psychology 51, 1173–1182 (1986)

Bernard, R., Abrami, P.L., Lou, Y., Borokhovski, E.: How does distance education compare with classroom instruction? a meta-analysis of the empirical literature. Rev. Educ. Res. 74, 379–439 (2004)

Campanella, S., Dimauro, G., Ferrante, A., Impedovo, D., Impedovo, S., Lucchese, M.G., Modugno, R., Pirlo, G., Sarcinella, L., Stasolla, E., Trullo, C.A.: E-learning Platforms in the Italian Universities: The Technological Solutions at University of Bari. WSEAS Transactions on Advances in Engineering Education 5(1), 1790–1979 (2008)

Chumley-Jones, H.S., Dobbie, A., Alford, C.L.: Web-based learning: sound educational method or hype? A review of the evaluation literature. Acad. Med. 77, 86–93 (2002)

Cook, R.G., Ley, K., Crawford, C., Warner, A.: Motivators and inhibitors for University Faculty in distance e–learning. British Journal of Educational Technology 40(1), 149–163 (2009)

Correa, J.M., Paredes, J.: Cambio tecnológico, usos de plataformas de e–learning y transformación de la enseñanza en las universidades españolas: la perspectiva de los profesores. Revista de Psicodidáctica 14(2), 261–278 (2009)

De la Cruz, O., Olivares, M., Pagés, C., Ríos, R., Moreno, F.J., López, M.A.: RED. Revista de educación a distancia, 1–15 (2005), http://www.um.es/ead/red/M2

Gibbons, A., Fairweather, P.: Computer-based instruction. In: Tobias, S., Fletcher, J. (eds.) Training & Retraining: A Handbook for Business, Industry, Government, and the Military, pp. 410–442. Macmillan, New York (2000)

Graf, S., List, B.: An Evaluation of Open Source E-Learning Platforms Stressing Adaptation Issues. Paper presented at Fifth IEEE International Conference on Advanced Learning Technologies, ICALT, pp. 163–165 (April 2005)

Greenhow, C., Robelia, B., Hughes, J.E.: Learning, Teaching, and Scholarship in a Digital Age. Web 2.0 and Classroom Research: What Path Should We Take Now. Research News and Comment. Educational Researcher 38, 246–259 (2010)

Leidner, D.E., Jarvenpaa, S.L.: The Use of Information Technology to Enhance Management School Education: A Theoretical View. MIS Quarterly, 270–291 (1995)

Letterie, G.S.: Medical education as a science: the quality of evidence for computer-assisted instruction. Am. J. Obstet. Gynecol. 188, 849–853 (2003)

Liaw, S.: Investigating students' perceived satisfaction, behavioral intention, and effectiveness of e-learning: A case study of the Blackboard system. Computer & Education 51(2), 864–873 (2008)

Littlejohn, A., Falconer, I., Megill, L.: Characterising effective eLearning resources. Computers and Education 50, 757–771 (2006)

Littlejohn, A., McGill, L.: Detailed report on effective resources for e-learning. Effectiveness of resources, tools and support services used by practitioners in designing and delivering E-Learning activities. JISC E-pedagogy Programme Project (2004), http://cetis.ac.uk:8080/pedagogy

Mahdizadeh, H., Biemans, H., Mulder, M.: Determining factors of the use of e–learning environments by university teachers. Computers and Education 51, 142–154 (2008)

Marshall, S., Mitchell, G.: Potential Indicators of e–Learning process capability. Educause in Australasia, 99–106 (2003)

Martínez Caro, E., Gallego Rodríguez, A.: El aprendizaje como ventaja competitiva para las organizaciones: Estilos de aprendizaje y e-learning. Direccion y Organización 33, 84–93 (2007)

McPherson, M.A., Nunest, J.M.: Critical issues for e–learning delivery: what seem obvious is not always put into practice. Journal of Computer Assisted Learning 24, 433–445 (2008)

Prenski, M.: Digital Natives Digital Immigrants. On the Horizon 9(5), 5–25 (2001)

Ruiz, J.G., Mintzer, M.J., Leipzig, R.M.: The Impact of E-Learning in Medical Education. Academic Medicine 81(3), 207–212 (2006)

Sclater, N.: Large scale open source e–learning systems at the Open University UK. EDUCAUSE, Research Bulletin, Is 12, 1–13 (2008)

Sharples, M.: The design of personal mobile technologies for lifelong learning. Computers and Education 34(3-4), 177–193 (2000)

Sun, P., Tsai, R., Finger, G., Chen, Y., Yeh, D.: What drives a successful e–Learning? An empirical investigation of the critical factors influencing learner satisfaction? Computers and Education 50, 1183–1202 (2008)

Wills, G.B., Bailey, C.P., Davis, H.C., Gilbert, L., Howard, Y., Jeyes, S., Millard, D.E., Price, J., Sclater, N., Sherratt, R., Tulloch, I., Young, R.: An e–learning framework for assessment (FREMA). Assessment and Evaluation in Higher Education 34(3), 273–292 (2009)

The Enhancement of Students' Interests and Efficiency in Elementary Japanese Learning as a Second Language through Online Games with Special Reference to Their Learning Styles

Steven K.K. Ng, Charles K.M. Chow, and David W.K. Chu

Caritas Bianchi College of Careers

Abstract. The introduction of online games in the implementation of Japanese language education at the elementary level is both desirable and challenging. It meets various demands from the population amongst many learners of Japanese language as a second language who are motivated mainly through playing online games but without any knowledge of Japanese language and also underlines some practical issues which involve the actual operations in Japanese classrooms, with respect to the possible outcomes realized through second language acquisition. In this paper, authors attempt to relate Fleming's model of VARK with its applications in different learning styles in elementary Japanese learning. They are illustrated with two different kinds of online games in each of the VARK strategies, namely visual, aural, read/write and kinesthetic. Above all, this article can as well be a reference for those Japanese teachers who are struggling in conducting elementary Japanese lessons in a more pleasant way as perceived by the learners.

1 Introduction

In traditional Chinese social philosophy, playing has always been perceived as an anti-thesis of studying. Hong Kong parents' minds have for a long time been instilled with a concept that pupils who enjoy playing are not able to perform well in their studies. Undoubtedly, they have been brought up with this kind of belief, which is seen as having been proved to be out-fashioned in recent years. The last few decades have seen a new generation who hardly survive without modern technologies such as mobile phones, computers and online games. They are in most cases presented as entertainments in front of the youngsters nowadays whereas they also have potentials to be developed as an effective but challenging medium for learning.

Some researches (see below) have so far been conducted to supplement English learning as a second language in classroom settings with the use of online games. It is a question of whether the same can also be applicable to Japanese learning as a second language, which has been motivated to a great extent through online games designed by Japanese toy makers. The successful use of online games in accelerating the pace of their learning Japanese as a second language can thus be highly expected and is also welcoming.

R. Kwan et al. (Eds.): ICT 2011, CCIS 177, pp. 305–318, 2011.
© Springer-Verlag Berlin Heidelberg 2011

2 Types of Learning Styles

Learning style has long been renowned as an important determinant for effective learning. As Kolb (1984) defines, "learning is the process whereby knowledge is created through the transformation experience" (p.38). Educators have often ignored the fact that students should have their own favorable learning style but not many of them are aware of their own learning preferences. Instead they tend to standardize their teaching approach for all their students, without paying attention to their heterogeneity. For example, Hawk and Shah (2007) comment that many of the higher education teaching staff are either unfamiliar with learning style models or uncomfortable to utilizing different learning styles other than their own inclinations since they are reluctant to leave their own comfort zone. Still, Felder and Silverman (1988) point out that the mismatch between traditional teaching styles and students' learning styles often results in students becoming bored and inattentive in their study; they will then perform poorly on examinations, being discouraged from the courses, or even drop out of colleges. For pedagogical reasons, it is thus obvious that educators need to gain knowledge of their student's favorable learning styles (Breckler, Joun and Ngo, 2009).

Nowadays, educators have been advised to shift their paradigm from the traditional teaching roles assigned to them. Educators are no longer the teaching authority in their classrooms, but they have to position themselves as a facilitator of learning, or the advanced learner of the knowledge which they are supposed to deliver (Tsang, Kwan and Tse 2008). For instance, Fleming and Baume (2006) suggest that educators and learners need a starting place for thinking, understanding as well as the ways of learning. In other words, a learning style is a description of preferences or of a process which encourage learners to understand the most effective step in the way in which they learn towards understanding and hence improve their depth of learning.

Nevertheless, Murphy et al. (2004) postulate that every student has his/her own learning style. They further their conclusion that if educators can adapt their teaching approaches to accommodate students' own learning style, improved learning outcome can be anticipated in addition to their own learning style. Tsang, Kwan and Tse (2007) also comment that the majority of students have more than one learning style; the natural learning style of the students is closely related to the students' community of learning. Thus, Hawk and Shah (2006) advocate that higher education teaching staff should vary their teaching approaches to match various learning styles of students so as to enhance their learning capability and performance.

As Hawk and Shah (2007) propose that there are six well-known and widely available learning style instruments in education sector, they are:

- Fleming VARK Model (Fleming, 2001)
- The Revised Approaches to Studying Inventory or RASI (Entwistle & Tait, 1995)
- Dunn and Dunn Learning Style Model (Dunn & Dunn, 1989)
- Felder-Silverman Learning/Teaching Style Model (Felder & Silverman, 1988)
- Kolb Experiential Learning Theory (Kolb, 1984)
- Gregorc Learning / Teaching Style Model (Gregorc, 1979)

In the last few years, lots of researches have tested the impact of all these six learning styles on students' learning improvement, and proved that each model has their own advantages and limitations. Since there is no one particular learning style which is better than others, the discussion will be based on Fleming's VARK model as the learning style to develop related learning apps in order to help students to acquire elementary Japanese language.

3   Review of VARK

As mentioned before, there are various learning styles introduced in the academic sector. Dobson (2009) comments that sensory modality is one of the most preferable approaches used in learning. Sensory modality consists of four different learning modes through which students can comprehend information which are "Visual", "Aural", "Read / Write" and "Kinesthetic". On this basis, New Zealand educator Neil Fleming has explored the concept by developing the VARK survey in 1998 so as to assess people's learning style preferences (Murphy et al., 2004; Dobson 2009). As Hawk and Shah (2007) quoted, Fleming's defines VARK learning as "an individual's characteristics and preferred ways of gathering, organizing, and thinking about information. VARK is in the category of instructional preference because it deals with perceptual models. It is focused on the different ways that we take in and give out information" (p.6).

VARK is an acronym for "Visual", "Aural", "Read / Write" and "Kinesthetic" (Fleming, 2001). A learner can take a free self-assessment with the completion of 16 questionnaires online or on paper by visiting VARK's official website: "http://www.vark-learn.com/english/index.asp". As Fleming (2006) comments, "VARK is a catalyst for metacognition, not a diagnostic or a measure" (p.2). The questionnaire is deliberately designed to be short in length for students' sake. They are encouraged to complete the questionnaires from their own experience rather than from any hypothetical situations. Educators and learners can self-assess, self-score, and self-interpret the VARK test and results on their own (Hawk and Shah, 2007).

Student's VARK learning style(s) can be classified by "unimodal" and "multimodal". In "Unimodal" learning style, the learner has a single or strong learning preference mode; whereas in "multimodal" learning style, the learner has multiple learning preference mode (i.e. more than one preference mode) (Breckler, Joun and Ngo, 2009). As Fleming (2001) suggests, relevant teaching approach for matching with correspondent learning styles as stated in Table 1:

Table 1. VARK Learning Styles versus Teaching Activities

VARK Learning Styles versus Teaching Activities			
Visual	**Aural**	**Read/Write**	**Kinesthetic**
Charts	Audio Tapes	Bibilographies	Constructing
Corls	Convesations	Books and Texts	Demonstrations
Designs	Debates & Arguments	Essay	Field Trips
Diagrams	Discussions	Handouts	Guest Lecturers
Different Fonts	Drama	Multiple Choic	Physical Activities
Graphs	Music	Note Taking	Real-life Examples
Spatial Arrangement	Seminars	Readings	Role Play
Wirtten Texts	Video & Audio	Written Feedback	Working Models

Source: Fleming (2001).

However, VARK model is hard to be validated statistically. There is scarcity of researches supporting its validity and reliability. Besides, several researchers also criticize that knowing one's learning style does not necessarily guarantee the improvement of their learning (Fleming, 2006). In despite of the above limitations and critics, Fleming (2006) argues that knowing students' learning style can still be beneficial if students can take their next steps, and then they can determine how and when they learn, as part of a reflective and meta-cognitive process, with appropriate learning actions followed. At the end, learners will have the possibilities and opportunities to make a distinction as well as an improvement in their learning process.

4   Enhancing Learning Efficiency through Online Games in Post-secondary Colleges

Generation Y, or the millennium, or "N" Generation (Network Generation), are usually defined as those who were born in the 1980s and early 1990s. This group of people is mainly those students who are studying at their colleges and universities at present and live in the computer and internet age. Also their major consumption focuses mainly on consuming cell phones, computers, online movies, online music, online games and online apps. They are reported to spend nearly 20 hours a week in average in playing online games (Blackwell, Miniard and Engel, 2006; Mesiter, 2008; Schrader and McCreery, 2008). It is thus commonly agreed that online games are pervasive in this generation.

Tsang, Kwan and Tse (2008) comment that the general public is relying more and more on internet due to the fact that internet has been integrated as a part of our everyday life. As Schrader and McCreery (2008) state, in the last two decades a dramatic change in learning environments on internet has been realized. Therefore, educators nowadays also need to consider utilizing internet and multimedia channel in their teaching. Hussain and Griffiths (2009) state that students will feel pleasant and satisfied at the time when they are playing online games. The online game is one of the multimedia channels which can be considered as an effective teaching platform to this group of students. Even though online gaming teaching mode is still at a relatively new area of activity in the education field, and using online games for training and education purposes are still limited in the current stage, some educational institutions and training organizations have already begun to use online game as a potential context in learning and education in the last decades. (Freitas and Griffiths, 2007; Schrader and McCreery, 2008). This corresponds to the instrumental motivation as coined by Robert Gardner and Wallace Lambert (1972). It refers to the language learning aiming at realizing some immediate or practical goals.

As Oliver and Carr (2009) reveal, online games have been recently considered in the mainstream education policy and it is needed to integrate appropriate games into related educational contexts. Yip and Kwan (2006) have also conducted a research on using online games for teaching and learning English vocabulary, and they have found that online game is an effective tool for vocabulary learning. They have concluded that students prefer more online games as a learning tool to a traditional face-to-face learning lesson. They have also discovered that in order to maintain the interests of students, online games can make students gain satisfaction and achievement (p.247). Henceforth, the following parts will be devoted to the study of how to match the online games and learning apps with the VARK learning styles in learning elementary Japanese language.

5   Enthusiasm of Using Mobile Technologies in the Youth

Language learning may be hard and frustrating for many students. However, some of them find playing games interesting and entertaining, which in turn can be an effective motivation for their learning. Nowadays, teenagers are more immersed in mobile technologies, including gaming of various types. According to Nielsen's recent report (Kellogg,D, 2011) on mobile youth globally, there are high percentages of young people owning smartphones. In Hong Kong, there are 47 percent of young mobile subscribers (age 15-24) owning a smartphone. In this way, apps take a critical role in the popularity of mobile technologies such as smartphone. They have undoubtedly an extensive reach to a huge population.

According to the TNS Global Telecoms Insights survey 2010 (TNS, 2010), Facebook is used extensively by Hong Kong consumers amounting to 17 percent, followed by Yahoo (14 percent) and Google (14 percent). Numerous apps are too available on it nowadays. Therefore, it might be a fantastic tool for learning as well and it is important to select appropriate apps which can be adapted to the learning styles of the game players. They will enable learners to take control of their learning modes. They can then choose the types of apps that match their interests, practice at times that fit their schedules, as well as adjust the levels that match their learning progress.

6   Types of Apps and Online Games

Generally speaking, there are as many as twenty categories of apps, ranging from games to social networking. Taking MOBILETUT.com (www.mobiletut.com) as an example, apps can be consolidated to four major categories, namely serious tools, fun tools, fun games and serious entertainment. Among them, fun games are believed to have high potential in facilitating an elementary stage of language learning.

The main reasons for deploying apps are their mobility and simplicity, but compatibility and portability are also key considerations. From the view of portability, use of apps is definitely an advantage. However, in terms of compatibility, there are still many concerns worth noting. Major operating systems like Symbian, Blackberry, Windows Mobile, iPhone and Android are deployed by smartphone makers. They are not compatible either from the users' end or the developers' end.

Systems like Symbian and Windows Mobile have existed for a couple of years. There have already been many custom applications built into their devices whereas Android is comparatively new. However, it is backed by one of the biggest Web players, Google, since it has been acquired by Google in 2007. There is strong momentum in picking up the market rapidly. Statistics of Worldwide Smartphone Sales to End Users by Operating System in 2010 (Gartners, 2011) shows that Symbian devices comprised a 37.6% share of smart mobile devices sold, with Android having 22.7%, RIM/Blackberry having 16%, and Apple iOS having 15.7%.

7   Matching of Learning Apps to Learning Styles

To facilitate learning of elementary Japanese, here comes with some recommendations on different types of apps. From the perspectives of learners, we have identified some types of games that match the learning styles of individual learners. Based on the VARK model, there are four categories of learning styles, namely Visual, Aural/Auditory, Read/Write and Kinesthetic. Eight types of apps, two sub-types for each style, are recommended here for each of the four learning styles.

For the Visual style, it is good for learners who prefer reading pictures or graphs. Therefore, "Puzzle" and "Real-time Strategy" apps are suggested. For the Aural/Auditory style, learners are stronger in listening to illustration, conversation, stories or music. Apps of "Music/Rhythm" and "Speech Recognition" are suggested. For the Read/Write style, learners prefer interacting with outside through reading and writing. Apps like "Act to Response" and "Handwriting Practice" are suggested. Lastly for the kinesthetic style, learners prefer more hands-on activities in their learning. Therefore "Role-playing" and "Shooting" games are suggested. Four types of apps suggested and their corresponding examples of game apps are summarized in Table 2.

Table 2. Examples of game apps for players of different learning styles

VISUAL Puzzle Real-time Strategy	**AUDITORY** Music/Rhythm Speech Recognition
READ/WRITE Act to Response Handwriting Practice	**KINESTHETIC** Role-playing Shooting

For the Visual style, puzzle games require players to re-arrange a scrabbled 5-by-10 matrix of 45 Japanese letters into right order. Real-time strategy apps require players to identify the right vocabulary from a cluster of words once a picture is prompted on screen. According to Lyster (2004)'s hypothesis, prompts 'can enhance control over already-internalized forms' (p.406) and in the words of Lightbown and

Spada (2006), they 'can push learners to retrieve a target form that they have some knowledge of but do not use reliably and to compare it to their interlanguage form.' (p.173). For the Aural/Auditory style, music/rhythm apps will play a Japanese song and the players should click on a particular phrase once it is played.   Speech recognition apps require players to speak out a Japanese word or phrase once it is prompted on screen. For the Read/Write style, Act to Response apps require players to read an instruction prompted and take the corresponding action by moving the objects to the target location. Handwriting practice checks if the player can write Japanese characters that corresponds to the picture prompted on screen. Lastly, for the Kinesthetic style, role-playing apps allow players to select a predefined scenario, and then the player is requested to select the right responses to a series of prescribed situations. Shooting games will play a conversation or a phrase and then the players need to compose the phrase by hitting the corresponding characters to complete the conversation. Detailed elaboration of the suggested apps will be given in the following sections.

By recommending relevant apps to the learners, students may learn the target language through those learning apps that match their learning styles. Although there are still critiques on the effectiveness of various models on learning styles, this project is not aiming at proving the effectiveness of a particular model. Instead, we attempt to relate the concept of understanding an individual's learning styles with a more preferable language learning tool for the learners.

Though compatibility problems among different operating systems are still ahead, cross-compatibility mobile development tools are on the way.   Notwithstanding the longer historic operating system Symbian or the rapidly growing operating system Android, it is generally believed that the development of apps that fits novice language learners provide alternative ways of language learning, especially at the elementary stage, with ease and fun.

8   Review the Difficulties Encountered in Learning Elementary Japanese for the Youth

Over the past few decades, there has been a growth in the Japanese language learning programmes in Hong Kong in terms of the education organizations which offer them and the levels at which learners study them. In this paper, focus will be on the elementary learners of Japanese language who attempt to attain the level of N5/N4 (equivalent to the Level 4 before 2010) at the Japanese Language Proficiency Test as organized by the Japan Foundation.   The past experiences of the author on teaching elementary Japanese for more than a decade has revealed some kinds of difficulties encountered by them in various aspects.

Firstly, some elementary learners of Japanese language are lack of solid foundation on the Japanese letters table (Gojuonzu五十音圖). This entails an important issue that they have found it hard to write down the correct letters once they have listened to the words spoken. Moreover, without sufficient knowledge of Japanese letters table they will be puzzled in the process of verb conjugations (Doshi no katsuyo 動詞の活用) in written form.

Secondly, second language learners are weak at the lexical understanding of a word in the aural form. Most of them tend to acquire the meaning of a word in visual form. It is rather unnatural for them to relate a sound with a visual object or any concept in their minds without time lag. The second language acquisition should be enforced more in this aspect.

Thirdly, situational learning is also insufficient when one discusses the second language acquisition. Having no obvious motivation to learn a language such as Japanese do not bring them to a situation of how Japanese language can be used effectively and efficiently. The introduction of specific scenarios will assist learners in the exploration of the ways in which they become more interested in using Japanese more appropriately.

9   Review Types of Online Learning of Japanese Language

1   Visual

a. Puzzle

A scrabbled 5-by-10 matrix of 50 Japanese letters (actually 45 letters) is presented to the game-takers who are asked to put them into right order according to the requirements named at both the vertical and horizontal axis. An example (Table 3) is provided below:

Table 3. Scrabbled version

	あ段	い段	う段	え段	お段
あ行	こ	え	つ	く	お
か行	て	ち	す	と	も
さ行	せ	や	れ	そ	け
た行	た	あ	い	の	よ
な行	は	う	な	ゆ	か
は行	さ	ひ	ふ	ろ	ほ
ま行	に	し	る	へ	わ
や行	を	X	ら	X	り
ら行	み	む	ね	め	ま
わ行	ぬ	X	X	X	き

Game-takers are supposed to change the example above into the following one (Table 4) as soon as possible. It is advised to add a time machine on the screen so as to enhance the degree of excitement on the part of the game takers.

Table 4. Correct version

	あ段	い段	う段	え段	お段
あ行	あ	い	う	え	お
か行	か	き	く	け	こ
さ行	さ	し	す	せ	そ
た行	た	ち	つ	て	と
な行	な	に	ぬ	ね	の
は行	は	ひ	ふ	へ	ほ
ま行	ま	み	む	め	も
や行	や	X	ゆ	X	よ
ら行	ら	り	る	れ	ろ
わ行	わ	X	X	X	を

Notes: Game takers are not required to put any letters into cells with 'X'.

b. Real-time strategy

Game takers are presented pictures which show some objects of everyday life. They are asked to choose one word from a list of alternative choices (usually 4) similar to each other in terms of their pronunciation which should correspond with the picture presented. Only one picture will be prompted at one time. Ten items will be tested for one game taker and the score is to be shown to the game taker once all the items are answered. The instruction is supposed to be given in Japanese read by a native speaker with female voice. An example is given below:

右の写真を見てください。　　　(Please take a look at the picture at the right)
それはなんですか。　　　　　　(What is that?)
左の選択肢から選んでください。(Please choose the right answer from the choices)

1. くるま
2. くまる
3. まるく
4. るくま

2 Aural/Auditory

a. Music

The game taker listens to a famous Japanese song and s/he is asked to click on a particular phrase once it is heard. An example is given below:

- たどりついたら みさきのはずれ
- あかいひがつく ぽつりとひとつ

- いまでもあなたを　まってると
- いとしい おまえの よぶこえが
- おれのせなかで　かぜになる
- よるのくしろは　あめになるだろう
- ふるいさかばで　うわさをきいた
- まどのむこうは　こがらしまじり
- はんとしまえまで　いたという
- なきぐせ　さけぐせ　なみだぐせ
- どこへ　いったか　ほそいかげ
- よるのはこだて　きりがつらすぎる
- そらでちぎれる　あのきてきさえ
- ないてわかれる　さいはてみなと
- いちどはこのてに　だきしめて
- なかせて やりたい　おもいきり
- きえぬおもかげ　たずねびと
- よるのおたるは　ゆきがかたにまう

b. Speech Recognition

A game taker is presented with a word containing up to five letters. Then s/he is asked to listen to 4 speakers pronouncing 4 different sounds respectively and choose the right one which corresponds with the one presented visually. An example is offered below. The instruction is given in Japanese read by a native speaker.

この単語を見てください。　(Please look at the following word)

ちかてつ　　　　　　　　(meaning: underground rail)

この単語の発音は以下のどれですか。　　(Which of the followings is its pronunciation?)

1番：フェリー　　　(meaning: ferry)

2番：バス　　　(meaning: bus)

3番：ひこうき　　　(meaning: plane)

4番：ちかてつ　　　(meaning: underground rail)

3 Reading/Writing

a. Act to response

The game taker is asked to read an instruction (in Japanese) prompted and required to take the corresponding action by moving some objects to the right places. An example is given below:

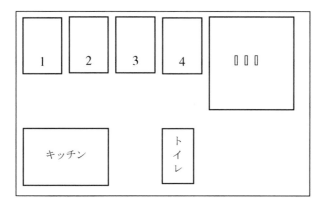

うえの　えを　みて　ください。　(Please look at the picture above)
かばんを　へやいちに　おいてください。(Please move the bag to Room No. 1)

b. Handwriting

A picture is prompted on the screen and the game taker is asked to write a word with its meaning corresponding to the picture. In order to limit the number of model answers, it is advisable to specific the number of letters to be used. For example, when the follow picture is presented, there may be more than one answer. Then, when the answer is limited to two letters, it is easier to identify the right one:

Model answer:

2   Kinesthetic

a. Role-playing

At the start screen, game taker selects a pre-defined scenario such as shopping, restaurants or tourist information counter. Then, a role will be allocated to the game taker, be a shop keeper, waiter or tourist information officer. The game taker is then presented with a question asked by a customer in the chosen situation. S/he is required to choose the most appropriate response to be expected there. An example is given below:

場面 ： レストラン	(Situation: Restaurant)
役割 ： ウェイター	(Your role: Waiter)
お客様の質問 ： いくら？	(Question from the customer: How much?)
あなたのお答えは ：	(Your answer should be:)

1. ありがとうございます　　(Thank you.)
2. どういたしまして　　　　(You are welcome.)
3. ごじゅうドルとなります　(It is 50 dollars.)
4. さようなら　　　　　　　(Goodbye.)

b. Shooting

The game taker listens to a word spoken by a native speaker. Then, s/he should follow it by shooting an object represented by the word. An example is given below.

りんごを　撃ってください　　　　(Please shoot the apple)

10   Relating Proposed Different Learning Outcomes in Each Type of the Game to Various Types of Learning Style

For learners with visual preference, the puzzle game aims at building up a more solid foundation for learners to use Japanese characters more effectively and efficiently. On the other hand, the real time strategy game attempts to explore game taker's segmental differentiation at the phonetic science.

For learners with aural/auditory preference, the song text at the music/rhythm game will be presented without the use of Kanji (Chinese character) in order to lessen the effect of Contrastive Analysis Hypothesis as advocated by some second language linguistics while the speech recognition aims at training the game taker's reading and aural proficiency at the lexical aspect.

For learners with reading and writing preference, the learners can comprehend some instructions in the way in which they are asked to do something. Through the game, it is easier for learners to enhance their confidence in reading Japanese paragraphs. In addition, through handwriting game, learners can improve their writing habits of Japanese language.

For learners with kinesthetic preference, they can know the reasons for which they are learning Japanese language. Furthermore, the shooting game can train their simultaneous response to an instruction spoken by a Japanese interlocutor.

11   Conclusion

In short, effective learning has sprung from effective teaching and learners' learning preference alike. The preference has normally been expressed in terms of their learning styles which vary from person to person. It is teachers who act as facilitators in adapting their teaching modes to the exploration of different learning preference such as visual, aural, read/write and kinesthetic, through which, learners are comparatively confident enough to collect, synthesis as well as process the information delivered to them.

Since most of Hong Kong learners are inclined to acquire Japanese language as a second language so as to prepare playing online games, the introduction of Japanese language via various kinds of these online games can provide an impetus to effective learning. Distinct from the last generation of Japanese learners who focused more on using Japanese in business transactions, the N Generation cling themselves upon learning it in the way that proved to be pleasant and satisfied.

12   Limitations of the Study and Further Research

As aforesaid, no one proven learning style works perfectly in enhancing all students' learning process. One of the limitations for this paper is that authors have so far not applied all the six learning styles to develop correspondent learning apps so as to help students in learning elementary Japanese language. Besides, they are still preparing to conduct a physical survey to testify if the said learning style can match the proposed learning apps. In this way, further research is recommended in the elaboration of the above learning apps to match other learning style models. In addition, a physical survey is desirable to validate the extent to which learners can improve their efficiency and effectiveness in elementary Japanese language learning as a second language through the suggested learning apps with their preference learning styles. Lastly, it should be supplemented by a research on the comparison of elementary Japanese learning between classroom setting and online game setting with respect to its efficiency and effectiveness.

References

1. Blackwell, R., Miniard, P., Engel, J.: Consumer Behavior. Thomson Higher Education, Mason (2006)
2. Breckler, J., Joun, D., Ngo, H.: Learning styles of physiology students interested in the health professions. Advances in Physiology Education 33, 30–36 (2009)
3. Dobson, J.: Learning style preferences and course performance in an undergraduate physiology class. The American Physiological Society 33, 308–314 (2009)
4. Dunn, R., Dunn, K.: Learning style inventory. Lawrence, KS: Price Systems (1989)
5. Entwistle, N., Tait, H.: The revised approaches to studying inventory. University of Edinburgh Centre for Research on Learning and Instruction, Edinburgh (1995)
6. Felder, R., Silverman, L.: Learning and Teaching Styles In Engineering Education. Engineering Education 78(7), 674–681 (1988)

7. Fleming, N.: Teaching and learning styles: VARK strategies. N.D. Fleming, Christchurch (2001)

8. Fleming, N., Baume, D.: Learning Styles Again: VARKing up the right tree! Educational Developments, SEDA Ltd. 7.4, 4–7 (2006)

9. Freitas, S., Griffiths, M.: Online gaming as an educational tool in learning and training. British Journal of Educational Technology 38(3), 535–537 (2007)

10. Gardner, R.C., Lambert, W.E.: Attitudes and Motivation in Second Language Learning. Newbury House, Rowley (1972)

11. Gartners, Worldwide Smartphone Sales to End Users by Operating System in 2010 (2011), http://www.gartner.com/it/page.jsp?id=1543014

12. Gregorc, A.: Learning/teaching styles: Their nature and effects. In: NASSP Monograph, pp. 19–26 (October/November 1979)

13. Hawk, T., Shah, A.: Using Learning Style Instruments to Enhance Student Learning. Decision Sciences Jounrnal of Innovative Education 5(1), 1–19 (2007)

14. Hussain, Z., Griffiths, M.: The Attitudes, Feelings, and Experiences of Online Gamers: A Qualitative Analysis. CyberPsychology & Behavior 12(6), 747–753 (2009)

15. Kellogg, D.: Among Mobile Phone Users, Hispanics, Asians are Most-Likely Smartphone Owners in the U.S., neilsenwire (2011), The Nielsen Company, http://blog.nielsen.com/nielsenwire (February 1, 2011)

16. Kolb, D.: Experiential learning: Experience as the source of learning and development. Prentice-Hall, Englewood Cliffs (1984)

17. Lightbown, P.M., Spada, N.: How languages are learned. Oxford University Press, Oxford (2006)

18. Lyster, R.: Differential effects of prompts and recasts in form-focused instruction. Studies in Second Language Acquisition 26(3), 399–432 (2004)

19. Meister, J.: Learning From Multiplayer Online Games. Chief Learning Officer. MediaTec. Publishing, Inc. (2008)

20. MOBILEtut.com (2010), Web http://www.mobiletut.com

21. Murphy, R., Gray, S., Straja, S., Bogert, M.: Student Learning Preferences and Teaching Implications. Journal of Dental Education 68(8), 859–866 (2004)

22. Oliver, M., Carr, D.: Learning in virtual worlds: Using communities of practice to explain how people learn from play. British Journal of Educational Technology 40(3), 444–457 (2009)

23. Schrader, P., McCreery, M.: The acquisition of skill and expertise in massively multiplayer online games. Education Technology Research Development 56, 557–574 (2008)

24. TNS (2010) Smartphone usage set to dominate Hong Kong mobile market. TNS Global Telecoms Insights Survey (2010)

25. Tsang, P., Kwan, R., Tse, S.: Enhancing Student Learning Through Technology: A Case Study of "Online Game" and "Webgame" Experiment. Enhancing Learning Through Technology – Research on Emerging Technologies and Pedagogies, pp. 233–249. World Scientific, Singapore (2008)

26. Yip, F., Kwan, A.: Online vocabulary games as a tool for teaching and learning English vocabulary. Educational Media International 43(3), 233–249 (2006)

Using Web 2.0 Technologies in K-12 School Settings: Evidence-Based Practice?

Khe Foon Hew and Wing Sum Cheung

National Institute of Education, 1 Nanyang Walk
637616 Singapore
{khefoon.hew,wingsum.cheung}@nie.edu.sg

Abstract. Evidence-based practice involves making pedagogical decisions that are informed by the available relevant research evidence. This paper reviews the current literature on the use of Web 2.0 technologies in K-12 school settings in order to discuss possible evidence-based practice that could inform educators and researchers who are interested in fostering student learning through Web 2.0 tools. A search of the literature was performed across the Academic Search Premier and ERIC databases. Empirical studies were included for review if they specifically examined the impact of Web 2.0 technologies on learning outcomes in primary and secondary school (including high school) settings. Articles that merely reported anecdotal or self-reporting survey studies (student perceptions or attitudes toward using Web 2.0) were excluded. Results tentatively suggested that a dialogic and/or co-constructive pedagogy supported by activities such as Socratic questioning, peer and self-critique, appeared to increase student achievements in blog- and wiki-enabled environments. A transmissive pedagogy supported by review activities appeared to enhance student learning of vocabulary when using podcast. However, given the limited number of studies currently available, as well as methodological concerns, further research is required to establish clear recommendations on evidence-based practice in Web 2.0 supported learning environments.

Keywords: Web 2.0, Evidence-based practice, K-12, Elementary education, Secondary education.

1   Introduction

Ever since the creation of the motion picture in 1922 educators have been intrigued with the potential of technology to transform education and improve student learning [1]. With the recent explosion in the number of Web 2.0 technologies, many educators are now spoilt for choice of use with their students. Many claims and suggestions have been made about the educational potential or benefits of these technologies. However, it is important to note that such claims and suggestions are often not based on research evidence.

This paper reviews the current literature on the use of Web 2.0 technologies in K-12 school settings (including primary and secondary schools) in order to discuss possible evidence-based practice that could provide educators and researchers with

R. Kwan et al. (Eds.): ICT 2011, CCIS 177, pp. 319–328, 2011.
© Springer-Verlag Berlin Heidelberg 2011

informed direction to achieve specific learning goals. This paper is organized as follows. It begins with a brief definition of Web 2.0, followed by a description of some related technologies. Then there is a description of data sources, analysis, and findings. There is a focus on several directions for future research related to the use of Web 2.0 technologies in K-12 settings.

1.1   Defining Web 2.0

Surprisingly, despite its popularity, there is no one widely acceptable definition of Web 2.0 [2], [3], [4]. Despite this lack of a consensus over what is actually meant by "Web 2.0", many educators concur that Web 2.0, in its most basic form, refers to a concept which allows individuals to collaborate with one another and contribute to the authorship of content, customize web sites for their use, and instantaneously publish their thoughts [3], [5]. Web 2.0, enables individuals with little technical know-how (e.g., using a Web editor or write HTML code) to contribute to the Internet. As a result, individuals can become contributors to the Internet, not merely readers of the contributions made by others [3].

There is currently a large range of Web 2.0 technologies available for educators to use with their students. One possible way to make sense of this ever-expanding number of technologies is to classify them by their modalities of representation and the degree of synchronicity they enable [2]. A summary of some Web 2.0 technologies (not exhaustive) is presented in Table 1.

Table 1. Examples of some Web 2.0 technologies, adapted from [2]

Technology	Example	Modality	Synchronicity
Weblog	Blogger, Edublogs, Glogster	Text, Image	Asynchronous
Wiki	PB wiki, Wetpaint, Wikispaces	Text, Image	Asynchronous
Social network	Facebook, Twitter	Text, Image	Synchronous, Asynchronous
Podcast	Houndbite, Chirbit	Audio	Asynchronous
Audio discussion board	Wimba voice, Voicethread	Audio, Text, Image	Asynchronous
Video sharing	YouTube	Video	Asynchronous
Social bookmarking	Delicious, Diigo, Simpy	Text	Asynchronous

2   Sources of Data

A search of the literature was performed across the Academic Search Premier and ERIC databases. Academic Search Premier is considered one of the most prominent databases in academic institutions [6]. Academic Search Premier and ERIC databases are frequently used by other researchers conducting literature searches [1], [7], [8], [9]. These databases were searched for articles using an open-ended search period (up until March 23, 2011). The search strategy used for searching the databases is listed in Table 2. The snowball method was used and the authors examined the references in relevant articles for additional studies. Article searches were limited to publications that were experimental in design. The Fraenkel and Warren [10] conceptualization of experiment research was adopted. This may include the following designs: (a) randomized control and treatment groups, (b) one-group pretest and posttest, and (c) quasi-experiment. Selected articles explored the impact of using Web 2.0 technologies on learning outcomes. Articles that merely described anecdotal or student self-report studies (student perception toward learning or toward Web 2.0) were excluded. Additionally, study participants either had to be elementary/primary students or secondary (including middle school and high school) students to be included in this review.

Table 2. Search strategy used for the Academic Search Premier and ERIC databases

Sequence	Keyword
1	Web 2.0 AND K12
2	Elementary education AND Web 2.0
3	Secondary education AND Web 2.0
4	Blog AND elementary education
5	Blog AND secondary education
6	Wiki AND elementary education
7	Wiki AND secondary education
8	Podcast AND elementary education
9	Podcast AND secondary education
10	Facebook AND elementary education
11	Facebook AND secondary education
12	Social bookmark AND elementary education
13	Social bookmark AND secondary education
14	YouTube AND elementary education
15	YouTube AND secondary education
16	Twitter AND elementary education
17	Twitter AND secondary education
18	Wimba AND elementary education
19	Wimba AND secondary education
20	Voice thread AND elementary education
21	Voice thread AND secondary education

3   Method

The basic unit of analysis was each individual empirical article. Each article was read and its content analyzed and classified into the following categories to help describe the key features of the study:

(1) Discipline (e.g., language arts, social studies);
(2) Web 2.0 technologies (e.g., blog, podcast, wiki);
(3) Learning goals or objectives (e.g., improve English narrative writing);
(4) Knowledge dimension (see subsequent paragraph for details);
(5) Cognitive process (see subsequent paragraph for details);
(6) Types of pedagogy (see subsequent paragraph for details); and
(7) Specific instructional/learning activities (e.g., peer critique, self critique).

Anderson and Krathwohl [11] created a taxonomy of learning, teaching and assessing that could help educators conceptualize learning. This particular taxonomy includes a knowledge dimension which incorporates the following categories:

(1) Factual knowledge – discrete pieces of basic information, essential facts, or terminology that people must know in order to be acquainted with a discipline and solve problems in it;
(2) Conceptual knowledge – inter-relationships of factual knowledge, including knowledge of classification, principles, and generalizations;
(3) Procedural knowledge – knowledge of procedures, processes, algorithms, or particular methodologies; and
(4) Metacognitive knowledge – knowledge of one's own thinking as well as that of other people.

In addition to the knowledge dimension, the taxonomy [11] includes the cognitive process dimension, which consists of the following:

(1) Remember – retrieving relevant information from memory; includes recognizing, identifying, recalling, listing, naming;
(2) Understand – constructing meaning; includes interpreting, paraphrasing, illustrating, instantiating, classifying, summarizing, predicting, comparing;
(3) Apply – using a procedure in a given setting; includes implementing, executing, carrying out;
(4) Analyze – breaking material into its component parts and examining how these parts relate to one another and to an overall structure; includes organizing, deconstructing, finding coherence, integrating;
(5) Evaluate – making judgments based on certain criteria or standards; includes testing, critiquing, checking, monitoring; and
(6) Create – putting things together to form a functional whole; includes planning, designing, producing, constructing, making, generating.

Finally, although there are many different types of pedagogies that can determine the success of a learning episode, these pedagogies can be distinguished by their degree of negotiation and production [2] (p. 182), as shown in Table 3:

(1) Transmissive pedagogies – transmissive-based information delivery approaches, where a stream of information is broadcast to learners;
(2) Dialogic pedagogies – centered on discourse between participants, and often involving exemplars followed by periods of activity and feedback;
(3) Constructionist – where learning occurs by developing a product; and
(4) Co-constructive – groups of learners complete a series of goal-related tasks to produce an artifact.

Table 3. Pedagogies categorized based on their degree if negotiation and production, extracted from [2], p. 183

	Non-negotiated	Negotiated
No product	Transmissive	Dialogic
Product	Constructionist	Co-constructive

4   Results

Four articles were eligible for inclusion for this review. One study investigated the impact of using wiki in a high school setting. One examined the effect of blog in an elementary school. One study explored the impact of blogging and podcasting on secondary school students' social studies achievement. One examined the impact of podcasting in a primary school setting. Table 4 summarizes the key features of these studies.

Table 4. Key features of the reviewed studies

Study	Discipline	Web 2.0 tools	Objectives	Knowledge dimension	Cognitive dimension	Pedagogy	Specific activity
[3]	history	Wiki	Improve learning of facts	Factual	Remember, understand, analyze, create	Dialogic, co-const.	Developing an e- scrapbook, peer critique
[12]	language	Blog	Improve narrative writing	Factual, meta-cognitive, procedural	Remember, understand, apply, create	Dialogic, co-const.	Writing model guide, peer critique, and reflection
[13]	social studies	Blogcast	Enhance critical thinking	Factual, conceptual, meta-cognitive	Remember, understand, evaluate, create	Dialogic, co-const.	Socratic questioning, peer and self critique
[14]	science	Podcast	Enhance learning of science vocabulary	Factual, conceptual	Remember, understand	Transmissive	Listen and review content

4.1   More Detailed Description of the Studies

Impact of wiki on retention of history facts. Heafner and Friedman [3] utilized a quasi-experiment design to test high school students' retention of World War II (WWII) facts. Participants were eleventh grade USA history students. One teacher taught two sections of the same class; whereby in one section students developed a wiki as an electronic scrapbook, while in the other section, the same teacher taught the class using a teacher-centered format in order to pass the end-of-course test. The number of students in the wiki and control groups was unreported. Data were collected from the following sources: observation, teacher interview, test scores, and student questionnaire. The duration of the study was not explicitly stated, but was judged to be over one semester.

Specifically, students in the wiki group visually presented and explained events that occurred in WWII. Student wikis consisted of eight pages reporting key themes of the war such as: the causes of WWII, USA entry, home front, holocaust, war in Europe, war in the Pacific, and outcomes. Within each page, students posted primary source images, as well as their analysis of each visual and a rationale for its inclusion in the page. Students in the control group, on the other hand, were assigned nightly readings from a textbook that strictly followed a department pacing guide for USA history. The pacing guide dictated what content would be covered on each instructional day, as well as the related textbook readings. Class instruction usually involved teacher centered map work, reading quizzes, teacher lectures and question-and-answer sessions.

End-of-course test scores revealed that students in the control group on average scored higher than their counterparts in the wiki group. No effect size was reported. Yet, interestingly, in a delayed test about eight months after the course, students in the wiki group remembered more (had greater content retention) than students in the control group. The authors concluded that a co-constructive pedagogy that required students to create an e-scrapbook (via wiki) was able to help students retain more content knowledge of WWII over the long term.

Impact of blogging and scaffolding on narrative writing achievement. Wong and Hew [12] utilized a one-group pretest and posttest experiment design to investigate if the use of blogging and scaffolding could improve students' English narrative writing. Participants of the study were 36 primary five (equivalent to grade five) students, consisting of 18 boys and 18 girls. Data were gathered using a pretest and posttest, student reflections, and face-to-face interviews. The study was conducted over a three-week period.

In the first week, students were given a pretest consisting of a narrative writing task in order to establish baseline data about the students' initial writing ability. Students were also introduced to a blog maker (Blogger, www.blogger.com).

In the second week, the students were provided with a scaffold – a writing model guide [15] which could be used as an outline or mind-mapping guide during the planning process of the writing. Essentially the writing model guide consisted of useful linking words, helpful phrases that dealt with action and ending, as well as questions for planning the story. Students individually wrote a draft of their story in their own individual blogs with the assistance of the writing guide. Students then read peer blogs and gave comments about each other's draft (peer critique). Next, students individually reflected on these comments and produced a final version of their stories.

In the third week, a posttest was conducted to test the narrative writing ability after the blogging and scaffolding treatment. Both the pretest and posttest questions were examined by the school's Head of Department for English language to ensure that they were similar in terms of difficulty. Completed pretest and posttest writings were marked by two teachers (to ensure reliability of marking) using a national English examination marking rubric. The total possible maximum score was 40. The marking scores for each student did not differ significantly at the 0.05 level of significance. All 36 students completed their reflections about the use of blogs. Individual face-to-face interviews were carried out with six students to clarify unclear issues surfacing from their reflections as well as to seek more in-depth understanding about their perceptions of using blog for writing.

Results showed that posttest scores were significantly better than pre-test scores at the 0.05 level of significance. The effect size was medium ($d = 0.47$). This suggested that the blogging and scaffolding treatment could help improve student narrative writing ability. Additionally, the standard deviation of the posttest scores had decreased, suggesting that the spread of the scores had reduced and that student scores were more consistent.

Effect of blogcast and Socratic questioning on ability to evaluate information related to controversial social studies issues. A one-group pretest and posttest study by Salam and Hew [13] investigated the impact of using blogcast with Socratic questioning on secondary school students' critical thinking in evaluating controversial social studies issues. (The ability to critically evaluate the credibility of information sources and facts revolving around political and social issues was considered a major component of the social studies curriculum). A blogcast is a combination of a blog and podcast into one single website.

Participants of the study were 27 secondary four (or grade ten equivalent) students (15 females and 12 males) between 15 and 16 years of age. Data collection included students' pretest and posttest critical thinking ability, and students' reflections. The study which was carried out over a period of three weeks comprised six key stages.

In the first stage, a pretest was administered to gather baseline data about the students' critical thinking ability in evaluating the credibility of information. Second, the teacher enrolled students in Quick Blogcast (https://app.quickblogcast.com), a web domain with blogging and podcasting capability.

In the third stage, the blogcast with Socratic questioning treatment was introduced. Students were requested to study some background information on political events (e.g., the Sri Langka Liberation Tigers of Tamil Eelam) as well as other relevant sources of information (e.g., a political cartoon drawn by a Tamil artist about university admission in Sri Langka, and the views of a Sinhalese who disagreed that discrimination against the Tamils was the real reason for the Liberation Tigers to kill people). Students were required to answer the following question: "How reliable is the political cartoon as a piece of evidence to suggest that the Tamils formed a militant group due to the unfair university admission criteria?" Students individually answered the question orally (think-aloud) and recorded their immediate evaluation of the source using Audacity. Students then uploaded the unedited version of their podcasts onto their respective blogs.

In the fourth stage, students were introduced to a set of Socratic questions (see Table 5 for some examples). Using these questions, students individually listened to and reflected (self-critique) on their initial evaluation thoughts (podcasts). Next, students typed out their thoughts in text and posted them to their own respective blogs.

In the fifth stage, students invited their classmates to comment on their thoughts. The classmates used Socratic questions to challenge ideas and assumptions. The peer critics' comments in text were posted on the respective student's blog. In the sixth stage, students studied their peers' comments, and their own prior reflections before revising their evaluation of the source in text. Finally, students ended the blogcast activity by inviting their peers to visit, and post any final comments for their blogs. A posttest was conducted to measure the students' critical thinking ability in evaluating information sources. Both the pretest and posttest questions were examined by two experienced social studies teachers for construct validity. Two teachers marked and scored the pretest and posttest scripts. The percent agreement between the two markers was 81.4%.

Table 5. Examples of Socratic questions [14]

Socratic question	For self critique	For peer critique
Questions about the question	Did I assume the question correctly? Why?	I am not sure I understand how you are interpreting the main question.
Questions of clarification	What is my main point?	Let me see if I understand you; do you mean _____ or _____?
Questions that probe assumptions	What am I assuming?	All of your reasoning depends on the idea that ____. Why have you based your reasoning on ____ rather than ____?
Questions about viewpoints	Is my opinion of the source one-sided?	Why have you chosen this rather than that perspective?
Questions that probe reason and evidence	What examples or evidence can support my opinion?	Can you explain how you logically got from____ to_____?

The result of a paired sample *t*-test indicated a statistically significant difference between the post-test scores and pre-test scores at the 0.05 level of significance. The effect size was computed to be 0.67, which was a medium effect size. The results suggested that the blogcast with Socratic questioning approach improved critical thinking ability.

Effect of podcast on learning of science vocabulary. Putman and Kingsley [14] employed a quasi-experiment design to investigate if the use of podcasts could improve elementary school students' learning of science-specific vocabulary. Participants were 58 fifth grade students. About half the students received access to the podcasts while the rest received class instruction only. Data collection included student pretest and posttest of science terms, and a student questionnaire.

All 58 students had the same class instruction of science vocabulary. Specifically, instruction began each week with an introduction to the vocabulary and textbook definitions through teacher-led classroom discussions. Students read textbook passages both inside the classroom and as homework to reinforce the content introduced in class. Students also wrote vocabulary cards each week; these cards included definitions of the vocabulary in their own words and sentences that featured the word in context. Throughout the week, students viewed demonstrations of the ideas and concepts pertaining to the vocabulary in experiments or with visual aids, followed by question-and-answer sessions where students explained the processes associated with the experiments using the vocabulary. Finally, near the end of each week, application specific questions were asked by the teacher and students were required to answer using appropriate vocabulary terms.

About half of the 58 students had additional lessons via podcasts for seven consecutive weeks, with one new podcast per week. All podcasts were created by the teacher. Each podcast began with an engaging introduction (e.g., a relevant song), followed by a review of the vocabulary (students mentally recalled the definitions) that was featured in previous podcasts. This was then followed by a review of the new vocabulary. To reinforce the definitions, passages that featured the vocabulary in context were included in the podcasts. Certain activities were also incorporated. For example, students were required to mentally supply a missing word to complete a sentence or write a sentence using the selected word. Each podcast concluded with a review of the definitions for the current week's vocabulary (e.g., some common definitions were presented verbatim, while some words were reviewed with mental response exercises, such as asking students to define a term in their own words).

Results of an ANCOVA analysis suggested that students who had access to the podcasts scored significantly higher in the science vocabulary tests than students who received only classroom instruction. No effect size data was reported.

5   Discussion and Conclusion

So does using Web 2.0 technologies enhance K-12 student learning? At this moment, our conclusions are limited due to the scant available literature focusing on K-12 use of Web 2.0 technologies. Indeed, our review of research found that many articles tend to target higher education settings, are predominantly anecdotal in nature, and merely provide examples of Web 2.0 use in classrooms.

Based on the review of the four studies, the following conclusions are offered. First, it is impossible to determine actual *causal effects* of Web 2.0 technologies on gains in student achievement. Two of the studies [12] and [13] did not employ control groups. The students in the wiki group in study [3] had three licensed social studies teachers present in the computer lab to address content questions raised by the students, but students in the control group had only one teacher. This presented a potential limitation because it created a change in the student-teacher ratio. Finally, the gains reported in study [14] could be attributed to students spending more time on the vocabulary (through podcasts *and* classroom instruction) compared to students who had only classroom instruction on the words. These potential confounding factors suggest that the conclusions of the studies should be interpreted with caution.

Second, despite the limitations, the findings are still useful because these studies attempted to examine the link between use of Web 2.0 technologies and achievement gains, an important issue given the current focus on accountability. At the very least, the fact that the findings were statistically significant suggests that there is potential for using Web 2.0 technologies for student learning. It can be inferred from the current findings that a dialogic and/or co-constructive pedagogy supported by activities such as Socratic questioning, peer and self critique appear to increase student outcomes in blog- and wiki-enabled environments (see Table 4). With regard to podcasting, a transmissive pedagogy supported by review activities appears to enhance student learning of vocabulary, probably because it allows students to listen to content that they missed out in class or did not fully understand. These findings could offer educators and researchers some informed directions for use of technologies to achieve specific learning goals.

The following recommendations are made for future research. First, studies examining the use of Web 2.0 technologies hitherto were limited to blogs, wikis, and podcasts. Research addressing other technologies (e.g., audio discussion boards) is needed. Future research should focus on examining where and how to best use these technologies as an instructional and learning media in order to build the evidence-based practice knowledge base. Second, longitudinal studies are required to mitigate the novelty effects of the Web 2.0 technologies. Current studies were short in duration, ranging from three weeks to about one semester. Novelty effect is a potential confounding variable following the tendency of participants to pay increased attention to technology that is new to them [16]. Conducting a longitudinal study can also provide researchers the opportunity to investigate any detrimental effects of using Web 2.0 technologies over a long period of time.

References

1. Hew, K.F., Brush, T.: Integrating technology into K-12 teaching and learning: Current knowledge gaps and recommendations for future research. Educ. Tech. Research and Dev. 55, 223–252 (2007)
2. Bower, M., Hedberg, J.G., Kuswara, A.: A framework for Web 2.0 learning design. Educ. Media International 47, 177–198 (2010)
3. Heafner, T.L., Friedman, A.M.: Wikis and constructivism in secondary social studies: Fostering a deeper understanding. Computers in the Schools 25, 288–302 (2008)
4. Norton, P., Hathaway, D.: On its way to K-12 classrooms, Web 2.0 goes to graduate school. Computers in the Schools 25, 163–180 (2008)
5. Alexander, B.: Web 2.0 – A new wave of innovation for teaching and learning? http://www.educause.edu/EDUCAUSE+Review/EDUCAUSEReviewMagazineVolume41/Web20ANewWaveofInnovationforTe/158042
6. Blessinger, K., Olle, M.: Content analysis of the leading general academic databases. Library Collections, Acquisitions, & Technical Services 28, 335–346 (2004)
7. Luppicini, R.: Review of computer mediated communication research for education. Instructional Science 35, 141–185 (2007)
8. Rinke, C.R.: Understanding teachers' careers: Linking professional life to professional path. Educ. Research Rev. 3, 1–13 (2008)
9. Wang, J., Odell, S.J., Schwille, S.A.: Effects of teacher induction on beginning teachers' teaching: A critical review of the literature. J. of Teacher Educ. 59, 132–152 (2008)
10. Fraenkel, J.R., Wallen, N.E.: How to design and evaluate research in education. McGraw-Hill, New York (2006)
11. Anderson, L., Krathwohl, D.: A taxonomy for learning, teaching and assessing: a revision of Bloom's taxonomy of educational objectives. Longman, New York (2001)
12. Wong, R.M.F., Hew, K.F.: The impact of blogging and scaffolding on primary school pupils' narrative writing. Int. J. of Web-based Learning and Teaching Tech. 5, 1–17 (2010)
13. Salam, S., Hew, K.F.: Enhancing social studies students' critical thinking through blogcast and Socratic questioning: a Singapore case study. Int. J. of Instructional Media 37, 391–401 (2010)
14. Putman, S.M., Kingsley, T.: The atoms family: using podcasts to enhance the development of science vocabulary. The Reading Teacher 63, 100–108 (2009)
15. Hallenbeck, M.J.: Taking charge: adolescents with learning disabilities assume responsibility for their own writing. Learning Disability Quarterly 25, 227–246 (2002)
16. Clark, R.E.: Reconsidering research on learning from media. Rev. of Educ. Research 53, 445–459 (1983)

Going Beyond Face-to-Face Classrooms: Examining Student Motivation to Participate in Online Discussions through a Self-Determination Theory Perspective

Wee Sing Jeffrey Sim, Wing Sum Cheung, and Khe Foon Hew

National Institute of Education, 1 Nanyang Walk
637616 Singapore
frey66@yahoo.com, {wingsum.cheung,khefoon.hew}@nie.edu.sg

Abstract. Current trends in education favor the use of collaborative learning environments. Social technologies such as an asynchronous online discussion board (AOD) enable students to communicate without time or place constraints. Unlike many past studies that merely focused in student posting, this study examines what motivates graduate students to log in, read and post in an online discussion board. The Self-Determination Theory (SDT) was used as a theoretical framework to investigate the various motivators. Results suggest that students' motivation to log in, read and make a posting shifts from one that is more externally regulated to one that is more integrated regulated. In addition, the availability of time and accessibility to the internet influenced students' motivation to log in to the AOD. Factors such as AOD design influence their motivation to read the discussion postings. Insofar as making a posting is concerned, results suggest that students' decision to make a posting in an AOD was largely found to be identified or integration regulated.

Keywords: motivation, online discussion, self-determination theory.

1 Introduction

Contemporary educational theory favors the use of collaborative learning environments that emphasize student discussion. Social technology tools now afford students to ability to communicate beyond the traditional face-to-face classroom environments. Currently, there are many types of social technology tools including facebook, blog, wiki, and asynchronous online discussion (AOD) board. Of these tools, the AOD board may be considered the most established and commonly used tool in online learning context.

An AOD board may be defined as a text-based human-to-human communication via computer networks. There is a growing body of literature that suggest discussion boards can be an effective instructional strategy to promote student critical thinking, problem solving skills, and knowledge construction [1], [2]. This is mainly due to the premise that AODs offer students time to think before contributing to the discussions, unlike that of synchronous discussions.

R. Kwan et al. (Eds.): ICT 2011, CCIS 177, pp. 329–341, 2011.
© Springer-Verlag Berlin Heidelberg 2011

Typically, in the context of an AOD, a student may participate in the discussion in a number of ways as shown in Figure 1. To culminate in making a posting, a student would have gone through a sequential 3-stage process of (1) logging into the discussion board, (2) reading the postings with regard to the topic or subject discussed, before (3) making a posting. Notably, students' participation may stop at any of the stage. For example, a student may log in but not read, or a student may log in and read but not post or a student may log in, read and make a posting. We posit that the motivation behind a student's decision to proceed to the next step may be influenced by a variety of factors. An understanding of what these factors are will allow an instructor to better incorporate motivational strategies when he or she designs the discussion board environment.

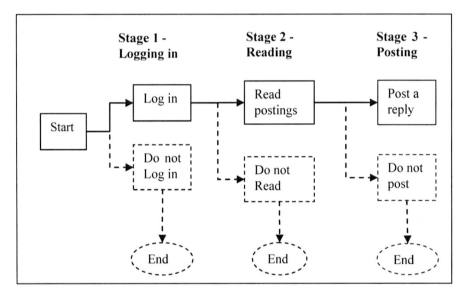

Fig. 1. The 3-stage process in discussion board participation

1.1 Research Questions

The research questions asked are as follows: (a) What motivates a student at the different stages of the phases (e.g., to log in into the discussion board, to read a post, and to make a post)? and (b) As the student progress from stage 1 to stage 3, are there changes in the student's motivation?

This case study will focus on these questions by firstly, providing an overview of the Self-Determination Theory (SDT) [3], [4] as a frame to discuss learner's motivation. It will then discuss the findings from the survey conducted on a class of graduate students who enrolled in the Master of Arts – Instructional Designs and Technology (MA-IDT) program SE802 module titled `Design of Asynchronous Online Discussion'. This case study differed from many other previous studies in the following two aspects. First, unlike many studies that focused merely on student posting, the current study examined students' motivation to log in and read, and not just post messages. Second, it examined the specific motivation related to each of the three phases.

2 Self-Determination Theory (SDT)

Deci and Ryan [3] proposed the Self-Determination Theory (SDT) as the theoretical framework to explain motivation. Under this theory, it proposes that a person's motivation may be classified within the range of intrinsic to extrinsic and amotivation (see Figure 2).

Intrinsic motivation is defined as the purpose of doing an activity for its inherent satisfactions rather than for some separable consequence [4]. Put simply, intrinsic motivation refers to motivation that is derived from factors that are inherent in the learner itself (e.g. the need to be competent) rather than from externally applied rewards, such as money, grades or praises. A person who is intrinsically motivated is moved to act purely out of interest or the enjoyment of that activity.

Ryan and Deci [4] also noted that there are a variety of conditions that would elicit or sustain as well as subdue and diminish these intrinsic motivational tendencies and put forth a sub theory called the Cognitive Evaluation Theory (CET). This sub theory argues that intrinsic motivation can be enhanced by social-contextual factors that facilitate a sense of competence as well as conditions that promote a sense of autonomy. That is to say, an intrinsically motivated person's motivation could be enhanced if there are provision of positive feedback, communications and/ or rewards (sense of competency) and that their resultant behavior must be perceived to be self-generated or self-determined.

On the other hand, a person who is moved to act with a specific intention of attaining some separable outcomes may be referred to as extrinsically motivated [3], [4]. These outcomes may be in the gaining of positive returns such as rewards, incentives or avoidance of negative returns such as punishments or consequences.

Within SDT, a second sub theory, usually referred to as the Organismic Integration Theory (OIT), was introduced to describe the different types of extrinsic motivation (see Figure 2) [4]. OIT further discusses extrinsic motivation in four categories – namely, *external regulation, introjection, identification* and *integration*. The *external regulation* category is the least autonomous form of extrinsic motivation. Under this category, a person engages in an activity solely for the purposes of rewards (e.g., earning marks in the context of the student/ learner) and/ or to avoid punishment. A second type of motivation is *introjected regulation* or *introjection*. Under this sub-category of extrinsic motivation, the student's behavior is governed by his perception of pressure in order to avoid guilt or anxiety or to attain ego-enhancement or pride; or to maintain self-esteem and the feeling of worth. This contrasts with the third category of extrinsic motivation, *identified regulation* or *identification*, where the student's behavior is governed by his perception that his actions will contribute to his achievements or his own goals. For example, a girl who memorizes Chinese characters because she considers it as relevant to reading, writing, and speaking, which she values as a life goal, has identified with the value of this learning task. The last sub-category of extrinsic motivation, *integrated regulation* or *integration*, is the most autonomous form of extrinsic motivation and occurs when identified regulations have been fully assimilated to the self. Such motivation occurs when there is a very high degree of internalization of the perception of values of the action in relation to the tasks, that is to say, the student feels that his behavior is in sync with his personal values and senses of self.

Using the concept of locus of control or locus of causality, which refers to the individual's perception of what controls life events, one can see a shift in the locus of causality shift from one that is purely external (e.g. provision of rewards of punishment) in the externally regulated extrinsic motivation to one that is largely internal to the learner (e.g. synthesis of self-learning goals). The continuum of the different type of motivation from amotivation (i.e., unwillingness to act) to passive compliance (the various forms of extrinsic motivation), to intrinsic motivation where there is an active personal commitment provides a frame to explain why a person acts in a certain manner.

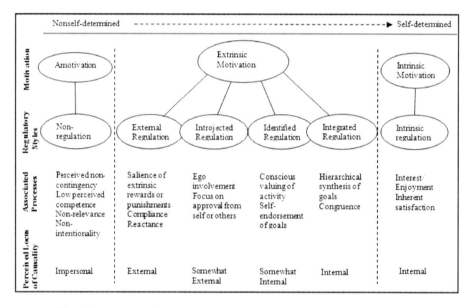

Fig. 2. A taxonomy of human motivation. Extracted from Ryan and Deci [4]

3   Methodology

The case study was conducted using the discourse in an online discussion board of the students participating in the Masters of Arts – Instructional Designs and Technology (MA-IDT) program MA-IDT SE802 module titled 'Design of Asynchronous Online Discussion'. The module focused on how the AOD can be used as an effective instructional strategy. The topics covered include the integration of the asynchronous collaborative online discussion environment with the F2F approach, the role of the teachers in designing and evaluating the environment, and the use of scaffolds in the online discussion environment to facilitate critical thinking skills.

The SE802 module was conducted over a 13-week period from Jan – Apr 07. It was conducted by two lecturers and attended by a total of 14 working adult students. Classes were conducted once a week (every Thursday evening) except in Week 5 (first week of Feb 07) where lessons were conducted in an online environment as part of the NIE's e-learning week initiative. As part of the fulfillment of the module, students were required to design, conduct and evaluate an AOD and to submit a project report after the completion of the AOD.

The instructors of the module mandated that students should post their project outlines in the NIE Blackboard (an online learning management system) before the execution of their AOD plan in early-Feb 07. This was carried out with the intent to allow them an experiential learning in facilitation and managing an AOD as well as to allow students to seek their classmate's feedback to improve their AOD plan before they execute their respective AOD plan. To facilitate the use of the AOD, students were put through a warm up activity during an F2F lesson in the Week 3 (last week of Jan 07). Students were also informed that their participation in the AOD would be assessed as part of their overall project.

The conduct of the AOD started in Week 4 (1 Feb 07). Week 5 coincided with NIE's e-learning week where no F2F lessons were conducted. F2F lessons continued in Week 6 (15 Feb 07) of the module. While no dateline was imposed for the AOD *per se*, students were asked to reflect on their experience when the class reconvened after the e-learning week. A new discussion forum was also created to allow students to post their reflections.

3.1 Participants

A total of 14 students participated in the MA-IDT programme. All students had at least 5 years of working experience at the time of the course and possessed at least a Bachelor degree. Eleven (78.6%) of the students are teachers with at least 4 years of teaching experience while the remaining 3 (21.4%) students are/ had been previously involved in teaching-related roles in the respective industry they came from. The average age is 37 years old and the age ranges from 29 to 49 years. Of the 14 students, 11 (78.6%) are males and 3 (21.4%) are females. All students had previous experiences in using AOD.

3.2 Procedure

The first author was a student of the MA-IDT program and participated in this case study as a participant-observer. This enables him to access to the data on the class' AOD forums which otherwise would not have been possible. However, consents from other students were first sought and obtained. The study of students' motivation when they go through the different stages of AOD participation and the factors behind it was conducted after the e-learning week from 21 Feb 07 onwards. The procedure involves the physical collation of data from the AOD, administering of a survey and the conduct of an interview on selected students who had the highest number of postings in the class AOD. The survey and interview questions were designed to elicit from individual students an understanding of what motivates them to log in, read and make postings in their own and their classmate's AOD and the factors that influence their motivation.

3.3 Data Collection

Data on Participant's Postings. The documentation of each participant's (both students and instructors) posting data was conducted after the 3-week AOD period. The data documentation process involved the physical counting of postings for the class per day, posting by every individual participants by the date and time of the post as well as the frequency of each participant's posting in the AOD over the 3-week period from 1 Feb 07 (start of the AOD) to 21 Feb 07 (one week after the F2F lesson).

Design of Survey. The survey questions were developed after a preliminary analysis of the data collated on student's postings. This preliminary analysis was carried out to provide an understanding on whether each student's posting in the AOD follows a specific pattern in terms of time of the day, day of the week as well as the frequency in which he makes a posting in his or his peer's AOD). With this understanding, an interview was conducted with three randomly selected students to provide further clarity on the motivation and the factors that affected their posting patterns during the 3-week period. The model in Figure 1 provides the frame to which questions were developed so as to understand the motivation and the factors affecting students at each stage of the AOD participation.

Questions on motivation were developed using SDT [3], [4] as the theoretical framework (See Appendix). The survey adopted a five-point Likert-type scale (1 for 'strongly disagree', 2 'disagree', 3 'neutral', 4 'agree' and 5 'strongly agree') for each of the questions developed. In addition, all questions posed were open-ended and students were encouraged to provide additional inputs wherever appropriate.

Conduct of survey and interview. The survey was conducted during the F2F lesson on 15 Mar 07. Twelve students completed the survey. The survey results and posting patterns of seven students who had the highest postings in the AOD were analyzed. Further questions were drafted whenever there were any observed areas of inconsistencies between the survey results and the posting data patterns and/or when there was a need to clarify the student's response of the survey. These questions were emailed to the individual students and F2F interviews were arranged for students whose responses need further clarifications. Six students responded and were interviewed. After the interview, member checking was done. Consolidated transcripts of the interviews were verified by interviewees.

4   Results

4.1   What Motivates Students to Log In to the AOD?

The data reflected in Table 1 shows a very distinct indication that the locus of causality for the motivation to log in to the AOD was largely external. Apart from one student (8.3%) who posted neutral, all students (91.7%) replied positively that their motivation to log in was either because it was a course requirement (extrinsic motivation - external regulation) or because he wanted to find out who had posted into his AOD (extrinsic motivation – introjection). The response was similar (83.3%)

for students who agree/ strongly agree that they logging as there are things they could learn and apply (extrinsic motivation – identification) or that they wanted to contribute to their peer's learning. Compared with the different sub-categories of motivation, there was also an observed highest percentage of students who are either neutral (25.0%) or disagree (25.0%) that they logging to AOD because they find enjoyment/ satisfaction doing it.

Table 1. Students' motivation to log in to the AOD

Motivation	Statement	SD	D	N	A	SA
External Regulation	It was a course requirement	0.0%	0.0%	8.3%	66.7%	25.0%
Introjection	I want to find out who has posted in my AOD	0.0%	0.0%	8.3%	58.3%	33.3%
Identification	There are things I can learn and apply	0.0%	8.3%	8.3%	50.0%	33.3%
Integration	I want to contribute to my peer's learning	0.0%	8.3%	8.3%	58.3%	25.0%
Intrinsic	I enjoy doing so	0.0%	25.0%	25.0%	33.3%	16.7%

4.2   What Were the Students' Perceptions of Their Behaviour When They Logged In to the AOD?

At least half of the students responded that they usually read every of their peer's AOD or read selectively when they logged into the discussion board.   25.0% (3 students) indicated that they will only read their own postings (Table 2).

Table 2. Students' perception of their behavior when they logged in

Behavior when logged in	SD	D	N	A	SA
I go through every classmate's postings	0.0%	41.7%	8.3%	25.0%	25.0%
I only read my peer's AOD selectively	8.3%	25.0%	0.0%	66.7%	0.0%
I will only read the postings in my AOD	25.0%	41.7%	8.3%	16.7%	8.3%

4.3   What Motivates Students to Read the Postings in the AOD?

The data from Table 3 suggests that there is a general trend towards an introjection or identification sub-categories of extrinsic motivation when it comes to reading discussion posts. 66.7% of the students responded that they would read an AOD because they wanted to learn as much as their classmates (extrinsic motivation – introjection). 75.0% of the students indicated that they would do so because the topic is / would be useful to them (extrinsic motivation – identification). This compares with only 58.3% of students who responded that they do so because they wanted to contribute to their peer's learning (extrinsic motivation – integration) and 50% who indicated that they do so out of pure enjoyment (intrinsic motivation).

Table 3. Students' motivation to read the discussion postings

Motivation	Statement	SD	D	N	A	SA
External Regulation	I want to minimize the highlighted (unread) posts when I next log in	25.0%	25.0%	8.3%	41.7%	0.0%
Introjection	I want to learn as much as my classmates	0.0%	16.7%	16.7%	50.0%	16.7%
Identification	I want to learn as much as I can about the subject/ topic as it is useful to me	0.0%	16.7%	8.3%	66.7%	8.3%
Integration	I want to contribute to my peer's learning	0.0%	8.3%	33.3%	50.0%	8.3%
Intrinsic	I enjoy doing so	0.0%	16.7%	33.3%	33.3%	16.7%

4.4   What Motivates Students to Post in an AOD?

From Table 4, the two highest motivations that students reported insofar as making a posting is concerned were that they wanted to help their peers improve on the project (extrinsic motivation – integration) (91.6%) and/ or that they want to learn as much as they could from the AOD so that they could apply in their project (extrinsic motivation – identified) (75.0%). This contrast with only 58.3% students who indicated that they made a posting in the AOD because they knew they were being graded (extrinsic motivation – external regulation). About 41.7% would consider ego (I want to show I know the topic) (extrinsic motivation – introjection) that motivated them to make a posting. This egoism-related motive was probably due to the existence of peer-pressure in the course; hence one might post in order to gain recognition as a knowledgeable individual.

Table 4. Students' motivation to post in online discussion

Motivation	Statement	SD	D	N	A	SA
External Regulation	I am being graded	8.3%	0.0%	33.3%	50.0%	8.3%
Introjection	I want to show I know the topic	8.3%	33.3%	16.7%	25.0%	16.7%
Identification	I want to learn as much as I can from the AOD so as to apply to my project	0.0%	16.7%	8.3%	58.3%	16.7%
Integration	I want to help my peers improve on his/ her project	0.0%	8.3%	0.0%	83.3%	8.3%
Intrinsic	I enjoy doing so	0.0%	8.3%	25.0%	50.0%	16.7%

5   Discussion and Conclusion

5.1   Motivation as a Social Construct

Despite the general positive attitude towards AOD, student's postings in the AOD were not even. It was observed that all students showed a highest number of posts in their own AOD and that the number of postings between students varies significantly. For example, Students F, H, L and M contributed a total of 203 postings (57.8%) from the class's total of 351 postings in the 3-week period of AOD. From interviews, it was also found out that many students (e.g. Student A, F, H, J) chose to read and not make any postings in the AOD when they participate. Student A, in the interview mentioned: "Perhaps I was careful that I should not come across as a strong opinionated person because most students knew of my professional background. So I was careful not to engage in those forums where I felt the tone of facilitator was rather aggressive. Secondly, I also did not want to engage in my classmate's AOD especially if he is in the same profession as me. The reason being that I did not want the other participants to think that people of my profession think alike should there be a convergence of views amongst us. Thirdly, I chose to engage in those AOD forums where I felt that I could contribute different perspectives rather than agreeing with others and echoing their views. Perhaps due to my logging in at odd hours, similar views were already echoed throughout the day, and there were only few perspectives that I thought different.

Similarly, some participants felt that there was no need to contribute further to ideas in AOD where there was on-going conversation between some of their fellow-participants. Students have also feedback in the interviews that often, they chose to read and not post any feedback and that they derive learning outcomes just by reading the many postings and feedback from their peers discourse in the AOD (e.g. Student F).

These feedbacks reflect the dynamics between the learner's motivation and the social context of learning. In the AOD environment, the findings suggest that learning often takes place without active postings in the AOD. This could be through the through reading of other student's postings and self-reflection [5]. This was also reported by Kruger [6] and one can easily infer that student's learning in the AOD can only take place if there are sufficient postings made in the AOD.

5.2   Motivation Shifts During the 3-Stage AOD Participation

The data in Table 5 and Figure 3 suggests a shift in the students' motivation during the 3-step process of logging in, reading and posting.

Table 5. Comparison of motivation during log in, reading and posting

Motivation	Log in	Read	Post
External Regulation	4.17	2.67	3.50
Introjection	4.25	3.67	3.08
Identification	4.08	3.67	3.75
Integration	4.00	3.58	3.92
Intrinsic	3.42	3.50	3.75

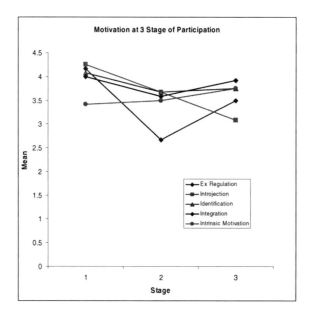

Fig. 3. Change in mean values of different motivation types at 3-stage of online participation

During the logging in process, there was a reported tendency for students' motivation to lean towards an external locus of causality whereby motivation was more externally regulated or introjectively regulated (e.g., I log in because it is a course requirement). This was similarly observed by Benfield [7] where he found that linking student contributions in the online discussions to assessment has been a useful mechanism to improve student participation and that the most active and effective online discussions are highly purposeful and task-oriented. This was best perhaps exemplified in the F2F interview with Student L where he mentioned: "We are assessed partly by our participation in the online discussion. So, I need to logon to participate in order to gain assessment points."

Other factors cited by interviewees that had a strong influence on their decision to log in included the availability of time and accessibility to the Internet. Given that the participants in this study were adult students holding full-time jobs, the time factor appeared to explain the observed posting patterns, where spikes in postings occurred mainly during the periods of 6 – 9 am (before work hours), 12 – 3 pm (typical lunch hours) and 9pm – 12mn (after work or class/family resting hours). Such a pattern is expected and could possibly be seen in other part-time programs involving working adults with similar work hours.

However, once logged-in, students showed lesser degree of being influenced by externally regulated motivation to read an online discussion posts. Instead, student's survey feedback found that the main motivation behind reading an AOD centered more towards the need to fulfill their ego (introjection regulation), learning for a self-centered reason (identification/ identified regulation) or to help their peers (integration/ integrated regulation). Interview data further suggested that students would generally want to read an AOD if they found the title interesting and the discussion threads well organized. Conversely, students reported that they were less likely to read if they were overwhelmed by too many postings.

Insofar as making a post is concerned, interview feedback suggests that most student's motivation were either identified regulated (I want to learn ... so that I can apply in my project) or integrated regulated (I want to help my peers improve on his/her project). This was reiterated in the F2F interviews where Student L's mentioned that "the main reason (he posted) is because there were certain issues in Student's G's threads that I was curious to find out. Those issues were probably related to my own assignment".

The observation that there is a shift in motivation during a learning process and that this shift in the motivation was related to some goals was also suggested in Dörnyei & Ottó [8] where they proposed that "motivation is not a static state but rather a dynamically evolving and changing entity, associated with an ongoing process in time; thus, had a featured temporal axis."

There are several limitations in the conduct of this study. First, the small population size limits the transferability of the study's findings. Second, due to system limitations, the author was not able to obtain data on the student's time spent in the AOD as well as the patterns in which student navigate from one AOD to another. Knowledge of this data would provide understanding in the behavior of the student when he participates in the AOD.

In conclusion, the results of this case study suggest that student's motivation to log in, read and make postings changed at each of these different stages of participation. It also showed that there were a variety of factors that influenced the students' motivation through the 3-stage process of AOD participation. Most significantly, the findings suggest that AOD-designs were the most cited reasons for influencing the student's motivation to read an AOD. Therefore, strategies to arouse a student's attention to the online discussion might be useful. This include strategies relating to arousing the student's perception (how titles of threads should be worded, postings should not exceed a specific number of words, one idea per post, etc) and variability (such as starting a new thread if there is a new concept/ context to be discussed, creating of different activities).

References

1. De Wever, B., Schellens, T., Valcke, M., Van Keer, H.: Content analysis schemes to analyze transcripts of online asynchronous discussion groups: A review. Computers & Education 46, 6–28 (2006)
2. Hew, K.F., Knapczyk, D.: Analysis of Ill-Structured Problem Solving, Mentoring Functions, and Perceptions of Practicum Teachers and Mentors Toward Online Mentoring In A Field-Based Practicum. Instructional Science 35, 1–40 (2007)
3. Deci, E.L., Ryan, R.M.: Intrinsic motivation and self-determination in human behaviors. Plenum, New York (1985)
4. Ryan, R.M., Deci, E.L.: Intrinsic and extrinsic motivations: Classic definitions and new directions. Contemporary Educ. Psychology 25, 54–67 (2000)

5. Garrison, D.R.: Cognitive presence for effective asynchronous online learning: The role of reflective inquiry, self-direction and metacognition (2003),
   `http://oit.hostos.cuny.edu/socialnetwork/effectiveonlinelearn`
   `ing/files/2009/09/Learning-Effectiveness-paper-Garrison.pdf`
6. Kruger, S.: Students' experiences of e-learning: Issues of motivation and identity (2006),
   `http://www.edgehill.ac.uk/Sites/SOLSTICE/`
   `ResearchandDissemination/documents/`
   `Studentsexperiencesofe-learningFebruary2006.pdf`
7. Benfield, G.: Designing and managing effective online discussions. Oxford Center for Staff and Learning Development, Oxford Brookes University (2002)
8. Dörnyei, Z., Ottó, I.: Motivation in action: A process model of L2 motivation. Working Papers in Applied Linguistics, Thames Valley University, London (1998)

Appendix: Questions on Motivation

Purpose	Question	Motivation subcategory	Answer
To understand the motivation behind logging into AOD	I **LOG IN** because…	Extrinsic – External Regulation	It was a course requirement
		Extrinsic – Introjection	I want to find out who has posted in my AOD
		Extrinsic – Identification	There are things I can learn and apply
		Extrinsic – Integration	I want to contribute to my peer's learning
		Intrinsic	I enjoy/ find satisfaction doing so
To understand general perceived behavior when students **LOG IN** to the AOD	When I **LOG IN** to the discussion board…	NA	I usually go through every classmate's postings
		NA	I only read my peer's postings selectively
		NA	I will only read the postings in my AOD
To understand what motivates students to **READ**	I **READ** the postings the AOD because…	Extrinsic – External Regulation	I just want to minimize the highlighted (unread) posts when I next logging
		Extrinsic – Introjection	I want to learn as much as my classmates
		Extrinsic – Identification	I want to learn as much as I can about the subject/ topic as it is useful to me
		Extrinsic – Integration	I want to contribute to my peer's learning
		Intrinsic	I enjoy doing so
To understand what motivates students to **POST**	I will **POST** because…	Extrinsic – External Regulation	I am being graded
		Extrinsic – Introjection	I want to show I know the topic
		Extrinsic – Identification	I want to learn as much as I can from the AOD so as to apply to my project
		Extrinsic – Integration	I want to help my peers improve on his/ her project
		Intrinsic	I enjoy doing it

Uncoupling Mobility and Learning: When One Does Not Guarantee the Other

Shelley Kinash, Jeffrey Brand, Trishita Mathew, and Ron Kordyban

Bond University, Gold Coast, Queensland, Australia
{skinash,jbrand,trmathew,rkordyba}@bond.edu.au

Abstract. Mobile learning was an embedded component of the pedagogical design of an undergraduate course, *Digital media and society*. In the final semester of 2010 and the first semester of 2011, 135 students participated in an empirical study inquiring into their perceptual experience of mobile learning. To control for access to technology, an optional iPad student loan scheme was used. The iPads were loaded with an electronic textbook and a mobile application of the learning moderation system. Eighty students participated in ten-person focus groups. Feedback on mobility and the electronic text was positive and optimistic. However, the majority of students were not convinced that the trial made a difference to their learning. This result was interpreted to indicate that the presence or absence of mobile devices does not guarantee or preclude student learning.

1 Introduction

There are two components of the coupled term, mobile learning. Mobility refers to the untethered nature of the student experience. Devices such as smart phones, tablets, netbooks, and iPads make learning materials light-weight and portable. Mobility also means that students can access the internet anywhere, anytime, provided that they also have access to a wireless or 3G network. "Mobile devices open up new opportunities for independent investigations, practical fieldwork, professional updating and on-the-spot access to knowledge" [1]. Mobile access to the internet can provide the opportunity to engage in the tasks that these authors listed. These pedagogical processes are part of the repertoire of the constructivist educator, engaging the students in hands-on inquiry [2-6]. These tasks are part of the pedagogy of the higher educator and intended to promote learning.

Learning is the second element of the compound term. Educational theorists argue against offering a blanket definition of the term, writing that "learning is always the learning of something" [7]. In other words, to say that a student has learned communication, one of the measured components is the demonstration of oral and written proficiency. In accordance with this theoretical perspective, the generalised assumption of mobile learning is problematic from the outset. "The feature of 'mobility' can seem a curious way to delineate a field of research on learning" [8]. The definition of mobile learning cannot be simplified into compounding the two terms [9]. The problem is that in English grammar, the side-by-side arrangement of the two

R. Kwan et al. (Eds.): ICT 2011, CCIS 177, pp. 342–350, 2011.
© Springer-Verlag Berlin Heidelberg 2011

words makes mobile the adjective of the noun learning. So, just as *quiet riot* means silent chaos, *mobile learning* connotes the meaning of portable educational process. The problem is that mobile learning may be just as much an oxymoron as quiet riot.

Belief in the legitimacy of the combined term, mobile learning, is widely apparent in the literature. Many educators claim student use of mobile technologies improves their learning [10]. Many of the reviewed studies in mobile learning "assume that handheld computers will be beneficial in a classroom environment" without rigorously considering and testing this assumption [11]. An example of the linking of mobile devices and learning is demonstrated in a quote such as, "with the proliferation of mobile devices, there is also great potential to harness mobile technologies to enhance learning" [12]. Some researchers claim mobile learning is distinctive from previous approaches to teaching and learning with technology because mobile devices liberate the learner to realise enactment of anywhere, anytime learning [4]. The widespread belief in the efficacy of mobile learning necessitates a research call to investigate the propositions, perceptions and outcomes.

While the literature revealed numerous claims that there was a pedagogical link between *mobile* and *learning*, there did not seem to be robust empirical evidence that this assumption was tested. Research into mobile learning is described as "maturing" as no "explicit frame exists as yet to guide the choice of research methods and the tools for data analysis" [13]. This depiction of the state of mobile learning research necessitates an exploratory study.

Four key questions emerged during analysis of the mobile learning literature. The first question is whether students perceive that the use of mobile devices in their university education makes a difference to their learning. The second question is whether students are already using mobile devices in their learning experience and if so, which students. The third question is whether the students' assignment scores are higher when they are using mobile devices (as an indicator of heightened learning). The fourth question is whether there is a significant difference in the final grades of students who do and do not use mobile devices.

All four questions cannot be comprehensively addressed in a single paper. Therefore, this paper has been designed to address the first question regarding student perception of learning related to the use of mobile devices. The final three questions regarding extent of student technology use and the effect of mobile learning on achievement and grades will be addressed in subsequent papers.

2   Method

The undertaken project was framed as design-based research (DBR) [14-15]. Design-based research is a method geared towards bridging educational theory and practice, with the aim of understanding how students learn within their natural settings (school/university). One of the main advantages of this method is that research and learning have a symbiotic relationship, as research can be enhanced through the study of scholarship, which in turn can enrich and refine the learning process [14]. In order to answer the defined research questions regarding the students' actual experiences and their perceptions of those experiences, it was important that the research conditions did not interfere with the integrity of their phenomenology as undergraduate university students. The primary reason DBR was selected as research methodology was that there is no manipulation of experimental conditions. The students, as volunteer research participants, spent no more time than normally spent engaged in class activities, and the conditions of the study were naturalistic, or what one would ordinarily expect in a university classroom facilitated by this particular educator. The only difference was that a loan scheme ensured that all students had use of iPads loaded with the electronic textbook and a mobile application of the learning moderation system (LMS). Also in keeping with the DBR method, student use of mobile devices must be consistent with regular timeframes and locations. Use of mobile devices spans formal and informal settings [16]. In other words, it is not normative for students to only use mobile devices while at university and only for the applications defined by the educator. In order to be true to the methodology of this study, students had free reign with the mobile devices during the loan period. They were free to take them home and to load whatever applications they wished during the loan period.

A total of 135 students enrolled in an undergraduate subject titled *Digital media and society* in the final semester of 2010 and the first semester of 2011. The pedagogical design of this subject was such that the educator used a combination of face-to-face teaching methods such as lecture and discussion and online methods such as immediate internet search and online formative assessment. The students were invited to use their own mobile devices such as laptops, smart phones and tablets to participate in the digital components. To ensure that every student had access to mobile technologies, each student was also assigned to a loan schedule whereby an iPad was made available for university and home use for a two-week period. The iPad was loaded with an electronic copy of the normally assigned textbook and an application to afford mobile access to the LMS.

As the key data collection instrument of the DBR process, the students were invited to participate in focus groups conducted during regularly scheduled tutorial times. The focus groups were designed to enable interpretive inquiry using a phenomenological hermeneutic framework [17-18]. Phenomenology means the actual lived experience of the participants. Hermeneutics is named for the Greek Hermes who was the mythical messenger for the gods, translating meaning so that mortals could understand. Combined with phenomenological experience, hermeneutics enables participants to describe experiences, and researchers to interpret meanings of those experiences. Specifically, students were not asked survey-type questions with multiple choice or closed-ended responses. Instead they were asked to comment on and discuss their experiences. This allowed the respondents to reflect on their actual experiences and co-created meanings through shared discussion, as opposed to forced choices or being influenced by the theoretical propositions of the researchers. Researchers writing about DBR emphasized that interaction among students, such as that through the focus group process was instrumental to the formation of subjective interpretation. The synergy and collaborative nature of group discussion is a key catalyst in the creation of an ongoing, cumulative discourse [19]. With respect to learning, it is more revealing to ask students to describe their experiences and perceptions of the use of mobile devices and observe whether learning emerged as a volunteered topic, rather than directly ask students whether they learned, which would force their response.

There were eight focus groups in total. Each had ten participants. The ten participants were those who had just returned iPads from the loan scheme. Each focus group was one-hour long. Set general themes were pursued in each focus group. The focus groups were designed to inquire into the students' experience of using the iPads and other mobile devices, and their opinions about mobile learning. Beyond these general themes, the group members carried the conversation in unique directions. All discussions were recorded on a voice recorder and transcribed for analysis.

The data was coded and analysed using NVIVO 8, a qualitative data analysis software. Two levels of analyses were conducted. At the first level, five common themes in the transcripts were identified by the researchers: utility of the iPad, advantages of the iPad, disadvantages of the iPad, experience of using the electronic textbook, and opinions on mobile learning. At the second level of analysis, these five themes were recorded as 'nodes' in NVIVO 8 and students' opinions were coded under each respective node.

3   Results

3.1   Class Demographics

There were 135 students, predominantly female (64%) undergraduates enrolled in a required subject for a major in communication and media in one of two semesters between September 2010 and May 2011. The mean age was 22 years with a range of 19 and standard deviation of 3.9 years. Almost all (96%) brought a mobile phone to class, almost half (48%) brought to class a laptop (only 4% of these were netbooks) and few (4%) brought a tablet computer to class. Mobile phones used by students were mostly internet enabled (73%). Of those phones with either Wi-Fi or 3G or EDGE Internet access, students reported that 80% were primarily used for social networking, 75% for web browsing and 68% for email.

All but one student came to class stating that they were already subscribed with a Facebook account.   Half had a Twitter account and one fifth had Linkedin accounts. Use of mobile phones and laptops were evenly split during class time with half stating they regularly use their phones and half use their laptops. Of the students who state they bring their laptops to class, half stated that primarily, they used the university's LMS, half that they use their laptops to take notes, half state that they go on Facebook, a third stated that they access Wikipedia and a third texted at some stage during class. Screens were used heavily for composing and reading, although e-books were preferred by few (11%).

Despite these tech-heavy frequencies among this sample of students, only 14% identified themselves as "power users" of information and communication technologies and 36% described themselves as tech-savvy. The majority (46%) said they were merely "tech-users." Tellingly, none self-identified with the label "tech-resister."

The final grade distribution for these students was slightly skewed with 40% earning a "Pass", 28% a "Credit", 20% a "Distinction", 7% a "Fail" and 5% a "High Distinction."

3.2   Applications Loaded on Loaned iPads

As a sample of the research participants, 38 students were asked to identify which applications they downloaded on the loaned iPads. The majority (28 students) failed to indicate any downloaded applications. Ten students indicated that they downloaded applications. There were a total of 25 downloaded applications, four of which were downloaded by more than one student. The most popular applications at three downloads each were: Angry Birds and Words with Friends. Two students indicated that they downloaded Facebook. Notably, two students indicated they downloaded the Blackboard Mobile Learning Application, even though this was pre-loaded on all of the loaned iPads. Single downloads were indicated for: Seek, Air Asia, Fruit Ninja, Piano, Workout, TED, The Age, Google Earth, Dropbox, Skype, WordPress, Bejewelled, Paradise Island, Friendly Facebook, eBuddy, Wall Street Journal, Twitter, ESPN Magazine, Hearts, Euchre and Solitaire.

3.3   Focus Group Results

Eighty of the students elected to loan iPads and participated in a focus group at the conclusion of their loan period. The major themes that appeared through qualitative analysis of the focus group transcripts were: the utility of the iPad, the advantages and disadvantages of the iPad, the experience of using the e-textbook and general opinions on mobile learning.

Utility of the iPad. Students reported using the iPad for seven functions. Four of these can be categorized as education-related activities. These functions were: checking the LMS, browsing the internet, checking emails and reading blogs. The students did not indicate the proportion of the sites they browsed that were related to their studies, nor the extent to which emails were sent to and/or received from their educator and peers related to curricular content and process. The three other non-educational functions were playing games, internet shopping and social networking. Notably, social networking is now increasing in popularity as a vehicle for higher education pedagogy. This was not the case in the researched *Digital media and society* subject; this function was therefore classified as non-education activity.

Advantages of the iPad. Overall, many of the students were enthusiastic about their esteem for the iPad. Two of the descriptors used by students were "sick" [a slang expression meaning excellent] and "revolutionary." No limits were imposed on the students in regard to use of the iPads. Students with iTunes accounts loaded additional apps on the devices and commented on "seeing all the cool stuff it can do." Other volunteered attributes of the iPad held in esteem were the "long battery life" and the screen size, said to be "good for games." Some students specifically addressed learning using iPads, describing interactivity and "learning-on-the-go" as advantages.

There was extensive discussion on the potential use of iPads as a lightweight library of textbooks. Numerous students commented on the size and weight of the iPad, saying that it was easily portable. A student said, "if it had all our text books in there, I wouldn't need a back pack." Another student said, "you know, like we're in a class here and then you got to go to the library to study. It's just easier to carry one little thing than like a stack." One participant linked the iPad to sustainability, in that fewer books would be published in the future, thereby reducing use of paper.

Disadvantages of the iPad. While the students listed numerous advantages of the iPad, as described above, the students were no less vocal regarding their perception of disadvantages. The majority of the complaints regarded features that the students believed that the iPad should have, but does not. These missing features included: USB port, Microsoft Word, camera, flash, chat functions and 3G. It should be noted that a word processor is available as an app on the iPad and that iPads may be purchased with or without 3G, but that these features were not made available on the loaned iPads. Numerous students also commented that typing on the touch-screen keyboard is not comfortable and is error-prone.

A number of students volunteered the information that they will not be purchasing iPads. Some students said that they prefer their laptops. Others said that the iPad did not hit a target function in that it is "not quite a computer and not quite a phone." Some students indicated that they were reluctant to buy soon because Apple will "keep updating them." A common theme was that the iPad was a novelty, but not a valid educational tool. "I enjoyed the novelty of it, um, but I didn't use it for any sort of work or any study." Some other students described the iPad as a "massive distraction."

Experience of Using the Electronic Textbook. Whereas there were minimal comments specific to use of the mobile LMS application, the electronic textbook provoked extensive commenting, the majority of which was positive. A minority of students criticized the electronic version of the book, stating that navigating through the book was "awkward" and/or stating that they prefer to read from paper.

The general portability of the electronic textbook was addressed and numerous design features held in high esteem. In regards to portability, one of the students who commented on this element said, "I liked it because it just sort of gave a different screen - sit in bed and read it rather than having to sit on a desk under the light." Other students described the electronic textbook as "easier." Some of the functions they commended were: highlighting, searching, dictionary and bookmarking. Numerous students described the format of the book as "engaging." One student said, "people will engage with already doing something, like it's a game."

Opinion on Mobile Learning. Overall, general opinion about mobile learning was positive. Emphasis was on the functional capacities of mobility. Students stated that use of mobile devices is more efficient than that of immovable and print resources. Many students forecasted that mobile devices would replace textbooks. Students particularly liked the environmental impact, saying that there would be "no need to be killing trees." Other forecasts were for the lowering of costs of devices and electronic books. They believe that more material will be available online and thus, mobile learning will become more convenient. Some students said that mobile learning was a good way to engage students, as it was interactive. Some students said that mobile learning should be integrated into the curriculum and that there should be tutorials on how to "use it." Others stated that mobile learning was "not vital" with still others qualifying that it is "more beneficial to take pen and paper notes."

4   Discussion

The overall impression of the summarized transcripts is that students were device-focussed. They considered the utility of what it could and could not do, and much of the discussion of functions considered non-educative features, such as the screen-size being large enough for good game graphics. Much of the dialogue clustered into themes that might be summarized as mobility features. Students discussed portability and compared the light-weight feature of the devices compared to bags filled with heavy texts. There was very little discussion about how students used the mobile devices in learning activities. The comment that it is "more beneficial to take pen and paper notes" might be interpreted to mean that the only student-perceived purpose of having a mobile device in class would be to key-in notes. Students did not address collaboration, intellectual debate or comparing and contrasting online sources of information. Higher level learning tasks did not appear to be made salient through the loan of iPads.

While there are numerous educational apps available for download, these are not what this group of students downloaded. Those students who downloaded apps, downloaded games. This is particularly notable when considered in context with the student profile. This group of students were positively skewed towards high grade achievement. They were almost unanimously frequent technology users.

The results might be interpreted as somewhat disappointing. The impetus for this research was assurance of learning. The researchers wanted to know whether the introduction of mobile devices into teaching would positively impact student learning. The hypothesis of this component of the study was that students would perceive a qualitative correlation between the use of mobile devices and learning. While the students enjoyed the experience of trialling the iPads, there was no strong evidence that they perceived a significant contribution to their learning. The question to consider is why not? To unpack this question, we look to the promise of mobile learning. Researchers wrote, "mobile technologies can support learning that is more situated, experiential and contextualised within specific domains and they support the creation and use of more up-to-date and authentic content" [1]. In other words, the authors are advocating an inquiry-based pedagogy, which means that the students are engaging with real-world content in active processes that resemble those used by industry professionals [20]. Herein rests the answer to the puzzle of why the students did not report a substantive difference to their learning. Sometimes a failed hypothesis is more informative than a confirmed hypothesis, because the puzzlement disrupts established relationships between phenomena and set patterns of thinking. The failed hypothesis causes us to look at the data in a new way.

In this case, the reason why students may not have reported enhanced learning as a result of iPad use is because the conceptions of teaching and learning, and therefore the implicit pedagogy, overrides the specificities of whether the teacher and learners are or are not using mobile devices. In other words, this particular educator is going to teach in creative ways, and the majority of learners enrolling in a class on *Digital media and society* are going to be open to thinking outside of the box no matter what. Researchers examining multiple mobile learning empirical studies wrote, "while new technologies can offer new and creative modes of learning, the primary educational goals remain the same: to equip students with a set of skills and knowledges that will help prepare them for later life" [11]. Evidence from student evaluation of teaching surveys and from peer observation of teaching pro-formas indicate that the educator in question has a developed philosophy of teaching, engages his students in active learning and provokes thinking through approaches such as Socratic questioning. The educator in question was the Head of School of Communication and Media. He was brought to the university in order to design and develop a program in emerging technologies and he started a multi-media, active learning lab for the students. In student evaluation of teaching surveys conducted over 3 years (2007-2009), 14 subjects, and 432 students, he achieved a mean score of 6.4/7 in response to the question, "All things considered, how would you rate the effectiveness of this teacher in this subject." In summary, the introduction of mobile devices into this particular classroom did not make a significant difference to pedagogy or perceived learning.

5 Conclusion

The conditions of the described design-based research were such that 135 students enrolled across two semesters of an undergraduate class in *Digital media and society,* were invited to borrow iPads for two-week periods. The results of qualitative analysis of their post-loan impressions revealed that they enjoyed the experience. What the data did not indicate was that the students perceived a large-scale impact on their learning. Interpretation of the results led the researchers to re-examine the context of the inquiry. It is believed that the perception of learning impact was not present because the pedagogy was not shifted by the use of mobile devices. The students experienced the same quality of teaching and therefore perceived an equivalent contribution to their learning.

Was this therefore a failed trial? Should the researchers have selected a less experienced educator with a weaker pedagogy? The emerging hypothesis is that student perception of learning impact would still be absent. The lesson is that mobility does not equate to learning. The introduction of mobile devices into the classroom is not a 'golden ticket'. The authentic independent variable is the collection of pedagogical decisions that the educator puts into play in deciding whether, when and how to use the mobile devices. There was value-added in this educator introducing the iPads into his undergraduate class. The benefits, however, did not magically appear by virtue of their being mobile devices. The strength of the approach was that the introduction of new technologies provoked the educator's thinking about how he could apply the affordances of a searchable text and same-time access to the internet by multiple users. For the students, particularly in the context of digital media, introduction of mobile devices provided another opportunity for reflection and critique. This exploration into mobile learning revealed that this term is more than hyperbole when grounded in mindful pedagogy.

References

1. Kukulska-Hulme, A., Traxler, J.: Mobile Learning: A Handbook for Educators and Trainers. Routledge, New York (2005)
2. David, B., Yin, C., Chalon, R.: Contextual Mobile Learning Strongly Related to Industrial Activities: Principles and Case Study. International Journal of Advanced Corporate Learning 2(3), 12–20 (2009)
3. Cavus, N., Uzuboylu, H.: Improving Critical Thinking Skills in Mobile Learning. Procedia Social and Behavioral Sciences 1, 434–438 (2009)
4. Motiwalla, L.F.: Mobile Learning: A Framework and Evaluation. Computers & Education 49, 581–596 (2007)
5. Chao, P.Y., Chen, G.D.: Augmenting Paper-Based Learning with Mobile Phones. Interacting with Computers 21, 173–185 (2009)
6. Chen, G.D., Chang, C.K., Wang, C.Y.: Ubiquitous Learning Website: Scaffold Learners by Mobile Devices with Information-Aware Techniques. Computers & Education 50, 77–90 (2008)
7. Ramsden, P.: Learning to Teach in Higher Education. RoutledgeFalmer, Oxon (2003)
8. Laurillard, D.: Foreward. In: Vavoula, G., Pachler, N., Kukulska-Hulme, A. (eds.) Researching Mobile Learning: Frameworks, Tools and Research Designs, Peter Lang, Bern, Switzerland (2009)
9. Guy, R.: The Evolution of Mobile Teaching and Learning. Informing Science Press, Santa Rosa (2009)
10. Johnson, L., Levine, A., Smith, R., Stone, S.: The 2010 Horizon Report. The New Media Consortium, Austin (2010)
11. Finn, M., Vandenham, N.: The Handheld Classroom: Educational Implications of Mobile Computing. Australian Journal of Emerging Technologies and Society 2(1), 21–35 (2004)
12. Kadirire, J.: Mobile Learning Demystified. In: Guy, R. (ed.) The Evolution of Mobile Teaching and Learning, pp. 15–56. Informing Science Press, Santa Rosa (2009)
13. Pachler, N.: Research Methods in Mobile and Informal Learning: Some Issues. In: Vavoula, G., Pachler, N., Kukulska-Hulme, A. (eds.) Researching Mobile Learning: Frameworks, Tools and Research Designs, Peter Lang, Bern, Switzerland, pp. 1–15 (2009)
14. Middleton, J., Gorard, S., Taylor, C., Bannan-Ritland, B.: The "Compleat" Design Experiment: From Soup to Nuts. In: Kelly, A.E., Lesch, R.A., Baek, J.Y. (eds.) Handbook of Design Research Methods in Education: Innovations in Science, Technology, Engineering, and Mathematics Learning and Teaching, pp. 21–46. Routledge, New York (2008)
15. Wang, F., Harrafin, M.J.: Design-based research and technology-enhanced learning environments. Educational Technology Research and Development 53(4), 5–23 (2005)
16. Sharples, M.: Methods for Evaluating Mobile Learning. In: Vavoula, G., Pachler, N., Kukulska-Hulme, A. (eds.) Researching Mobile Learning: Frameworks, Tools and Research Designs, Peter Lang, Bern, Switzerland, pp. 17–39 (2009)
17. van Manen, M.: Researching Lived Experience: Human Science for an Action Sensitive Pedagogy. Althouse, London (1997)
18. Alvesson, M., Sköldberg, K.: Reflexive Methodology: New Vistas for Qualitative Research. Sage, Thousand Oaks (2000)
19. Rasmussen, C., Stephan, M.: A Methodology for Documenting Collective Activity. In: Kelly, A.E., Lesch, R.A., Baek, J.Y. (eds.) Handbook of Design Research Methods in Education: Innovations in Science, Technology, Engineering, and Mathematics Learning and Teaching, pp. 195–215. Routledge, New York (2008)
20. Jardine, D.W., Clifford, P., Friesen, S.: Back to the Basics of Teaching and Learning: Thinking the World Together. Routledge, New York (2008)

e-Assessment System as a Positive Tool in the Mastery of Putonghua

Kitty Siu, Y.T. Woo, Kat Leung, Kenneth Wong, Reggie Kwan, and Philip Tsang

Caritas Bianchi College of Careers, Hong Kong
{ksiu,ytwoo,kleung,kwong,rkwan,ptsang}@cihe.edu.hk

Abstract. Assessment in whatever format has not been favourably received by students at all levels since the beginning of time. There is a misconception that assessment is always regarded as a means to make judgments about student performance and grade allocation. It is often thought to have little, if anything, to do with learning. This paper introduces the design of a self-regulating and diagnostic e-Assessment system in learning Putonghua as a second language. The beauty of the newly developed system is its embrace of the spirit of "assessment for learning" and its demonstration of how well-planned web-based multiple choice test items can be used to facilitate self-directed learning so as to enable students to learn Putonghua Pronunciation independently outside the classroom. It is also an example of the Computerized Adaptive Tests (CATs), which is based on the Item Response Theory (IRT) model capable of adapting to an individual student learning needs and learning pace. The key distinguished features of such an e-Assessment system are specified and the paper concludes by providing a list of potential uses of the system in the context of language teaching and learning.

Keywords: assessment for learning, Putonghua learning, computerized adaptive testing.

1 Introduction

The application of Assessment for Learning (AFL) to the education environment is not a new trend [1] [2] [3] [4]. AFL has, in fact, been increasingly adopted during the past decade by various educational institutions as a positive tool to enhance student learning and boost the motivation to learn. Many efforts have been made to explore the effect of AFL on student learning and positive results were reported in face-to-face classroom settings [5] [6] [7]. Though [8] [9] [10] put this to use empirically, research on its learning effectiveness in the online teaching and learning environment is still in its infancy and the current pedagogic evidence base about this assessment tool in language education is scarce.

To embrace the trend of AFL and make use of the benefits of information technology to Putonghua learning in full, the Caritas Bianchi College of Careers (CBCC) has actively participated in the development of various e-learning platforms. Since its introduction in 2001 the e-assessment system for Putonghua using the concept of AFL demonstrated satisfactory learner performance. The aim of this paper

R. Kwan et al. (Eds.): ICT 2011, CCIS 177, pp. 351–365, 2011.

is to give an account of how learners can benefit from the system. In the first part, the background in developing the system will be discussed, followed by a brief introduction of its system design and architecture. The second part provides scenarios in the application of the system with conclusions.

2   Literature Review

The types of "assessment" have been widely discussed in the western literature and three models of "assessment" have been identified in the past decades. These are: (i) "assessment of learning", (ii) "assessment as learning" and (iii) "assessment for learning" respectively. The different prepositions used in the above terms between the nouns "assessment" and "learning" explicitly highlight the unlike principles behind these three models and the different purposes for which the assessment is designed.

Assessment in most classrooms, worldwide, is dominated by elements of "Assessment of learning" (AOL). AOL is an event designed merely for the purpose of evaluating student performance, assigning grades, sorting and ranking students. It is also used to collect evidence to evaluate programmes, curricula effectiveness, and school achievement. AOL normally happens at the end of a school term or a school year in order to inform teachers, students and their parents what a student has learned and how much he/she has achieved during the assessment period. In the classroom where AOL is practiced, teachers are the sole assessors, taking full control of how, what, and why students will or will not learned or be assessed, Students play their roles as passive participants both in the learning and assessment process. The spirit of AOL is clearly reflected in the writing of Stiggins and his research team [11] in which they viewed AOL as "a measurer of the impact of instructional interventions". Such an interpretation is similar to that of Chappuis & Stiggins [12]. They described AOL as "an index of school success". In the AOL model, assessment, to a large extent, is equated with the meaning of "measurement" which can be viewed as a process of estimating the amount, extent and level of student learning [13].

As opposed to "Assessment of learning", the practice of "assessment as learning" (AAL) is always completed and carried out by students instead of teachers with the emphasis on the involvement of learners in assessment in the midst of the learning process. Dann's definition of "assessment of learning" is considered as one of the best illustrations of its kind [14]. According to his definition, AAL "is not merely an adjunct to teaching and learning but offers a process through which pupil involvement in assessment can feature as part of learning" (p.153). The concept of AAL also reminds us of the idea of "meta-cognitive process advocated by Brown (1981) focusing on student ownership and responsibility for moving his or her thinking forward and teachers act as facilitator to provide support for students during the learning process [15].

The application of Assessment for learning (AFL) into the day-to-day classrooms has been one of the main concerns in the educational arena, both internationally and locally. The main difference between AFL and the other two assessment models largely lies in its primary purpose of use. The primary purpose of AFL is to use assessment as an instructional tool to enhance and improve student learning. Unlike

AOL, the AFL model is not just the index of change but apparently, the change itself [11]. It occurs throughout the learning process focusing on promoting learning rather than ranking students; boosting student confidence and motivation to learn with special reference to progress rather than enhancing student achievement and performance[12] [17]; getting students involved in the assessment process rather than assigning teachers to play a dominant role; and providing students with descriptive and corrective feedback by emphasizing strengths, identifying challenges and pointing to next steps rather than giving them grades or scores.

Mixed opinions were found in the available literature when it comes to the question whether the practice of AFL equates with that of "formative assessment". On the one hand, AFL and formative assessment are interchangeable in some publications [13] [16]. Similarly, AOL is also called "summative assessment" in the extant literature. On the other hand, some researchers with the opposing view believe that AFL and formative assessment are not the same. As suggested by Stiggins [17] and Stiggin et al. [11], an easy way to distinguish AFL from formative assessment is to ask the following questions: First, "what kind of feedback are teachers using in assessment? Is it descriptive in nature? Second, "Do students get involved in assessment?" If both replies are yes, then the assessment can be called AFL. If not, then the assessment practice is more likely to fall into the category of formative assessment. In short, AFL has a broader meaning than formative assessment [11].

2 Background

Since the handover of Hong Kong's sovereignty to the Mainland China, the status of Putonghua has been rising in Hong Kong as it is not only the national language of the Mainland China, but also the national lingua franca among speakers of various dialects. Together with English and Cantonese, Putonghua has already grown to be another important powerful and essential language in local schools and colleges, where regular Putonghua lessons are offered. It is even used as the medium of teaching in place of Cantonese, which has dominated the Chinese language lessons for many years.

Facing the soaring number of students and the congenital limitations of Putonghua learning within fixed bounds of a physical classroom including insufficient time to interact with learners which may further lead to an inability to understand their needs, information technology has offered a good solution with more powerful software and applications, along with mobile devices such as tablet computers, personal digital assistants (PDAs) and laptops. The Internet, being a powerful and affluent resource of learning materials and a convenient means of communication, can be effectively utilised as a desirable learning platform to overcome the limitations with the support of the suitable software and mobile devices so that learning can occur regardless of time and place and according to individual progress.

The idea of developing a self-regulating and diagnostic e-Assessment learning system stems from our interaction with sub-degree students in which severe problems in their self-learning abilities in the mastery of Putonghua after school were noticed. It is apparent that they have difficulty in locating and choosing the appropriate learning materials at a level with which they are comfortable within a self-paced environment. They are always weak in the identification of their own Putonghua levels, not to mention they are not knowledgeable and confident enough to design an individualised study plan to meet their diverse learning needs and learning pace. This situation can always be found in the learning of tone (聲調) as learners always distinguish the four tones in Putonghua according to those in Cantonese, which have nine tones of inexact equivalence. What is even worse is that most of the self-access Putonghua learning resources in the market are not well-classified according to the language abilities of the learners and the difficulty level of the questions. All the above-mentioned can be seen as barriers to the learning of Putonghua independently outside the classroom or for consolidation of work done inside the classroom.

In light of this, an online assessment learning system (e-assessment system) was developed to enhance the self-learning abilities of learners in the acquisition of Putonghua through a considerable amount of listening exercises regarding tone in the form of multiple choice questions, based on the idea of Computerized Adaptive Testing and Item Response Theory. The system also aims to help individual learners diversify and customize various approaches to learning "how to learn" languages through self-directed, self-controlled and, to some extent, individually packaged "assessment" opportunities. The purpose of doing this is to reshape their ideas concerning "assessment". Assessment in whatever format has long been unwelcomed by learners at all levels as there is a misconception that assessment is merely a means to make judgments about their performance and through which grades are allocated. These elements have little to do with learning. Therefore, the design of the e-assessment system is mainly focused on how learners can understand their weakness through feedback so as to seek apt and specific ways to improve their proficiency in Putonghua, rather than producing grades for teachers. The feedback can also be useful for Putonghua teachers, in gauging individual student ability and therefore providing them with a basis to re-visit topics in the face-to-face classroom and to thereby develop follow-up prescriptive instruction.

3   System Design and Architecture

Development of Data Bank

The main design concept of the data bank is to develop an e-Assessment system that accommodates the diverse learning needs of sub-degree students. The system will not only help solve the problem of teaching a class with considerable variation in language ability, it will also encourage students to improve their language skills on their own, as they would not feel the pressure of learning next to the high achievers or within the fixed time schedule of a lesson.

The system will be designed as multiple choice assessments for Putonghua with item response theory implemented inside. Item bank number for Putonghua will have about 800 sets of questions. The multiple-choice questions are categorized under the curriculum domain, which denotes the "breadth" of the e-Assessment system. They are then further divided into the skill domain, which denotes the "depth" of the system. Four choices will be provided for each question, one of which is the correct answer. Specifically, there will also be an audio file attached to each of the Putonghua questions (Figure 5).

The item database and the codes of the system will be designed using a 3PL parameter model. However, in actual implementation, a 1PL parameter model will be used ("discrimination" will be set to 1 and "pseudo chance parameter" will be set to 0) i.e. only "difficulty" will be demonstrated. This will leave space for further extensibility when the 3PL model is actually required.

Development of the Web Interface

When the user enters the system, the login page (Figure 1) will be shown first and if the validation fails, a popup will be displayed. If the validation is successful, the main panel (Figure 2) will be displayed. The system panel will be in Chinese for the subject of Putonghua. An Introduction message will be displayed to describe each of the assessment sets (Figure 3). Users will be able to continue with a previous ability level or begin with a default level. Explanations will be provided for the users after carrying out the assessment.

The result records will include the skill areas needed to be improved upon, the total number of questions answered, the total number of correct answers, ability values, a conclusion on a user's overall ability quotient and the related skill descriptions. Users will be able to access the last five assessment result records they previously undertook.

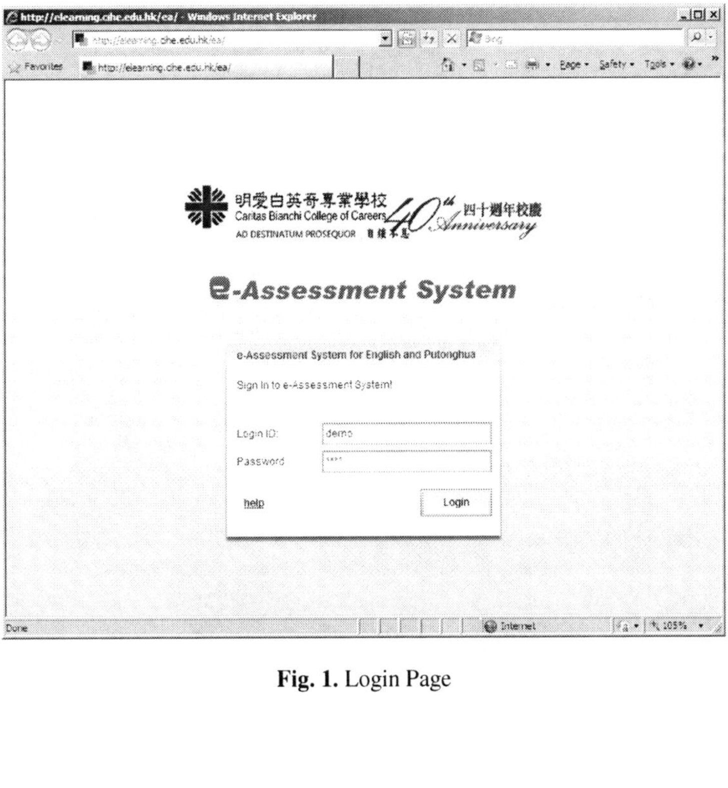

Fig. 1. Login Page

Fig. 2. Main Page

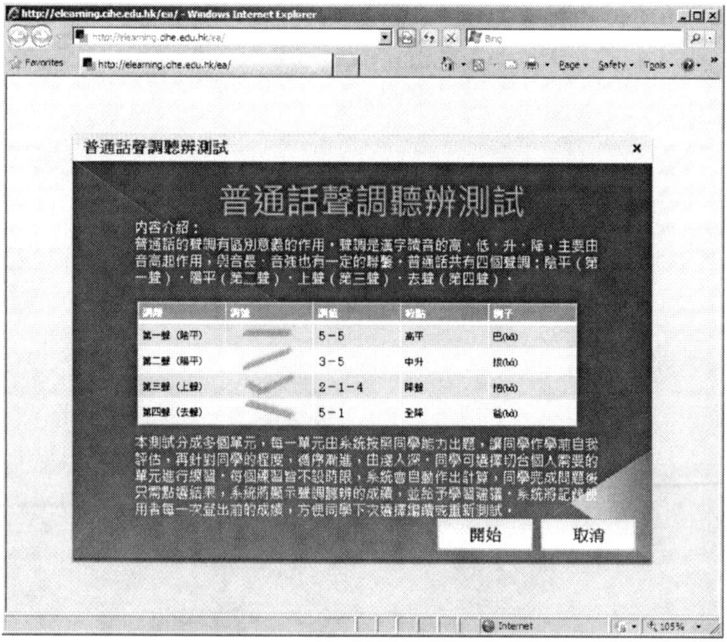

Fig. 3. Putonghua Introduction Page

Curriculum and Skill Design

Based on the common mistakes made by local students, the curriculum of the Putonghua e-Assessment System covers the main areas in Phonetics (Curriculum 1 – C1). Students should have a strong grasp of the concepts in those areas in order to master the speaking skill.

There are various skills involved in the curriculum. Phonetics (C1) has been selected to demonstrate the design of the questions in *Figure 4*. The three main skills involved in C1 are: Tone (聲調) (Skill 1 – S1), Vowels (韻母) (S2) and Consonants (聲母) (S3). To use S1 as an example, different levels of questions with audio files are set to test a user's ability to distinguish between the four tones of Putonghua individually as well as in combinations, such as two characters of the same tone put together (*Figure 5*), the first and second tones, the first and third tones, the first and fourth tones and so on.

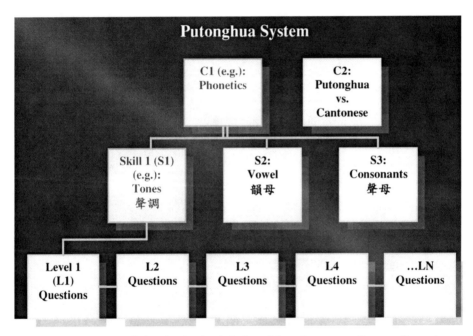

Fig. 4. A flowchart outlining the data bank design of the e-Assessment System - Putonghua

System Rationale

All users will first be treated as equals regardless of the level of their studies. A random question will be generated from the data bank as a reference point of the user's language standard. Every time a user logs in, he/she can choose to begin the assessment at a new level or continue with the previous level if there is history saved. There is no time limit set for each assessment. If the user exits before the end of an assessment, he/she can choose to finish the remaining questions of the previous test or

Fig. 5. A question that tests a user's ability to identify the first tone in Putonghua

commence new ones next time. The system will calculate the ability of the users when they have successfully submitted an answer. The difficulty of the next question will be based on the users' answer history. Once the standard error of successive answers calculated is less than a defined value (e.g. 0.01), the system will prompt the user that the assessment has been finished successfully.

Wrong @ Q392

user_id	quiz_id	question_id	time_spent	answer_history	result_history	difficulty	ability	test_information_value	standard_error	status
2	2	328	30	C	1	-2.20925844	3.5	0.000176	75.361939	1
2	2	417	19	D	0	3.5	0.65	0.044423	4.744537	1
2	2	397	22	B	1	0.673924085	2.1	0.441918	1.504282	1
2	2	430	24	A	0	2.024107789	1.3	1.129543	0.940911	1
2	2	457	10	C	0	1.294398146	0.85	1.6864	0.770051	1
2	2	404	10	B	0	0.841754858	0.45	2.014605	0.704539	1
2	2	392	17	C	0	0.431195234	0.1	2.201916	0.673906	1
2	2	381	43	C	0	0.121460645	-0.2	2.367092	0.649969	1

Correct @ Q392

user_id	quiz_id	question_id	time_spent	answer_history	result_history	difficulty	ability	test_information_value	standard_error	status
2	2	328	30	C	1	-2.20925844	3.5	0.000176	75.361939	1
2	2	417	19	D	0	3.5	0.65	0.044423	4.744537	1
2	2	397	22	B	1	0.673924085	2.1	0.441918	1.504282	1
2	2	430	24	C	0	2.024107789	1.3	1.129543	0.940911	1
2	2	457	10	C	0	1.294398146	0.85	1.6864	0.770051	1
2	2	404	10	B	0	0.841754858	0.45	2.014605	0.704539	1
2	2	392	20	D	1	0.431195234	0.75	3.00877	0.576508	1
2	2	399	113	A	1	0.743514485	0.95	3.75908	0.515774	1

The above analytical report shows the user's scores and ability levels. The first table indicates a wrong answer to Question 392 with the next question marginally lower in the level of difficulty, and the second table indicates a right answer to Question 392 with the next question marginally higher in the level of difficulty.

Fig. 6.

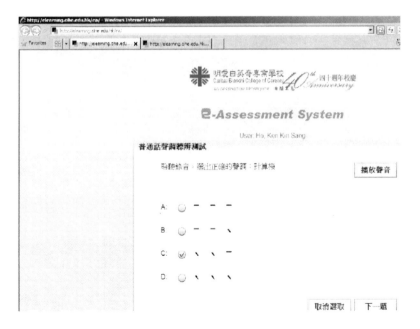

Fig. 7.

If the user answers correctly (Figure 6), the next question (Figure 7) will be generated at a higher skill level.

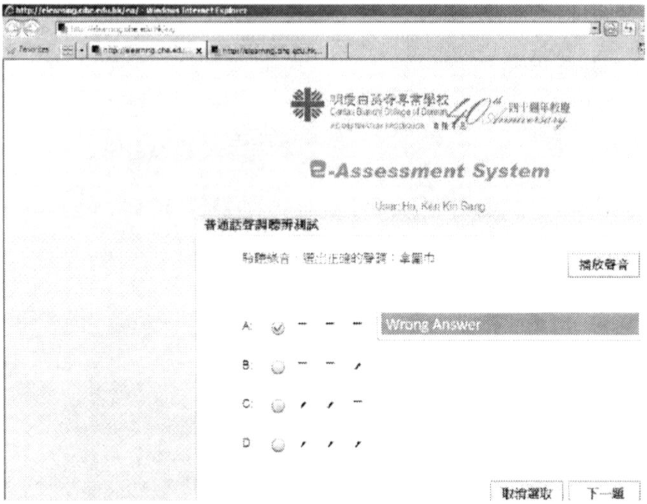

Fig. 8.

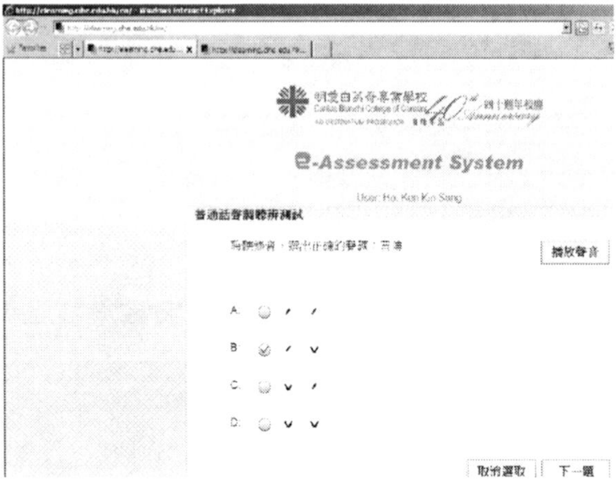

Fig. 9.

3If the user answers wrongly (Figure 8), the next question (Figure 9) will be generated at a lower skill level.

Assessment Reports with Explanations

After carrying out an assessment, users can navigate to the results window to review their assessment record. Analytical reports on the user's strengths and weaknesses are available and information includes skills that need to be improved upon and related suggestions on further reading will be displayed. Users can click on the advice web link for further information.

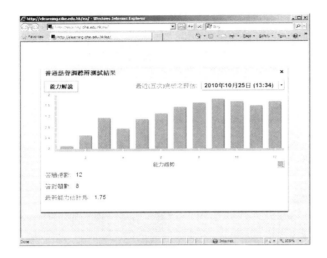

Fig. 10. Assessment results with the total number of questions answered, the total number of correct answers, ability values and a conclusion on a user's overall ability quotient

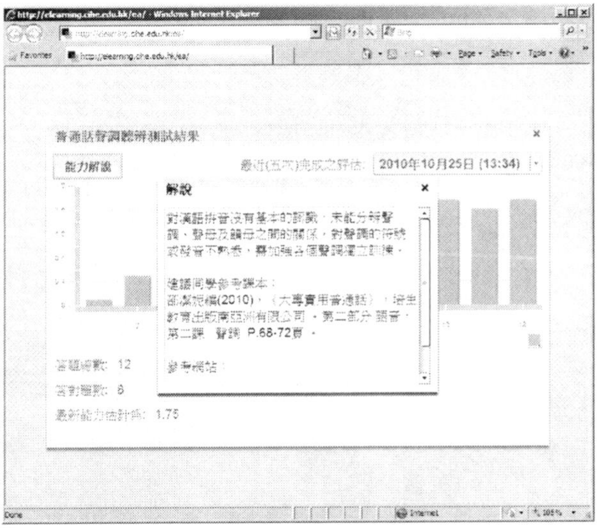

Fig. 11. A screen capture showing the assessment report and suggestions on further reading

4 Scenarios and Potential Use of the e-Assessment System

The **e-Assessment system** is specially designed to provide a supplementary aid to enhance the teaching and learning of Putonghua Phonetics to complement the existing formal assessments during the academic semester. The system can serve the following purposes:

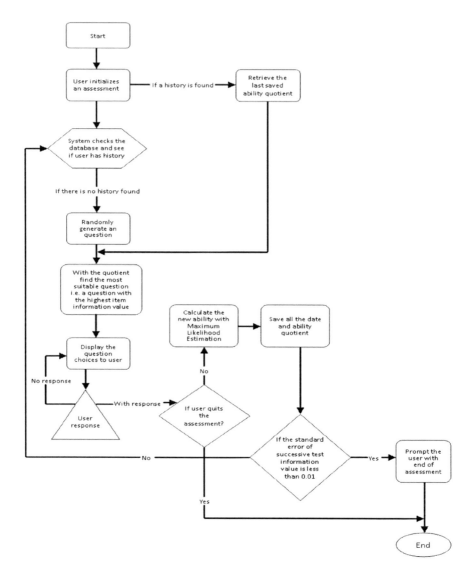

Fig. 12. System Flow Chart

1.   It can be used to boost student motivation to learn

With the e-Assessment system, students become more motivated to learn Putonghua pronunciation and are able to regulate their own learning pace in a step-by-step manner. The e-Assessment system is self-regulating in nature and is capable of adapting to each user's language ability and skill levels. This is different from traditional web-based multiple choice tests with identical question sequence and time limit. The system generates questions according to the user's performance with some random factors to avoid an identical question sequence. The number of questions, the type of questions and the respective levels of difficulty, will thus vary across different people as well as across time for the same person. As a result, it is difficult for a user to perform well just by memorizing the test answers. The user will only be able to improve his/her subsequent performance through "genuine competence". Every attempt leads to a brand-new learning experience and presents a real challenge to the user.

2. It can be used to facilitate self-directed learning

The conventional face-to-face language assessment and classroom learning is a time consuming process. The e-Assessment system is able to offer a diagnostic function to provide an immediate feedback for users which enables them to recognize their strengths and weaknesses in Putonghua phonetics. Detailed study guides with full explanations, follow-up exercises and recommendations for self-improvement, and email addresses of Putonghua teachers for individual tutorial advice are available in the system. Analytical reports on overall performance on the tests will also be generated to give a clear indication of mistakes and deficiencies. Users can plan personalized study for self-improvement by directing their future learning effort to the problem areas. In particular, users are able to select the appropriate learning materials from the library or the Language Centre at a level that is matched with their progress without the need for instructor guidance. Users can repeat this self-learning process in the following cycle: e-Assessment, Diagnosis of weak areas, Improvement, Reassessment.

3. It can be used to collect evidence to revise classroom instruction

The performance report generated by the e-Assessment system is also very useful to the instructors. The report contains a detailed record of each student's performance/progress on the online tests, thus providing valuable information for the instructors and helping them decide which topics to be re-visited in subsequent face-to-face classes. Follow-up prescriptive instructions can be developed accordingly. For example, learners will be referred to enroll in a short course in "Putonghua Toning" offered by the Language Centre of the College if they are found to have difficulty in differentiating between the first and the fourth tones in Putonghua on the e-Assessment system.

4. It can be used to form the basis for curriculum design and development

The e-Assessment system is able to identify the weak patterns among students with different programmes and at different years of study. By comparing the test performance among students according to their levels of study, types of programme enrolled (Higher Diploma, Associate Degree, Top-up Degree, Bachelor Degree) and nature of programme enrolled (Design, Business, Hospitality Management, Language, Social Work), specific patterns of strengths and weaknesses in terms of programme, course and level of study can be identified eventually through repeated testing. These empirical findings can help the programme/course developers in future curriculum design and development.

5 Conclusion

This paper stems from the 24-month project of developing an e-Assessment system in English and Putonghua learning funded by Hong Kong Education Bureau under the Quality Enhancement Grant Scheme, and reports the progress of the project's first year with special reference to Putonghua learning. Since the test item banks and web interface have been fully-developed, effort will be made to test the validity and reliability of the test items in the remaining project period. On top of this, during the coming year, questionnaire surveys and focus-group interviews will be conducted among the students and instructors in order to evaluate the learning effectiveness of the e-assessment system.

Acknowledgements

This project was funded by the Education Bureau of Hong Kong SAR Government under the Quality Enhancement Grant Scheme.

References

1. Black, P., Harrison, C., Lee, C.: Working inside the black box: assessment for learning in the classroom. Open University Press, Maidenhead (2003)
2. Black, P.: Assessment for learning: putting it into practice. Open University Press, Maidenhead (2003)
3. Chappuis, S., Stiggins, S., Arter, J., Chappuis, J.: Assessment for learning: an action guide for school leaders. Assessment Training Institute, USA (2004)
4. William, P.: Assessment for learning: why, what and how. University of London, UK (2009)
5. MacLellan, E.: Assessment for learning; the difference perceptions of tutors and students. Assessment & Evaluation in Higher Education 26(4), 307–318 (2001)
6. William, D., Lee, C., Harrison, C., Black, P.: Teachers developing assessment for learning; impact on student achievement. Assessment in Education: Principles, Policy and Practice 11(1), 49–65 (2004)
7. Marshall, B., Drummond, M.: How teachers engage with assessment for learning: lesson from the classroom. Research Papers in Education 21(2), 133–149 (2006)
8. Kwan, R., Wong, K., Yu, C.-w., Tsang, P., Leung, K.: Building an Assessment Learning System on the Web. In: Fong, J., Kwan, R., Wang, F.L. (eds.) ICHL 2008. LNCS, vol. 5169, pp. 91–102. Springer, Heidelberg (2008)
9. Kwan, R., Wong, K.: e-Assessment Learning as a Learning Tool. In: Handbook of Research on Hybrid Learning Models: Tools, Technologies and Applications, pp. 105–114. IGI Publishing (2009)
10. Wong, K., Leung, K., Kwan, R., Tsang, P.: E-Leaning: Developing a Simple Web-based Intelligent Tutoring System Using Cognitive Diagnostic Assessment and Adaptive Testing Technology. In: Tsang, P., et al. (eds.) Hybrid Learning, pp. 23–34. Springer, New York (2010)
11. Stiggins, R.J., Arter, J.A., Chappuis, J., Chappuis, S.: Classroom assessment for student learning: Doing it right using it well (retrieved 30 January 2011 from Google Scholar)

12. Chappuis, S., Stiggins, R.J.: Classroom Assessment for learning. Educational Leadership 60(1), 40–43 (2002)
13. Hargreaves, E.: Assessment for learning? Thinking outside the "black" box. Cambridge Journal of Education 35(2), 213–224 (2007)
14. Dann, R.: Promoting Assessment as learning: Improving the learning process. Routledge Famler, London (2002)
15. Brown, A.L.: Metacogniton: the development of selective attention strategies for learning from texts. In: Kami, M. (ed.) Directions in Reading: Research and Instruction. The national Reading Conference, Washington, DC (1981)
16. Hoover, K.: Open door to learning with keys to assessment. Innovations Perspectives (May 10, 2010)
17. Stiggins, R.J.: Assessment Crisis: the absence of assessment for learning. Phi Delta Kappan 83(10), 758–765 (2002)

Reconciling "human touch" with "high tech"?

Madeleine Tsoi, Reggie Kwan, Kat Leung, and Sandy Tse

Caritas Francis Hsu College, HKSAR
mtsoi@cihe.edu.hk

Abstract. With the increasing proliferation of technology in education, especially in the higher education sector, educators face the dilemma of reconciling "human touch" services, such as academic and personal advising, with the "high tech" environment. Extensive research has indicated that advising and other support services form a critical part of a student's success. This is particularly applicable to the sub-degree student population in the Hong Kong Special Administrative Region (HKSAR) where the top 18% of high school graduates get into state funded and cash rich universities while the rest choose from a wide range of sub-degree providers with abundant places. This paper reports the establishment of an online advising and learning support system that allows interactivity between teachers and students in a community College with multiple campuses. The system supports activities in the areas of *academic advising and course registration, online language training, career counseling and general counseling.*

As there seems to be as many places as students in the sub-degree sector, the language standards of these students are quite diversified, ranging from poor to excellent, which make the task of teaching them exceptionally difficult. Through videoconferencing equipment, native speaking English tutors based on the main campus are able to conduct online language activities and tutorial sessions with students on the same location or other branch campuses, either in the form of one-on-one basis or in groups. The system is also designed to support online job matching between potential employers and job applicants. In fact, a number of postings have generated much interest and have attracted applications. Virtual job interviews have been conducted on various occasions for employers to evaluate the suitability of the applicants. Online career counseling and tutorials on composing job application letters and curriculum vitae are also available for students to practice in their own time. The system has so far registered positive feedback from students as most of them consider it a more efficient, convenient and less intimidating way of seeking advice from both academic and counseling staff. If funding permits, the system has the capability of further expansion to incorporate users from other local, as well as overseas tertiary institutions.

1 Introduction

This paper describes a government-funded project for the establishment of an Online Advising Support and Interactive Study System (OASISS) by a community college in

R. Kwan et al. (Eds.): ICT 2011, CCIS 177, pp. 366–374, 2011.
© Springer-Verlag Berlin Heidelberg 2011

the Hong Kong Special Administrative Region (HKSAR) which offers sub-degree programmes, mainly Associate Degree and Higher Diploma programmes. The system offers online advising and interactive learning support to sub-degree students who do not make the top 18% of high school graduates. These students exhibit a diverse range of language standards, especially in their English proficiency, for some students, their English standard poses a major hurdle for them to pursue and progress in their studies. Besides, these students from diversified backgrounds approach tertiary studies with different mindsets, motivation levels, career aspirations and intentions. There is a genuine demand for appropriate advising over different aspects of college life in order to help these students to achieve their academic and career goals.

2 Technology and Student Support

With a growing nontraditional student population with diverse educational needs and career aspirations, academic advising plays a prominent role in guiding students towards the achievement of their education goals. Sloan, Jefferson, Search and Cox (2005) claim that with any higher education institution, academic advising forms a critical part of a student's success and advisers provide academic guides. Simpson (2002) proclaims that online advisers face the additional difficulty of making a genuine connection with students which their face-to-face counterparts do not have to. Despite the difficulties they encounter, online advisers still have to guide their students through the educational process to the success of academic gradation, job selection and life management. Sayles (2005) insists that the ultimate responsibility of an adviser is to provide academic guidance so that students gain the most from their education. A Web-based academic advising system is put to practice (Kwan and Chan 2004) and even statistical techniques, such as six sigma, have been incorporated to enhance the quality of the advising process (Kwan, Chan, and Lui 2005). Cohen and Brawer (1987) argue that students in community colleges are faced with more problems than their counterparts at universities and at times these problems pose "insurmountable barriers" to their academic success.

  Current research reflects that the infusion of technology into advising and student support services seems to lag behind the penetration of technology into classroom teaching and curriculum design. Universities and colleges vary in their development of web-based advising and support services, some of which are just beginning to assess the use of technology to cater for the diverse needs of students. This situation is far from satisfactory in an increasingly digitized world of mass education, especially in community colleges and institutions offering sub-degree programmes. An article published by the Arts and Humanities Department at Atlantic Cape Community College reports that personalized advising can help to increase the rate of student retention. Research in this area (Winston, Miller, Ender and Grites, 1984; Pace, 2001) demonstrates that greater faculty-student interaction leads to higher levels of student satisfaction with college experience and consequently, to a higher student retention rate. The National Association of Academic Adviser (NACADA) in America insists that a personalized and individualized advising process forms a critical link between students and their institutions. It promotes learning and assists students "to develop intellectually, physically and personally". In accordance with NACADA's guidelines for developing online advising, there should be one-on-one access to advisers, a more personal environment and more opportunities for interaction.

3   The OASISS Project

With government sponsorship, a community College with multiple campuses has established OASISS, a system which facilitates online interactivity between students, teachers, employers and other users. The necessary hardware and software to install and operate such a system include web servers, audio-visual and videoconferencing equipment, communication software housed in a physical OASISS laboratory located on the main campus of the College, with booths being built to enable remote access from other "satellite" campuses. Specifically, the system supports activities in the following areas:

a)   Academic advising and course registration

Students from the three College campuses are able to log onto the OASISS and make appointments with academic and administrative staff seeking advice relating to course selection, planning of their studies, course requirements and study guides. Since all the programmes offered by the College incorporate elements of General Education (GE) as required and elective courses, GE selection and registration has become a daunting task that puts a lot of pressure on manpower. In the past years, the selection and registration of GE courses is done manually which proves to be very demanding in terms of time and manpower. The problem has now been addressed by the system which allows online course selection and registration. For instance, in October 2010, a total of 706 vacancies for elective GE courses were selected by students in the College. The online system enabled all the students to make their choices and complete the process within 10 minutes of the registration period on each Registration Day (3 days) by using computers at the College or at home, i-phone and Wi-Fi. Most students were familiar with the computer technology and did not require any technical support during the process, thereby relieving manpower for other urgent tasks (see Figure 1).

b)   Online language training

Besides course advising and selection, the system is also designed to conduct online language training between instructors and students. Using the videoconferencing equipment, native speaking English and Putonghua tutors based on one campus are able to hold online language advising and training sessions with students based on the same or other campuses in the form of one-on-one basis or in groups. In group sessions, students share the same online learning materials with other participants on screen and they can engage in real time discussions with the tutors and other participants. In individual sessions, students are able to discuss their learning problems and difficulties with the tutors and the tutors offer plausible solutions.

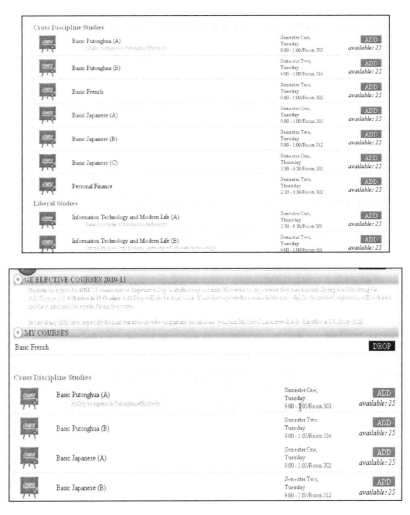

Fig. 1. Screen dumps of online registration in progress

About 170 students, mostly from Business, Social Work and Translation programmes of the College have so far used the online advising function and attended the language clinics. The system is regarded as an additional online platform for students to interact with the instructors as well as with one another in order to improve on their language skills (see Figure 2).

c)   Career counseling and recruitment postings

The system is particularly designed to support online job matching between employers and job applicants. With the consent of the employers, the uploading of job pages and postings in various industries enable students in the College to select the positions they wish to apply for. They can then send their CVs directly to the

Fig. 2. Screen dump showing a language training session

Fig. 3. Screen dump showing CV composition

employers. Although the system is designed to store students' profiles and CVs for prospective employers to view them, most students prefer to apply directly to those employees. In fact, a number of postings have generated much interest and have attracted applications. Virtual job interviews have been conducted on various occasions for employers to evaluate the suitability of potential job applicants. Both employers and job applicants have been reassured that these virtual interviews will be kept strictly confidential. Online career counseling and tutorials on composing job application letters and curriculum vitae are also available for students to practice in their own time (see Figure 3).

d)   General Counseling

Based on the initial success of the system, the web-based counseling system has since been expanded to include student counseling in other areas. With the help of the Student Affairs Office of the College, counseling on other aspects, such as learning difficulties, financial and family problems, and adjustments to College life has been offered. Student opinions about campus facilities, teaching effectiveness, etc have also been solicited in these sessions. An online booking system is currently available for students to make appointments with advisers of their choice. A survey done on this aspect of the system indicates that students tend to be more outspoken about such

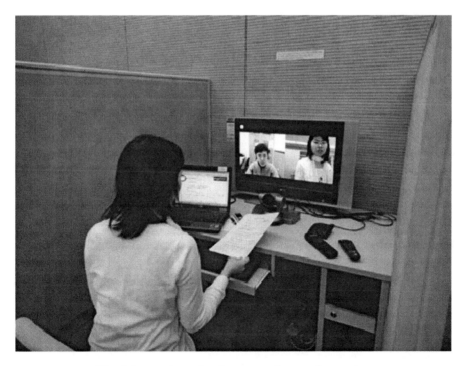

Fig. 4. Screen dump showing a general counseling session

problems as learning difficulties, College facilities, etc and less forward about personal and family problems. Perhaps this is understandable as people tend to opt for face-to-face counseling when it comes to "matters of the heart" (see Figure 4).

4   Effectiveness of the System

The system has impacted greatly on the students as a tool for counseling, learning and interaction.   Three rounds of evaluation have been conducted inviting users to give opinions on such aspects as the outward design of the system on-screen, user friendliness and its effectiveness as a platform for interactive activities.   Up to the present moment, positive feedback opinions seem to outnumber negative opinions, some of which are as follows:

"The outward design is not spectacular but the instructions are clear. However, when I put on my headphone to listen to my instructor, I miss some of the instructions on screen. As a matter of fact, I concentrate more on the incoming sound and what everybody has to say rather than focusing on the colour or the background images. In group discussions, I only focus on the close-ups of the other participants, their facial expressions and what they have to say. I must say I do find the zooming in and out of faces a little distracting (one of the distinct features of the system is that the camera automatically zooms in the face of the person speaking at the time)."

"Sound delay happens sometimes and the image does not synchronize with the voice of the speaker. I guess it is because the Wi-Fi connection may not be stable all the time and the location of booths in an outdoor space may cause extra interference. Perhaps the access points should better be located indoors."

"I'm in one of the smart classes where a lot of other students, especially girls, are bright, chatty and chirpy. When it comes to classroom discussion and interaction, they just dominate the scene and I can't even put a word in because I'm either too slow or perhaps too dumb. I feel so left out most of the time. But OASISS has changed all that. For the first time in my life, someone (the tutor) actually paid full attention to me, to me alone and listened to what I had to say. OASISS not only boosts my self-confidence but also my ego!"

"Awesome! I don't have to physically go to TKO to meet my tutor face-to-face. Since I am doing my top-up year in Business, I have a tight schedule running between job and class, this kind of system really works for me!"

"I am very shy and I would rather communicate with tutors online than meeting them face-to-face because I suffer from anxiety when I have to speak English with them in person."

"I can talk to my tutor online about my Putonghua pronunciation problems and she demonstrates to me the lip and mouth movements on the screen close-ups which are more helpful than in class when she stands from a distance and there are other people interrupting. The beauty of it all is I can talk to her directly on the screen without having to make the trip to the TKO Campus."

"I hope the system can be extended to my home so I can chat with tutors and advisers from home and not in the booths."

On the whole, staff members and students are highly satisfied with the online course selection and registration process because it is efficient, convenient and hassle free. The electronic online process can be completed by students themselves without any assistance from staff members and thus saving staff time and manpower. The academic advising and language training sessions have also proved to be useful and convenient, as students from the satellite campuses are able to join in the training sessions. Since the system also facilitates online booking, students can check for the time availability of each tutor and make online booking leaving little room for errors and time wastage.

Students in senior years find the career advising and job matching service useful as the tutorial sessions walk them through the process of job applications, and give them useful pointers about job requirements, interview etiquette and body language. The virtual interviews held so far have enabled a couple of students to secure job offers.

Though some advising sessions and interactivity are occasionally marred by technical problems and weak signal reception due to the instability of the Wi-Fi reception and the echoes in the headsets students are wearing, the initial feedback from students and academic staff has been overwhelmingly positive. The fact that OASISS has won the "Stockholm Challenge Award", an international award for innovation because of its unique features and some of its pioneering aspects, is another affirmation of its effectiveness in the most gratifying way.

5 Future Directions

As indicated by the users, the image and sound transmission sometimes fail to be satisfactory due to weak signals. Numerous trial runs seem to pinpoint at the location of the booths and the stability of the Wi-Fi reception. These problems need to be addressed and more importantly, there should be more access points, both indoors and outdoors added for the convenience of the users. Ideally, student users should be able to access the system from their homes and this will take the system to a new level of user friendliness. Although initial success indicates that the system is indeed useful for interactive advising and learning, further expansion of the system warrants a substantial injection of funds into it.

As the system is equipped with audio-visual equipment, it can be expanded for use to capture "real-time" images and sound for staff training and orientation programmes. Staff members based on different campuses can participate in those sessions and interact with the speakers and the trainers in real time. In future years, it may be possible to license out the system for both academic and commercial training applications.

Ultimately, the OASISS and the accompanied technology should be shared with other local or even overseas tertiary institutions. This can be achieved through a "license issue" arrangement, making this effective online system available not only to local users, but also to global users.

Endless research has indicated that advising and student support play a significant role in fostering a congenial college environment, generating a stronger sense of belonging in students and consequently, giving rise to a higher student retention rate. With ample student places and a wide variety of programme choices, the problem of getting enough students to fill those places and more importantly, retaining those students appear to be matters of urgency among institutions offering sub-degree courses in the SAR. In future years, the College should consider diversifying levels and types of online advising. Departments and faculties should make use of the system to advise students on faculty-related matters and promote extracurricular activities which help to boost student satisfaction level. Faculty staff should work towards the common goal of making college life a unique and meaningful experience for students.

Acknowledgement

This project has been funded by the Education Bureau of Hong Kong SAR Government under the Quality Enhancement Grant Scheme.

References

1. Cohen, A., Brawer, F.: The collegiate function of community colleges: Fostering higher learning through curriculum and student transfer. Jossey-Bass, San Francisco (1987)
2. Kwan, R., Chan, J., Lui, A.: Application of Six Sigma Methodologies in Student Advising. In: International Conference on Quality Management and Six Sigma, Hong Kong, China, pp. 99–104 (2005)
3. Kwan, R., Chan, J.: A Web-based Academic Advising System (WAAS). In: International Conference of Distance Education (ICDE 2004), Hong Kong SAR, China (2004)
4. McArthur, R.: Faculty-based advising: an important factor in community college education. Atlantic Cape Community College Review (2007), http://www.findarticles.com/p/articles/mi_moHCZ
5. NACADA. Standards and Guidelines, http://www.nacada.ksu.edu/Profes/standard.htm
6. NACADA. Statement of Core Values of Academic Advising, http://www.cacada.ksu.edu/Profes/corevalu.htm
7. Steele, G., Leonard, M., Haberle, C., Lipschultz, W.: NACADA. Technology and Advising Commission. Technology and Advising, http://www.psu.edu/dus/ncta/techartc.htm
8. Sachs, S.: Best practices - Using Technology to Deliver Instructional Support Services (2005), http://www.nvcc.edu/oit
9. Sayles, S., Shelton, D.: Student success strategies. ABNF Journal 16(5), 98–101 (2005)
10. Simpson, O.: Supporting students in online, open and distance learning, 2nd edn. Routledge Publishing, United Kingdom (2002)
11. Sloan, B., Jefferson, S., Search, S., Cox, T.: Tallahassee Community College's progressive advising system: An online academic planning and resource system for individualized student advising. Community College Journal of Research & Practice 29(8), 659–660 (2005)
12. Winston, R., Miller, T., Ender, S., Grites, T.: Developmental academic advising: Addressing students' educational, career, and personal needs. Jossey-Bass, San Francisco (1984)

Author Index

Albano, Giovannina   214
Albors-Garrigos, José   291

Barcelos, Ricardo José dos Sanos   71
Bernardo II, Danilo Valeros   37
Beutelspacher, Lisa   109
Brand, Jeffrey   342

Chan, Selena   243
Charles, Chow Kin Man   305
Chen, Carole   177
Cheung, Wing Sum   319, 329
Chua, Bee Bee   37

David, Chu Wai Kee   305
Drachsler, Hendrik   22

Earnshaw, Rae   200
Ebner, Martin   22
Eustace, Ken   226
Excell, Peter   200

Fotouhi-Ghazvini, Faranak   200
Fox, Robert   1

Gao, Helena Hong   186

Hedges, Claire   152
Hew, Khe Foon   319, 329
Hirata, Yoko   138
Hirata, Yoshihiro   138
Ho, Alex C.H.   280
Huang, Chao   85

Ivanova, Malinka   123

Kinash, Shelley   342
Kordyban, Ron   342
Kwan, Reggie   351, 366
Kwong, Theresa   268

Lam, Hoi Ching   51
Lau, Kai Kwong   51
Lau, Wilfred   51
Leung, Kat   177, 351, 366

Lim, Kin Chew   167
Lui, Andrew Kwok-Fai   96, 280

Mathew, Trishita   342
Maxwell, Gordon   177
Moeini, Ali   200

Ng, Vanessa Sin-Chun   96, 280

Park, Jae   51

Ramos-Carrasco, José Carlos   291
Robison, David   200

Sapargaliyev, Daniyar   63
Schön, Sandra   22
Segarra-Oña, María-del-Val   291
Shrestha, Prithvi   152
Sim, Wee Sing Jeffrey   329
Siu, Kitty   351
Steven, Ng Kwan Keung   305
Stock, Wolfgang G.   109

Tam, Vincent   85
Tan, Christopher Eik Chor   8
Tan, Keng T.   268
Taraghi, Behnam   22
Tarouco, Liane Matgarida Rochembach   71
Tsang, Eddy K.M.   280
Tsang, Philip   22, 351
Tse, Sandy   366
Tsoi, Madeleine   366

Vivian, Rebecca   254

Walsh, Christopher S.   152
Wong, Eva   268
Wong, Fu-Hong   96
Wong, Kenneth   351
Woo, Y.T.   351

Yu, Mingmei   51
Yuen, Allan H.K.   51